FILMMAKERS SERIES
edited by
ANTHONY SLIDE

The Hammer directors, executives, and production heads, together with Peter Cushing and Christopher Lee, outside the Green Room at Pinewood Studios on the occasion of the presentation of the Queen's Award to Industry—Wednesday, May 29, 1968.

A History of Horrors

The Rise and Fall
of the House of Hammer

Denis Meikle

with
Christopher T. Koetting, Research Associate

The Scarecrow Press, Inc.
Lanham, Md., & London

SCARECROW PRESS, INC.

Published in the United States of America
by Scarecrow Press, Inc.
4720 Boston Way
Lanham, Maryland 20706

4 Pleydell Gardens, Folkestone
Kent CT20 2DN, England

British Cataloguing-in-Publication Information Available

Library of Congress Cataloging-in-Publication Data

Meikle, Denis.
A history of horrors : the rise and fall of the house of Hammer / Denis
Meikle ; research associate, Christopher T. Koetting.
p. cm. -- (Filmmakers ; no. 51)
Filmography: p.
Includes bibliographical references and index.
1. Hammer Film Productions. 2. Horror films--Great Britain--History and
criticism. I. Koetting, Christopher T. II. Title. III. Series: Filmmakers
series ; no. 51.
PN1999.H3M45   1996   384'.8'0941--dc20   96-13939 CIP

ISBN 0-8108-2959-2 (cloth : alk. paper)

⊖™ The paper used in this publication meets the minimum requirements of
American National Standard for Information Sciences—Permanence of
Paper for Printed Library Materials, ANSI Z39.48–1984.
Manufactured in the United States of America.

This book is respectfully dedicated
to the memory of

MICHAEL HENRY CARRERAS

who died before he could see it in print

The best of men cannot suspend their fate:
The good die early, and the bad die late.

—Daniel Defoe

Contents

Foreword — Peter Cushing

Perhaps it was because Bray Studios started life as a large mansion standing in its own grounds that it always seemed to me like "going home for the hols" whenever I went to work there—just like "Tom Merry" and "Harry Wharton" in those splendid schoolboy yarns by Charles Hamilton in *The Gem* and *The Magnet*, which made such an impression upon me in my salad days.

In 1957, when I made my first picture for Hammer, there was no motorway as such; we took the more romantic-sounding Great West Road, via Hammersmith and Brentford, over the bridge at Kew, and then, soon, out into open country at Cranford, on to Colnbrook, Datchet, Windsor and so to the studios at Bray, nestling beside the silver Thames. What a halcyon start to the day's work!

Then there were the familiar faces to greet us with mutual affection—like a family party, with lots of old friends all gathered together: dear Rosemary Burrows and Mrs. Molly Arbuthnot, who looked after the wardrobe department, at the same time dispensing endless and most welcome cups of tea. (Later, Rosemary married Eddie Powell, who "doubled" for my very dear friend Christopher Lee—two more names synonymous with Hammer's success story.) Although I didn't need a toupee thirty years ago, Monty Montsash was established as resident hairdresser and kept us all in good trim.

Then there was that delightfully shy man and exceptionally clever director, Terence Fisher! What a joy it was to work with him. He knew exactly which suggestions to accept from his actors and which to discard, and was invariably right in his selection. Being somewhat inarticulate, he had an endearing idiosyncrasy. "Peter," he would say, wagging his forefinger at me and then pausing for such an inordinately long time that I began to imagine he was trying to think of some polite way to tell me that my idea stank. When I could hardly bear the suspense any longer, he'd suddenly

give voice to his verdict—"This is good!"—and then he immediately proceeded to improve upon it!

Jack Asher was another magician, and it was rightly said of him
that he "painted with light." His cinematography added to those
productions a lushness that belied the thrifty budgets imposed
upon them. That was Hammer's secret weapon, I reckon—getting
experts in their particular fields for key positions, backed up by the
best possible supporting personnel. Two more stalwarts of similar
expertise were John Wilcox and Arthur Grant, and Len Harris's
unique operating of the camera can still be enjoyed by all who
watch old films on television.

Anthony Hinds was one of a pool of producers in constant
demand. (He was on the board of directors of the company, as well
as being an accomplished writer for the screen, using "John Elder"
as his pseudonym.) Another Tony—Anthony Nelson-Keys—
worked in the same capacity on many of the productions in which
I appeared, and we often had fascinating chats about his father
Nelson "Bunch" Keys, who was the toast of the town in his heyday
as a comedian, appearing in many of the musicals so popular at the
turn of the century and into the twenties.

Phil Leakey did wonders in the makeup department, and the
stills taken by the excellent Tom Edwards have become collectors'
pieces. As a bonus, to look after the inner man, there was the
indefatigable and enchanting Mrs. Thompson. She and her staff all
qualified for the *cordon bleu,* and had her restaurant been open to
the general public, Egon Ronay would have given it the maximum
number of stars!

The "Big Boss" of Hammer Productions was the late Sir James
Carreras. Wisely, he seldom visited the studios, preferring to leave
those he trusted to deliver the goods while he got on with promot-
ing the products and raising the financing necessary to meet an
ever-increasing demand. I met him only once at Bray (during
nearly a decade), but enjoyed his hospitality and enthusiastic
comments many times elsewhere. His son, Michael, often acted as
producer and became the managing director in 1971. Michael's
wife, Jo, is such a dear lady, and I shall always remember her kind
thoughtfulness during a rather gruelling period when filming
Dracula and the Legend of the 7 Golden Vampires in Hong Kong and,
subsequently, the days I spent with the family in their lovely house,
deep in the heart of Gloucestershire's glorious countryside.

The adjective *horror* has a strong pull at the box office, but I prefer "fantasy," because that is what those films are. To my way of thinking, *horror* conjures up events that actually happen, whereas most of the capers we got up to were mere figments of the fertile brains of imaginative writers who set out to take people's minds off everyday unpleasantnesses, if only for ninety minutes or so. *Captain Clegg, She, Sword of Sherwood Forest* and *Cash on Demand* were pure adventure stories and proved to be just as popular as the films given an "X" certificate.

It is a lovely feeling for an actor to be associated with any success and I count myself lucky to be one of the many who contributed to the output of the "fabulous factory" which has given—and still gives—such pleasure all over the world.

I now leave Denis Meikle to fill in many gaps and thus keep in perpetuity the memory and name of a filmic empire that came and saw and conquered.

Peter Cushing, O.B.E.
Whitstable, Kent 1990

"When the screen gives us severed heads and hands, eyeballs dropped in a wine glass and magnified, and brains dished up like spaghetti, I can only suggest a new certificate—'S.O.' perhaps, for Sadists Only."

Campbell Dixon
reviewing *The Curse of Frankenstein*
The Daily Telegraph, May 1957

Acknowledgments

I would like to express my sincere thanks to the following individuals and institutions for their help and cooperation in the writing of this book: Peter Cushing O.B.E., Oliver Reed, Christopher Lee, Jimmy Sangster, Kenneth Hyman, Brian Lawrence, Anthony Hinds, Wolf Mankowitz, Bryan Forbes, Mike Raven, Frank Godwin, Michael Ripper, Len Harris, Roy Skeggs, Aida Young, Christopher Wicking, Tom Sachs, Hugh and Pauline Harlow, James Ferman and the staff of the British Board of Film Classification, Mark Deitch of Programme Acquisition Group at BBC Television, Boston University and the Mugar Memorial Library, Princeton University Library, University of California Los Angeles, Peter Gray of Bray Management Limited, the staff of the Oakley Court Hotel, Mrs. Jean Tsushima, Archivist of the Honourable Artillary Company and, of course, the staff of the BFI.

A special thanks must go to Richard Klemensen of *Little Shoppe of Horrors*, who almost single-handedly has kept the name of Hammer alive to fans around the world since 1972, whose practical contributions have been constant and considerable, and whose faith in the project has been unwavering throughout. For the rare illustrations, I must again thank many of those mentioned above, while other stills were provided by Doug Murray, Teddy Green, and BFI Stills, Posters and Designs, and for information or the loan of materials from personal collections, Fred Humphreys, Harvey Clarke, Gary Smith, and Marcus Hearn.

I would like to single out Chris Koetting, who was responsible for much of the research at the BFI and at the American end (among many other things), and whose selfless and unflinching support was an inspiration and saw me through the bad times. Above all, I am grateful for the collaboration of Michael Carreras, who opened so many doors that would otherwise have remained closed and whose patience, generosity, and enthusiasm made this book possi-

ble: a very special man. I must also add a word in praise of David
Biesel, my editor at Scarecrow, whose deft touch worked wonders
on an unwieldy text. And finally, I would like to thank my wife,
Jane, who has been steadfast in the shadow of Hammer for far too
long, all in the name of love, and my daughter Sarah—prettier than
the rose—who, quite without knowing it, has been the best inspiration of all.

Introduction

A HAMMER Film: three words that on the turn of a single overnight success took on a life of their own and came to symbolize an entire genre for a whole generation of cinemagoers: horror.

For some of those involved, Hammer's dedication to "terror and disgust" (as the dictionary defines horror) was never acknowledged as such. Peter Cushing: "I don't like the word horror; I think fantasy is a much better word." Christopher Lee: "I prefer to call them films of fantasy—particularly the ones I have made." Director Terence Fisher: "I object to my films being called horror pictures. I prefer my work to be known as macabre."

But the public thought differently. They were not concerned with such fine distinctions. To them, Hammer made *horror* films, pure and simple. And so, for twenty-one years, horror was to be Hammer's stock-in-trade.

In that time, the company produced more than sixty features tailored for or sold to the horror-thriller market. Of these, the majority were set in a dislocated but quintessentially Victorian Gothic hinterland: hybrid period pieces that more or less evolved a distinctive generic style of their own. The first of them was *The Curse of Frankenstein*. That it marked a watershed—perhaps *the* watershed in the history of the horror film—is now beyond dispute, but the stylistic unity they all shared would come to be appreciated the world over and designated by the eponymous sobriquet of *Hammer Horror*. In terms of a body of work being so identified with one company or individual as to become entirely indivisible from them, only the thrillers of Alfred Hitchcock have been the recipients of a similar accolade.

Critics of the time hated everything that Hammer did and stood for. When it introduced blood into its films, they complained about the blood; when it introduced sex, they complained about the sex. And when—unpalatably—it mixed the two, then the end of civilization as we knew it was deemed to be at hand. It was the same reaction that greeted Matthew Gregory Lewis in respect to his Gothic splatter-piece *The Monk* some 160 years before.

Despite this, Hammer Films would grow to be one of the most successful British film companies of its day, be the first to receive the Queen's Award to Industry, become the subject of numerous retrospectives—including a 1971 "Tribute" at London's National Film Theatre—sire countless international fan clubs, and foster a devotional following around the globe. It would live to take its rightful place second only to Ealing in the ranks of the great postwar British independents.

The cinema of Hammer is one of castles and crypts, of blushing virgins and blood-lusting vampires, of fanatical scientists and rapacious aristocrats, of ascetic *savants*, and of vengeful spirits from beyond the grave. It is a cinema rich in opulent decor and steeped in romantic extravagance, and it lies in direct line of descendency from the literary tradition established by the more morbid fancies of Horace Walpole, Dickens, and M. R. James. From Wilkie Collins's "The Woman in White" (1860) to Susan Hill's "The Woman in Black" (1986), the wheel turns full circle. Yet despite a total of 157 feature films and a Queen's Award to Industry to its credit, no biography of the house that horror built exists.

This book aims to correct that omission and, in so doing, provide insight into a thematic collective that has proved to be both unique in British cinema and singularly influential on fantasy cinema throughout the world. It is the untold story of the modern Prometheans who brought "Hammer Horror" into being.

The Hammer Horrors

By the mid-1950s, a new age was dawning.

It was an era of hope, of rebuilding, of new-found prosperity. It was the era of rock'n'roll. But it was also a time of anxieties and unspecified dreads. The countries of the world were decamping into ideological territories, aided by the emergent superpowers: the United States and the USSR. The bogeyman of communism was hiding under every bed. The prospect of war still tantalized. And television was on hand to remind that while life in general may have begun to look increasingly good, never before had man seemed so mortal as he did then, when over him hung the appalling specter of the hydrogen bomb.

The cinema reflected these national psychoses. By the middle of the decade, *Invasion of the Body Snatchers* was vying with *X The Unknown* for box-office attention and, as in any art with a populist bent, communal paranoias were writ large and reactionary. Science was the villain of the piece, and radiation was the name of the nightmare. Its spawn were invariably colossal, mutant, and prone to dolling out the most spectacular feats of destruction on the heads of humankind.

As always, efforts to dampen such fears centered on sublimating their expression. "Horror comics" had already been banned. The still-youthful "X" certificate was being granted with the same reluctance as the "H" it had replaced. The artistic imaginings that were now at work exploring and analyzing the postwar, postatomic psyche stood accused of pandering to base instinct.

Against this backdrop, and in the face of a cinematic fad for ever-more-outlandish examples of the Armageddon that awaited the world around the next corner of discovery, a small British film company resurrected a half-forgotten myth and gaudily repackaged it for the sensation-seeking present.

The Gothic obsessions of Mary Wollstonecraft Shelley were to provide a welcome relief from the all-too-real terrors of the nuclear age. The fruit of a sibling rivalry at the Villa Diodati during an idyll in Geneva in 1816 was to be revived and revitalized for an audience desperate for a fantasy that did not look to predict only the following day's headlines.

On May 2, 1957, *The Curse of Frankenstein* opened to a largely vitriolic press and a worldwide commercial reception of unprecedented enthusiasm. After twenty-three years in and out of the business, Hammer Film Productions was finally on the map.

And with the wholly unexpected arrival of the modern horror film, a legend was also born: Hammer itself. What follows is the truth behind that legend.

Chapter 1

The Rebirth of Frankenstein

1947-1957

"We had a head floating in a jar showing the skin peeling off. It had to be cut."

James Carreras
on *The Curse of Frankenstein*

"One morning, six hours after dawn, the first manned rocket in the history of the world takes off from the Tarooma range, Australia. The three observers see on their scanning screens a quickly receding Earth. The rocket is guided from the ground by remote control as they rise through the ozone layer, the stratosphere, the ionosphere— beyond the air. They are to reach a height of fifteen hundred miles beyond the Earth, and there learn…what is to be learned. For an *experiment* is an operation designed to discover some unknown truth. It is also a risk.

"When it is fourteen hundred miles up, all contact with the rocket is suddenly lost…"

With these words, to the accompaniment of "Mars, the Bringer of War" from Holst's *The Planets,* the first episode of a six-part television serial began transmission at 8:15 P.M. on Saturday, July 18, 1953, with a vista of earth as viewed from the nose cone of a V2 rocket far out in the deep blacks of space. They were a last-minute addition to the script, designed to better contextualize events for an audience entirely unprepared for what was about to confront them in the deceptively titled "The Quatermass Experiment."

The serial was to hint at what might be lurking in the darkness beyond the kindling flame of technological advance, and its effect on viewers was immediate and unparalleled. Among those held in thrall was a 29-year-old film producer named Anthony Frank Hinds, whose latest low-budget outing—*The Flanagan Boy*, with Tony Wright—was just being readied for release. Hinds persuaded James Carreras, managing director of Exclusive Films and a senior partner in their production-arm subsidiary, Hammer, to tune in to future episodes, and while the serial was still on air, the young company negotiated the rights to turn it into a feature film. At the time, it was simply one more in a long line of similar deals, but within fifteen years, Tony Wright would be a sales rep and Hammer would be the recipient of a Queen's Award to Industry for dollar earnings in excess of 4.5 million as a result of what Quatermass and Hinds had found in that dark: horror.

Horror as a genre had been all but dead since the end of the war. With a few notable exceptions—Robert Florey's *The Beast With Five Fingers*, Ealing's *Dead of Night* (both 1946)—Gothic cinema had become a thing of the past by 1951. With the new British "X" certificate limiting the audience even more, the literary monsters of yesteryear were gasping their last to the exorcising spoofery of Abbott and Costello and Old Mother Riley. [1]

With the advent of the fifties, the archetypes of horror may have retreated into the shadows, but their legacy was still to be felt amid the technological marvels of the new age and the new cinema of science fiction, which had been heralded in by the docudrama *Destination Moon*. But once the cinemagoing public had seen one lunar crater, it had seen them all, and *things* were required to be found lurking under the moon rocks. As a result, Frankenstein's monster soon resurfaced in the guise of *Invaders From Mars* (1953), while the spoor of Dracula had already transmuted into the blood-sucking *The Thing From Another World* (1951).

In response to this sea change, cinema's new archenemy, television, had also decided to embark on an exploration of the more uncharted regions of deep space. Against the background of public euphoria that was to mark the summer of 1953, the British Broadcasting Corporation had put Manx staff writer Nigel Kneale to work on an original science-fiction project intended to form the basis of a serial of six thirty-minute instalments: "The Quatermass Experiment." It was in the antiquated BBC studios of Alexandra Palace that the real foundation stone of the Hammer House of Horror was to be laid.

True, the company had been around in one form or another since the thirties. Its first incarnation had imported Dracula actor Bela Lugosi for *The Mystery of the Mary Celeste* (1936; *The Phantom Ship* in the U.S.), but Hammer as it is known today was not formed until 1949 (the company was incorporated as Hammer Film Productions on February 12). It was while embarked on a series of second features which were using the services of Hollywood stars past their prime that Hammer successfully negotiated its deal with the BBC for the rights to the serial that caused such a stir during July and August.

Hammer's history prior to this had been colorful and convoluted. The name itself was that of entrepreneur William Hinds, who—aside from his array of retail business interests—had somehow found time to dabble in variety theater. Hinds was one half of a comedy duo called Hammer and Smith (after London's Hammersmith) and had come to be better known by his stage name of Will Hammer. Hinds/Hammer had interests in music publishing (Moon Music), show business promotion (with Jack Payne), and hotel and theater management in Surrey, East Anglia, and elsewhere (including Clacton's West Cliff Gardens Theatre), and the move into films was seen as a logical development of his theatrical concerns. In November 1934, he and four others—George Mozart, George A. Gillings, producer Henry Fraser Passmore, and James Elder Wills—formed Hammer Productions Limited.[2] They embarked on their first feature in 1935, which would trade unashamedly off Alexander Korda's *The Private Life of Henry the Eighth* and be called *The Public Life of Henry the Ninth*. After only two years in the business (with one notable film to their credit: the Paul Robeson starrer, *Song of Freedom*, in which Hinds had played the role of the Potman), further production was abandoned and the company was allowed to lapse.

As Hinds was forming Hammer Productions, a Spanish émigré named Enrique Carreras was looking for additional financing for *his* new venture, a film distribution company called Exclusive. Enrique had come to Britain with his wife and brother Alfonso in 1907. In 1909, Dolores Carreras had given birth to a son, and in 1913, after a spell in the family tobacco business, the brothers bought the first of what would later become a seven-strong chain of cinemas, with "Blue Halls" in such diverse locations as London, Putney,

Brighton, and Manchester. By 1932, Enrique had sold his interest in the halls to develop a brand of toothpaste, but a promotional scheme in breach of the Lotteries Act had incurred a fine that had bankrupted the enterprise. The twin-screen flagship of the Blue Halls had been in Hammersmith, however, and he and Hinds had met. Hinds was approached and, having already established a production company, agreed to take a stake in Exclusive to add to his portfolio of thirty other directorships.

Exclusive Films was founded in December 1934, with a staff of four: Enrique, Jack Spratling, James Dawson, and a secretary, Mrs. Burnham. As a result of the association, Hinds's 16-year-old son Anthony was employed as a booking clerk prior to his war service, and he was followed in 1943 by Enrique's grandson, Michael Henry Carreras. Enrique's *son* had served time in the Blue Halls as an assistant manager, after having trained with Gaumont at the Astoria Charing Cross Road. (He had arrived on his first day to find that the manager had absconded with the takings!) But James Enrique Carreras was content, for the moment, to pursue a career as a car salesman for Bert Henley in Warren Street, off London's Tottenham Court Road.

At the outbreak of war, Exclusive was already ensconced in the heart of the film community, with logging, barring, and sales conducted from 93 Cinema House in Wardour Street, and accounts and publicity handled from 60-66 National House opposite.[3] The company prospered throughout the hostilities and, in 1945, the trio of Enrique, Spratling, and Dawson were joined by Anthony E. "Brian" Lawrence, who formerly had been with the Anglo-American Film Corporation and was now to assist circuit manager Spratling. Before entering into the business, Lawrence had studied for the priesthood. His devotional bent would find new succour with Exclusive, Hammer, and James Carreras, above all. There may have been only "a handful of clerks with a few accounts clerks across the street," according to Lawrence, but they were to have their work cut out for them, since Exclusive's annual turnover would soon begin a steady rise from five figures to six.

After his "demob" from the army, James Carreras at last decided to join the family firm.

"Doodlebug Jim" had had a good war. He had entered service as private 1472308, attached to 273 battery A.A. Regiment of the Honourable Artillary Company as a gunner. His progress through the ranks had been rapid, if not meteoric. By the end of 1940, he had made Second Lieutenant; by October 1942, he was a Captain; by December, a Major. Eventually, he had been posted to command 450 (mixed) Heavy A.A. battery, a showpiece antiaircraft unit that would entertain King George VI and Queen Elizabeth, as well as Soviet Marshal Rossoloff. This battery scored such a marked success against the V1s aimed at London during the Battle of the Flying Bomb (78 kills) that "Hair-trigger Jim"—as he was to be nicknamed by General Sir Frederick Pile—had earned the rank of Lieutenant-Colonel R.A. by the end of September 1944.

While stationed at Rye on the Kent-Sussex border, Carreras and his battery had been the stars of a Gaumont-British documentary on the bringing down of the bombs. On September 12, 1944, he had found time for a trip to Wardour Street with his father to publicize the film—a calling card for what he had now determined was to be his future in civilian life.

Jack Spratling—who occupied his time between films by selling "smokeless chimneys" and the occasional Rolls-Royce—was the first to depart under the new regime, and Carreras appointed Lawrence and Morris Young to sell Exclusive's catalog of shorts and British and American reissues. "Surround yourself with good lieutenants and you can't go wrong," Colonel James would counsel the man who was to become his right arm in the years ahead. Brian Lawrence never wanted to be anything other than a "good lieutenant," but he would certainly never be anything less.

Will Hinds continued to be a source of financing for budding independent producers whose films could be distributed through Exclusive. One such venture was Vernon Sewell's *The Jack of Diamonds* (1948). Consequently, the beginning of authentic postwar Hammer production is confused and erratic.

When Anthony Hinds was persuaded (by his father) to rejoin Exclusive, after serving with an R.A.F. photographic unit in the Far East, his first project was along similar lines. "Two likely lads came along and said, would we like a film made," he recalls. The two were producer Hal Wilson and cameraman Brooks-Carrington, who were affiliated with actor John Blythe. A coproduction deal was struck, and the film in question became *Crime Reporter*, which was followed in quick succession by another of the same—*River Patrol*. These were succeeded by a fictionalized account of the criminal exploits of one Henry Thurston, a notorious thief and jailbreaker, but this fared less well. On completion, it was judged morally questionable by the British Board of Film Censors and denied a certificate of exhibition. The film was reedited to remove all references to Thurston (who had actually appeared in it), wrapped in a spurious American linking narrative, and released as *The Dark Road*. Of those who had participated, only a young Michael Ripper managed to survive the affair with dignity intact. Producer Henry Halsted and his Marylebone Studios (in reality, a disused church) had been coopted to provide the goods on *The Dark Road* and, with his help, the company next embarked on *Death in High Heels* with Don Stannard, though still under only the nominal guise of "Hammer."

Anthony Hinds soon found himself with an unexpected producer credit of his own when he was called on to add some scenes to a radio-inspired featurette that had recently been abandoned due to lack of funds. This was *Who Killed Van Loon?*, and the film had been shut down before anyone thought to provide the answer to the title question. Hinds called back three of the principals and made up the remainder as he went. In the nature of such "quota quickies," no one noticed or cared.[4]

In August 1947, the government imposed a punitive 75 percent import tax on American films, in an attempt to stem the flow of currency out of the country. This was to lead to a retaliatory export ban, and with domestic production curtailed by fuel shortages due to the severe winter, cinemas soon became starved for product. It suddenly seemed opportune for Exclusive to initiate some genuine production of its own, and with the added incentive of an encouraging word from D. J. "Jack" Goodlatte (bookings supremo of Associated British Cinemas, purchasers of the Blue Halls), James Carreras began to cast around for subjects to fit the bill.

These were radio days, when the nation's cultural icons were heard but not seen, and the notion of giving form to popular characters from successful radio series was a logical move in the quest for screen stories. One such was "Dick Barton," who had captivated listeners with his first airing on the Light Programme between October 1946 and May 1947. The BBC was approached and *Dick Barton, Special Agent* was readied to go before the cameras at Marylebone, with Stannard rallying to the now familiar strains of "The Devil's Gallop" in radio's Noel Johnson's stead. *Dick Barton, Special Agent* was a success. When the tax was abandoned in March 1948 in favor of the Anglo-American Agreement, British supporting features were still in short supply and James Carreras was encouraged to plan more of the same. The result was *Dick Barton At Bay*, but on this occasion, Halsted farmed out the actual producing to Mario Zampi and his technicians at Alliance (at the behest of Enrique Carreras). Just as *At Bay* was due to go onto the floor, Zampi disappeared—along with the budget!—and Exclusive was forced to take over this second Barton adventure itself. "It was unplayable," said Anthony Hinds of the outcome. The experience at Marylebone convinced Carreras that control should remain firmly in the hands of Exclusive in the future, so Hinds was allocated the task of finding a crew, and several of those who had worked for Zampi were persuaded to join the new outfit, including a young third assistant director named Jimmy Sangster.

"More of the same" was to become a hallmark of the Carreras strategy, and *Dick Barton and the Silent Plague* (released as *Dick Barton Strikes Back*) was announced to the waiting world for immediate production on location in Blackpool. In the interim, the distribution side of Exclusive had continued to grow apace, so the move into feature films meant that a separate company would be required to act as a safeguard against the risks involved. The decision was taken to reregister Hammer as the name of Exclusive's production arm. This time, the directors would be Enrique and James Carreras (who between them were to hold a 48 percent stake) and William and Anthony Hinds (who would take up an equivalent 48 percent, with 40 of that going to the senior Hinds). James Dawson was to be the company secretary, and Hammer's sales manager would be the 28-year-old Brian Lawrence.

While shooting exteriors for *Dick Barton Strikes Back* at Blackpool's famous tower, electrician Jack Curtis had mooted the idea of renting a country house as a base of operations. Hinds had been greatly attracted to the prospect of a studio of his own, and by the end of 1948, the unit found itself installed in "Dial Close," Winter Hill, at Cookham Dean in Berkshire. The youngest Carreras, fresh from his stint in the Grenadier Guards, had now become part of the team again and was seconded to Hinds to help oversee future production. "It was wonderful," Michael Carreras recalls. "We had a butler and a maid. Tony and I used to be sitting there having our toast and butter in the morning and the unit would come down by bus from Hammersmith. They were wonderful days."

They were also formative days. As the winter evenings grew long, lasting friendships were struck. Michael remembers that time with particular affection. "The first true Hammer film was 1948— November, at the house in Cookham: *Dr. Morelle*. That's where it started. It wasn't Hammer, it was Exclusive, but that's where it started. That's where Tony, I, Jimmy Sangster reported for work."

In point of fact, *Dr. Morelle* was the first film to be accredited solely to Hammer on screen (in association with Edward G. Whiting), implying that this was the production of a *company* (especially as it was made with NFFC money[5]) as opposed to one that was partly financed by Will Hinds or Exclusive. The film serves as a symbolic beginning in any event. *Dr. Morelle: The Case of the Missing Heiress* was another radio-inspired melodrama, and the story is dark and mysterious, with a grotesque villain (the wheelchair-bound Kimber: Philip Leaver) and a corpse disposed of in an incinerator. Dr. Morelle was a hypnotist-sleuth in the haughty, conceited, and inherently mysoginistic mold of Sherlock Holmes or Bulldog Drummond—a typical product of class, empire, and the public school system—and had been created by Ernest Dudley for the radio show "Monday Night at 8." But he was never likely to make it past the mid-fifties, and Hammer's next hero was much more down to earth. The first film to be produced after the formation of Hammer Films proper was *The Adventures of P.C.49*, made in February 1949, but the *advent* of production in the house studios is commonly held to be the starting point.

It was an innovational move, and by the spring of 1949, it had caught the attention of the trades. "Since the experiment began a few months ago at Cookham," ran one report,

"shooting schedules have been tightened and production costs trimmed. Producer Anthony Hinds plans to put the first screen versions of *Meet the Rev.* and *The Man in Black* on the floor at Cookham when *Celia* is complete in about a week's time. He is still a trifle undecided whether or not to introduce bigger artistes names to the credits alongside his all-star technical crew. At the present rate of production, allowing five weeks' shooting for each film and two weeks' rest and planning breather between pictures, he could maintain an output of about eight pictures each year—at least until 1951, when the present production programme for Cookham Dean expires."

The "all-star technical crew" was headed by director Godfrey Grayson, his two equally talented brothers (writer Ambrose and composer Rupert), and screenwriter A. R. Rawlinson (who had coscripted Hitchcock's *The Man Who Knew Too Much;* 1934). Camera operator Peter Bryan and director Francis Searle had also been appended to the growing list of Hammer luminaries, and any "indecision" about the use of star names was about to resolve itself with the company's next step forward.

Further production at Cookham was to be thwarted by residents' objections and the company's failure to acquire a land-development license for the property, and Hammer Film Productions was forced to move from Dial Close in May 1949, even before the outcome of the planning appeal was known (September 1950). *Meet the Rev.* (released as *Meet Simon Cherry*), *The Man in Black*, and five others would actually be shot at Oakley Court, a Gothic "folly" (dating from 1859) on the banks of the Thames near the village of Bray, downstream from Windsor. The house was owned by Ernest Olivier, and Hammer rented it for a mere fifty guineas a week. From there, the thirty-strong unit would venture to the fifty-acre Gilston Park Country Club near Harlow in Essex for a further two features, before transferring back to Oakley Court and, at the close of 1950, rapidly decamping to a more favorable arrangement next door at Down Place—a ramshackle manor house that had provided them with facilities during the shooting of *The Lady Craved Excitement* in March of that year.

In a few short years, Exclusive had grown from a purveyor of esoteric shorts such as *A Night in Old Seville* to a major-league distributor. Its success was due in part to the aggressive marketing techniques that James Carreras would later apply to Hammer; the company offered theater owners 50/50 participation on exhibition material, but provided *free* posters, showcards, and foyer displays. Despite the incursion of the Hammer name and the recent branching out to feature production, it would remain the mainstay of the Hinds-Carreras business empire for a long time to come.

The operation had moved to the fifth floor of Nascreno House at 113 Wardour Street (which would later become Hammer House with Will Hinds's acquisition of the whole building), and Exclusive had expanded from a motley crew of commission agents to a well-oiled machine with 13 branch offices and a total staff (at its peak) of well over 100. In another decade, it would be entirely forgotten—swamped by the success of the affiliate it had sired to feed itself. But for the moment, it continued from strength to strength, fostering annual conferences at which Brian Lawrence would outline strategy and Will Hinds would deliver witty, if predictable, addresses to the troops, to rally them to even greater achievement. The outcome was to be year-on-year of record-breaking success during the early fifties under the auspices of Lawrence and sales supervisor Harry Bernow, an idiosynchratic Russian Jew "as round as he was tall," as his manager would joke.

By now, Enrique Carreras was "a little out of his depth," in Lawrence's view, and effective control of the fast-expanding concern had already passed to his son. With the sudden death of Enrique on October 15, 1950, James Carreras became the major shareholder in Exclusive and officially its managing director, with William Hinds remaining as chairman.

Hinds operated out of frugal offices at 261 Goldhawk Road, in Fulham, an address known jokingly as "Bleak House" to his associates in the less austere surroundings of Wardour Street. With his existing chairmanship of the Goldhawk Building Society, his "summer shows," and sundry other interests, Hinds already had enough to occupy his time, and Exclusive was never high on his list of priorities, in any event. (Hinds entertained a profound distaste of the film business.) As a result, *his* son had also risen rapidly in the ranks of the company.

Anthony Hinds's office was at an even more distant remove. But Down Place, at Water Oakley, Windsor, was a location that would soon begin to figure prominently in the plans of James Carreras— the new Head of Hammer.

Colonel James Carreras

" Suddenly we saw the reflection of the doodle on the radar screen enlarge and disappear, and we knew that another flying bomb had been hit and disintegrated in mid-air. This went on, hour after hour, from nine in the morning until ten at night, when the final score came through for that day—101 launched, 98 destroyed."

Extract from a broadcast by Colonel Carreras
August 16, 1944

When Hammer first settled into Down Place, Colonel "Jimmy" Carreras was 41 years old.

Carreras was a man who excelled at everything he did or tried to do. (He had been awarded the M.B.E.[6] in 1944, at the age of 35.) He loved sports, and whether it was cricket, rugby, or golf, he played superbly, with single-minded determination. "A man of tremendous energy, enormous enthusiasm, and great fun to be with," was actor Christopher Lee's opinion. He was also brash, self-motivated, and competitive to a fault. But he had an easy manner ("could charm the birds from the trees," Michael Carreras considered) and was as much at home with commoners as with kings. More particularly, he was a salesman without peer. During his time at Henley's, he had sold bandleader Joe Loss a Buick without an engine, just to prove a point! With his drive, his charisma, and his overriding ambition to reach the very top, Carreras would have been an asset to any company. "The most brilliant promoter and entrepreneur I've ever come across," Lee adds. In another life, he could have been a captain of industry, but fate had decreed him Hammer, and James Carreras had every intention of taking it to the heights.

As an indication of what was to come, Carreras had already secured a useful source of domestic funding for Hammer by fostering ties with James Lawrie, head of the newly enfranchised National Film Finance Company. *Dr. Morelle* was the first film to be wholly financed by NFFC money (at a modest £14,169), and Carreras was to ensure that this and future loans would be swiftly repaid, in order to promote a similarly benevolent response the next time round. ("We were the only people who didn't quite understand that you never had to pay them back," he was subsequently to quip at a press conference.)

Carreras was equally shrewd with the production costs. Key personnel, such as leading players and directors, were offered profit participation (usually around 5 percent) by way of deferring part of their salaries, and Hammer staff were required to work cheap. Both Michael and Tony took an annual wage, regardless of what the budget sheet may have shown as payment for their individual contributions to a particular film. All such "charges" went into the general coffers. If he had a fault as a businessman, it was an inadequate rewarding of worth. If he had a fault as a salesman, it was an inability to think for the longer term. Hammer

lived on the fee that each of its films could generate. It made them
to a price, and rarely was it party to a slice of the action.[7] "He wasn't
the best deal-*maker*," Michael admits, despite what was to become
an unrivalled ability to open any door. It is a sentiment shared by
Hinds. "James Carreras was never interested in the making of the
films, only the making of money; unfortunately, he wasn't that
good at it, and none of us came out of it rich."

But what would come to be recognized as James Carreras's
unique brand of salesmanship was now being honed to perfection
in the cut-and-thrust of postwar expedience. To encourage interest
in a Hammer project, the Carreras technique was to offer a title, a
poster, and a promise. To maintain interest, he would show potential distributors a presentation reel of highlights from the film while
it was still in production. Through a procession of ever-more-astute
maneuvers (such as packaging titles when demand was at its peak,
so that those with pulling power could only be sold as part of a
multiple purchase with features of more limited box-office appeal),
James Carreras would keep Hammer in continuous production
almost single-handedly throughout the years of reconstruction
that were to mark the beginning of the fifties, and well beyond.

> "Night seems closer to us—it never comes too soon for
> me....Quite soon, you'll understand what I mean...."
>
> —Doctor Fell
> *Room to Let*

A total of ten features were actually produced between the
summers of 1949 and 1950, with Grayson and Searle directing the
bulk of them. Searle, in particular, was a good actors' director, and
these early films were often smoothly made and solidly absorbing.
Many of them were dramas of adulterous or unrequited love—*The
Rossiter Case*, *To Have and To Hold*—but a notable exception was
Room to Let, based on a Margery Allingham radio play that had trod
much the same path as Mrs. Belloc-Lowndes's *The Lodger* in its tale
of a house guest who turns out to be Jack the Ripper. Neither an
uneasy script by John Gilling nor melodramatic direction by
Grayson quite manage to subdue an effective idea that even em-
braces the odd reflexive line—"Curious that *I* should be the *lodger*,"
muses Doctor Fell—and an unsettling harpsicord aids the air of

menace. But the real triumph of this very first example of Hammer Horror is the enigmatic beauty of Connie Smith, quite striking in her only outing for the company. *Room to Let* had been built around the malign persona of the Man in Black, Valentine Dyall. He was an actor of chilling presence in the whisker-twisting tradition of Tod Slaughter, and could easily have played either Frankenstein or Dracula, had the opportunity arisen. But the film itself was more of an aberration than a portent of things to come. If such signs *were* in the air, they were winging their way in from the west rather than the east.

There were now some 4,700 cinemas in the U.K., but of the thirty operational studios, only thirteen were presently in production, and an eligible workforce of 8,000 technicians was soon to be reduced to a little over 5,000. The Eady Plan had proposed a levy on ticket sales to help to subsidize British film production but, in the view of James Carreras, the industry had already "fallen on its face," and he was intent on doing something about it in his own way.

To take advantage of the continuing transatlantic standoff over quotas, Carreras decided to abandon Hammer's flirtation with homespun radio dramas and pursue a more vigorous hands-across-the-sea policy of coproduction with an American partner, the idea being that such an arrangement might provide the company with a foothold on the U.S. market for supporting features. First on the scene was Alexander Paal. Paal was a Hungarian émigré with contacts at United Artists through a previous association with Alexander Korda and Steven Pallos. The result was *Cloudburst* with Robert Preston, but Paal was soon followed by Sol Lesser and RKO, and on May 11, 1951, the first of many informal press luncheons was held at the Savoy Hotel to launch *Whispering Smith Hits London* as the spearhead of what was planned to be a nine-film affiliation with Hammer. [8]

The deal with Lesser was ultimately to prove abortive, [9] but a producer of twelve-day quickies named Robert L. Lippert was on the lookout for an additional line of supply for the shadow company he operated on behalf of Twentieth Century Fox. Lippert was, first and foremost, an exhibitor, with more than sixty theaters to his name. But since 1948, and the Cinecolor western *Wildfire*, he had also been Exclusive's main supplier of American product through his own Screen Guild Pictures. (Exclusive had built its reputation as a provider of low-budget action spectacles, many of which were culled from the Lippert stable: *Savage Drums, FBI Girl, The Dalton Gang, Unknown World, Tales of Robin Hood, The Return of Jesse James).*

With the blessing of Fox President Spyros Skouras, Lippert contracted to coproduce with Hammer. Indigenous American stars were required to make the deal feasible, but Fox was one of a number of companies with funds in Britain that had been frozen as a result of the Anglo-American Agreement of 1948. By using these funds, Lippert undertook to provide two stars and the script for each film, in return for distribution rights in the U.S.

Hammer was the first domestic producer to secure such a guarantee. In the wake of it, it would commence a whole series of formula thrillers styled along Hollywood lines and starring the likes of Paul Henreid, George Brent, Dan Duryea, Alex Nicol, Lloyd Bridges, and others who had not yet found a niche for themselves on American television. The first of these was *The Last Page,* which went onto the floor on July 9, 1951. It was to be followed by sixteen more over the next four years.

The deal with Lippert was intended to complement a coproduction arrangement that had already been arrived at between Carreras and James Brennan, a wealthy Manchester exhibitor who had also long been associated with Exclusive. Both were in addition to a continuation of Hammer's own program.

With the possibility of production tripling, the benefits of shooting in country houses were less apparent. Tony Hinds was alert to the shortcomings: "The camera is restricted and new angles are difficult to find with immobile scenery." The prospect of two new strings to the corporate bow forced Hammer to consider an offer to base itself at the Riverside Studios in Hammersmith. Hinds had his doubts, but a return to a more conventional studio-based operation seemed to be in the cards, and three permanent groupings of craftsmen and technicians (totaling 140 in all) were envisaged, to allow for simultaneous production at Manchester with Brennan, Riverside with Lippert, and Bray—until the expiration of the lease on Down Place at the end of 1951.

The deal with Brennan went only as far as the ironically titled *Never Look Back,* the house at Bray went begging for takers to occupy its empty corridors and, as a third Lippert film went onto the floor at Riverside, the ever-belligerent technicians' union—the ACT [10] —called a job action. With equal belligerence, James Carreras threatened to suspend indefinitely all his 1952 production unless the dispute was resolved. *Stolen Face* overran its schedule in the course of the job action, but good sense prevailed, and grudging cooperation was returned. Hammer had been given reason to reflect on its decision to leave Down Place, however. "It just wasn't economical," said Hinds. Carreras promptly made an offer to purchase the property outright, and in return for permanent tenancy of part of the west wing, the Davies family (who owned the house) accepted. This Thames-side mansion was to become Bray Studios, and it would be the headquarters of Hammer Films for the next sixteen years.

With Hammer in a home of its own at last, production could begin in earnest—more or less. "The nicest thing about arriving at Bray in the morning—my memories of Bray in the early morning are always of it freezing, absolutely freezing! —was that you got out of the car and walked into the kitchen. And if there was nobody there to give you bacon-and-eggs, you fried your bacon-and-eggs yourself!...It was that kind of atmosphere," recalled Aida Young, who had just arrived at Hammer as a young second assistant director on *Mantrap* for producers Michael Carreras and Alex Paal.

The restructuring of Down Place into a functioning film studio meant equipping it with dressing rooms, wardrobe, makeup, and a restaurant. It was further extended to incorporate sound, camera, and props departments, and the other necessary technical adjuncts—all in addition to the various administrative offices, two small sound stages, and an exterior lot of some 35 acres. It was a tight squeeze, and despite their designations, few of these areas would be left untouched by an art department forever on the lookout for suitable locations that could be adapted into sets. Expansion on this scale would not be repeated until 1957, when the success of *The Curse of Frankenstein* would see most of the above dispersed from the main building in favor of enlarging the stages. But Bray was to remain a country house in essence, and the ambience of gentrification would linger on.

By the end of 1952, the liaison with Lippert was underpinning Exclusive's business strategy with a solid foundation of Anglo-American cooperation. According to Michael, it had opened up the United States as a potential market in "one fell swoop," but it was also investing the small company with some significant talent on the side. The works of Max Catto, Leo Marks, James Hadley Chase, Elleston Trevor, Jon Manchip White, and even actor George Sanders were now reaching the screen via Hammer's films, and Terence Fisher was rapidly becoming the company's house director.[11] The American stars who were feeling the pinch of the B-picture might have had to work for "short salaries," but they were afforded generous expenses, and the tripartite nature of the Hammer operation had come into its own to make the most of the situation: James Carreras did the deals, Tony Hinds did the bulk of the producing, and Michael did everything else—casting, story editing, and public relations, including "pubbing and clubbing" the stars. Paulette Goddard may have had to put up with only one new outfit for *The Stranger Came Home* (1954), but she made a Hammer film, nonetheless—as did Zachary Scott, Cesar Romero, Forrest Tucker, and all the others who joined the wagon train from Hollywood to Bray.

There was still little formal structure to the company. Hammer was a loose association of talents where affinities were struck and people gravitated to the roles that best suited them. But as the Lippert films got into their stride, all that began to change, and a more businesslike approach took its place. In January 1953, a new policy was enacted whereby two teams, each consisting of a director, production manager, first assistant director, and editing staff, were formulated to work in rote. One was to be headed by Tony Hinds and the other by Michael Carreras. Hammer was beginning to take shape.

The deal with Lippert had now proceeded on its uninterrupted way for almost two years, and the experience had been an invaluable one for all concerned. It had enabled Tony Hinds to perfect the art of low-budget production—"You worked long hours for very little money," said Aida Young—and Michael Carreras to finally marry his love of jazz to a Hammer film (*Face the Music*, in which Alex Nicol's trumpet solos were performed by Kenny Baker). By June 1953, with Bray's third stage nearing completion, it was announced that arrangements had been made with Lippert for certain of Hammer's future productions to be shot in color, to meet the growing threat from television, and that the first of these would probably be Robert Louis Stevenson's *The Weir Of Hermiston*. (This was a nominal response to Disney's 1950 *Treasure Island*, and the upcoming *The Master of Ballantrae*. Robert Louis Stevenson was *in*.)

The remarkable change in the fortunes of Exclusive had turned James Carreras into something of a celebrity in his own right, and he was now intent on making similar strides in the world of show business, particularly through its charity conduit—the Variety Club of Great Britain. In 1954, he attained the post of chief barker, and he would become president of Variety Club International seven years later (the first to serve two terms). His new found philanthropic bent would also come to embrace the London Federation of Boys' Clubs (as president), the Friends of the Duke of Edinburgh's Award (as chairman), and the Royal Naval Film Corporation, through which he would provide free films to the Navy, ultimately persuading others in the industry to follow suit. He was to hold eight more board and council seats, chairman and trusteeships, but his interest in charitable works would be strictly limited to the facility they offered for making friends and influencing people. Whether it meant arranging strawberry teas on the sundrenched lawns of Oakley Court for the benefit of visiting bigwigs from the Bank of America, or creating the position of "personal assistant" for Terry O'Neill (son-in-law of C. J. Latta, one of the "founding twelve" of the Variety Club and managing director of AB Pathé[12]), Carreras would become supremely adept at using his largesse on Hammer's behalf with the increasing number of contacts that such magnanimity was to attract.

With James Carreras immersed in "the getting to know you syndrome," as Michael would put it, "especially where money might be available," and Hammer/Exclusive expanding their respective operations by the day, an adjustment in corporate thinking was again in the cards. "Quite early on, Jim Carreras wanted Michael and I to pack up producing and become executive producers and work in London with him," Hinds said. "I didn't fancy it at all—I never liked the Wardour Street bit, and I wouldn't do it." But someone had to, and Michael was obliged to take the duty on his own shoulders after Hinds declined. "Tony didn't want to be an executive producer any more than I did," Michael recalls. "He wasn't the slightest bit interested in the paperwork." As a result, the role of line producer would now be Hinds's alone.

The incursion onto Hammer's stages of American associate producers such as Julian Lesser had not been to Hinds's liking, however. "I liked the setup before we got the Americans in," he said. "I didn't like not having things absolutely under my control."

He had responded by upping and leaving on a six-month sabbatical, ostensibly to embark on more formal training in the lower echelons of the industry. "I'd never been in another studio, ever—never even stood on the floor and watched." Hinds had been offered the post of third assistant to Leslie Norman on Ealing's *West of Zanzibar.* "Jimmy Carreras thought I was mad to try and find out how other films were made." He went, regardless, but he never became third assistant. Tony Hinds was a director of Hammer Films and partner of the combative James Carreras, and the ACT refused to grant him a work permit.

Michael Carreras had used the occasion to spread his cinematic wings a little further afield. While Terence Fisher was at Brands Hatch in Kent, directing Richard Conte in a humdrum motor-racing thriller called *Mask of Dust* for associate producer Mickey Delamar, Michael had taken a unit to Bodiam Castle in Sussex for *The Men of Sherwood Forest* and to the fishing village of Polperro in Cornwall for *Break in the Circle.* In a significant departure from form, both films were in color (though not for Lippert). "I was constantly trying to make each one a little more interesting," he explains. But the reins of production were not to stretch this far for long. By the end of 1954, the day of the "intrusive" coproduction was coming to a close, and when Hammer began to consider its next move, Anthony Hinds was once more back at Bray, and back in control.

Under Hinds, Bray was now to welcome a multiplicity of talents through its refurbished Regency portals, and in a few years, it would be playing host to the ensemble of actors and technicians who together would turn Hammer into a household name. For the moment, though, such a grouping was only in embryo, and several of those who were about to play key roles in that process were still plying their craft elsewhere. A more pressing concern beckoned as the unit looked toward 1955: Cinemascope.

When Tony Hinds first began to contemplate *Quatermass,* it was a time of *Picture Post, Reveille,* and *Eagle,* when the most popular authors were Mickey Spillane and James Hadley Chase and the most popular film stars were Alan Ladd, Richard Todd, and Jane Russell. Radio comedy was king, and the kings of radio comedy were "Archie Andrews" and The Goons. Wilfred Pickles and his Mabel were jovially entreating the listening public to "Have a Go," and *film noir* in British terms meant *Fabian of the Yard* or the prurient criminological reconstructions of Edgar Lustgarten.[13]

Hammer was not entirely a stranger to science fiction, having dipped three toes in its virgin waters with *Stolen Face* (1951), *Four Sided Triangle* (1952), and the more overt space operatics of Charles Eric Maine's *Spaceways* (1952). The first was a plastic-surgery thriller of the change-the-face-but-the-personality-remains-the-same variety (a plot that would resurface under the guise of *Frankenstein Created Woman* in 1967). The third was a murder mystery made marginally less routine through the device that the body in question is thought to have been stowed away on a *spaceship*. By far the most interesting of the trio was *Triangle*—a mad-lab confection from a 1949 novel by William F. Temple, starring Barbara Payton, who had achieved a certain notoriety through a triangle of her own. It had been only the fourth film for Michael Carreras as producer, but with its story of a scientist who clones the woman he loves, its *Metropolis*-inspired laboratory, and its fiery climax, it was uncannily precognitive of the Gothic alchemy to come. "The direction is uneven," said one reviewer, "but the science scenes are tense enough for anyone." In addition to these, Exclusive had handled the British release of Lippert's 1950 ground breaker *Rocketship X-M*, among its many less-notable offerings from other producers—*Robot Monster* (1953); *King Dinosaur* (1955).

The signs for a positive box-office reception for *Quatermass* were good. The year 1954 had witnessed the arrival of *The Creature From the Black Lagoon, Godzilla, Them!,* and British opus *Devil Girl From Mars*. The trend looked set to continue into the following summer with *This Island Earth, Tarantula,* and *It Came From Beneath the Sea.* "Dan Dare" was still a popular feature on Radio Luxembourg, and Charles Chilton's "Journey into Space" (which had embarked on the Light Programme on September 21, 1953, in the wake of "Quatermass") was continuing into series after series, so a film version of Nigel Kneale's science-fiction opus seemed a reasonable short-term bet, in view of its potential to cash in on a boom that was still pulling in the crowds, especially in America. As a bonus, the company's long-standing connections with the BBC through its many adaptions from radio had already ensured the project a smooth transition to the screen. On a budget of no more than £42,000, *The Quatermass Experiment* was now to become Hammer's forty-third feature (according to the *official* count, which began with *Dr. Morelle*).

> "It's the Quatermass experiment. I'm afraid you'll have to take it right to top level, sir—I need troops and the civil defence."
> —Inspector Lomax
> *The Quatermass Experiment*

The director's chair was offered to Val Guest, who had already helmed four films for Hammer: *Life With the Lyons* (1953), *Men of Sherwood Forest, The Lyons in Paris* (aka *The Lyons Abroad*), and *Break in the Circle* (1954). The breezy Londoner was unimpressed with the idea at first, his only experience of science fiction having been to cowrite and direct a comic fantasy called *Bees in Paradise* for Gainsborough in 1944, but he was eventually persuaded to join the project by his actress wife Yolande Donlan. The script was offered to American Richard Landau, who had written the last three of Hammer's Lippert coproductions. It was to be a fortuitous pairing, since the combined talents of Guest and Landau were to bring a frenetic pace and stark American neo-realism to *Quatermass* that would see the film sit comfortably alongside the very best of the current crop of sci-fi extravaganzas.

The all-important role of Professor Quatermass had gone to American *noir* heavy Brian Donlevy.[14] An able and proficient second-leaguer in the Hollywood gangster mold, Donlevy's particular brand of slit-eyed deviousness made him a curious choice. But like so many actors who had broken their teeth on the slick pulp thrillers of the forties, he carried an easy authority and came endowed with a screen presence that belied his stature. This would be used to great effect to give the belligerent scientist the air of a man who could walk through doors without opening them—a trait ideally suited to the faster pacing of the film.

Character actor Jack Warner, who was to play Inspector Lomax, was under contract to J. Arthur Rank. Warner had already played similar roles in *Dear Murderer* (1949) and *Valley of Eagles* (1951),[15] but at the time, he was better known to British audiences as the voice of Joe Huggett, amiable patriarch of the long-running radio sit-com family "The Huggetts," who had themselves been sired from an initial outing on the big screen. Warner was fast becoming identified with sympathetic authority figures, and he was therefore admirably dispositioned to carry the adversarial weight of the common man against unknown forces from outer space.

Finally, there was Richard Wordsworth (then a relative unknown), who would be Guest's choice for the monster. His excellent mime ability was to bring a pathos to the part of Carroon that would be worthy of Karloff himself, and it is arguable that he could have gone on to play the creature in *The Curse of Frankenstein*—perhaps even Dracula.[16] Needless to say, he did not (due in part to his expressed antipathy toward repeating such a role), and thus he would assure Christopher Lee of *his* place in film history.

Prior commitments had already taken up most of the production schedule for 1954, so *Quatermass* had to wait until the very end of the year before being prepared to go in front of the cameras. It just made it. By then, a backlog of unreleased films had built up—and not only at Exclusive.

The deal with Lippert had reached its natural end, but cinema attendance was now significantly on the decline, thanks mainly to TV and despite the short-lived gimmick of 3-D. This had led to the first closures among independent theaters, which further limited the domestic market for the second features that hitherto had been the stock-in-trade of both Hammer *and* Exclusive.[17] All indicators were pointing to the fact that a radical rethink was required, if the company was to go on repeating the record turnovers of preceding years. Radical, the Hinds/Carreras partnership was not. Theirs had been a no-risk strategy. They had followed established patterns and traded on proven success. Their strength was in sales and promotion, and their business had been founded on the simple principles of supply and demand. Suddenly, that demand was abating.

Despite the typically upbeat announcement of a plethora of new productions for 1955, Hammer would make only one more feature over the next twelve months: *Women Without Men*—and that, simply because it was too late to stop it. Theater owners desperate to combat the creeping menace of television were becoming unanimous in their demand for something different to offer their reducing numbers of paying customers. Something different was increasingly coming to mean color and scope. But switching to what was effectively *first*-feature production overnight was a gamble that James Carreras was not prepared to take. Shooting in color was one thing, but shooting in color *and* scope was a high-risk strategy that flew in the face of his natural business conservatism.

Many of Hammer's earlier black-and-white features were now being sold off to an intermediary in readiness for a new life on the very medium that was threatening to engulf the industry.[18] Bray Studios—with an advocated *nine* workable stages, according to the latest specification—was currently the subject of speculation about its *own* imminent sale to one of the new ITV franchisees. James Carreras confirmed that there had indeed been an offer and that the Hammer board would be meeting to consider the situation. "We *never* had any policy," Tony Hinds recalls. "We had directors' meetings at which Jim Carreras would announce what was happening and that would be that. There was never any discussion." Michael is more forthright about his father's style of management: "He did all the talking, and we did the nodding."

Face the Music had been the first Hammer film to respond to the advent of the new technology by being made available in both the standard (Academy) ratio of 1 to 1.33 and 1 to 1.85 for wide-screen showing, and other productions had followed suit. But by November 1954, Warners was signalling the end of this dual-format compromise by restricting the release of *A Star Is Born* to the Cinemascope version only. Since many more theaters were being forced to install wide-screen equipment, they were naturally desirous of using it. Despite the touch-and-go nature of events, the usual exhibitor presentation reel for *The Quatermass Experiment* augured unusually well, and as the combined staffs of Hammer and Exclusive made their way to the Grand Hall of the Criterion Hotel in Piccadilly to attend a December 3 ball in celebration of Exclusive's twentieth birthday, it was a time to take stock, retool, and wait and see.

The original 1953 serial of "Quatermass" had transmitted live, as did the sequel two years later (before the introduction of videotape in 1956), and it had been one of television's early popular successes.[19] Written by Kneale and produced by Rudolph Cartier, "The Quatermass Experiment" had caught the public's imagination like nothing before it and little since. Word spread fast, and on each Saturday of its six-week airing, it "had the nation grinding to a halt," in Michael's words, as pubs emptied and streets cleared. The reason lay in the sheer believability of a serial thriller, that in the days before Sputnik, and in the comforting domestic environs of living rooms throughout the land, had sent a manned rocketship to breach the cloud cover and leave Earth's safe embrace for the dark unknowns of space, only to have it become infested with a cosmic virus that was to absorb two of its crew and turn the third into a voracious mutation capable of ingesting entire populations. Of course, Hollywood had done it all before, but never with such matter-of-fact realism—never with such *immediacy*. To a nation already agog with postwar spectacle—the Festival of Britain, the crowning of a new queen, the conquest of Everest as jewel in that crown—"The Quatermass Experiment" had not only been a technological triumph in televisual terms, it had been a nightmare vision of just where that technology might be taking it.

Kneale's serial had struck a chord—even the name of its benign scientist was to become synonymous with horror—and its very unrepeatability invested it with the sort of legendary quality that was normally reserved for the most enduring of folk myths. When Hammer came to exploit its version of the story for a public eager to recapture the vicarious terrors of that portentous summer of two years before, it was to emphasize the horror element by dropping the "E" from Experiment in advertising campaigns (and the title card of the film itself on its initial release) and amplifying the "X," to underline the fact that *Quatermass* was only the twelfth such film to qualify for an "X" since the inception of the certificate. [20]

The film would turn out to be hugely popular and unknowingly prophetic. When the Quatermass rocket made its nosedive into a Berkshire field in the opening sequence like an immense steel dart finding the bull's-eye, it was to bring more than the threat of contagion from space. With it, Hammer Horror would also arrive on the scene, and that would go on to make an altogether bigger impact.

> *A space-probe launched by Professor Bernard Quatermass crash-lands back on Earth after a 1,500-mile voyage into the unknown, with two of its crew missing and the third in the grip of a strange disease. With the help of Inspector Lomax, Quatermass discovers that the two men were absorbed by a life-form that is using the survivor, Carroon, as its carrier on Earth. His arm now deformed through fusion with a cactus plant in his hospital bedroom, Carroon escapes and goes foraging for food: he is transmuting into a monster that is able to reproduce itself at cyclical intervals. The search*

culminates during a television outside broadcast, when the result of the Professor's "experiment" is spotted in the eaves of Westminster Abbey. The entire generating power of London is diverted to fry the monster before it has time to spore and endanger all life on the planet. With the threat defeated, Quatermass determines to press on with the exploration of space.

Considering the industry's predicament at the time of its pro-duction, *The Quatermass Experiment* opens on an appropriately ominous note. The credits roll against an overcast sky, to the accompaniment of the first of James Bernard's many doom-laden scores for Hammer. From this point on, Guest goes straight for the jugular. The film abandons Kneale's exposition and begins by crashing its rocket at "Oakley Green," in the process, making full use of every facility at hand. These scenes were shot around Bray village itself. The rocket's hull was built on the Bray back lot, as was the exterior of Westminster Abbey for the finale. The abbey interiors were constructed on Bray's new "large" stage, with much use of glass painting to disguise the innate poverty of the set. Less effective was Les Bowie's tripe-and-rubber monster at the climax, but since it was produced on an effects budget of almost zero, the fact that it works at all can be considered an achievement. Other scenes were filmed at Windsor, and second-unit shooting around London added breadth to the narrative that would soon be notice-able by its absence, as later horrors became more studio bound.

While the general thrust of the plot remains the same, few individual sequences from the TV serial crossed to the screen intact. The tale's main *frisson*, the episode of the cactus, is given a more viable dramatic charge in the screenplay, as are other horror ele-ments, such as the death of a chemist, who lived to tell the tale on television. The film's corpses are suitably shocking. So much so, that shots of them were excised from many British reissue prints by the more squeamish local watch committees.

The serial was something of a science-fiction hybrid. The initial optimism of Kneale's professor had given way to doubt and uncer-tainty in the course of the story (in the time-honored tradition of "mad" scientists) and in a climactic display of recant and penitence, Quatermass had offered to sacrifice himself to the monster in return for the salvation of a world that *he* had placed in jeopardy to begin with. And despite its origin as an organic protoplasm floating in the cosmic vacuum, the serial's monster was ultimately regarded as evil—a vampiric essence that had fed on the astronauts fear ("You will overcome this evil. Without you, it cannot exist upon the Earth"); it was the last trace of their humanity, inhabiting its consciousness still, that was called upon to vanquish the "beast."

These mythic undertones of the cosmic struggle between good and evil are jettisoned from the film with some dispatch by Landau's screenplay. While Kneale may have deplored the change of characterization wrought on his scientist, there is no question that Donlevy's Quatermass is more surefooted when it comes to dealing with catastrophic accident. Landau's shift of emphasis was in tune with other science-fiction films of the fifties which, despite their predilection for exploring the possibilities of apocalypse at every turn, were invariably at pains to emphasize that nothing was beyond the improvisations of postatomic man.

If American science fiction had sounded an occasional note of caution, Kneale's "Quatermass" had trumpeted an unequivocal warning. But while the television serial had been designed for a British audience, the film was targeted for an American one, and *its* script gives short shrift to any soul-searching: Donlevy's professor knows what he's about, and despite a hiccup or two, the world was to be persuaded to realize that. In the teleplay, the Celtic dreamer in Kneale had taken issue with the headlong rush to oblivion that he felt was inherent in the threat of superpower technology; the film redresses the balance in favor of the technocrats.

Viewed from this distance, the plot of *The Quatermass Experiment* throws up some curious anomalies in the way this new technocracy was perceived. Quatermass is a scientific buccaneer who owes no allegiance to government and appears to be quite capable of launching a space probe without so much as a by-your-leave from his local authority. This produces the idiosyncrasy that a civilian police force is brought in to investigate what is self-evidently a scientific accident—one that has taken place outside of the Earth's atmosphere—as if it were a simple case of murder.[21] It is a notion that harks back thematically to *Spaceways* (which was also partly scripted by Landau), and it was allowed to remain in the film to provide the mandatory conflict-of-opposites through which its writer could ultimately restate his faith in the scientific hierarchy, despite that hierarchy having to resort to a bout of total mobilization every now and again in order to correct the occasional "glitch" in the system.

> "...Every experiment is a risk, and there will always be those who accept the risk, the challenge to meet and conquer that which might lie ahead...."

From Richard Landau's draft of
The Quatermass Experiment

The Quatermass Experiment had its West End opening at the London Pavilion on August 26, 1955. Reviews in the press were surprisingly favorable, and with the *News Chronicle* graciously providing the sales pitch—"This is the best horror film since the war"—it proceeded to clock up an astonishing £3,500 a week, to become the biggest hit in town. Hammer's publicity folder for the film had characterized its producer as "serious-minded, rather inclined to the soberness and gravity of people and things." If it was meant as a joke, then it was to be entirely appropriate, for *things* were exactly what Tony Hinds would be inclined toward from here on in.

Hammer's Christmas 1954 communiqué to the trades had promised a total of seven color features and eight scope shorts, but the hard-times year of 1955 saw the company produce not much more than the latter, on a borrowed lens, while the industry in general waited for the coup de grace that many felt certain would inevitably be delivered by the September 22nd inauguration of commercial television. The once mighty Ealing Studios, bastion of British film production, had already given up the ghost (its new owners would be the BBC), so Bray had been busily turning its facilities and personnel to other things.

In place of the promised features, the studios had been leased out to anyone brave enough to venture into production, though there were few of them. The ACT had done its bit by backing *Stolen Assignment*, which had made use of Bray (and Terence Fisher) before "The Errol Flynn Theatre" stepped in to save the day by occupying its limited stages for a six-month stint. Camera operator Len Harris had found himself dispatched to do jobbing work for television (such as shooting variety acts at the Adelphi Theatre for

"Jack Hylton Presents"), while others on the permanent staff of 68 had been subcontracted to the likes of the Danzigers.[22] As Hammer waited for a sign, Michael Carreras was able to indulge his passion for big bands and big stages by filming *Cyril Stapleton and the Show Band*, the first of six musical shorts in scope, at the Horticultural Halls in Victoria before switching the remainder to Elstree. But color and Cinemascope were also to be used for a pair of shorts of a less frivolous nature, as both of Hammer's house producers were forced to mark time. Following the pattern set by *The Men of Sherwood Forest*, Michael was to opt for the light-hearted escapism of *Dick Turpin—Highwayman*, but Tony Hinds chose to try out the format on a thriller subject—*A Man on the Beach*. A surplus of film stock allowed the eight announced shorts to be expanded to ten, and a quick trip to Denmark produced *Copenhagen*, as well as providing some location footage (and the backdrop) for *The Right Person*. In the uncertain climate, even the success of *Quatermass* would not be enough to convince James Carreras to put all Hammer's eggs into one basket, and this scatter-gun approach was to remain the order of the day until something much more tangible than Les Bowie's glass-painted spaceship appeared on the horizon.

The release of *The Quatermass Experiment* was timed to cash in on prepublicity for the BBC's sequel to the original serial: "Quatermass II" (the first episode of which was to be broadcast on October 22). With the character once more fresh in the public mind, returns from the new Exclusive release were nothing short of spectacular. When it came due for a circuit booking in November through ABC, its nominal West End support—*The Eric Winstone Band Show*—was waived in favor of the obligatory second feature which, because of the limited number of "X" certificate films in distribution, turned out to be Jules Dassin's acclaimed *Rififi*. The combination saw Hammer's fortunes firmly on the up again by Christmas.

For Hammer and Bray, a slow death had been narrowly avoided. The next step was speedily to exploit what had become a *solo* success for the company which had only been formed as an outgrowth of Exclusive in the first instance. For Hammer's aging parent, *The Quatermass Experiment* was to mark the beginning of the end. Exclusive had found itself in the shadow of something much more exciting and potentially more profitable, and nothing at 113 Wardour Street was ever going to be quite the same again.

At Bray, schedules were reshuffled to make way for another stab in the direction of a feature that even the *New Statesman* had been moved to concede was "a better film than either *The War of the Worlds* or *Them!*" Having wiped the slate clean of every project that had been announced for 1955-56,[23] Hinds readied his next full-blown science-fiction opus with the formula exactly as before, even to the extent of using the highly marketable "X" factor for a second time around. The result was to be *X The Unknown*.

> "Let's not conjure up visions of nameless horrors creeping about in the night."
>
> —Dr. Royston
> *X The Unknown*

Visions of horrors were exactly what Hammer was intent on conjuring up but, bankrupt of original source material for an encore to *Quatermass*, Hinds turned to the apprentice screenwriting talents of one of his own.

Jimmy Sangster had been working his way up through the ranks at Hammer and been alternating assistant director duties with those of production manager. He had always nurtured a desire to be more creatively involved (though he himself would put a different perspective on it: "I figured writing had to be a nice easy way of making a living if you could do it"), and he had already submitted one treatment with the encouragement of Tony Hinds. But the cutback in production during 1955 had afforded the 27-year-old his first real crack at what would soon prove to be his forte. For the usual reasons of economy, Sangster had been allowed to adapt the Victor Canning short story "A Man on the Beach" for American director Joseph Losey, who was now working in Britain as a result of the persecution of U.S. left-wing sympathizers by Senator Joe McCarthy and his House Un-American Activities Committee (HUAC).

To cash in on *Quatermass*, what Hammer needed was a variation on Kneale's theme of an extraterrestrial invader. With time at a premium, Hinds asked Sangster if *he* could come up with something. The young production manager took it literally and, with the ingenuity that was subsequently to become his trademark, created the screen's first *ultra*terrestrial threat, in the form of a living magma that disgorges itself from the Earth's molten core. Sangster was to mix the requisite ingredients with an aplomb that largely belied his novitiate status, and his script for *X The Unknown* would engineer a surprisingly effective addition to the monster-on-the-loose cycle begun by *The Thing From Another World* (1951), and serve as the prototype for *The Blob* (1958). A grateful Hammer rewarded his initiative with a princely £750 for providing story and screenplay, which was sufficient to enable him to whisk his wife and child from Seymour Place in Marylebone to the greener pastures of a brand-new house at Ascot.

On this occasion, the obligatory American presence would be furnished by Dean Jagger, a Hollywood veteran whose career dated back to 1929 but who had appeared in the company of Spencer Tracy and Robert Ryan as recently as 1954 in *Bad Day at Black Rock*, and with Ida Lupino and Steve Cochran in the Exclusive release, *Private Hell 36*. In support would be a trusty band of contract stalwarts and some newer faces from television. Edward Chapman's career went back to *Things To Come* (1936)—he was soon to foil for Norman Wisdom—and John Harvey was a long-time friend of producer Hinds. On the other side of the coin, William Lucas was making a name for himself on the small screen, and ex-child actor Tony Newley was about to do the same in the Top Twenty. (His two day's work on the film would earn him £100.) Ironically, it was to be the presence of the other *American* in the lineup which would hint that Hammer's transatlantic dealings were never again to be quite as smooth in the future as they had been in the past.

An Army exercise on a desolate Scottish moor triggers off an explosion that results in the opening of a large fissure. Atomic scientist Dr. Royston is called to investigate and discovers the soldiers suffering from radiation burns. After the death of a local boy and the theft of materials from a hospital radiography unit, Royston concludes that the fissure has released a form of energy from the Earth's molten core that feeds on radium, that this "X" will require ever-larger doses to survive, and that its next target will be the research station. A search confirms the creature's existence, and Royston tries to evacuate the plant's cobalt phial. Before this can be achieved, the thing attacks the plant, consumes the cobalt, and returns to the fissure. Royston has been experimenting with neutralizing radioactivity by means of sonic waves, and he is now persuaded

to test his prototype against the monster. The Unknown is lured from
its lair and destroyed. But for how long?

X The Unknown commenced in January 1956, with the exiled Joseph Losey set to direct (under the pseudonym of Joseph Walton). But warning voices threatened. It was quickly made plain to Hammer that any film which involved someone on the HUAC "blacklist" would have the rug pulled out from under it in terms of its potential distribution in the U.S. Losey obligingly contracted pneumonia, and within the week, he had been unceremoniously replaced by hard-nosed Ealing producer-director Leslie Norman.

The filming itself was a distinctly unpleasant experience for all concerned. The location unit was based at Beaconsfield Studios, and much of the action involved night exteriors in a nearby gravel pit. Tony Hinds, who had been thrown off his stride by the debacle over Losey, found himself working with a director with whom he had little rapport. Norman was known as a "difficult gentleman." Despite being faced with a crew up to its galoshes in freezing mud, he insisted on "miles and miles" of camera track, much of which promptly disappeared into the slurry, never to be seen again. Hinds was soon inclined to disappear himself. More than once, Michael Carreras was called away from his office to try to ease the ill-tempered transition of X to the screen, a task in which he was aided and abetted by associate producer Mickey Delamar (uncredited) and assistant director Chris Sutton. "That was a miserable picture," he said later. It was a sentiment that would be echoed by Jimmy Sangster, who had not yet given up his day job as a production manager.

The January shoot can be witnessed in a pronounced change of mood from its predecessor: *X The Unknown* swaps the high-key neon of the big city for the cold and foreboding winter light of Scottish moors (Buckinghamshire, in reality). It is infused with an entirely different ambience from the more familiar "tomorrow's world" look of the majority of mainstream American science-fiction films it unashamedly attempts to emulate. Like the irradiated slime that provides the script with its quota of thrills, there is a genuine flavor of the Gothic bubbling just below the surface in *X The Unknown.* Just as Nigel Kneale had done before him, Sangster allows this echo to undercut the tale's superficial air of pseudoscience, to resonate and disturb on a deeper, more primal level. A succession of sequences almost sees the film's notional science-fiction tag dispensed with altogether and replaced by the more traditional *motifs* of the eternal struggle between good and evil: the thing emerges from a bottomless pit; it is encountered near an eerie tower ruin at dead of night; it menaces a church. Sangster's monster may be made of mutated toxic mud, but it is an old-fashioned demon at heart—albeit wrought in atomic hellfire.

In a departure from the more reticent approach of its contemporary competitors, the film's "bowel-loosening" horror effects (as one reviewer referred to them) are fully dwelt upon. The "melting" head of the unfortunate radiographer is unexpected and (still) shocking, in accordance with the precedent set by *Quatermass*. In fact, it remains the single most horrific shot that Hammer ever committed to film.

X The Unknown was to introduce an element that had been absent from Kneale's more sober entry into the science-horror stakes. The vein of sardonic humor that would run through many of Sangster's later screenplays for Hammer is clearly in embryo here. "Is there anything in the fact that the only one killed was a National Serviceman?" a reporter enquires of the Army brass in charge of the search-and-destroy operation. "It's changed direction!" an airman screams in alarm on seeing what he takes to be an alteration in the monster's trajectory; "Turn the map the other way up," his mate replies, deadpan. But the *femme* presence is strictly token. Even allowing for its subject matter, *X The Unknown* is unreservedly mysoginist in outlook (a characteristic that would remain in Sangster's subsequent work), and the film's lack of a love interest may have helped to account for what would ultimately be a poorer box office compared to that of *Quatermass*.

In the meantime, James Carreras remained convinced that the road to international success ran through the U.S., and even before the completion of *Women Without Men* — the last of the Lippert/Fox coproductions—he had actively been seeking a new American partner who would be similarly placed to promote the company's wares on the other side of the Atlantic. By early 1956, through the auspices of Variety Club International, he found one in Eliot Hyman and Associated Artists, whose address alone (345 Madison Avenue) testified to his ability to wield power behind the scenes, particularly at Warner Brothers. In point of fact, Hyman had

much more influence at the court of King Jack than Robert Lippert
had ever held with Spyros Skouras.

The Quatermass Experiment had gone out via United Artists on
its stateside release (and taken a title change in the process, to *The
Creeping Unknown*, to accommodate American unfamiliarity with
the television serial). *X*, on the other hand, had originally been
destined for Sol Lesser and RKO, but a title dispute would see the
distribution rights pass from RKO to Warners (in time for them to
cobill the film with *The Curse of Frankenstein*). While the second
Quatermass would follow on the heels of the first and also be
handled by United Artists, this was a temporary agreement, at best.
James Carreras was looking for something a good deal more solid
than a transatlantic version of *La Ronde*.

To their credit, the hierarchy at Hammer had now begun to
realize that part of the success of *Quatermass* had lain in the essential *humanity* of that film's monster, and they began to cast around
for subjects of similar appeal. As *X The Unknown* went into post-
production under the aegis of Tony Hinds, Eliot Hyman was
approached by Milton Subotsky and Max J. Rosenberg—who were
later to found Hammer's rival, Amicus Films—with a view to him
financing a remake of Mary Shelley's horror classic *Frankenstein*. To
Hyman's way of thinking, the two New Yorkers had little experience of the business (their main claim to fame to date had been a
children's television series called "Junior Science"), and he begged
off. But he offered to prospect the idea to an associate in Britain
whose company had begun to specialize in much the same area—
Colonel James Carreras. Carreras, in turn, sounded out Jack Goodlatte who, recalling a *Daily Sketch* review of *Quatermass* that had
referred to the film as "a poor man's Frankenstein," indicated that
such a subject was likely to find favor in his eyes. The opportunity
was seized, and Subotsky and Rosenberg were instructed by Hyman to submit an outline. Carreras agreed to enter into a 50/50
partnership with Hyman on the venture, and by March 1956, James
and Michael Carreras had begun negotiations based on a working
draft of the screenplay. With the project sanctioned as part of the
program, Hammer announced its intention to remake *Frankenstein*
in the trades.

Response was swift. The company was informed in no uncertain
terms that it faced litigation from Universal Studios, makers of the
first Frankenstein film series, if any part of this "new" *Frankenstein*

infringed on copyrights held by Universal City, including Jack Pierce's makeup for Boris Karloff.

By the end of May, with *Frankenstein* undergoing some hasty revision in view of the threat from Universal, shooting was to commence on *Quatermass II*. United Artists having had its corporate arm twisted by James Carreras to foot almost three-quarters of the bill, Tony Hinds was allotted a leisurely six-week schedule this time, and a considerably upgraded budget of £92,000, to mount Hammer's version of the second Quatermass serial in the more expansive surroundings of Borehamwood.

> "God knows how many infected people they've got in high places."

> —Professor Quatermass
> *Quatermass II*

On the production side, the team was much as before, an exception being the addition of Anthony Nelson-Keys, who was later to figure prominently in the company's affairs by becoming general manager of Bray Studios in 1959. With the budget now doubled from the previous film, more care could be taken over production values. Three weeks of exteriors were ordered, with locations to include Hemel Hempstead New Town, the South Downs, and the Shell Haven oil refinery on the Essex coast, near the Isle of Grain. Since 100-foot monsters were required to lumber at the climax, the effects crew was enlarged appropriately. Over and above the luxury of increased fiscal freedom, a quieter revolution was about to turn the art department on its head: *Quatermass II* would be art director Bernard Robinson's first film for Hammer.

Robinson was a man of unique talent. A twenty-year industry veteran, his previous assignment had been *Reach For the Sky* (the bio-pic of fighter pilot Douglas Bader). With the popularity of the stiff-upper-lip war film or social drama that had always formed part of the staple diet of Ealing and others now coming to an end, along with the studios that made them, Robinson had been encouraged by Keys to lower his sights and move to where the work was. On June 22, he set up office at Bray, and throughout the next decade, he would become as responsible as any single individual could be for the intangible quality that would go to make a Hammer film.

Robinson's personal contribution to *Quatermass II* was minimal; he had to pick up a film already on the boards and run with it. But he would maintain a strong sense of identity with the previous production, which had been designed by James Elder Wills. In any event, the sets were carbon copies of those in the BBC production, as were the "Zombie" costumes, which were *literally* borrowed.

> *His funding temporarily suspended, Quatermass turns his attention to meteor-like objects falling in the vicinity of Winnerden Flats. Investigation reveals the existence of a vast construction at the site that replicates Quatermass's own "Moon Project"—an artificial environment designed to enable man to exist in an alien atmosphere. Quatermass discovers that the meteors come from an asteroid orbiting on the dark side of the Earth, and that they contain parasites capable of controlling their human hosts. It soon becomes apparent that the alien control extends to the government itself and that this "synthetic food plant" has been built to house these invaders. Quatermass and Lomax alert the workers to the danger and together they gain entry into the plant, where they take over the pressure control and flood the alien containers with lethal oxygen. The Quatermass 2 rocketship is launched toward the asteroid, its reactor substituting for an atomic warhead; it hits its target just as the collective organisms, in their poisoned rage, begin to destroy the plant.*

The admen had a field day—"A creeping terror of destruction! A nightmare of horror and fear!"—and before the titles, the film unfolds onto the screen at a fever pitch of excitement never quite attained in the previous adventure. The relentless pace that Val Guest brings to *Quatermass II* is helped considerably by James Bernard's strident scoring, which orchestrates elements introduced in *The Quatermass Experiment* into a symphony of sustained hysteria. Bernard had been singularly favored in reviews of the original film, and Hammer was never slow to capitalize on success.

From this opening sequence—in essence, not much more than a traffic accident with its ensuing garbled exchange between Quatermass and a young couple in another car—to the bravura finale of humankind at the mercy of a marauding toxic intelligence, *Quatermass II* provided an abundance of the kind of thrills that the audience had now come to expect, if a touch more cerebrally than before. The monsters themselves are splendidly staged, though the equivalent of the first film's "cactus" scene—the death of "Broadhead" in a cocoon of poison sludge—was handled with more subtlety at Lime Grove.

This time, Nigel Kneale had scripted from his own teleplay (having left the BBC and obtained his ticket from the Screenwriter's Guild), but Guest had further condensed the result into a tight 85 minutes by dovetailing some of its exposition into the cunningly crafted precredits sequence and completely abandoning the serial's anticlimactic ending, in which Quatermass himself flew the Q-2 rocket to the offending asteroid and destroyed the invader. (In the film, the rocket is turned into a nuclear bomb to perform the task by proxy.)

Kneale was less than happy with the end result, not least because Brian Donlevy had been asked to reprise the role of its scientist hero. As he was later to note in the introduction to the published version of his television script for "Quatermass and the Pit,"[24] "The first two serials...had reappeared in shortened cinema-film shape. The American actor Brian Donlevy, once an excellent comic heavy but quite gone to pieces, bawled his way through them in what was meant to be the role of poor Quatermass." Despite such objections, there is no doubting the robustness of Donlevy's portrayal or the power of the film. It more than matches the serial's strong subversive undertow and heightens its all-pervasive mood of paranoia.

> "Secret!—You put a label like that on anything and law and order goes out the window, is that it?"
>
> —Professor Quatermass
> *Quatermass II*

Kneale had adapted George Orwell's *1984* for the BBC prior to writing "Quatermass II" in 1955. The play had caused an outcry (partly because it had been transmitted on a Sunday) and the less successful film version had followed a year later, hot on the heels of an adaption of Orwell's *Animal Farm* by the animation team of Halas and Batchelor. While the totalitarianism addressed in these works was generally viewed as being of the Iron Curtain variety, their author had been more concerned with delivering a warning about a future that might know no such frontiers. This point was not lost on Kneale, and Orwell's futuristic parable on the Secret State found new and more topical form in "Quatermass II."

Nuclear power plants such as Doonreay on the coast of Caithness and Windscale (now Sellafield) in Cumbria had begun to appear on the horizon—structures the like of which had never been seen before. These constructs were viewed as the harbingers of a monstrous new technology. Contained within them were the atomic elements that in coalition could destroy the Earth.[25] They were the Gothic castles of the modern age, and it was fear of them that had given Kneale his inspiration for a striking assault on the icons of the new establishment. In the film, the "synthetic food plant" is depicted with an unnerving sense of the unearthly by photographer Gerald Gibbs, and it is only on entering this other-worldly domain that the nightmare really begins. The climactic battle that results as the workers rampage through this very heart of the techno-state has parallels throughout film history (most notably in *Metropolis*; 1926), but never was the ideological message so pronounced. In pursuing its polemic without compromise, the Kneale-Guest script overturns the accepted conventions of the genre. Science is no longer responsible. Its secrets have been plundered by the bureaucrats and turned into tools with which to suppress the masses. The science-fiction film was coming of age. Coincident with *Invasion of the Body Snatchers* (which was made at much the same time, but without the impetus that an impending Suez Crisis would provide to hone the point with more precision), *Quatermass II* posits a conspiracy theory that would have far-reaching implications. The formula was to resurface with little diminution of its impact in John Carpenter's *They Live!* (1988), a thinly veiled attack on "Reaganomics" and the politics of capitalism.

The radical theme of *Quatermass II* still resonates today, when propaganda and newspeak are as contemporaneous a currency as they were in 1956, but the film also managed to engineer a significant role reversal in the process. Embodied in its protagonist's lone struggle to avert the encroaching darkness of fascism (which the story encompasses by using all the trappings of the Big Brother state—loss of identity, mind control, paramilitary policing) is the resurgent notion of the scientist as *hero*.

Ironically, Nigel Kneale's more studied and imaginative essays into the realms of science fiction were unwittingly ringing the death knell on the giant monster cycle. In *Quatermass II*, the "infection" from space is merely a catalytic sideshow; the politicians are the villains of the piece. The monsters and the metaphors were no longer needed now, and within a year of the film's release, the cycle would be dying on its radioactive feet. As Kneale was to make unequivocal in the third and best of his Quatermass adventures ("Quatermass and the Pit"; 1959), the message was clear: the threat that man had been inspired to fear was revealed to be... *himself.*

> Lomax: "What worries me is how am I going to make a final report about all this?"
> Quatermass: "What worries *me* is, how final can it be?"
>
> —*Quatermass II*

Pretty final, was the real answer to that question, at least until another decade had passed. Reflected in the eventual box office would be the fact that the central theme of alien possession in *Quatermass II* had been progressively done to death by a whole series of American sci-fi thrillers —from *Invaders From Mars* (1953) and *It Conquered the World* (1956) through to the apotheosis of the breed, *Invasion of the Body Snatchers* (1956)—prior to the film's release in June 1957. A doubling of the budget was not to produce a corresponding increase in business. Returns would be good, but not *that* good and, in common with *X The Unknown*, not nearly as good as those of the original film. After the relative financial bonanza of Hammer's first excursion into the field, the comparatively lackluster performance of the follow-ups would begin to sow the seed of doubt, and *Quatermass II* was to confirm to the company that the science-fiction cycle was rapidly drawing to its close. But before that could happen, subjects that featured obsessive scientists were still much in favor, and having supped once of success, Hammer's executives were intent on repeating the experience. With *Quatermass II* in postproduction and *X The Unknown* ready for release (as the lower half of another double bill, with Clouzot's *Les Diaboliques* [*The Fiends*]), all eyes turned back to Subotsky's *Frankenstein* script.

When Anthony Hinds was introduced to what was now to be his next project, Milton Subotsky was still hard at work on the elimination of anything in his script that even sniffed of Universal copyright. Hinds found the Subotsky script "unusable" and casually pointed out to James Carreras that since the novel had been published in 1818, it was in the public domain and open to anyone to adapt. Consequently, Hammer had no need of outside writers. In reality, Hinds was simply not interested in any sort of *remake*. "Firstly, the script was just a complete steal—secondly, I couldn't do it in the budget—thirdly, I really didn't *want* to do it," he said later. The best efforts of both parties had achieved little to alleviate ongoing concern about the threat of litigation, and since most of the bright ideas at Hammer were springing from the enthusiasm of fledgling screenwriter Jimmy Sangster, Hinds suggested it might be judicious to terminate the arrangement with Subotsky and let he and Sangster be entrusted with the task of bringing *Frankenstein* to the screen from scratch. "[26] I wanted Jimmy because he was a friend. And because I knew he'd do what I told him!"

To everyone's relief, Sangster produced a draft of the story in three weeks. It turned the structure of the novel upside-down and made Frankenstein himself the main focus of attention. As an *aide memoire*, he and Hinds had gone back to Shelley and found characters that they could satisfactorily substitute for some of those in present employ: Krempe, Felix, Justine. Krempe would stand in conveniently for Universal's and Subotsky's use of the more preeminent Doctor Waldman, though Sangster did inadvertently retain at least one of Universal's original ideas in the concept of a *Baron* Frankenstein; in the novel, he is never more than a medical student. But a nod to all this back-peddling still managed to filter through into the synopsis of the film, which would note that Frankenstein's creature was "the result of experiments he had conducted from notes and formulas left by his father, the old baron, *who had been the creator of a former monster.*"

The film—now provisionally entitled *Frankenstein and the Monster*—had already been cast on the basis of the original script. It was duly revised to accommodate the changes Sangster had wrought. But the pirating of the work as an entirely British venture had begun to worry Eliot Hyman, who—on the strength of a successful June 1956 stateside opening for *The Quatermass Experiment*—had now arranged for the remainder of the production budget to come from the mighty Warner Brothers. There was still concern over the specter of Universal's attorneys-at-law. Hyman expressed severe reservations about the *Britishness* of the film and was keen that at least the baron should have the requisite American profile, a notion to which Hammer was not unsympathetic. The suggested use of Boris Karloff had been abandoned in the wake of the copyright threat, but while the talking continued, two more innovations were introduced, *sans* Sangster, that would take Hammer's *Frankenstein* as far away from the 1931 version as it was possible to get. It would be filmed in period, and Hinds was to be persuaded that it should also be shot in color, if only so it could be released that way in America.

To make absolutely sure that they were now in the clear, Hammer registered the film with the BFPA[27] as *The* Curse *of Frankenstein* (having been advised that such a form of words would better represent an original item), and followed this up by taking out an indemnity to protect their American interest. Hyman was happy, except for one thing: a sudden reticence on the part of Carreras to discuss any details about the cast, beyond the inexplicable remark in a memo of September 3 that stated they would naturally be first class and "have *no trace whatsoever* of a British accent."

To bring what had become *The Curse of Frankenstein* to the screen, Hammer needed a director conversant with the twin requirements of color and Gothic romanticism. Its two previous features in color—*The Men of Sherwood Forest* and *Break in the Circle*—had both been directed by Val Guest, but Guest had been lined up to direct *The Abominable Snowman* from another Nigel Kneale script. Joseph Losey had shot *A Man on the Beach* in color, but he was now out of the question. Michael Carreras had helmed a number of shorts in both color and scope for the company during the hiatus of 1955, but Michael had his mind on other things: the reshaping of the future of Hammer production. Of the available regulars, that left Terence Fisher.

Fisher had directed numerous features for Hammer, going back to the Lippert days, including all its earlier entries into the science-fiction arena prior to *Quatermass*. More importantly, he had served part of his apprenticeship at Gainsborough, whose productions were noted for their lush period detail and heavy romantic flavor, which was exactly what Tony Hinds now had in mind for *Curse*. "I asked for Terry because I thought he would get this 'Victorian melodrama' flavor," said Hinds. With the departure of Grayson and Searle in the wake of the company's "Americanization" in

1951, Fisher had become Hammer's most prolific house director. There was the added benefit that he had worked with both Michael Carreras and Tony Hinds as producers, so both men were well aware of his capabilities and method. Since his brief flirtation with fantasy, Fisher had been angling for something grittier to get his teeth into, and with the cancellation of all features originally scheduled for 1955 prior to the unprecedented success of *The Quatermass Experiment*, the company nominally owed him a film. The 52-year-old Fisher was given the job.

The Curse of Frankenstein was new ground for all who were party to it. Notwithstanding a modest budget of some £65,000 and typically short shooting schedule of less than five weeks, a lot had begun to ride on Hammer's decision to go the road of a horror freed from any pretense of a contemporary scientific "rationale." With that in mind, more than the threat of court action from across the water, Terence Fisher was offered the opportunity of viewing the Karloff version of the story, to familiarize himself with the territory. Fisher, who had neither seen the original nor read the novel on which it was based, declined. It was a decision that was to bring a freshness of approach to the piece that, when coupled with Sangster's adaptive ingenuity, was comprehensively to sever the umbilical cord to the past and produce a work destined to become as influential in the shaping of the horror films of the future as Karloff's *Frankenstein* had been before it.

> More than a hundred years ago, in a mountain village in Switzerland, lived a man whose strange experiments with the dead have since become legend.
> The legend is still told with horror the world over....It is the legend of...
> THE CURSE OF FRANKENSTEIN.
>
> —Screen caption
> *The Curse of Frankenstein*

Under the increasingly heady influence of rock 'n' roll, American cinema had now become putty in the hands of stars such as James Dean, Marlon Brando, and Montgomery Clift—the more especially since the 24-year-old Dean had seen fit to die at the wheel of his Porsche Spyder toward the end of the previous year. Youth culture was on the march, and a new freedom of artistic expression was following along behind. John Osborne's *Look Back In Anger* had already caused a storm of controversy at the Royal Court Theatre; the concept of "Free Cinema" was germinating in the minds of Lindsay Anderson, Karel Reisz, and Tony Richardson; and only three days before Hammer's *Frankenstein* would go onto the floor at Bray, *Love Me Tender* was to open in New York and teenagers throughout the world would find voice in the drawl of a young rockabilly singer from Tupelo, Mississippi, named Elvis Presley. [28]

All of this was shaping the Hammer Gothic to come. With Hinds's notion of "making Frankenstein a *shit*" very much in mind, Sangster had envisaged his baron to be in his early 20s—a coldly intellectual, arrogant dandy, disdainful of his contemporaries and driven by the twin furies of pride and ambition. The character, as written, had few redeeming features. He was a nineteenth-century rebel *with* a cause, self-centered and egotistical—Jimmy Porter out of Oscar Wilde. As if to mitigate the harsh, one-dimensional approach, the script exhibited a marked propensity for sending the material up every now and again. Fisher chose to ignore this aspect and opted instead to play it totally straight. (The tongue-in-cheek lines remain, but they are delivered deadpan and consequently pass as literal.) With the tone set and production scheduled for the end of 1956 after a somewhat shaky start, only one part of the puzzle remained—the role of the baron himself.

As preparations were being finalized for the film to commence shooting on November 19, Hammer was contacted by John Redway, the agent for an actor who had soared to prominence in December 1954 with his portrayal of Winston Smith in Nigel Kneale's television adaption of *1984*. Redway's client had played the lead in 31 subsequent TV plays and two serials within the space of two years; he had recently won Best Television Actor of the Year awards from two daily newspapers (the *Chronicle* and the *Mail*), as well as the Guild of Producers and Directors; he had since played opposite Alan Ladd in *The Black Knight* and, more importantly, Deborah Kerr in *The End of the Affair;* but he was now going through a "quiet patch." Redway had been asked to inform Hammer that his client had seen the trade announcements and expressed interest in the role of the baron, and to inquire if they would be interested in *him*.

The actor in question was Peter Wilton Cushing, and Hammer was delighted, especially since James Carreras had actively been courting him for some time in relation to other projects, so far without success.

By now, Eliot Hyman had begun to sense the maverick nature of this small British independent with whom he had allied himself —although he had not been prepared for the kind of cavalier responses he was receiving to the rapid-fire memos that were still winging their way by telex to 113 Wardour Street, in an attempt to clarify the situation. Hyman's queries with regard to the nature of the cast were stalled or deflected by tactics such as the suggestion that a *fourfold* increase in the leading actor's salary would now have to be contemplated, if an American played the role. Meanwhile, Carreras organized a meeting with Cushing that included a screening of the completed but as-yet-unreleased *X The Unknown*, to give him an idea of the sort of production qualities that Hammer could bring to a fantasy subject. Cushing, the absolute epitome of the English gentleman and most inoffensive of men, declared himself more than happy with the company and its product.

The deal was done; the last piece of the jigsaw that was to become *The Curse of Frankenstein* was now in place. Despite there being a twenty-year age gap between Cushing and the original Shelley (and Jimmy Sangster) conception of the character, Hammer had found its baron.

> As Baron Frankenstein languishes in prison awaiting execution, he relates the events that led to his downfall. The scene flashes back to Frankenstein and his tutor, Paul Krempe, discovering the secret of life through experimenting on animals. Frankenstein desires to breathe life into something that has never lived: a man built of parts from dead bodies. In the meanwhile, his cousin Elizabeth has arrived at the castle to prepare for a marriage of convenience to the baron. To furnish his creature with a brain, Frankenstein kills a fellow scientist. Krempe discovers the truth and threatens to expose Frankenstein's guilt. The creature is brought to life, but it escapes to kill a blind man and his grandson in the woods. Frankenstein and Krempe track it down, and Krempe shoots it. Frankenstein subsequently reanimates the creature and uses it to murder a maid. On the eve of his wedding, it escapes again and attacks Elizabeth on the castle roof. The baron hurls an oil lamp at the creature, who falls through a skylight and is destroyed in a vat of acid. Krempe arrives at the jail, and Frankenstein pleads with him to confirm that it was the creature who killed the maid and not he. Krempe refuses, and Frankenstein is led away to the guillotine.

Peter Cushing's portrayal of Victor Frankenstein was innovative. It is both authoritative and assured, easily overcoming some of the inconsistencies thrown up by the characterization of the script. Through technical skill and sheer force of personality, Cushing manages to submerge the calculated callousness of the man beneath a glaze of guile and persuasive charm and make him both attractive and compelling, in spite of himself. By the time he reached the screen, Hammer's baron was a veritable serpent in a silk dressing gown.

The character of Frankenstein was to soften with succeeding films,[29] giving rise to the common view that he is merely an obsessional, blind to the sensibilities of others in pursuit of great and worthy goals—a man ahead of his time, restricted by prejudice and hampered by fear and superstition. There is, frankly, no trace of this in *The Curse of Frankenstein*. The baron is a devious schemer who will tell any lie, contrive any situation, put anyone's life or livelihood at risk in order to get his own way. He contemplates and commits murder with an unpalatable ease. He exercises his *droit de seigneur* with the chambermaid as to the manor born. He conspires to deceive his innocent cousin Elizabeth for the thinly veiled purpose of some future, unspecified, experimentation on her, also. (When asked by Elizabeth if she could ever be of help to him in his work, Frankenstein replies sardonically, "Who knows, my dear? Perhaps you will...one day.") He spends his nights in necrophilia, and his days in plotting and indulging in illicit sex.

This Faustian Oppenheimer is scarcely redeemed by the high-minded ideals he espouses to justify the immorality of his methods. He is a danger to society much more than a benefactor of it. Yet Cushing's pronounced ability to convey mortal fear (not to say cringing terror)—used so convincingly in the BBC's "1984"—is deployed here in counterweight. As the baron faces execution in the film's final frames, the actor manages to extract a measure of sympathy for the character that is disproportionate to what might otherwise be expected of this arrogant psychotic, for whom the value of human life is equated only against its usefulness in provisioning him with the spare parts required of his surgery. In Sangster's crafting and Cushing's portrayal, Hammer's baron promised to go where no Frankenstein had been before him. Whatever age this Rabelaisian fiend actually belonged to, by 1957, his time certainly seemed to have come. They were going to explore the forbidden, these new antiheroes of horror, and where Frankenstein would leave off, Dracula would soon follow on.

Terence Fisher's direction is uncertain at first, safe and unadventurous and preferring to rely on long, single takes, with setups changing only as characters move from room to room. (Sangster's device of a first-person narrative interspersed with vignettes of dialogue to get the story underway was to find a better outlet in *Dracula*.) But as Fisher's confidence increases, so, too, does the fluidity of his camera and the extravagance of his compositional effects. Whether by design or not, the first part of *The Curse of Frankenstein* consists of little more than a series of static tableaux that depend entirely on *mise-en-scène* to do the work. But with the arrival of "the creature" three-quarters of an hour into the film, everything changes, and the whole production comes more vividly to life.

Much of *The Curse of Frankenstein* is photographed theater. It is not a frightening film, as such—it gets too much value from its Eastmancolor for that—but its quota of visceral thrills would leave a satisfied public clamoring for more, and it does contain at least two effectively staged "shock" scenes: the literally stunning death of Professor Bernstein, and our first sight of the creature itself. Only the finale ultimately disappoints, when the poverty of the staging becomes apparent as Frankenstein, his cool detachment seeming suddenly to desert him, illogically attempts to shoot the creature to "save" Elizabeth. This having failed, he flings an oil lamp at it instead. Engulfed in flames, it promptly falls through the skylight into a convenient vat of acid. The whole is an excuse to gather the principals for purposes more to do with publicity than purge.

Hazel Court and Valerie Gaunt do their best with the typically underwritten Sangster females. Gaunt, as the maid, appears to have slightly more of the breath of life in her body than does poor, passive Elizabeth. Court had trifled with the genre before, and she would make something of a name for herself as a heroine of horrors in the years to come—both for Hammer and for Roger Corman—but her encounter with the creature in *The Curse of Frankenstein* is cursory at best, and her presence a mere contrivance to bring matters to a head after the requisite eighty minutes have passed.[30] Its absence from *X The Unknown* makes the *femme* interest more significant in this instance, although the film remains male dominated. The women function simply as victims or potential victims, their roles being stereotypical in the literal extreme—the virgin and the slut.

Christopher Lee, an actor not known for his reticence in detailing the suffering he endured for his art, had landed the part of the creature because of his height (6'4") and a talent for mime, and through the recommendation of John Redway. He reportedly found the process of monster playing supremely uncomfortable, but in *The Curse of Frankenstein,* he was doubled during the fiery finale by Captain "Jock" Easton, who was given the added distinction of posing in the identical makeup for some of the publicity shots with Court.

The makeup for the creature *is* gruesome—so much so that at the time of the film's release, it was universally condemned for resembling nothing more than the victim of a road accident. Technically, Phil Leakey's work is not far short of excellent, especially considering that his orders were to avoid comparison with the original, at all cost (or at *no* cost). A lack of suitable materials and the constrictions of space under which he labored were to stretch his talents to the limit, and while the mask he created in no way evokes the cadaverous phantom of the novel, it undoubtedly comes closer to that concept than Karloff's Hollywood designer head. Few critics of the day bothered to take this into account, even where they were aware of the difficulties that Hammer had been under in this respect, but Lee's performance was generally well regarded. The *Daily Herald*'s Paul Dehn was particularly eloquent. "If Mr. Karloff suggested that vitality had imperfectly become a part of him, Mr. Lee gives the impression that life itself had been pumped into his ill-assembled body and not had the mistiest notion what to do there."

The mask's failure lies in its inability to convey something of the grand design embodied in this Gothic fable of creation. What was missing was any vestige of the fantastic. Here was no mythic monster in the making. This Frankenstein was merely presiding over the carnage of a casualty ward. The creature had been sculpted to disgust, and disgust it duly did. Allied to a film that had as its protagonist, if not its nominal hero, a man willing to mutilate and murder at the drop of a scalpel in pursuit of his ambitions, and surrounded as it was by the grisly accoutrements of its maker's chosen trade, Lee's creature—as much as anything in *The Curse of Frankenstein*—was to assure the production a grim notoriety.

Hammer was not to acquire its new, larger Stage 1 until July 1957, so the film's meager laboratory set forced Fisher to skirt around the grandiloquence of the original's creation scenes. The art direction is similarly scant (nearby Oakley Court can clearly be seen standing in for Castle Frankenstein by night), and a helping hand from Bernard Robinson, who had been called on partway through the production, can be witnessed in the design of only a single rooftop set. But it was Britain's first color horror film— "unique...and in colour!" as the June issue of the *ABC Film Review* was to announce.

An early spring screening of the finished product for Warner executives ensured that what had originally been intended for Exclusive release was now to receive worldwide distribution by an American major of the first order. It was Hammer's biggest coup to date, but it would be one more nail in the coffin of Exclusive Films.

With the might of Warners behind it, *The Curse of Frankenstein* premiered in the West End of London on May 2, 1957, and immediately settled into a record-breaking run. In another week, it would be playing the Ritz, Leicester Square. In ABC release, it was less ostentatious (if just as successful), although in parts of the country, it would be consigned to cinemas with a reputation for art-house or exploitation trade. This did not help to combat the campaigns of vilification that would now be directed at Hammer's executive heads from all corners. It was not so much that the film had elected to show gore, it was the impression given—and it is only an impression—that the camera was *dwelling* on it.

The viewer *is* privy to a small catalog of brutalities: a half-glimpse of a severed head; eyeballs in a jar; a pair of dismembered hands. And the film betrays a certain callousness toward matters of the flesh in devices such as the vat of acid for the disposal of bodies. But even in 1957, none of these could be considered excessive by the standards of a populace inured to atrocity after two wars. Certainly there is nothing in *The Curse of Frankenstein* to rival Leakey's "melting head" in the earlier *X The Unknown*. America's National Legion of Decency found itself more concerned with the suggestive costuming, and considered the film to be "morally questionable" on this score, but it was divested of much of its bloodletting in Chicago, and all of it in Canada. The British censor, harking back to the rule book of the thirties, asked only that the shot of the head be shortened. Nevertheless, the reviews were unrelenting. "Disgusting" and "degrading" were the two adjectives in most prominent use, although *Picturegoer's* Margaret Hinxman was notionally kinder. "Lee's monster is not so monstrous," she demurred, noting in passing, "Although this shocker may not have created much of a monster, it may well have created something more lasting: a star!"

The reference was to Cushing, but it was soon to embrace Hammer Films itself. The more bad notices the film received, the more the public desired to see it. What had started life as a modest period piece with few concessions to the Gothic, or even to its own literary source, was a sensation that would go on to appear on more American screens than any British film ever. Curiosity, in this instance, would cause the goose to lay a golden egg, for *The Curse of Frankenstein* was a Cook's Tour of the charnels, and audiences turned out in droves to be revolted by the spectacle. What they found when they got there was a work steeped in decadence and reeking of the paraphernalia of the slaughterhouse. Like *The Texas Chainsaw Massacre* of twenty years later, there is relatively little to be seen onscreen, but the atmosphere of butchery pervades all.

> "Well, the birds didn't waste much time anyway....The eyes...Half the head is eaten away—"
>
> —Paul Krempe
> *The Curse of Frankenstein*

A more subtle attraction was the sheer clarity of the photography. Ex-Gainsborough regular Jack Asher's meticulous lighting had married to the precision mechanics and superb results that could be obtained from Hammer's aged Vinten-Everest camera (with its combination Cooke lenses) to produce images of stunning realism. All the better to see you with, my dear.

The *leitmotif* of the film is blood; more accurately, the color of blood. Rather than *Dracula*, where one might have expected it, it is *The Curse of Frankenstein* that is suffused with scarlet: the floral decoration on Hazel Court's funereally black dress; Frankenstein's instrument case; Krempe's silken robe; the contents of a smashed phial; the beakers of bubbling liquids. Where *Dracula* would unfold in sepulchral greens and blues, in the picaresque colors of the grave, *The Curse of Frankenstein* brandishes a palette culled from the very stuff of life. From its opening titles to its sunrise-emblazoned final shot of the waiting guillotine, it is a film wrought in the luminous hue of bright Eastmancolor red—as vivid a symbol for the beginnings of Hammer's color Gothics as the plummeting of the Quatermass rocket had been for the inauguration of the whole cycle of Hammer Horror.

Almost nine months of complex and often tense negotiations had led Hammer to take no chances with what small investment it had in the film. Uncertainties over the all-British cast— including a leading man who had come to Hollywood's attention only by standing-in for Louis Hayward (prior to him being optically doubled) as far back as James Whale's 1939 production of *The Man in the Iron Mask*—had meant that by the second week of shooting, Hyman's Associated Artists had still not come up with its part of the monies. Despite it being a color production and much touted in the press, the budget had been appropriately pared to two-thirds of what had been expended on *Quatermass II*. Convinced that the film would sell on the name of Frankenstein alone, no matter who was playing the role, Hammer had gone ahead, regardless. Even when shooting had begun, the company's troubles were still not over. No sooner had the first scenes gone into the can than word had come that Universal was attempting to prevent the registration of the title in America. The attempt was to prove futile, and six months later, *The Curse of Frankenstein* would have opened at the Paramount Theatre on Times Square in New York.

By then, it would have become crystal clear to all involved with the film that their instincts were correct: *The Curse of Frankenstein* was a bandwagon just waiting to roll.

Chapter 2

New Blood for Old

1957-1959

"I told her, 'Listen, you should imagine you have had one whale of a sexual night, *the* one of your whole sexual experience. Give me that in your face!'—And she did, of course."

> Terence Fisher
> on directing Melissa Stribling
> in *Dracula*

"No one who saw it lived to describe it!" screamed the advertising slogan for *The Curse of Frankenstein*. Other than the critics, that is, who described it variously as "the film to end all horror films" or a "revolting exhibition" that would surely mark "the end of the thriller-film proper." But while there was a general sense of outrage at the excesses sanctioned by Hammer in its treatment of the tale, there were good words, too, and no noticeable disquiet about where this new trend might lead. That was to become more apparent with *Dracula*.

The critics were supercilious, dismissive, patronizing, bemused, or simply contemptuous, but they were *not* universally shocked, nor were they averse to suggesting that for a horror film, *The Curse of Frankenstein* was on a par with the better of them. Paul Dehn liked it. "Philip Harben, preparing *Tête de Veau Vinaigrette* from a live calf on TV could hardly be more explicit," he observed. *Punch* was the bravest of all, calling it a "straightforward and conscientious version of the novel...unusually well done." They were also kindly disposed toward praising the playing, the craftsmanship, and the overall quality of the film—but then it was *British*-made—with a

few exceptions. The *Sunday Times's* Dilys Powell wrote, uncharac-
teristically, "For years I have rushed to defend the cinema against
the charge that it debases. In the case of the current series of horror
films I have changed my mind."

That so many notables would even bother to put pen to paper
about the subject in question was striking in itself, but not representative of a rush to judgment. Hammer's film had been released
in a week when the only other feature on offer was a minor western
called *The Quiet Gun*, starring Forrest Tucker. But the effect could
hardly have been more pronounced had it been a major international studio hyping a blockbuster.

The film opened to "some amazing scenes in Leicester Square,"
said Michael Carreras. The upstairs foyer at the Warner had been
kitted out in facsimile of the baron's lab, complete with bandaged,
headless torso in a glass tank, and this apparatus was subsequently
made available for other key locations around the country. "You
should see the audience," James Carreras typically informed Milton Shulman, then at the *Sunday Express*. "They squeal, gasp, and
shriek. Some of them even run out of the cinema in panic. It's
wonderful!" So wonderful, in fact, that Hammer lost no time in
announcing a sequel: *The Blood of Frankenstein* would commence
production straightaway, using the same team as before—Cushing,
Fisher, Sangster, and, most importantly, Hinds. "Tony was the man
in tune—I was not enamoured of that type of material," Michael
would confess, and certainly Hinds had been singularly responsible for the bringing together of the talents who had helped make
what was fast becoming something of a phenomenon.

Anthony "Quatermass" Hinds, as publicity handouts had
dubbed him prior to *The Curse of Frankenstein*, promptly set about
preparing the sequel. This time, there would be no need of Lee.
Hammer had created a new archetype in the Byronesque figure of
the baron himself. But had he not been judicially beheaded in the
film's closing moments, Shulman inquired? No problem, James
Carreras assured him. "We sew his head back on again."

The man who was charged with making literal that promise was
as surprised as anyone by the enthusiasm with which his own
creation was being received around the world. "We didn't know
we were breaking new ground; we were just making a living," said
Jimmy Sangster. But if imitation is the sincerest form of flattery,
then it would be another year before the glut of like-minded

vehicles arrived to pay homage to the success of *The Curse of Frankenstein*.

When the news broke in the summer of 1957, dies had been cast, and more conventional fare was still the order of the day. There was *The Daughter of Dr. Jekyll, I Was a Teenage Werewolf, Blood Is My Heritage* (aka *Blood of Dracula*), and the more aptly titled *The Dead That Walk* (aka *The Zombies of Mora-Tau*), each of which was tied to the other not by genre blood links but by murky photography, a lack of budget, an equivalent lack of ideas, and plots that insisted their monsters make obeisance to the great god Superscience, from whom they were all still springing. One exception would be the first British horror to swing into production as a direct result of the Hammer breakthrough: *Cat Girl*. Starring Barbara Shelley as the shape-changing panther woman in the thrall of a bestial lust, this thinly disguised reworking of Jacques Tourneur's *Cat People* (1942) was also among the first to elaborate the notion of suppressed sexual desire that was to find fuller form in Hammer's *Dracula*. Another exception would have more lasting value but, released in the wake of the quite different demand that was being engendered by *The Curse of Frankenstein*, its black-and-white atmospherics would find themselves at odds with an audience sated on the antics of the Baron of Blood. This film was *Night of the Demon* (aka *Curse of the Demon*), based on a short story by M. R. James [1] and coincidentally directed by Tourneur himself. But it would go unnoticed in the brouhaha that surrounded the opening of *Curse* and thus ensure that Hammer would look no further than Shelley—and soon Stoker—for its future horrors.

The upturn of the preceding year had seen Hammer's production program reinstated without interruption. When *The Curse of Frankenstein* was delivered to Warners in New York on April 8, *The Steel Bayonet* and the newly complete *The Abominable Snowman* had gone with it. James Carreras announced that from here on, he would be "concentrating on films for global consumption." After the summer, things began to happen fast at Bray. Having smelled the money in blood, Universal announced that it would have no further need of its lawyers and would be turning its back catalog of horror titles over to Hammer Films for the remake treatment. *Dracula* was already in the planning, so the first of these "joint" ventures was to be *The Mummy*, though Hammer would still be free to go wherever else its collective nose might take it.

With four horror films already in distribution and a fifth about to open, *The Snorkel* and true-life horror *The Camp on Blood Island* in production, and both *Dracula* and *The Blood of Frankenstein* in preparation, Tony Hinds's nose would now take him to Hollywood and the dark fantasies of writer Richard Matheson.

Matheson was enjoying a cult success with his hit, *The Incredible Shrinking Man*, and seemed just the right choice to distill the heady brew of science and horror that Hammer was fast coming to think of as its own. Three years before, he had written a novel called *I Am Legend*, about a global plague that turns the Earth into a world of vampires. The story appeared to be perfect for the Hammer treatment and Hinds took out an option on the book, inviting Matheson to London to work on the screenplay.

By the time the author was greeted at Waterloo Station by James Carreras, Anthony Nelson Keys, and a contingent of interested press, Hammer was preparing to unleash the Yeti on the world.

> "It's a new age of awareness. A big age. You've got to measure up to it, Doc."
>
> —Tom Friend
> *The Abominable Snowman*

The Abominable Snowman would fail dismally in this respect, although the homily was to guide Hammer's production policy for some time to come. Operating to a schema dictated by the reception accorded to *Quatermass* rather than *The Curse of Frankenstein*, *Snowman* was the result of another Nigel Kneale television play being adapted for the screen ("The Creature"; 1956), but with a marked lack of similar success.

The Snowman himself had little cinematic pedigree: *The Snow Creature* (1954), *Half Human* (1955), and *Man Beast* (1956), the latter two of which had been simply a potpourri of dissociated Mexican and Japanese footage married to American linking narratives. But with Eric Shipton's 1951 Yeti-footprint photographs still fresh in the public's mind, the very idea of such a creature carried a resonant terror that was buoyed by lurid articles in the popular press. Accordingly, Kneale's play had been perceived to be just this side of the possible, and it had been enacted on television in a creepy atmosphere of snow mist and oil lamps, its unseen menace remaining, for the most part, just beyond the dim, campfire light of man's understanding. Had this story amounted to more than the single twist in the tail that it had been engineered to encase, it would still have been destined not to translate well to the demands of the new horror cinema. But like the beast that it purported to portray, Hammer's *The Abominable Snowman* was a throwback. It promised a monster, with or without its parent play's consent; it delivered a mouse.

> Botanist John Rollason is persuaded to join a Himalayan expedition in search of the Yeti, or "Abominable Snowman," by American showman Tom Friend. Friend's motives are less than scientific: he intends to capture a Yeti and put it on display to a paying public. Eventually, a creature is shot, and the party makes plans to transport it back to base, but the other expedition members are killed in mysterious circumstances. Friend falls victim to an hallucination orchestrated by the Yeti and is also killed in an avalanche. Rollason— alone now—is given sight of the Yeti; he realizes that they are a superior race and blacks out. When he recovers from his ordeal, he confirms that no such creatures exist.

Kneale's script for what also started life as *The Snow Creature* in feature form was left virtually intact by Val Guest, who was shooting too fast on a hectic schedule that took him from Bray to the French Pyrenees and then on to Pinewood for the studio interiors of the mountain. The film's television origins show all too clearly in the long expository sequence of character interplay at the Tibetan retreat, where the tensions implicit in the written word are dispersed in *Regalscop*ic midshots of tedious uniformity. It takes a full twenty-five minutes to get the protaganists out of the monastery and onto the snow, where they encounter inconsistent sound recording, discontinuity between the studio work and the location footage, and floor effects that mark an unhappy return to the days before *Quatermass.* By this time, audiences were expecting more from Hammer than the benign and sagacious pussycat that the film ultimately disgorges as its beast of the Himalayas. (A full-scale model of a dead Yeti roped to a sled *was* constructed, but it is barely glimpsed in the release print.)

Several good ideas are lost in the transfer from the claustrophobic intimacy of the medium for which "The Creature" was originally written—the revelation of a psychic link between the monastery's Lhama and whatever it is that inhabits the mountain, and the unnerving "hallucinations" suffered by Rollason and Friend toward the climax (a broken radio suddenly sputters to life to vouchsafe a warning; a dead comrade cries for help in siren sound, beckoning Friend to *his* death as a result). Peter Cushing actually reprised the role of Rollason from the BBC version of the tale, but the play's Friend, British actor Stanley Baker, was expediently replaced by Forrest Tucker for the big-screen adaption. (If anything, Tucker actually *subdues* the ruthlessness of Friend and makes the point of the fable less obvious.) Director Val Guest captured the haunting isolation and eerie other-worldliness of the mountain at night, but not the bigger game that he was really aiming for.

The Kneale play was typically thought-provoking, but it transcribed to the wide screen as flat and undramatic, singularly burdened by the weight of its intellectual preoccupations. The "Snowman" is the Ghost of Christmas Future for the new age— a vision of promise for a dead world, presided over by a race of telepathic Neanderthals. Even though the pill was sugar coated, the moral at the heart of it remained the same. The notion of a breed of Snowmen produced through parallel evolution and waiting, Godlike, on a Himalayan Olympus to inherit an atomically debilitated Earth was little more than a cerebral reworking of the ant threat in *Them!*

Coming hot on the heels of *The Curse of Frankenstein*, *The Abominable Snowman* had seen Bernard Robinson elevated to the position of production designer over *Curse*'s Ted Marshall, who was shortly to leave and join Woodfall, instead. The monastery set is an excellent construction on Bray's back lot—the Pinewood mountains, less impressive. In another departure, James Bernard had given way to Humphrey Searle, who provided an atmospheric score that occasionally echoes of "Swan Lake" but lacks the majesty and drama required to really fire the subject to life.

Hammer's first "A" certificate for one of its horrors dampened enthusiasm for the film even before its story was allowed to unfold. The Yeti make their first appearance after nearly an hour. When they come more clearly into view at the close, revealed with them are the limitations of a plot that may have begun as well intentioned but concludes, like the creatures it features, as disappointing and uninspired.

"There is no Yeti!" intones the Lhama at fadeout, and on this showing, he was seen to be right. Cushing's botanist survives to tell the tale—unlike most of the cast—though it was a close call. But by the time the film opened, shooting was already underway on the much more assuredly "X" certificate story of *The Camp on Blood Island* at the instigation of Tony Nelson Keys, returns were pouring in from the record-breaking success of *The Curse of Frankenstein,* and *Dracula* was scheduled for a November start, so Hammer found itself in the same happy position as Dr. Rollason.

Whether or not *The Abominable Snowman* would break any ice at the box office, demand for the Frankenstein sequel continued to grow. James Carreras had decided to ask Warners for a cool $500,000 advance guarantee in return for the rights to distribute *The Blood of Frankenstein* in all territories except the U.K. and Japan. Concerned by the possibility that Hammer might have a one-hit wonder on its hands, Warners declined to meet the figure. Carreras, angered by what he perceived to be a lack of commitment on the part of both Warners *and* Hyman, chose to offer the film to the highest bidder as part of a package deal with *The Snorkel* and *The Camp on Blood Island.*

Of the majors in the field, Columbia had so far failed to participate in the bonanza. Mike Frankovich, their man on the ground in Great Britain, stepped in. By dangling the carrot that Columbia would be willing to coproduce a spin-off series for American television called "Tales of Frankenstein" through their subsidiary Screen Gems, Frankovich snapped up *The Blood of Frankenstein* and announced to the world on September 6 that Columbia intended to join forces with Hammer and coproduce three features a year for the next three years. When Hammer's Himalayan saga opened (on August 26, 1957), Warners had made a $2 million killing on *The Curse of Frankenstein* in the U.S. alone, but only ten days later, *The Abominable Snowman* would not be the only one out in the cold.

"Two months, the paper says. In two months it can cover the whole western hemisphere."

—Ben Cortman
The Night Creatures

As *Dracula* went into production, Hammer was to have its most serious run-in yet with that august body of arbiters in all matters of cinematic good taste—the British Board of Film Censors. Michael Carreras was summoned to an urgent meeting with Board Secretary John Nicholls in his office at 3 Soho Square.

The Matheson script of *I Am Legend*, duly completed by the author after a two-month sojourn in England (and now titled *The Night Creatures*) had been turned down flat—no revisions, no alterations. If the subject were made, it would not be passed for exhibition in Britain. The industry was self-regulating, and the BBFC was there to protect it from its own worst excesses before someone else decided to. Having just sanctioned *Dracula* with reservations, they were not about to unleash a veritable army of such creatures (or such films) on an unsuspecting world. The Motion Picture Association of America (MPAA), guardians of the Production Code, were no less concerned. In a letter of December 4, Geoffrey Shurlock drew attention to the script's "over-emphasis on gruesomeness," and submitted a detailed list of objections which included brutality, profanity, bad language, and immorality—all of which threatened to deny Hammer a Code "Seal of Approval" in the American market, as well. Despite having signed Val Guest to direct, Michael was left with no choice; the title was retained, but the project was aborted. It was not a complete write-off—the property was sold to Bob Lippert at a knock-down price—but it taught Hammer's young executive producer a salutory lesson. "From that moment on, we *never* made a film without submitting the script first."

After writing *The Curse of Frankenstein* for a mere £500 in October 1956, Jimmy Sangster had returned to more mundane duties, such as preparing *The Snorkel*, but the release of *X The Unknown* the following month had encouraged Tempean to hire him for the film of an ITV serial transmitted in the wake of "Quatermass"—*The Trollenberg Terror* (aka *The Crawling Eye*). Not long after, Sangster had found himself in the Audley Square offices of Warwick Films, where Irving Allen and Cubby Brocolli had commissioned him to write a script based on John Wyndham's novel, *The Day Of The Triffids*. Sangster had begun to moonlight, but the subterfuge had been uncovered, and he had been given an ultimatum. Either he was a production manager for Hammer or he was a writer for someone else. The pill was not a bitter one, however. If it was to be the latter choice, Michael would give him a script a year for three years at £750 a script. On that basis, Sangster decided to take his chances. But by May 1957, his future as a scriptwriter had begun to look decidedly bleak. Six months at the typewriter had produced little of consequence, and with *The Day Of The Triffids* since passed over, he was left with no alternative but to ask Michael for his old job back. An appointment had been arranged, but within two days of the proposed meeting, ATV had called with an offer for a serial that he had written, sent in, and subsequently forgotten about— "Motive For Murder. "

In context, Sangster's departure had meant little to Hammer at that stage (though Will Hinds had presented him with a gold watch), but the success of *The Curse of Frankenstein* soon put Tony Hinds on the phone again, pressing Sangster into service on *The Blood of Frankenstein* and the upcoming *Dracula*. He was to augment these with another for the Tempean team of Monty Berman and Robert S. Baker: a Gothic this time, called *Blood of the Vampire*.

Blood of the Vampire had ex-*Svengali* Donald Wolfit barnstorming his choleric way through the role of medical "vampire" Dr. Callistratus in an old-fashioned melodrama not at all like the Hammer *Frankenstein* that it was trying to ape. Though shot some months before, it would follow *Dracula* into theaters, but it was to have neither the count nor the sexual dimension of Fisher's film. Under Henry Cass's rudimentary direction, it would look dated even when it was new—something Hammer's *Dracula* was to be assiduous in avoiding.

> "At last I have met Count Dracula. He accepts me as a man who has agreed to work among his books as I intended. It only remains for me now…to await the daylight hours…when, with God's help, I will forever end this man's reign of terror…"
>
> —Narration of Jonathan Harker
> *Dracula*

Eschewing Sangster's scripted opening, which had followed in the footsteps of Universal by having Harker arrive at Castle Dracula in the company of a coachload of superstitious peasants portentously crossing themselves, Terence Fisher substituted a first-person narrative that went straight to the meat of the matter and wasted no time in alerting the audience to the librarian's plight. But this revision was merely a foretaste of the new life that he was to breathe into his version of the story, and if *The Curse of Frankenstein* had broken down the taboos on horror, then *Dracula* was to bang on the door of something more unsavory altogether.

When the film went onto the floor on November 11, 1957, Hammer was as unaware of the potential in the *character* of the count as it had been with that of the baron. He was the obvious choice to follow Frankenstein, nothing more. He was the other great Gothic archetype[2] —the vampire with the household name, the familiar ring. But Dracula killed with kindness, and in *boudoirs*. "Dracula has the power, in a twisted way, to make Lucy and Mina give a sexual reaction," Fisher noted in review of the film's core dynamic, and in his endeavors to bring this element of repressed sexual desire to the surface, he was to strip the superficial polite-ness of the Bram Stoker novel which had harnessed it bare to its Freudian essentials. Unlike its predecessor, Hammer's *Dracula* is not about the chill charm of a *bourgeois*, it is about the warm embrace of a demon lover. The presence of its vampire villain is felt rather than seen. It is an indelible in the *atmosphere* of the story, whereas Cushing's cold-fish baron had been an integral part of the architecture of its companion piece. It is in this fundamental that the two films differ markedly. But if *The Curse of Frankenstein* was predominantly Peter Cushing's triumph because of it, *Dracula* would be entirely Terence Fisher's, for the same reason.

The roles of the blood-drinking count and his nemesis Professor Van Helsing were naturally to be filled by the successful sparring partnership of Cushing and Lee. Remolding the professor from his literary persona of geriatric Dutchman into a quick-witted and agile vampire killer was simple expedient, but in transforming the count from an aged Romanian aristocrat (the novel) and a sinister Latin gigolo (the Universal film) into a young and virile seducer, Fisher was to enlarge on what had remained staunchly implicit in Sangster's script. By openly interpreting Stoker's subtextual fan-tasy of submissive sex, he would strike a chord—albeit not quite with the intended note. An Edwardian himself, he was to wrest from *Dracula* the notion of *machismo*—male sexual dominance— and the female pleasure that supposedly derived from it. This time round, the vampire was to be a misogynist wish fulfilment—a despoiler of female flesh, but with their *compliance*. And there's the rub. By altering the nature of the victim's response to his nocturnal advances, the rapacious sexual sadist of the novel was to be turned on his head, to become the answer to a maiden's prayer. The nightmare was to be reborn as a dream of desire. The fiend—once a figure of dread—would now be a figure of *fascination*.

The change was subtle, and it was enabled by the happy accident that, for the most part, the story has to focus on Dracula through the perception of his victims. If the film made a sex symbol of the count, it was accidentally. What we see is not the seductive charm of Dracula himself, but the sexual awakening of the women who become the objects of his ardor. Lucy awaits the vampire in her bed with a mix of uncertainty and expectation, while Mina, trapped in a marriage in which she is "not sexually satisfied" (to quote Fisher again), returns from an early morning encounter with the count wearing an expression akin to that of Scarlett O'Hara's after her first night of passion with Rhett Butler. "I feel perfectly well," she replies to her husband's concern. In context, it was to mean much more.

Paul Dehn would notice the transformation. "Whereas the Stoker heroines didn't like having their blood sucked, the Hammer heroines simply love it." The victims in the film are shown to be willing—*eager*, even—for Dracula's caress. They are sexual neophytes, unburdened by guilt or social mores. But in reality, it was to be the spin-off of sexual *parity* that would interest the female audience most. In Mina's case, she is seen to indulge in sex without shame. More pertinently, she is seen to enjoy it. In a day when female orgasm was barely discussed, let alone demanded, the fact that Dracula's women appeared to have a shared expectation of the experience would really hit home. [3]

The fan reaction was to take Christopher Lee by surprise. "Maybe it's because I tried to make Dracula a romantic and tragic figure. Someone you could feel sorry for," he said at the time, thinking it was something to do with him, when, in truth, it was to do with the sexual emancipation that was still some years around the corner of the next decade.

Of the novelties that *Dracula* was to bring to the screen, fangs and the vampire-hunter's kit-bag would be the two most obvious. Cushing's Van Helsing armed himself with neat little stakes and crosses—none of your makeshift remedies here. He would also be quick to dismiss a whole host of popular theories concerning the

"Undead," as he was predisposed to call them. Bat and wolf transformations were for Lugosi, not for Lee. *This* Dracula was a creature of flesh and blood—warm flesh and blood, at that. His potency lay in his *charm*—no need of "hypnosis" to subdue his victims. From a female perspective, he was an idol of *desire*. All this would reduce the likes of Peter John Dyer to indict the film for having "no atmosphere, no conviction, no respect for folklore." But it was nothing if not original.

> *Jonathan Harker has come to Castle Dracula to destroy its vampire overlord, but he is outwitted by the count and killed. When Dr. Van Helsing arrives in search, Dracula flees, but Harker's diary reveals that the count now has designs on Harker's fiancée, Lucy Holmwood. At the Holmwood house, Van Helsing finds the girl suffering from a strange illness; it transpires that she has been the victim of a vampire. Despite his precautions, she dies. Lucy, now a vampire herself, begins to prey on the family. She attacks her brother Arthur, but he is saved by Van Helsing, who traps Lucy in her coffin and releases her soul by driving a stake through her heart. He and Arthur Holmwood now join forces to seek out Dracula's resting place, but unbeknown to them both, Holmwood's wife, Mina, is under the spell of the vampire. Van Helsing uncovers the lair of the count, but Dracula escapes once more and returns to the safety of his castle, taking Mina with him. The two men give chase and arrive in the nick of time to save Mina from being buried alive. Van Helsing pursues the vampire to his throne room, and after a titanic struggle, Dracula is destroyed in a shaft of sunlight.*

"Research on the vampire—certain basic facts established. One: allergic to light—never ventures forth in the daytime. Sunlight fatal—repeat, fatal—would destroy them…Two: garlic—vampires repelled by odour of garlic. Three: the crucifix, symbolising the power of good over evil. The power of the crucifix in these cases is twofold—it protects the normal human being, but reveals the vampire or victim of this vile contagion when in advanced stages.…"

—Doctor Van Helsing
Dracula

In Jimmy Sangster's cleverly succinct script, Van Helsing's phonographic dicta both redefine the myth and establish the rules by which future Hammer vampire variants were to be played. Encapsulated in these precepts is the entire plot of the film, up to and including its climax. It is not true to say that by this restructuring the vampire was shorn of his supernatural abilities; he was simply relieved of the power to transmute into a bat. To Hinds's and Sangster's way of thinking, this had never been successfully achieved by earlier films, so they saw no need to repeat those errors. But in consequence of this pragmatic reinvention, new anomalies surface: the count crosses running water in his nightly quest for blood. While the changes would be ground breaking for *Dracula*, they were to prove too restricting for the sequels, where box-office dispensation was eventually to dictate a more spurious mix-and-match approach.

The storyline of Bram Stoker's Gothic epic remains as intact in Sangster's screenplay for Hammer as it did in the Universal version. All three begin by introducing the vampire in his lair, then proceed to bring him forth to drain the lifeblood from a Victorian family before returning him to his lair for the final confrontation with the forces of good. The alterations that Sangster wrings from the material are primarily ones of detail and emphasis, as much a product of the time of the film's creation as they are a reevaluation of the myth of the vampire. If *Dracula* is flawed, it is in its *Curse*-like rush to a climax (the count reveals himself to Van Helsing at the appropriate moment and the chase is on), and in the illogicalities that some of these changes were to produce: Harker is aware of the count's vampire nature from the start, yet he barely pauses to consider if the same might not be true of the woman in his castle! But it was Sangster's background in production that was ultimately to bring about one of the most striking attributes of Hammer Horror.

"I'd done budgets and I knew what a picture cost," Sangster explains, "so when I'd finished the script, I knew what it would cost to within the nearest penny." In *Dracula*'s case, the nearest penny was £82,000, and it had been achieved by compressing the *geography* of the tale. Castle Dracula is on the outskirts of Klausenburg, a coach ride away from Carlstaat and the home of the Holmwoods. Yet they have never heard of him, and their typically English-Victorian world does not appear to be in any way affected by the fact that it has been transplanted in Bavaria! It was to Sangster's credit that he managed not only to sew such diverse elements together, but that he did it so that you cannot see the joints. This expediency created that mythic country beloved of the fans—Hammerland—home of the monsters.

Hammerland was to be Bernard Robinson's territory, and he would cultivate it with loving care. For *Dracula*, the new stage 1 at Bray had accommodated no less than four of the castle's main sets: the vestibule, with its rococo arches; the banqueting hall; the library; and the stairway to the upper floor—as well as several secondary ones. But Robinson ("A very clever man at making a lot out of not very much," in the estimation of Tony Hinds) was also a master of seamless joints, and his sleight of hand passes similarly undetected. The designs are exquisite—from the great stone eagles and spiral pillars of the castle itself to the austere vaults where Van Helsing effects his handiwork; all are wrought to the smallest detail, and Fisher was to make much compositional use of foreground props to add an illusion of depth to stages already straining at the seams. If Sangster provided the bones on which the film was hung, then Robinson's sets are its flesh. But it is the lush Technicolor photography of Jack Asher that endows the whole with the breath of life. In *Dracula*, the shadows deepen; the velvet shades of mortuary drape mask the festering aura of death and decay that always lies just beyond the pinpoint pools of light in which the principals play. If *The Curse of Frankenstein* was a lurid comic horror, then *Dracula* was Gothic *grand guignol* of a very high order, indeed.

Much has been made of Dracula's imposing entrance. He descends the stairs and strides into giant close-up to deliver the obligatory introduction: "I am Dracula. Welcome to my house." In fact, it is a carbon copy of the same scene in Universal's original, the close-up being added for counter shock to emphasize the youthful urbanity of the Lee incarnation. The "real" entrance is given over to Van Helsing (and Cushing), the messianic vampire hunter who arrives late in the proceedings but is introduced via an over-the-shoulder shot, as all before him shrink under his steely gaze. Cushing's physicality as an actor is dutifully built upon to provide a considerable degree of movement within the confines of the restricted sets. He is forever darting about in elfin mobility, never walking where a single bound might accomplish a more dramatic effect (a trick learned from working with Laurence Olivier). Only a leap to the curtains from a refectory table at the climax is furnished by a stunt double. It was Cushing who was accorded top billing on the film, a position he would retain for most of his long association with the company. Peter Cushing was Hammer's *star*—Christopher Lee was only its monster.

What of Dracula himself? In 1957, the part was as much a godsend to Christopher Lee as it would become a burden to him ten years later. Unlike Cushing, who had already reached the heights by the time he played Frankenstein, Lee's career had been "moving very slowly," though as a direct result of *The Curse of Frankenstein,* he had just essayed his best screen role to date—that of the Marquis St. Evremonde in Rank's 1957 version of *A Tale of Two Cities.*[4] In *Dracula,* his time on screen is minimal, but he nevertheless provides Cushing with an oppositional force of considerable power, combining the preternatural strength and sentient threat of the count with a grace and poise of balletic precision. There are moments when his appearance evokes a genuine horror: the attack on the vampire woman, and the stalking of Van Helsing in the throne room. They are moments when Leakey's makeup and Asher's lighting blend with the art of the actor to transcend mere technique, and they were not to be repeated. With his eyes ablaze and his eye-teeth bared, his aristocratic nostrils flaring, and his cloak clutched tight about him like the wings of a giant bat trapped in mid-flight, Lee was to make Dracula his own as no actor had before him. He was to become as identified with the role of the count as Sean Connery would later be with that of James Bond, and he would spend a good deal of his time trying to prise himself free of it. For now, though, the moment was his. A huge close-up of Dracula's blood-caked face would launch him onto screens and into magazines with the cinema's most vivid realization of the vampire in action. The part had paid Lee "less than a thousand pounds," but it was to create a visage that would go down in film history: a remarkable "debut" by any standard.

The film had been shot on a six-week schedule, one more than Fisher had extracted from Hinds for its forerunner (though this had since become the norm). On completion, the sets had been struck to make way for *The Blood of Frankenstein* and Peter Cushing's next starring role for Hammer. For Christopher Frank Carandini Lee, however, fame—or notoriety—would take a little longer.

"In the year 1860, Baron Frankenstein was condemned to death for the brutal murders committed by the monster he had created....The whole continent breathed a sigh of relief when the guillotine was called upon to end his life of infamy."

—Screen caption
The Revenge of Frankenstein

By the time Hammer's "horror-sex blockbuster" (which was to be retitled *Horror of Dracula* in the U.S.) was ready for certification early in 1958, work was already complete on the sequel to *The Curse of Frankenstein*. An original concoction this time, it had been divested of its preproduction title to become the less provocative *The Revenge of Frankenstein* instead.

While Lee had busied himself in some useful prepublicity for his first major outing for Hammer, Cushing had been left free to recreate the role of the baron. There was the small matter of the monster, however, which the finite nature of the first film had inadvertently consigned to an acid bath. But did the monster matter? It was, after all, only a patchwork of collodion scar tissue beneath which the actor had barely been recognizable. Tony Hinds had decided that it did *not* matter; the baron would suffice to bridge the gap between the two and, in capable hands, he could be a good deal easier to resurrect. With another goldmine waiting around the corner, Hinds's hands had proved more than capable.

Frankenstein had gone to the guillotine at the end of *Curse*, but who saw him die? Jimmy Sangster had been instructed accordingly.

> Baron Frankenstein has escaped the guillotine with the help of Karl, a dwarf, and is back in medical practice. Dr. Kleve knows the baron's true identity and persuades Frankenstein to let him assist in the transplanting of Karl's brain into a normal body. The operation is successful, but Karl is unwilling to be a showpiece for the baron's skills and flees. While attempting to dispose of his former body, Karl is badly beaten, and his new body begins to acquire the warped characteristics of the old; in addition, he has developed a cannibalistic desire to eat flesh. Karl is now a monster. He kills a young girl and gate-crashes a party where the baron is in attendance. After pleading for help, he dies. Frankenstein stands accused, but he denies the charge. The authorities exhume the baron's body and find a decapitated priest instead. Convinced of his guilt, Frankenstein's patients beat him to the point of death. But he has an ace in the laboratory: he has built a second body for himself. Kleve transplants Franken-

stein's brain into the other body just as the police arrive to arrest them both. Now reborn as Dr. Franck, the baron begins a new practice in London's Harley Street.

Like Universal's *The Bride of Frankenstein* before it, Hammer's *The Revenge of Frankenstein* begins exactly where its predecessor leaves off. But in the manner of a serial cliff-hanger, what was seen at the close of the previous episode is *not quite* what is seen at the commencement of the next. The two anonymous jailers shown leading the baron to the guillotine at the climax of *Curse* are magically enjoined into the single figure of a hunchbacked dwarf, who promptly dispatches the officiating priest to his doom in Frankenstein's stead, in order that he can be rewarded with a new body and, more to the point, set in motion what was modestly claimed to be "The World's Greatest Horrorama!"

In scope and scale, *The Revenge of Frankenstein* is an epic among the early Hammers. The film opens in 1860, but the story proper takes place three years later, with the baron ensconced in a Carlsbruck medical practice under the alias of Dr. Stein. Sangster's grasp of his material is unquestionable here. Gone is the laboriously linear narrative of the first film, and in its stead, we have a multifaceted plot with all the strands required of its climax already in place at the beginning of the tale. A more confident production in every way, *Revenge* is even allowed a joke or two at its own (or others') expense. When Dr. Stein is quizzed as to his identity, he evades the issue by declaring that there is more than one "Frankenstein." "There are branches everywhere—even in America, I understand." (*Frankenstein's Daughter* and *Frankenstein 1970* were both in production stateside at the time, while *I Was a Teenage Frankenstein*—which, apart from its modern dress, was an outright steal from *Curse*—had already been released.)

Sangster's wit is equally in evidence when he is glossing over the inherent grotesqueries of his own plot. A pickpocket's right arm is zealously amputated, only to turn up later as part of Frankenstein's new self! If *Curse* was Cushing's film and *Dracula* Fisher's, then what *Motion*'s Philip Strick would claim "besmirches with strawberry blood the name of the original Mary Shelley creation" is Jimmy Sangster's most accomplished work.

Terence Fisher's direction is assured, if a touch perfunctory. *Revenge* betrays none of the visual stylishness of *Dracula*—in fact, it is often flat and theatrical, in the manner of the first Frankenstein film. In its slower middle section, Fisher seems to lose his grip on the material altogether for a time, indulging in *longueurs*, a penchant for eccentricities of characterization at the expense of pace, and a lethargy of composition that produces the familiar sequence of static tableaux whose sole point of interest becomes the decor in which they are framed.

Hazel Court is now replaced by Eunice Gayson, but to even less purpose than before. Gayson's Margaret is the most token of all Hammer's heroines. She has nothing whatever to do and is only occasionally seen doing it. She was not even included for her *décolletage* but only to be threatened by the monster (in the manner of Court) as he gate-crashes the baron's new social world. Gayson was a television personality (having originally been "discovered" by Hammer for *To Have and To Hold*), though her presence in the film is so negative as to be contemptuous—a view supported by the baron's dismissive *"interfering* women" in reference to her. But all this is compensated for by the fascinating structure of Sangster's narrative. And again, it is to the baron that the film so graciously submits.

In this second outing, Cushing wears the character like a familiar suit of clothes, despite the baron having undergone a radical metamorphosis in the interim. *The Revenge of Frankenstein* offers us a social climber—not averse to a bit of skulduggery, to be sure, but no callous murderer. Instead, we have a dedicated scientist, hungry for the recognition of his peers—an affable fellow, who spends his days treating the ungrateful sick, and building on a successful practice through charm and sheer sexual magnetism. In fact, so completely altered is the character of the baron that he has no trouble at all in eliciting audience sympathy when he finds himself accused by virtue of his family name. The "revenge" that Frankenstein seeks is the intellectual satisfaction that acclaim can afford him, not the crass eye-for-an-eye brutalities of his former self—but it made for a good title.

> "Frankenstein should have been accepted as a genius of science—instead, he was sent to the guillotine. I swore I would have my revenge. They will *never* be rid of me!"
>
> —Dr. Victor Stein
> *The Revenge of Frankenstein*

By adding the inexplicable dimension of cannibalistic tendencies to the monster's characteristics, Sangster was trying to inject something original into what had already become a relatively redundant metaphor. But the inclusion of this sensationalist afterthought did little to assuage concern about the way the new horror cinema was going. The very intrusiveness of this notion—a self-serving gratuity that was to be embraced by the more savage horror films of the late seventies—undermines what is otherwise a remarkably fine piece of mainstream fantasy. But it does provide the film with its one great *frisson* when "Karl" turns on the bullying janitor from whom he has received a beating and, after strangling the man, drools visibly as the realization of his new nature dawns upon him. It was to be the beginnings of *Hammer Horror*, as it would come to be appreciated: those isolated sequences, self-contained and separate from the whole, which by their horrific impact are remembered long after the details of what instigated them have been forgotten. Until now, the gore that Hammer films had contained had been integral to their plots. *The Revenge of Frankenstein* changed all that—an otherwise respectable Gothic blood-curdler had been given a "horror high" in the famous (or infamous) tradition of the French *Théâtre du Grand-Guignol*. This film, more than either of the company's previous Gothics, was to set the tone for the horrors to come.

Peter Cushing is treated as a star here, from his first cryptic but impeccably polite utterance—"Good evening, I am Baron Frankenstein"—to his final reemergence as Dr. Franck, complete with waxed moustache and monocle. But with Hammer's order book now filling with alternative monsters, courtesy of Universal's good graces, this would be the last Frankenstein for the foreseeable future, and the door was to close (literally) on the character in the most bravura style. In Sangster's cunning script, the baron's brain is transplanted into a second body, which he has built in contingency. The irony is complete: Frankenstein and his creation become one, and Mary Shelley's modern Prometheus is fused with the Nietzschean concept of the superman.

The film's *actual* monster is something of a throwaway. Its death does not even provide the story with its climax, but merely paves the way for it. In *The Curse of Frankenstein*, the trial experiment is conducted with a dog; in *Revenge*, the creation of the *monster* is the trial experiment—the creation of Dr. Franck, the real one. Had

Sangster written a further sequel, he would doubtless have done away with the notion of a monster altogether, and in that respect, *Frankenstein Must Be Destroyed* (1969) should be seen as the true successor to *The Revenge of Frankenstein* rather than the next, belated episode, *The Evil of Frankenstein* (1964).

While Jimmy Sangster was completing his script for *The Revenge of Frankenstein*, Michael Carreras had suggested that he might like to provide story ideas that could be used as a basis for the first six episodes of Hammer's proposed television series for Columbia-Screen Gems, "Tales of Frankenstein." Sangster came up with voodoo, mutations, and cryogenics as some of the avenues down which the baron could travel in his quest for the secrets of life, in what was now planned to be 26 half-hour adventures, thirteen of which were to be shot in Britain and the remainder in Hollywood. With the format finalized and set designing underway, Michael had flown to America's West Coast during Thanksgiving weekend in November 1957 to inaugurate Hammer's breakthrough into the brave new world of American television.

A Tale of Frankenstein

"From the beginning of time, many men have sought the unknown—delving into dark regions where lie those truths which are destined to destroy us...Of all these eerie adventurers into darkness, none was more driven by insatiable curiosity, nor went further into the unknown, than the unforgettable Baron Frankenstein....So infamous were his exploits that his name stands forever as a symbol of all that is shocking, unspeakable, forbidden!...Thus, in our day, any story which chills the soul and freezes the blood is truly a 'Tale of Frankenstein'...Now—join us in the mystery, the excitement, and the stimulation that comes when we tell a story so wierd, so dark, so harrowing...that it deserves to be called one of the many... 'Tales of Frankenstein'."

—Opening narration for "Tales Of Frankenstein"
spoken by a disembodied head in a crystal ball!

Unseen in Britain since the date of its completion, the half-hour pilot that followed this lurid introduction, and was to have opened the American airwaves to Hammer Horror, is a genuine curio.

The way things turned out, "Tales of Frankenstein" was not a pleasant experience for Hammer. A good deal of effort had gone into the preparation of the series, but Screen Gems had their own ideas on how the shows should be shaped for what they saw as essentially the domestic market. The Sangster scripts were rejected in favor of an indigenous writer. Horror-story specialist Henry Kuttner was drafted to pen the "Tales," and Curt Siodmak was hired to direct. (Siodmak was the author of *Donovan's Brain*, but among his more recent screen credits were *The Creature With the Atom Brain* [writer only; 1955] and [as both writer and director] *Curucu—Beast of the Amazon*; 1956.) As Michael would discover, there was to be little or no input from Hammer; only the name was required as a peg on which to hang another variation on the old "Shock Theatre" format. Alas, there would be no need. "Tales of Frankenstein" hung itself on conception, quite without any outside help. The pilot was shot in Hollywood, with London-based Austrian actor Anton Diffring playing the baron and Don Megowan playing the creature. The pilot was entitled "The Face in the Tombstone Mirror." It would be the face of failure, and the film was subsequently shelved. Kuttner died shortly after cowriting the first episode with his wife, and Jerome Bixby (*Curse of the Faceless Man* and *It—The Terror From Beyond Space*; both 1957) had been hired to concoct a second pilot, "Frankenstein Meets Dr. Varno." Too late; like Kuttner himself, "Tales of Frankenstein" was already dead.

> *Baron Von Frankenstein needs a brain for his monster. Enter the Halperts: he, terminally ill—she, begging for help on his behalf. Frankenstein declines, but when Halpert then dies, the baron decides to use Halpert's brain instead. The transplant is successful, but the monster catches sight of himself in a mirror. In a rage, he breaks free and pursues Frankenstein to a graveyard. Halpert's wife shows up, and pleads with her monster-husband to return from whence he came. Filled with remorse, the monster throws himself into an open grave. The baron is attempting to dig him out again when the police arrive.*

Conceived at a time when the singular baroque that would become established as a house style for Hammer was less than readily identifiable, the very idea of a series built around the exploits of Hammer's baron was destined from the start to be a stab in the dark. There was, as yet, no firm consensus as to what had made the Hammer *Frankenstein* unique, and as far as Columbia was concerned, all that could be seen were the trappings.

"Tales of Frankenstein" was a hasty and unsuccessful attempt at grafting the ephemera of Hammer period authenticity onto a typically clichéd and monster-oriented Hollywood version of the story or, to be more specific, onto Dick Briefer's pre-1954 *Prize Comics* incarnation of the Frankenstein myth (before the CCA stepped in and sent the concept back to the movies, where it had spawned[5]). As a result, the atmosphere of this pilot was unmistakably forties' Universal, the one-dimensional plot was pilfered from the horror comics of the early fifties, and the hybrid notion of having Diffring dress in the *mode* of Cushing's baron was merely an exercise in larding these with what was imagined to be the flavor and appeal of the Hammer product.

Even allowing for its restricted running time, "The Face in the Tombstone Mirror" rarely rises above the level of a revue sketch on the baron and his nefarious activities. It chooses to ignore the changes that Universal had been forced to ring on the theme, let alone the radical reappraisal wrought by Hammer. The episode is simplistic to the point of caricature, as naive in approach as many of the commercials that it was designed to showcase, and much too darkly European and depressing for the candy-floss tastes of the emergent "I Love Lucy" generation of postgraduate bobby-soxers. With Diffring's characteristically intense playing, Don Megowan's ominous presence (under a brutalizing and blatantly iconographic monster makeup—no problems with Universal copyright here), and the able Siodmak's deft handling of the shock elements, it is also exceedingly grim.

But while there was little feel for the material beyond the commonplace, there *was* an attempt to ape the Hammer design—the lab and staircase sets bear strong family resemblance to those in *Curse*—and the baron's amorality survives intact. Nevertheless, it is easy to see how hidebound the format would have become. To nail the casket lid tight, the script was strictly on a pay-as-you-view level. Michael Carreras was more abrasive: Siodmak, he said, was a "charming gentleman of the European school who wrote, produced, and directed a piece of utter *crap*."[6]

If it was not already obvious that this baron had his eye more on the creation of a network slot than the creation of life, then the Kuttners ram the point home in time-honored tradition: having been apprehended at the graveside, shovel in hand, by a local constable, Frankenstein turns to the camera and, without a trace of self-parody, commences a monologue of such high camp that to reprise it only dilutes the rich absurdity encapsulated in Diffring's deadpan delivery.

> "You have your job to do...and so have I—and I don't think either of us would let anything stand in the way of fulfilling our respective destinies...Time is of small matter...You see—there is always tomorrow."
>
> —Baron Von Frankenstein
> "The Face in the Tombstone Mirror"

Not in this case. By the end of the "pilot season" in 1958, Von was gone, and the series with him.[7]

In the wake of *The Curse of Frankenstein*, a rumor had begun to circulate that Hammer was producing "export-strength" versions of its horror films, encouraged by gleeful statements to the effect that had been made by James Carreras. This notion was to find fuel in *Dracula*, where publicity stills were to hint at horrors unseen in the finished film, and about which Tony Hinds had also seen fit to confess to *Picturegoer*'s Tom Hutchinson, in December 1957, "The Japanese want more blood so we're making them a special version."

Dracula would contain three instances of the supposed excess that this rumor has since enshrined in legend: the death of Jonathan Harker, the staking of Lucy Holmwood, and the destruction of the count himself. In the case of Harker, an emaciated corpse *was* constructed, but was abandoned during production on advice from Soho Square (although after its inclusion in promotional material). The remaining two were the result of Hammer's policy of closer cooperation with the BBFC and the censor's new and more vigorous interest in the company generally.

This time, a copy of the script had been sent one month before the start of production, and problems were apparent straightaway. The reader's report referred to "the uncouth, uneducated, disgusting and vulgar style of Mr. Jimmy Sangster," noting that the mix of blood and Technicolor were going to be intrinsically incompatible and that "some of the stake-work is *prohibitive.*" Sangster was wise to the ways of the censors. "I would put something in that I was sure wouldn't get through," was his technique for distracting their attention away from the general air of blood-letting in Hammer's films. The censors were even wiser, however. Referring to the excess of violence in Lucy's reaction during her staking, the reader was to conclude that this had probably been inserted "in order to make us think that we are being let off lightly in other scenes."

Objections at this stage were sniggering and primarily directed at the script's "near-illiteracy," but the preponderance of allusions to nudity (the vampire woman) or near nudity (Mina's "expanse of bare chest") were drawn to Hammer's attention, as was the amount of blood. The staking was disallowed, the climactic disintegration was considered to be questionable, and there was to be no shot of a hearse driver's cut throat. By October 1957, Hinds had received his instructions but, with one eye to the lucrative American and Japanese markets, he had promptly ignored Nicholls's "very strong caution" and shot to the script.

On February 5, 1958, a black-and-white print of the film was submitted to the Board with scenes missing. Nicholls was not pleased. A note from his examiner informed him that the producers had "ignored the script letter" and advised that the film should not be passed until it had been seen in color, and in the presence of the president of the board. Hinds was now *in absentia* at Screen Gems in Michael's stead, where he was watching, bemused, as Columbia made a complete hash of its Frankenstein TV pilot, so James Carreras put Tony Nelson Keys onto the phone to smooth talk their way out of the problem. The Board had seen the "American" version, Keys assured—the English version would be along shortly. On February 11, Hinds was back at his desk, and was immediately given the list of exceptions. He ordered editor James Needs to remove all the scenes that should not have been shot in the first place. Among other things, out went the close-ups of the staking and a shot of the count clawing at his disintegrating face. The remainder of the sequence was considerably reduced. By the following day, the board had another version of *Dracula.*

To no one's surprise in Soho Square, there did not seem to be much improvement. Now Nicholls demanded the removal of the scene showing Dracula's assault on Mina and all the shots of Lucy writhing in the coffin. He also asked for extra cuts in the climax, and the *music* was added to the growing list of objections. It was time for the personal touch. James Carreras finally put pen to paper and, in his best conciliatory tones, pleaded for a more tolerant approach, given "the very poor state our industry is in." The letter went on to advise that there had been no attempt to mix sex and horror in the film, as there was an entirely different audience for that kind of material. Later the same day, a personal visit by Carreras produced the desired result: Nicholls agreed to soften his stance.

Hinds resubmitted the film in color on April 3 and awaited his certificate, but he was unprepared for the face-saving that would now be required in order to grant it: the sequence in Mina's bedroom and a shot of Dracula's crumbling hand were still to go. He appealed, stating that he had already scored, dubbed, and prepared the negative on the assumption that everything in the film had now been approved; in other words, it was too late. At the BBFC, there was a drawing-in of breath. Hinds was summoned to account for his actions.

On April 14, Hinds was seen by John Nicholls and Chief Examiner John Trevelyan. After a polite dressing-down, his explanation was accepted—this time. Because of the misunderstanding, the scene in the bedroom would be allowed to stand, but a second shot still remaining of Dracula tearing at his face was to be deleted in place of the hand. Hinds had no option but to agree and left with the warning that he was *not* to repeat his mistake. Unfortunately for Hammer, he would ignore that, also.

Three weeks after the opening of *Dracula,* with some unsettling feedback arriving on his desk, John Nicholls was to receive a memo from one of his staff concerning an interview in *Vogue* with James Bernard, "a composer of film music." Bernard had scored *Dracula,* and was reported to have said that he was *specifically* asked to write 'sex music' for the film. Nicholls took note and attached the memo to the file; the board was not going to be fooled *again*.[8]

Hammer's *Dracula* premiered at the Gaumont, Haymarket, on May 20, 1958, and three months later, *The Revenge of Frankenstein* would open at the Plaza, Piccadilly Circus. In keeping with the bravura staging of its now-infamous predecessor, the giant billboard outside the Gaumont was engineered to drip a continuous stream of blood from the count's slavering lips through some ingenious trip-lighting, and the legend "The Terrifying Lover who died...yet LIVED!" was accompanied by the exhortation, "DO NOT SEE IT ALONE!" to add spice and aid ticket sales. At peak times, the queues extended up to a quarter of a mile beyond the box office, and the film would go on to break all records for a first-week take at the Gaumont since its opening in 1925.

But with success, come envy and spite—there were stirrings. Though none had condoned the emphasis on the graphic that had been the hallmark of the film, reviews of *The Curse of Frankenstein* had nevertheless commented favorably on the expertise with which it had been made. No such balance was to greet *Dracula*. The message had hit home now; the end of the road had been reached, if one believed Harold Conway of the *Daily Sketch*. Despite its immeasurable superiority over its predecessor, press reaction to this new Hammer Gothic was noticeably fiercer. Having had more than a year to mull over their earlier remarks, and a spate of gratuitous exploitation pieces to contend with in the meantime as commentary on their folly, the critics were less than kind.

Nina Hibbin of the *Daily Worker* set the tone. "Astute producers are realising that brutality and sadism have had their day at the box office. Michael Carreras—please copy!" she admonished. Since the public was turning out in vast numbers to enjoy what *The Observer*'s C. A. Lejeune had christened "a singularly repulsive piece of nonsense," this advice seemed premature. But it was to find echo among the highbrow. In a general condemnation of the trend, Derek Malcolm wrote, in *Sight and Sound*, "A sane society cannot stand the *posters*, let alone the films," while Peter John Dyer, in the effortlessly snobbish *Films and Filming*, noted, "There are boring horror films and tasteless horror films. This new version of *Dracula* is a boring, tasteless horror film."

Tasteless it may have been, but boring it was not, as *Dracula* was to prove by going on to repeat the same impressive results that had greeted *The Curse of Frankenstein*, which, according to Hinds, had now made over $3 million in America and more than its production budget from exhibition in Japan alone.

Dracula would be the first Hammer horror to go out via Rank, due to their distribution tie-up with Universal. Hitherto, the Odeon circuit had championed the cause of family entertainment, and its Chairman John Davis had to be persuaded to make *Dracula* an exception to the rule. James Carreras, now designated "The King of Nausea," had naturally been up to the task, though the film was consigned to the lower-profile Gaumont subsidiary. Rank explained their decision thus: "There has always been a considerable public demand for the type of entertainment which has also been popular on the live theatre stage under the general classification of *grand guignol.* We consider *Dracula* to be an example of this type of film and so we feel justified in departing from our normal policy," causing one critic to note that "if a film is going to be a guaranteed success then it is worthwhile departing from a policy." With thirty-five new horrors promised from Hollywood (in addition to a further seven announced by Hammer itself) and "family fare" in a seemingly irreversible decline, that policy was to undergo a more permanent rethink in the months to come.

At the time of *Dracula's* release, the arts were in the throes of a sexual awakening that would culminate in the sensational obscenity trial of *Lady Chatterley's Lover.* The intimacy of kitchen-sink drama on television was spearheading the trend, and in the cinema, the "new wave" and an influx of naturist films were coming hard on the heels of Brigitte Bardot's latest disrobings in the cause of realism. *The Curse of Frankenstein* had played in many of the same so-called "art" houses that had been home to Bardot and Lollobrigida in the past, and Hammer was aware of the connection *and* the appeal of spiced-up scenarios. *Frankenstein Created Woman* had already been announced in acknowledgment of Bardot's 1956 success, *And God Created Woman.*

The emphasis on cleavage that was to figure in all Hammer's Gothics was no more a product of Victorian dress design than was the inclusion of suitably large-breasted females to flesh out such apparel. Stribling's costumes in *Dracula* were hand-me-downs, but not her negligée, and while it was hardly diaphanous, it was still impressively backlit as an aid to the imaginative voyeur! Actresses were soon hired on the strength of a talent that owed little to the Royal Academy of Dramatic Art (RADA), and if Hammer shot a special version for abroad, it was not for added gore but for *erotics,* such as a nude of Hazel Court in the following year's *The Man Who Could Cheat Death.*

The disputed bedroom sequence makes it clear that Hammer knew exactly where the wind was and just how closely it was sailing to it. In style and staging, it parallels a similar encounter with Lucy earlier in the film. Silently, Mina "welcomes" Dracula to her room and retreats toward the bed. He enters, back to camera, as the music rises to a crescendo, and closes the door—thus providing the scene with a natural fade. But the camera does not *stay* outside the door or outside the count's blackout cloak, as it had previously. This time, there is a jarring cut to a point-of-view *inside* the room, beside the bed, as Dracula approaches. Again, the music wells up. The vampire caresses, then moves to ravish his victim as a second fade obscures what follows....

Hammer sometimes added footage that it could remove if the censor were to demand it—making unpredictable cuts could be an expensive and uncertain business. This is where the idea originated that there were multiple versions of certain scenes. At least two versions of some scenes *were* shot, but these were for the British censor and the "strongest" of them was always submitted *first*. They also took what were known as *protectives:* cutaways or reaction shots that could be inserted to substitute for anything that was disallowed. Had the contentious bedroom sequence been deleted as intended, its absence would have gone unnoticed—the film is intact without it. But the BBFC looked kindly on it, and it remains in place. It is the one sequence that was used in all subsequent publicity, and its purpose is plain—it was designed to test the water.

If Hammer sold horror, then it sold sex in equal measure. Three years later, it would not be so lucky, and that license would be withdrawn.

With its production roster expanding faster than vampire ash in a cup of blood, Hammer again turned to Eliot Hyman, who had been excluded from recent transactions. *Dracula* had been funded to the tune of £33,000 by the NFFC, with the remainder coming from Universal in return for distribution rights to the film, but the ubiquitous Connecticut businessman had since become a silent partner in Ray Stark's newly formed 7-Arts venture, and financing from Hyman offered a better range of options. This time round, he decided to take out some insurance. At the guarded invitation of James Carreras, Hyman's son Kenneth was decamped to Wardour Street and welcomed into the Hammer fold, ostensibly to learn the ropes of producing, but also to keep a partisan eye on the purse strings in relation to Hammer's American investors. He was to be less successful at the latter of the two tasks. Faced with the burgeoning list of offshoot companies that were now blossoming from the parent operation in all directions, Ken Hyman soon realized the futility of trying to unravel Hammer's intricate financial affairs: "We made a lot of money—but I don't think we made as much as we *should* have made."

Under the counsel of Brian Lawrence and accountant William Croft, Hammer had become well versed in the common industry practice of producing individual films through subsidiary companies especially set up for the purpose, to speed audits and offset tax—what in American-speak are "collapsible corporations." They would use more than thirty such subsidiaries over the years—Clarion, Concanen, Key, Cadogan, Hotspur, Merlin, Laverstock (formerly Lawrie), and so on[9]—but all were known by the name that was applied to one group in particular: the "bird" companies, which were composed of Falcon, Cormorant, Sparrow, Swallow, Woodpecker, Jackdaw, and others. Lawrence would crow his belief that there were "a hundred ways to make a deal," and accordingly, a multitude of sins were enabled to fly-by-night on the wings of a bird. Shortly before his death in 1959, company solicitor Donald McKelvie suggested that Hammer might go public. It was a proposition that held little appeal for James Carreras. Public companies required public accountability, and not all of Hammer's money was that easily accounted for.

To give himself a calling card, Ken Hyman had purchased the rights to the Sherlock Holmes evergreen, *The Hound of the Baskervilles*, from the Conan Doyle estate, and had already secured partial funding for the film from United Artists. By March 1958, the title had found its way onto the list of forthcoming attractions in place of a previously announced remake of *Dr. Jekyll and Mr. Hyde*, with James Carreras promising, "When Peter Cushing plays the part [of Holmes]…I shall get him to sex it up a bit." With Hyman seconded to Tony Hinds for the September production of the next Hammer Gothic (but without a British credit for union reasons), Michael Carreras was appointed to return the favor and oversee Hammer's interest in its first 7-Arts coproduction: the long-promised film version of Lawrence P. Bachmann's novel *The Phoenix*— one of Michael's pet projects.

Truly international in scale, this post-World War II bomb-disposal saga would star Jeff Chandler and Jack Palance and be filmed on location in Berlin. But Michael would reckon without the vagaries of its macho nominee director, Robert Aldrich, the formidable producer-director of *The Big Knife, Kiss Me Deadly* (both 1955), and most appropriately, *Attack!* (1956). In the attempt to take on Hollywood at its own game, he was to find himself as ill-equipped to navigate the political waters of 7-Arts as Ken Hyman had been with those of Hammer.

> Holmes: "My professional charges are upon a fixed scale—I do not vary them, except when I remit them altogether."
>
> —Script addendum
> *The Hound of the Baskervilles*
> (courtesy of Conan Doyle's "The Problem of Thor Bridge"[10])

It was appropriate that Hammer should choose *The Hound of the Baskervilles* as the film to return Sir Arthur Conan Doyle's Sherlock Holmes to the screen after an absence of thirteen years. It was this story that had returned the character to literary life in 1901 after his fatal encounter with Professor Moriarty at the Reichenbach Falls in "The Final Problem."

Naturally, Peter Cushing would play the great detective (fresh from a couple of interim non-Hammer roles—as the British naval officer who would hear Robert Stack's Independence privateer *John Paul Jones* exclaim, "I have not yet begun to fight!" and as the infamous Dr. Knox in John Gilling's *The Flesh and the Fiends*, coincidentally Cushing's professed role model for Frankenstein). Naturally, Hinds would produce and Fisher would direct.But Sangster was busy on other projects, such as *Jack the Ripper* and *The Siege of Sidney Street* (for Baker and Berman), so the task of grafting the gentleman sleuth onto a Hammer horror fell to Peter Bryan, in his first feature-length script for the company. Although the film's backers were United Artists, the plot—with Universal's consent—was to lean heavily on the Fox original of 1939, the rights to which had transferred to Universal when it took on the ensuing series after *The Adventures of Sherlock Holmes* (1940).

The Hound of the Baskervilles was to entrench the skills of Hammer's technical team and cement the alliance of all of those on both sides of the camera who, in unison, were to create a new *form* in British cinema. The style of future Gothics would be consolidated here, characterized by Robinson's inventive sets and Asher's richly saturated photography. The look and feel of Hammer Horror—that decadent textural elegance embryonic in *The Curse of Frankenstein*, proclaimed with vigor in *Dracula*, but held in abeyance again in the rush to *The Revenge of Frankenstein*—would finally take its first real bow.

> *According to legend, the Baskerville family is cursed by a "Hound from Hell" that will destroy all the heirs. Sherlock Holmes is hired to protect Sir Henry, new heir to the Baskerville fortune and last of the line. Holmes sends Dr. Watson to Baskerville Hall on Dartmoor. Meanwhile, Sir Henry has become attracted to Cecile Stapleton, the daughter of one of his tenants. An escaped convict is on the loose; while searching on the moor, Watson is surprised by Holmes and they discover the convict dead, in a suit of Sir Henry's clothes. Holmes deduces that the man was mistaken for Sir Henry, the clothes having been given as an act of charity. Finding some half-eaten bones in an old mine shaft, Holmes narrowly escapes death when the roof collapses. He establishes that the curse is a cover for a plot to kill Baskerville, and he allows the baronet to be led into the trap. Stapleton releases the "Hound," but both are shot by Holmes. Cecile perishes in Grympen Mire, and Holmes explains that Stapleton was the illegitimate heir to the estate whose murder spree was an attempt to claim his rightful inheritance.*

"Know then the legend of the Hound of the Baskervilles. Know then, that the great hall of Baskervilles was once held by Sir Hugo of that name: a wild, profane, and godless man. An evil man, in truth, for there was with him a certain ugly and cruel humour that made his name a by-word in the county...."

—Opening narration
The Hound of the Baskervilles

The flashback that follows this narration expands on that in the 1939 film (which was conveyed via a series of trite tableaux framed in the pages of the manuscript from which Lionel Atwill's Dr. Mortimer read), but since its role is that of a red herring in the tale, the proportion of the whole that it occupies is extravagant, to say the least. It was felt to be the one area where Hammer horrifics could more readily be applied to Conan Doyle's sedate mystery, however, as the vile Sir Hugo first tortures a stable hand, then wagers his cronies on a promise of gang rape of the servant girl that he has locked upstairs.

David Oxley's Hugo Baskerville is a genuine grotesque, a creature of frightening power. It is he, rather than the hound, who contributes the film's one great shock: Fisher first builds on the escape of the girl, then cuts abruptly to the crazed figure of Sir Hugo standing at the head of the stairs, his features illuminated by a lightning flash and contorted in demonic rage as he hisses, "The bitch has flown." This lengthy episode sets a mood that is never quite recaptured in the remainder of the film, but that is a minor quibble. The vivacity of its execution is enough to stamp the Hammer marque across the production, and it easily surpasses the similar expository opening in *Dracula* to provide one of the finest set pieces in the Hammer canon.

The sequence served to concatenate Hammer's growing narrative obsession with a diseased nobility whose time was coming to an end, and it is a pity that it did not find a film more worthy of it. With Bryanston and Woodfall Films about to chart a path to screen stories rooted in the working class,[11] so, too, did Hammer Horror reflect the new tide of socialism rising in the land, despite the fact that Bray was only a rugby ball's throw away from the playing fields of Eton. Monsters were no longer from space, they were from the ranks of the elite—the landed gentry—a corrupt aristocracy feeding off the lifeblood of the lower orders. The pendulum was swinging back in the wake of Suez and the "never had it so good" platitudes of the idle rich. As Cecile observes toward the end of *The Hound,* "I, too, am a Baskerville—descended from Sir Hugo—descended from those who died in poverty while you *scum* ruled the Moor!"

The film was on a much smaller scale than that of its predecessor at Bray, and it was to bear many of the hallmarks of a stopgap production. James Bernard contributed a reduced score to *The Hound,* fleshed out with borrowings from *Dracula.* With the necessity of location shooting at Frensham Ponds in Surrey, some minor inserts and other scenes were eliminated. In the absence of Sangster, and despite its shortcomings in purist terms, Hinds's protégé Peter Bryan[12] delivers a workmanlike script that offers up some welcome *femme* interest in the person of Cecile, to provide a splendidly vindictive *belle dame sans merci* in the shape of Italian actress Marla Landi (who had modeled under her real name of Maria

[Marcella] Scorafia). The bastard progeny of Sir Hugo remain the villains of the piece, but in tune with the times, and in line with Hammer's pronouncements on the nature of its revision, death is now a *woman*. The dated revenge motive of the novella is sublimated to a more appealing *motif* of sexual revenge in the film.

Less successful is the bending of the storyline to bring it within the parameters of Hammer's own thematic universe, and the corresponding attempt to mold Holmes into a kind of sub-Van Helsing figure. This only serves to produce some annoying inconsistencies in the great detective's psychology. "Do as the legend tells, and avoid the Moor when the forces of darkness are exalted," Holmes exhorts, in complete contradiction to the spirit of Doyle's rationalist. (In the story, this line *remains* in the "legend.")

This time, Cushing had precedent: he was following in the footsteps of illustrious forerunners like Clive Brook, Reginald Owen, Arthur Wontner, and Basil Rathbone. The Holmes of Rathbone overshadowed all others, but Gainsborough Pictures had also tried its hand at a version of *The Hound of the Baskervilles* in 1932, with Robert Rendel as the detective and Fred Lloyd as his faithful sidekick, Watson.[13]

In spite of a superficial appearance to the contrary and the actor's professed fondness for the part, Cushing's playing of Holmes is much less adroit than his Baron Frankenstein. His reading of the role is unnervingly variable—affected and obnoxious—offering only the slightest trace of the inner strength and undoubted genius that made Doyle's Holmes such a singularly unique fictional character. He is not helped by a screenplay that barely scratches the surface of the man and, in contriving that Holmes should glean most of the important clues in the case from the convict (rather than through his own powers of deductive reasoning), reduces the stature of the character to the point where he functions as little more than a plainclothes policeman, as opposed to the "foremost champion of the law of [his] generation" that he was in Watson's eyes.[14]

> "As I thought—Selden. The body's been mutilated. Some revolting sacrificial rite has been performed."
>
> —Sherlock Holmes
> *The Hound of the Baskervilles*

The climax with the hound is also mitigated by the fact that its presence throughout has been attested to only via an occasional howl (whereas the script had called for the *shadow* of the beast to shroud the action at intervals). When it does appear, it is distinctly anticlimactic, in the manner of *The Abominable Snowman*. In Fisher's hands, the innate docility of the obligatory Great Dane is only too obvious; it is equipped with an ineffective mask, and the stand-in can clearly be seen to grab it, in an effort to make it look as though he is being attacked. (A week of additional second-unit work with the dog and a *boy* in facsimile of Sir Henry's clothes, to try to make the hound appear more gigantic, was discarded when the hoped-for effect failed to convince sufficiently.)

It is because of such conceptual deficiencies that *The Hound of the Baskervilles* must remain a minor entry in Hammer's horror repertoire. James Carreras was to be his usual exuberant self in the *Daily Cinema* in defense of it: "The fact that the Sherlock Holmes Society in London rate it the greatest Sherlock Holmes film ever made, fully supports all our own high claims for it," he said. But the critics would be less enthusiastic—"Doyle and water," was one assessment. The film has all the right ingredients, but after a barnstorming opening, it somehow falls short of its central objective, despite an advertising campaign that was to announce it as "Sherlock Holmes' Most *Terrifying* Adventure!"

Dealing with a capricious Great Dane was nothing compared to dealing with the undisciplined bull terrier that Robert Aldrich had turned into during the shooting of *The Phoenix*. The director had become smitten with the sights and sounds of Europe, so British supporting players sat by unused, and Jeff Chandler whiled away his off-set hours in interminable phone calls home. When the still relatively inexperienced Michael Carreras found himself staring at an overbudget, over-blown epic of ever-expanding proportions— and with only a punch in the jaw to testify to his appeals for moderation on behalf of Hammer's American backers—he was forced to call for outside help. 7-Arts supremo Ray Stark had been summoned to mediate, in a last-ditch attempt to bring the unruly director back in line. This had not gone according to plan, however, and Stark's intervention had resulted in the young producer being removed from control while the wayward Aldrich was given *carte blanche* to finish the film exactly as he pleased.

That was only the start. Stuck with a grossly overlong and tediously indulgent piece that bore little relation to the novel from which it had sprung, United Artists demanded the Aldrich epic be cut to something more in tune with the original intent. This process was to last for several months, with Hammer eventually dispatching editor Henry Richardson to Los Angeles to make what he could of the resultant mess. A compromise was finally reached, and the film underwent a title change to *Ten Seconds to Hell*. It had been all of that, and more than a squad of angst-ridden conscripts were to be blown to pieces in the aftermath. "If it had worked, Hammer would have gone on to get some much bigger artists and some much better properties, and we would have been making really big pictures," Michael noted ruefully. "Aldrich killed us."[15]

When James Carreras flew to America to attend the May 28 world premiere of *Dracula* at New York's Mayfair Theater, he had carried with him a storyline for a sequel that he announced would "be completed in the next twelve months." This treatment had followed the pattern that Sangster had laid down for *The Revenge of Frankenstein*, and was to have returned Dracula to life in the briefest possible screen time. But resurrecting the count was not to be as simple as resurrecting the baron had been.

Cushing and Lee were aware of the precedent that had been set for them. In Lee's case, he was all-too-familiar with the life and tragic career of Bela Lugosi, the actor most identified with the role of the count, who had died in August 1956 after years of morphine addiction (and playing second-fiddle to the *real* star of Whale's *Frankenstein*: Boris Karloff). "We realized, both of us, that we had inherited the mantle of Karloff and Lugosi," he said. To ensure that the lesson of history was not lost, he had decided to try his hand at a variety of other roles before once more donning the cape of the vampire. Consequently, Hammer was to be forced to play a waiting game as far as its sequel to *Dracula* was concerned—for the moment, at least.

With the soaraway success of *Dracula* and *The Camp on Blood Island* (both would appear in British lists of the top 12 box-office draws for 1958) and a myriad of new thriller subjects in the planning, Hammer found itself in the enviable position of being able to attract no end of worthy acting talent to its door, like proverbial moths to the flame. "Actors like pantomime, and to do a horror film was a *fun* thing to do," said Tony Hinds. Hammer had not, as yet, achieved respectability, but it was acceptably *chic*, and its Bray Studios, deep in the Berkshire countryside on the banks of the River Thames, were now the place to be.

Camelot

"Bray Studios, situated on the main Windsor-Maidenhead road, are easily accessible from London by all modes of transport....The natural surroundings provide their own advantages. Wide, sweeping lawns leading to the banks of the Thames, adjoin part of the studio lot."

Advertising supplement
The Cinema, September 1957

Before Jimmy Sangster acquired his Bentley Continental (which he would lease to Hammer whenever the opportunity arose), his journey to work had been more mundane. "When I was living in Chelsea, I used to catch the tube from South Kensington station to Hammersmith Broadway. The company ran a bus; we used to leave the Broadway at 7:30 every morning." After *Dracula*, Christopher Lee was to drive there in his Mercedes, often in the company of other actors collected along the way. Oliver Reed would recall such trips. "Christopher used to pick Denis Shaw and myself up at Earls Court and we'd have to listen to him sing opera all the way down. *German* opera—all the time!" James Carreras, on the rare occasions when he ventured outside the confines of Wardour Street, sat in the back of a black Vauxhall Cresta and confined ostentation to a chauffeur—at least in the early days. The modes of transportation may have differed, but the roads all led to Bray.

The studios, and Oakley Court adjacent, lay on the river side of the through road between the small town of Maidenhead—with its narrow High Street (in the days before shopping malls), boating park, and Skindles Hotel to provide rest and sustenance—and the large town of Windsor, with its regal connections. Bray village, with its notorious *Vicar*, picturesque church, and pivotal garage (glimpsed briefly in *The Quatermass Experiment*) was the landmark, although a detour on the route. The rough track leading down to the house had been bordered to shield the inner sanctum from prying eyes on the road, but for those whose business it was to be there, the lot would lead them on to the car park, from where a short walk past the new Stage 1 and smaller Stage 2 (both to the right) would bring them to the administration block—actually the extended east wing of Down Place itself, which now had a maze of wooden adjuncts foisted on to it to the left, housing the sound and editing departments.

To the technician reporting for duty, this was the 8:30 A.M. start of an almost 10-hour day (if it was a Monday, Tuesday, or Thursday; a 9.5-hour day, if it was not). According to assistant director Hugh Harlow, Hammer "never deviated" from this basic pattern. Like any other business, the turnover of staff at Bray put different faces in place at different times, but many of the Hammer personnel enjoyed a longevity with the company that was rare elsewhere, and most of the best-known were already *in situ* by 1958.

If Hammer's horrors began with their opulent sets, then the sets began with Bernard Robinson and assistant art director Don Mingaye. Making them a reality was the province of construction manager Arthur Banks and plasterers such as Stan Banks and Mickey Lyons; Tommy Money was the props master. Animating them was the job of the actor or actress, and to breathe Gothic life into Hammer's "repertory company" required a small army of beauticians and couturiers. Their hair was currently in the hands of Henry Montsash (Frieda Steiger would soon step in), their appearance was in those of Phil Leakey (Roy Ashton waited in the wings), and their wardrobe was in the charge of Rose Burrows and Molly Arbuthnot. Backing *them* up was a technical staff whose task was to ensure that the assembled cast looked, spoke, and performed as they should on screen. Behind the lens was operator Len Harris and his focus-puller Harry Oakes; pumping up the volume was sound man Jock May; and splicing the results together was editor Jim Needs and his cutting crew. Any effects were still being conjured up by Sydney Pearson, and production was invariably managed by Don Weeks. The continuity girl was Shirley Barnes (Tilly Day and Pauline Wise were to follow in her footsteps), and engineering and electrics remained the responsibility of Jack Curtis. But these are just some; of the majority not mentioned in person, all can be deemed included in spirit.

A handful of individuals stood out, for reasons of idiosyncrasy or expertise—from camera-car driver Bill "Coco" Epps to stills man Tom Edwards, who had begun as a printer but had taken over the job from John Jay, and whose proficiency with a Rolleiflex was the envy of Michael Ripper, himself a keen photographer (but with a Leica in his case). "There was a certain ambience about the studio and all to do with it," Ripper asserts. "The whole atmosphere was *alive.*" The impression was shared by Christopher Lee. "Everyone was extremely friendly," he remembers. "The food was the best in England and the atmosphere in the studio was better than any other I've ever worked in." The first went some way to guaranteeing the second, since Mrs. Thompson's studio canteen had become as good a reason to do a Hammer film as anything else. Lee goes on, "There were never any disagreements on the set—never any rows or temperamental outbursts. We all got on together very well. It was a very happy time; probably the happiest time of my career." New boy Oliver Reed would put it more succinctly: "That was the most *amazing* place," he said.

If an air of cozy gentility hung over Bray, it was hardly diminished by the two studio cats who roamed the grounds, one of whom had made a more convincing attempt at the climactic leap onto Sir Henry during a rehearsal for *The Hound of the Baskervilles* than the Great Dane that had been employed for the purpose. But an air of quiet efficiency was also present, and the tranquility of the setting belied the ceaseless activity behind the scenes of Hammer's horror "factory." In the view of Len Harris, "Hammer had got together a lot of very good craftsmen. Very efficient people." Oliver Reed agreed. "They knew exactly what they were doing—and they were very quick, very professional. The staff they had there were very slick." "And very *keen* people they were too," Harris adds. As well they might be; they were from the cream of British studios. Several of the plasterers had worked at Denham, while other specialities had come from Gainsborough, as had Bray's general-manager-in-waiting, Tony Nelson Keys. "You very rarely saw producers on the set at Hammer," the irreverent Reed would observe. "They used to listen to everything through the boom, which was wired into Tony's office. When I got a bit more senior, I used to go in and have a drink with Tony, and you could hear all the chat in the studio. He was *earwigging* for the producers!"

But the keynote of success was a more constructive form of listening. "The drive behind it was Tony Hinds and Michael Carreras," Harris believed, "and they were very willing to listen to any ideas that would make the studio more efficient and easy running." Hinds concurs. "The chaps knew that if we went over budget or schedule then that was the profit gone. The attitude was good at that time about 'getting on'—there was no question of 'can we make it a bit better' or go on a bit longer; it was nice, the time around *Hound of the Baskervilles*. It was a nice period." "One big happy family," Christopher Lee would conclude.

The family feel for which Bray would be best remembered was no accident. Costumer Molly Arbuthnot was the sister of Don Weeks, and Stan and Arthur Banks were brothers, but many of the studio's other employees were closer still. Jimmy Sangster had married hairdresser Monica Hustler, while Michael Carreras had wed his grandfather's secretary, Yvonne Josephine Maccagno. Rose Burrows was to repeat the performance with Eddie Powell, Christopher Lee's stunt double (his stand-in was Eric Wetherell, whereas Cushing's was Paddy Smith), assistant director Hugh Harlow would do the same with Pauline Wise, and Bernard Robinson was to meet his wife, Margaret, by first engaging her to work in the model shop. Phil Leakey's wife found occasional employment in hairdressing, Colin Garde's in makeup with her husband, and Frieda Steiger's other half was called on as a stand-in. No doubt some have slipped the net.

This, then, was the Fantasy Land that Michael Carreras told his children was to be his destination each day as he drove down from his home at Boulter's Lock to begin to produce more of his own share of the roster of films—a perfect little corner of England, where dreams and nightmares went hand in hand, amid green fields and sleepy towns and villages, in the lazy, hazy summers of the late 1950s. But if Bray Studios still retained the look and feel of a cottage industry at the turn of 1958, that cottage was in the sights of the developers, and foremost among them was James Carreras.

Paramount now wanted to get in on the act and offered Hammer remake rights on a property from their own back catalog—the 1944 thriller *The Man in Half Moon Street*, which had starred Nils Asther. As the company looked toward the New Year with increasing optimism, the project was added to the lists and announced to the trades as *The Man in Rue Noire.*

"We must find a man to operate at once, or God help me!"

—Julian Karell
The Man in Half Moon Street

The original Paramount feature had been based on a play by Barré Lyndon about a scientist who discovered the secret of eternal life, which had itself drawn inspiration from the legend of the Count St. Germain, an eighteenth-century occultist at the court of Louis XV who was reputed to be in possession of the Elixir of Youth.[16]

The most poignant and revealing scene in the original film echoed the supposed real-life encounters between Germain and the Countess von Georgy, first in 1710 and then in 1760. In the scene, Asther's Julian Karell comes face-to-face with a former lover, in the person of the now-venerable Lady Aldergate. The lady is astonished by the similarity between Karell and her erstwhile suitor, Julian LeStrange (a previous alias of Karell's), and he teasingly recalls intimate details of their affair. The grande dame is shocked at the depth of the young man's knowledge about her *amour-triste,* but remains blind to the truth. Karell reassures her, passing off the indiscretion as a tale told him by his "grandfather," whose memory could at times be "embarrassingly accurate."

No such scene exists in Hammer's version of the story, and with Fisher none the wiser, Jimmy Sangster's purely functional screenplay would turn what had been an unusually thoughtful treatment of the *Dorian Gray* theme into a crude surgical thriller geared toward a single shock effect.

The film was offered to Peter Cushing, but the recent adverse critical reaction and similar doubts to those of Christopher Lee about "typecasting" were also giving him pause for thought—he turned it down. "Cushing did not think much of Jimmy Sangster as a writer and was always complaining about his dialogue," Tony Hinds recollects. "I didn't like the whole idea of it," Cushing said, in addition to which, he had been shown the script only days before shooting was due to commence on November 17, immediately on completion of *The Hound of the Baskervilles.* Cushing made meticulous preparations for a role, learning his part "from cover to cover" prior to filming. With no warning of the production, he had committed himself elsewhere, in any event. Losing interest by the day, Hinds relinquished the project to Michael, who promptly changed the title and turned to Anton Diffring. After his summary ejection from "Tales of Frankenstein," it was perhaps fitting that Diffring should play *The Man Who Could Cheat Death*.

> *Paris, 1890. Dr. Georges Bonner is awaiting Professor Weiss, who is to assist in the operation that Bonner must undergo and regular intervals. Weiss arrives but reveals that a stroke now prevents him from performing surgery. Bonner is distraught, but he manages to stave off his mysterious ailment with an elixir that he keeps locked in a safe. During one such treatment, he is interrupted by his current mistress, Margo; he accidentally disfigures her as a result of his condition. Bonner renews his affair with Janine, but fails in his quest to find a suitable replacement for Weiss. The police are interested in a series of murders spanning several decades, and it transpires that Bonner has found the Elixir of Youth, but that gland implants are needed as part of the process; this has led him to murder. Weiss decides not to continue with the experiment and smashes the phial of life-sustaining fluid. Enraged, Bonner kills him. He locks Janine in his cellar and blackmails her consort, Pierre, into performing the operation. Bonner reveals his secret to Janine but, to his horror, he starts to age; he realizes that Pierre has not replaced the gland! The police arrive as Margo sets fire to the cellar. Now reverted to his true age of 104, Bonner perishes in the flames.*

As an example of how an actor's personality can alter the essence of a drama regardless of script intent, one has only to compare Asther's misguided (yet understandable) desire to prolong his existence, despite the cost, with Diffring's monomaniac pursuit of the same goal. Diffring's paranoid and progressively psychotic obsession with the lifespan-enhancing operation makes a nonsense of the altruism that was meant to have been at the root of the discovery in the first place. A cold and unsympathetic actor at best, Diffring would spend most of his career playing the same nasty Nazi in a variety of war films, from *The Colditz Story* (1954) to *Where Eagles Dare* (1968) and beyond. His screen persona was the very epitome of self-seeking ruthlessness, coupled to an air of calculated indifference to human life. It would be perfectly suited to the surgeon-villain of *Circus of Horrors*, but it would leave *The*

Man Who Could Cheat Death without a center of empathy. The result was soulless and detached, and a lackluster showing at the box office would follow suit.

The film represented at least a partial change of pace for Hammer. Despite pushing its period back to 1890 and thereby sacrificing the fingerprint evidence that had been so integral to *The Man in Half Moon Street*, both plot and playing are stubbornly modernist. In production terms, it is typically slick—so much so, that Jack Asher's immaculate lighting supplies a profusion of atmosphere where none would exist without it. But concessions to speed are nonetheless everywhere in evidence. There is little incidental music, Richard Rodney Bennett's effective xylophonic title piece being used repeatedly throughout, and much of the action is of the talking heads variety, conducted via a minimum of sets. This leads to characters elucidating the plot as events progress, then updating their stories to fill in the gaps when the scenario suddenly decides to notch up a gear in its rush toward the desultory finale. But the script is not without the usual touches of Sangster black humor: "We don't want people to know the doctor is sick—it's bad for the morale of the patients," advises Professor Weiss.

Changes of emphasis apart, Sangster's adaption was as faithful to its source as the turning of a genteel metaphysical mystery into out-and-out horror film would allow. In constrast to the original film, *female* victims predominate, though Hammer was now aware of the censor breathing down its neck. The story afforded plentiful opportunity for violent death, as unsuspecting supporting actors gave of their "uter-parathyroid" gland to help stave off the effects of Bonner's malady, but only two of these are dealt with on-screen, and one of those is behind the credits.

There are also concessions of the exploitative kind. In response to more liberal censorship abroad in relation to female nudity, both Linda Cristal and Julie London had just bared (almost) all for special continental versions of *Cry Tough* and *Night of the Quarter Moon* respectively, in accordance with the precedent set by Jack Arnold's *High School Confidential*, and Michael Powell's *Peeping Tom* was about to take fuller advantage of the potential offered in this area. Michael Carreras had decided to adopt the strategy. "It was a trend we had picked up. Part of my job was to look for any sort of commercial tie-ins," he said. "And while you're shooting, why not shoot a second version that you've got in the drawer?" For

The Man Who Could Cheat Death, a waist-up nude of a posing Hazel Court was shot for inclusion in European prints, and the scene optically cropped for British and American release, adding more fuel to the publicists' fantasy of export-strength horrors. "It never really worked," said Michael, though he would continue to pursue the policy. But while Ms. Court's charms went unnoticed at home, the film's studied avoidance of suitably "X" certificate gore did not. The eventual reviews were uniformly vitriolic, from "feeble and cliché-ridden" to "horror-flop from the house of Hammer." If *The Man Who Could Cheat Death* was to have been entirely reliant on a single bang, then it had to be a big one.

> "I shall become the inheritor of all my one hundred and four years—of all the sickness I've never had—of every pain, blemish, disease…A lifetime of illness—in one moment!"
>
> —Dr. Georges Bonner
> *The Man Who Could Cheat Death*

Sadly, it is more of a whimper. The transformation of Bonner from eligible bachelor to diseased degenerate was used to good effect on the film's poster, but it was a promise left unfulfilled by Roy Ashton's unconvincing mask. In the 1944 version, Nils Asther's sudden ageing had been conveyed on camera using the same technique of preapplied, light-sensitive greasepaint that had been pioneered by Rouben Mamoulian in *Dr. Jekyll and Mr. Hyde* (1932). *The Man Who Could Cheat Death* was allowed no such refinements. Considerations of speed and economy were to override dramatic good sense, and Hammer's antipathy toward costly effects work would deprive the sequence of much of its shocking impact. Earlier intimations of the horror to come are similarly minimized—try as Asher does to make good the deficit. In Sangster's more science-fiction-oriented scenario, the doctor had fared more garishly.

> "His body seems infused with a strange inner light…allowing the bones to show clearly through the covering of his flesh. His hands are skeletal things, like two great spiders. And his face is a skull, a grinning, greenly-glowing skull, from out of which stare two incredibly bright eyes."

The budget would stretch neither to contact lenses nor the elaborate dummy that Ashton had prepared to construct, and the omission did not go unnoticed. "For once, the Hammer make-up man missed a stupendous chance," one critic would comment.

Terence Fisher made a point of not seeing any of the original versions of the films he directed for Hammer. With *The Man in Half Moon Street*, he might have profited by the experience. Barré Lyndon's tale of the scientist condemned to spend eternity alone as the price of his humanitarian ideals was an heroic tragedy in the grand manner, and since Fisher's stated desire had always been to make a love story, he need have looked no further for the peg on which to hang his romantic hat. At the climax of the Paramount version, Helen Walker promised Nils Asther, "I'll share your madness with you, because there's grandeur in it." In the Hammer remake, there was only the madness.

By 1959, which *Film Review* was to dub "the year of the horror film," hardly a week would go by without the marquees heralding fresh terrors in response to one of *Variety*'s typically quirky headlines—"Horror Pix In Global Clicks"—and the London Pavilion in Piccadilly Circus had become a mecca for the revival. While Michael took solace among friends on the set of his third World War II drama—*Yesterday's Enemy*—before planning a second Bernard Bresslaw comedy that was to use the temporarily jettisoned premise of Jekyll and Hyde as the basis for a lampoon of the genre called *The Ugly Duckling*, Hammer retrained its sights on the promised follow-up to *Dracula*.

Having ended the career of *The Man Who Could Cheat Death*, Christopher Lee was about to embark on a new one of his own. "I was convinced that if I could make myself known to the audiences of Europe...the day would come when they would be making coproductions with international casts, recognized and known to people of other countries," he explains. With this notion in mind, he had set off across the channel to spread the word of his newly acquired fame, making himself tactically unavailable to Hammer in the process. Tony Hinds had other ideas, which did not include pandering to the whims of actors. He asked Jimmy Sangster to script an alternative to the original treatment that would reduce the next film's dependency on Lee. "Despite the fact that Peter played

Van Helsing, I wasn't offered it," Lee said later of the sequel. "I was slightly surprised." He would not have been if he had *read* it.

> Dracula: "Baron Meinster…you know who I am?"
> Baron: "You are the Father."
> Dracula: "I am the Father."

—*The Disciple of Dracula*

The new screenplay was entitled *The* Disciple *of Dracula,* and it concerned a sub-Dracula vampire named Baron Meinster, who is kept imprisoned in an ancestral chateau and fed on stray morsels of female flesh by his doting mother. Two English girls, Margaret and Pauline, arrive on the scene. Margaret is invited to become the baroness's "companion," while Pauline proceeds on to a teaching post at the nearby academy. During her stay, Margaret unwittingly releases the young baron from his confinement; he turns his mother into a vampire and enslaves Margaret to his will. She then acts to procure a supply of victims from among the students in Pauline's charge. The stratagem is uncovered by a character named Latour, who has ultimately to summon the spirit of Dracula himself, to deal with the renegade.

Sangster had succeeded in marginalizing the count, but he had still felt obliged to *include* him in support of the title: Dracula had figured briefly at the climax of the piece, his appearance causing Meinster to *hemorrhage* to death. But in this story, the character of Van Helsing did not figure at all. With no role for Cushing and "Dracula" now playing hard to get, Hinds was forced to postpone the production again, until a way around the latest impasse could be found.

An American investment in Bray Studios had been in the cards ever since *Dracula* confirmed to the majors that Hammer was on a roll, and James Carreras had estimated its worth at £300,000. In October 1958, it had become a reality, when the friendship between Carreras and Frankovich had sanctioned the sale of 49 percent of the complex to Columbia. In return, three Columbia executives had been appointed to the board—the aptly named Anthony Bray, Kenneth Maidment, and Frankovich himself. On March 18, 1959,

Columbia consolidated the partnership by extending its earlier
coproduction deal to incorporate a further 25 features over 5 years.

The benefit to Hammer was clear, but the logic of the move was
equally unassailable to the Americans. A number of factors in the
U.S. had contributed to this collision of interest. Independent production was on the increase, with the demise of the mogul-oper-
ated studio system. There were loopholes in the tax laws that now
made it advantageous to produce overseas. And there were increasing problems with domestic union arrangements—not to
mention that Columbia was also faced with one of the worst fiscal
years in its history. In the view of Columbia's vice president of
publicity and advertising, Paul Lazarus,

> "Runaway production was the phrase that was being used in
> Hollywood. That's when companies like Hammer, who had proven
> track records, suddenly became desirable. Then if you put together
> experience in production, and a studio, and a source of continuing
> product—that's what we were looking for."

It had also been what James Carreras was looking for, and
correcting his letter to John Nicholls of less than twelve months
before, he now noted that the future for the industry was "very
rosy," while Michael announced a program of expansion for Bray
that would double its capacity and make it capable of handling
feature films and television production simultaneously. As part of
"phase two" of Hammer's long-term plan, all existing facilities
were to be allocated to television, and two new stages were to be
built, along with other "really big-scale developments" on which
work was "soon to begin."

The pact with Columbia was concluded at a cocktail reception
in the Cottage Room of New York's Hampshire House hotel, and
James Carreras used the opportunity to announce a plethora of
new subjects, one of which was *The Stranglers of Bengal* (also no-
tioned as *The Horrors of Thuggee* at this stage), and since the deal
permitted Hammer to produce one film a year for a company other
than Columbia, *The Invisible Man, The Phantom of the Opera,* and
Sangster's revised *Disciple of Dracula* were appended to the roster
of those intended for Universal. But as representatives of the Theater Owners of America Association toasted their honored guests—

"The Boys with the Golden Touch," James Carreras and Tony Hinds—one notable was absent from the celebrations.

Michael Carreras had been isolated from the decision making at Hammer at his father's instigation; he was to be isolated from the related social whirl, as well. "That was Jimmy's idea," Paul Lazarus says. "Jimmy and Michael didn't get along. They didn't travel in the same circles." To Lazarus, Michael was introspective and reserved, the complete opposite of his outgoing father; they were *different*, and there was nothing more to it than that. "Jimmy took care of Columbia—Michael took care of production." But still waters run deep.

In "taking care of production," Michael's nonconformist nature had immersed him in the whole art of fimmaking, and he had developed his own philosophy about what made good cinema. From behind his desk at Wardour Street, he would take an active interest in *all* of Hammer's films, not just those for which he was personally responsible, and the resulting differences of opinion did not always find favor with Tony Hinds. "To avoid any friction, we used to keep tactfully out of each other's way, because we didn't actually agree about things," Hinds recalls. "I remember some heated words about my policy," Michael admits. After having to put up with Ken Hyman coproducing on *The Hound of the Baskervilles*, and the recent appointment of Tony Keys as general manager of the studio, Hinds had begun to express his discomfiture more forcefully by taking extended leaves of absence from the day-to-day work at Bray.

By this time, Peter Cushing had his Jaguar MK 8, his Kensington flat, and his cottage by the sea, and he was feeling a good deal more secure. A starring role in "Cyrano de Bergerac" for BBC television having recently fallen through, he had accepted the next offer from Hammer without demur—particularly as it promised to reunite him with Fisher and Lee. But even the celebrated triumvirate would not be enough to persuade Tony Hinds to the film, and once again, a Hammer horror was about to go begging for a producer.

When Michael Carreras found himself catapulted into the breech for a second time, the script was already complete for what seemed to be little more than an old-fashioned monster-on-the-rampage melodrama. But the experience of *The Man Who Could Cheat Death* would encourage him to try his hand at the Gothic on his own terms. By expanding on an element of the story that Jimmy

Sangster's customary fiscal caution had seen fit to omit, he set
about creating what was to become Hammer's most exotic horror
fantasy to date: *The Mummy*.

> "I've worked in dozens of tombs; it seems the best part of my life
> has been spent amongst the dead—but I've never worked in a place
> which had such an aura of…menace. There's something evil in there,
> Uncle Joe—I've felt it."

> —John Banning
> *The Mummy*

In the ranks of fictional monsters, the concept of the living dead
man (or occasionally, woman) who rises from the tombs of Egypt
lacks the clear-cut lineage of a Frankenstein or Dracula. The literary
antecedents are various and arbitrary. "Facts, Mr. Banning, facts.
Not fantasy straight out of Edgar Allan Poe," says the inspector in
the film. Poe did indeed pen one whimsical mummy tale, but the
familiar image of the bandaged corpse kept alive throughout the
millenia thanks to a good dousing in the natron bath is more
identifiable from the likes of Hazel Heald's "Out of the Eons"[17] and
Conan Doyle's "Lot No. 249."[18] In fact, it was a second Doyle story
called "The Ring of Thoth" that was to supply most of the ingredients for Universal's original venture into mummery, and the two
were to create the bones of the archetype as it is now accepted. The
prolific Bram Stoker would add a mummy to his own catalog of
horrors with *The Jewel of the Seven Stars* and inspire two films as a
result: Hammer's *Blood From the Mummy's Tomb* (see Chapter 5) and
The Awakening (1980). But cinematic interest was actually awak-
ened by the supposedly ill-fated (though mostly media created)
Howard Carter/Lord Carnarvon expedition of 1922 that had discovered the tomb of Tutankhamen, and Universal had set the cycle
in motion a mere ten years later with *The Mummy*.

> This is the Scroll of THOTH.
>   Herein are set down the magic words by which Isis raised Osiris
> from the dead.

> —Screen caption
> *The Mummy* (1932)

This opening caption from Universal's original of *The Mummy*, may have been sublimely succinct in its explanation of the rudimentary plot, but it somehow failed to make the transition into the Hammer version. In that, it was exceptional. The new film would be unique for its borrowing from a cinematic rather than a literary source. The scenario married the first half of *The Mummy* (unrequited love that spans the centuries) to the center section of *The Mummy's Tomb* (revenge from beyond the desecrated grave; 1942), and topped it off with the climax to *The Mummy's Ghost* (1943). As Universal properties, Hammer was at liberty to plunder them as it saw fit, but by virtue of the resulting patchwork, Sangster's *Mummy* would betray a constructive flaw. In combining the stories into a single whole, motivation had become muddled. Kharis, the mummy, is now required to rethink his plight halfway through and make for the archaeologists instead of a reincarnated Princess Ananka. The remainder of the story is then given over to a belated revenge enacted against the defilers of the tomb by the current High Priest of "Karnak,"[19] and the mummy himself—unrequited lover or no—consequently becomes entirely incidental to that end.

Most authorities give John L. Balderston due credit in relation to the Hammer production, while omitting the poor hacks who had pieced together *Tomb* and *Ghost*—Griffin Jay, Henry Sucher, Brenda Weisberg. Balderston was screenwriter on the 1932 film (itself based on an original story by Nina Wilcox Putnam and Richard Schayer[20]) and contributor to several of Universal's other early horrors, but in the Sangster version, his central theme of the mummy's affection for Ananka is reduced to an overblown subplot, coincidental at best, and of no more importance to the whole than as the means by which the character of John Banning is enabled to escape his just desserts—twice.

Egypt, 1895. After opening the tomb of Princess Ananka, Stephen Banning suffers a breakdown and is committed to an asylum in England. Three years later, he recovers to warn his son John that the tomb was protected by a living mummy. A mysterious Egyptian arrives with crates of artifacts; one of these is lost in a swamp. Akhir reads from the Scroll of Life, and the mummy rises from the mud. It breaks into the asylum and kills Banning senior. John Banning now recounts the legend of Ananka and realizes that the mummy has been reanimated in order to kill the defilers of the tomb. His uncle dismisses the idea and is killed by the mummy. The police are called,

> *but they refuse to believe John's story. The mummy attacks again,*
> *but John is saved by his wife, Isobel, who bears an uncanny resem-*
> *blance to Ananka. He decides to pay Akhir a visit. The Egyptian is*
> *surprised to find that John has escaped death and once more dis-*
> *patches the mummy. Confused by Isobel's appearance, it kills Akhir*
> *instead and carries Isobel to the swamp. Armed with shotguns, the*
> *police surround it. John tells Isobel to order the mummy to release*
> *her. It does—and is destroyed in a hail of gunfire.*

Michael's contribution to *The Mummy* (aided and abetted by technical adviser Andrew Low) had been to expand Sangster's verbal account of the legend of Ananka into a long and elaborate flashback to ancient Egypt. The sequence would allow for some spectacular byplay—and the requisite alternative nude scene, again unused, involving some topless handmaidens.[21] But since the purpose of this flashback, like that in the 1932 production before it, is to point up the unrequited nature of the High Priest's love, it was to play havoc with the narrative continuity of a script that was already running in circles in the attempt to keep its flimsy storyline in one piece.

It fell to Terence Fisher to make what he could of a scenario that remained stubbornly joined at the hip, and compensation comes in the form of several sequences that are stunning directorial *tours de force,* as Kharis demolishes the various obstacles that are placed in his path with the unstoppable ferocity of a juggernaut. The main assault on the Banning household will stand as the high-water mark of Hammer Horror: the mummy crashes through the portico door (of Bray's ballroom stage) to take both barrels of Banning's shotgun full in the chest and a spear through his midrift, before snapping the spear off at the shaft like a twig and laying about the hapless archaologist as if he were a rag doll. The staging (and more especially the editing) of this sequence is precision itself, and the other rampages are treated with similar deference.[22] The tremendous energy with which these encounters are choreographed mark them among the great moments of fantasy cinema, even though the vehicle that conveys them is generally held in lower regard.

These set pieces apart, Fisher's film gives the appearance of being entirely composed of a series of routine dissolves, used to bridge what are often the briefest of vaguely interconnecting scenes in the hope of forcing some semblance of continuity between them. Banning senior discusses developments with Banning junior; Banning junior does ditto with Uncle Joseph, with the coroner, with the police—the inspector does the same, but with Banning junior again, with the villagers, with anyone else who will listen. And so it goes. Since the dissolves that begin and end these vignettes are an accepted grammatical device designed to slow the passage of narrative time (or compensate for a thin script), their use here has the unfortunate effect of making *The Mummy* seem even longer than its already stretched 88 minutes.

The padding can be evidenced throughout. The events leading up to the opening of the tomb are repeated in part in a *second* flashback. The police investigation turns up a variety of sundry characters who dutifully reprise incidents verbally that the audience has witnessed only minutes before. The entire police involvement serves as little more than a device to keep things moving—by itself, it produces nothing; explanation is ultimately provided via the impertinent cliché of the two conjectural flashbacks, which occur within minutes of each other. (The first recounts the legend of Kharis and Ananka and is sustained far beyond the bounds of contextual integrity.) Even Sangster's previous dexterity at time compression seems to desert him here. The main action takes place three years *after* the opening of the tomb (to allow the protagonists to return to Victorian England and the cheaper confines of Bray's standing sets), but it nevertheless jars as an inordinate length of time for a vengeful mummy to wait before exacting bloody retribution—even though he has already waited 3,000 years!

If its lack of internal cohesion ultimately leaves *The Mummy* unnaturally dependent on the effectiveness of its set pieces, it never fails to rise to the challenge, though it is not without the odd missed opportunity as a result: the curiously undramatic first entrance of the mummy as it stumbles out of the bog, and the bland and mechanical treatment of the script's best sequence, a tight piece of verbal sparring between Banning and Akhir that is designed to provoke the high priest into action. Against this, the numerous onslaughts on the Banning household are each uniquely arresting and all spectacularly staged. And they generate a surprising amount of suspense in prelude. While Sangster's weariness is plain—"He who robs the graves of Egypt, dies!" is all we get by way of a curse—his particular brand of tongue-in-cheek humor still shines through. The stage Irish duo who deliver the mummy to Akhir are irreverantly named Mick and Pat.

On the strength of having become a subcontractor to Universal (*The Mummy* was made for £96,000 and sold to Universal for £125,000), Hammer had pushed the *Sekhmet*-boat out. The film's supporting cast had been significantly upgraded, and the lavish sets had required an additional stage at Shepperton. Distinguished character actors Felix Aylmer and Raymond Huntley had also lent their prestigious weight to the proceedings in brief cameos—an indication of how Hammer's standing in the profession (if not in critical circles) had improved by 1959.[23]

Beyond the ethereal appeal of French-born Yvonne Furneaux, the latest of Hammer's horror heroines to originate *sur le continent*, there is no sex to speak of. The love interest is strictly of the domestic variety. But there *is* violence aplenty, though the film was to have been nastier still. The mummy's destruction by shotgun blast was abbreviated by the censor, but a scene showing Kharis being deprived of his tongue prior to mummification (which had been extended to include the severed appendage in shot as a pay-off) was removed before the film was submitted for certification.

Reviews were to be surprisingly indulgent. The film was considered "continuously entertaining," as well as "excellently mounted...well acted," though one commentator would strike an ominous note; "It has an odd, *old-fashioned*... charm." Its superbly executed surface gloss may have been predisposed to disarm critical response, but *The Mummy* can nevertheless be seen as a product of marked shifts in expertise. Things were moving at Bray, and the pressure of an increasingly hectic schedule was now beginning to reveal itself. *The Mummy* would be released within a month of *The Man Who Could Cheat Death*—ahead of it, in fact—but they were to be followed into theaters by Hammer's next horror in equally short order.

> ...For hundreds of years, there existed in India a perverted religious sect, dedicated to the wanton destruction of human life...
>
> ...So secret was this savage cult that even the British East India Company, rulers of the country at the time, was unaware of their existence...
>
> —Screen caption
> *The Stranglers of Bombay*

What had been announced as *The Stranglers of Bengal* was Ken Hyman's encore to *The Hound of the Baskervilles*. Originally, the film was to have been based on John Masters's 1952 novel *The Deceivers*, about Thuggee ritual killers in India during the 1820s, and it had not been intended for Hammer at all. But the screen rights had been owned by Rank, and their asking price had curtailed the idea of a more prestigious production, along with the involvement of John Huston as director. Not one to give up easily, Hyman had decided to scale the project down and go to the historical record, instead— namely the reminiscences of Major General Sir William Sleeman, the officer who had chiefly been responsible for the overthrow of the cult. Having found himself a writer in New York who could distill the brew, Hyman offered his alternative version to Tony Hinds.

The not-dissimilar result, which was to be awarded a surprising "A" certificate in spite of an advertising line that screamed, "Murder—their religion!" was now to be titled *The Stranglers of Bombay*. With George Pastell (who had played Akhir in *The Mummy*) performing a quick-change routine from fez to turban (but not from his villainous profile) to play a high priest of Kali this time, the film lensed in Megascope in July 1959, once again under the direction of Terence Fisher.

> *India in the 1820s, and the British East India Company is becoming increasingly concerned at the disappearance of thousands of travelers each year. Captain Lewis is appointed to investigate, and gradually pieces together evidence of a cult of stranglers who worship Kali—the goddess of darkness. After strangling their unwary victims with a silk cloth, these "Thugs" then rob them and inter their bodies in mass graves, prepared in advance. Narrowly escaping death at the hands of the Stranglers, Lewis is able to present the facts to Colonel Henderson. High-ranking Indian officials are implicated, but with Lewis now in charge of suppressing it, the days of the cult are numbered.*

The strictures to which Hammer's horror films were now required to conform were not only being entrenched, they were becoming immutable. In David Z. Goodman's simplistic script, history is reduced to basic essentials. Good, in the form of Guy Rolfe's East India Company official, combats evil, in the form of George Pastell's High Priest, in accordance with the model that

Fisher had evolved for his Gothics. All the expected juxtapositional devices are deployed—even to the extent of providing the high priest with a predatory female acolyte in the unlikely form of buxom fifties' pinup Marie Devereux, whom Hammer publicists had coyly described as "statistically exciting."

By confining its narrative to the formulaic guidelines of Hammer Horror, the film presents the aberrant Thug threat as nothing more comprehensible than the sum of the atrocities that it sanctions in Kali's name, and since "the innocent victims totalled over a million" (a screen caption advises), it quickly abandons its worthy premise to concentrate instead on regulation interludes of pure *guignol*. With brandings, eye gougings, amputation, and mutilation, *The Stranglers* was more gratuitous than any of the previous horrors. Perhaps because it purported to be history, reviewers in general would not see these as self-serving. They were to reserve the wrath that they still felt obliged to direct at Hammer for the censor, who, by awarding the "A" certificate (with cuts), was allowing children—albeit accompanied by a parent or guardian—to be exposed to such excesses for the first time.

Fisher himself considered the film something of a failure, subsequently blaming its lack of historical perspective and crude oppositional structure on an approach to the material that was overreliant on the narrow formalizations of Gothic fantasy. If *The Stranglers of Bombay* is *The Camp on Blood Island* played to the tune of *Dracula*, one sequence stands out. After a silent night attack on his encampment by Thugs, Captain Connaught-Smith (Allan Cuthbertson) wakes to find himself virtually alone among the dead ranks of his command. As the realization dawns, a distant chant of "Kali!—Kali!" rises to a roar, and the invisible nemesis returns to seek *him* out as well. In its depiction of imperial complacency faltering in the face of an alien culture, the sequence is genuinely unsettling, but even this would have been more at home in the metaphorical landscape of a Gothic. It was a blinkered entrapment in archetype that would return to haunt Fisher when he had once more laid Dracula to rest, and despite some soul-searching after *The Stranglers of Bombay*, he would go on to show that he had not learned the lesson.

"Great goddess—you have given a sign. I understand. Prepare a
funeral pyre!"

—High Priest
The Stranglers of Bombay

The deal with Columbia, coming on top of that already brokered
with Universal, was to spell the end of Exclusive Films. Hammer
had no further need of a self-owned distribution arm, and Exclusive was now "too big for the product" that remained to it. Since
some of its activities were also no longer in keeping with the more
scrupulous requirements of a major international company in any
event, it was closed down, though the name would remain until
1966, when James Carreras would announce that it was to be used
to form a new company—Exclusive Film Productions—within the
existing Hammer "Group." Nothing further would come of that.

With the closure went all the branch offices and the majority of
the staff, in addition to the Christmas parties and the summer boat
trips to Southend-on-sea. The small business was becoming a
larger business, and such frivolities had served their purpose.
Morris Young would join United Artists (where he was eventually
to rise to the position of managing director), but Brian Lawrence
would remain, to concentrate his energies exclusively on the business side of Hammer, with Croft and legal adviser Edwin Davis.
"No British distributor can match the international releasing facilities of a major American company," James Carreras informed
Variety. But he would be unable to stomach breaking the news to
the one man who had been equally responsible for Exclusive's rise
to prominence, and Donald McKelvie was subsequently dispatched to Brian Lawrence's office to "do the honors" in his place.
"Exclusive was very dear to me," Lawrence said. "I appreciated
him not being able to tell me himself."

After the success of the first of the ribald *Carry On* comedies
(*Carry On Sergeant*; 1958), Hammer continued to incorporate examples of the breed. The Val Guest coproduction *Further Up the Creek*
and TV spin-off *I Only Arsked* had been succeeded by *The Ugly
Duckling* (announced as *Mad Pashernate Love* in a nod to the small-
screen persona of its star, Bernard Bresslaw), and there was to be
financial participation in *Don't Panic Chaps!* and the later *Sands of*

the Desert. In the opinion of Ian Johnson, writing in *Films and Filming,* such films were breaking with tradition as comedy went back to its music-hall roots and became "freer and more robust...*and dirtier.*" But if 1959 was to be "the crucial year in British cinema," according to Johnson, it was not just to be in comedy. All manner of films were becoming more adult, and the so-called "social realism" that had invested the "X" certificate of *Room at the Top* with such tantalizing proletarian appeal was about to find its way into the field of horror, as well.

As part of his brief within the hierarchy, Michael Carreras had been charged with charting new paths for the company to travel and, at the end of 1958, had even forecast the first Hammer musical, in expectation that the fad for horror would soon be over. "Demand has become more selective," he informed the trades.24 After the disappointment of "Tales of Frankenstein" had come the setback of *Ten Seconds to Hell,* but Michael's vision for the future still included ideas that went far beyond things going bump in the night. *Ten Seconds to Hell* may have been a sobering experience for him, but not so the film that he had chosen to snap at its heels.

Yesterday's Enemy was the screen version of a controversial stage play by Peter R. Newman. Directed by Val Guest and starring popular tough-guy actor Stanley Baker, the harrowing antiwar tract represented Guest at a different and more somber pace. The powerful script (by Newman) was unremitting in its emotional browbeating about the nature of the Hobson's choices facing combatants caught up in the "total war" scenario of the Burma jungle's green hell. A top-notch cast engaged sympathy from the first—a ploy designed to maximize the impact of the fact that none of them made it past the last reel. The film's origins as a play were never far from the surface of its studio-bound set (along with its moral conscience), but it was to show a new side to Hammer and, for the first time, reveal the company as Michael Carreras would have liked to see it develop: the cinema as art form, every bit as much as entertainment.

After his intermediate sidesteps into fantasy and comedy, Michael was quick to follow the thematic direction of *Yesterday's Enemy* with an equally hard-hitting police thriller centered on the Manchester underworld, also with Guest and Baker. Scripted by Guest (from a novel by ex-Manchester policeman Maurice Procter), *Hell Is a City* was a tense and engrossing drama of the hunt for an escaped killer. It was similarly endowed with a superlative supporting cast and what had now become Guest's trademarks of unrelenting pace and a sharp documentary-style sense of realism, aided in this instance by authentic locations, the employment of some colorful local customs (such as the "tossing school," a form of gambling peculiar to the North of England that was staged for the film at Oldham Edge), and *cinema verité* tricks such as the use of overlapping dialogue. Just for a change, the *villain* of the piece was an American (John Crawford).

Yesterday's Enemy opened on October 12, backed by a massive promotional campaign in which General Sir Robert Mansergh (who had commanded the Fifth Burma Division, and was aide-de-camp to the queen) would tour Britain and the U.S. to accompany the film in release. On this occasion, Michael was to be lauded with as much fervor as he had previously been lambasted over *Ten Seconds to Hell*. "Brilliant and disturbing" was the consensus. "One of the most savage and certainly the most controversial films about war ever to come out of a studio." "Made by Hammer Films, it is a credit to the picture business." And from *Kine Weekly*, "A powerful stable companion of the phenomenally successful *Camp on Blood Island*. Outstanding British war fare and an infallible box-office proposition." (*Yesterday's Enemy* was to find itself nominated as Best British Film of the Year in the BFA[25] Awards of 1959, with two of its cast—Baker and Gordon Jackson—nominated for Best Actor. It would be beaten to the post by *Sapphire*, produced by Michael Relph.)

Such reviews were rare for a Hammer production and, cognizant of the sudden appeal of subjects of more contemporary concern, Tony Hinds now abandoned a plan to revive *Brat Farrar*, which as scripted by critic Paul Dehn (through his friendship with composer James Bernard) was showing every sign of abandoning him anyway,[26] and opted instead for the more unorthodox transport of *The Pony Cart*—a successful stage play by Roger Garis that dealt with the controversial subject of child molestation, and which Hinds was to translate to the screen as *Never Take Sweets From a Stranger*. Despite the sensitive nature of the subject matter, the film was a taut, responsible, and compelling affair, with a first-class script (by John Hunter), impeccable performances from a well-chosen cast, and sympathetic direction by Cyril Frankel. *Kine Weekly* again—"Stark and intelligent psychopathic melodrama...Skilfully blended from potent ingredients, it can't miss, provided it is given the exploitation it deserves."

"That was the only picture of mine that I ever got good notices on," Hinds recalls. Alas, they were not to be in the majority, and in a significant role reversal, Paul Dehn would renounce his previous support for Hammer and lend voice to the clamor of indignation that was to be raised against the company for having had the temerity to tackle such an issue in the name of commercialism. The combination of Hammer and pedophilia would turn out to be an unfortunate one,[27] and Hinds was quick to revert to type. But role reversals were now becoming the order of the day.

After years of playing in reserve for a team that had never given any indication that he might one day be called to the first eleven, Michael Carreras had finally come into his own. At the close of 1959, *Yesterday's Enemy, The Mummy,* and *The Man Who Could Cheat Death* were all on screen simultaneously in the West End of London, and Michael had produced the three of them. Even Tony Hinds was effusive in extolling the virtues of his onetime apprentice:

> "Michael was probably *the* most efficient producer in England. He knew his script backwards—he was very good with crews; he was very good with actors...I don't think he was always right in his ideas of what to make—and casting—but he was more efficient than I ever was."

Now accepted as one of the brightest lights in the industry, Michael was at last in the position to stamp his own personality onto the fabric of Hammer, and in a different way to that of his peers.

While Hinds set about tackling the belated sequel to *Dracula,* Michael had already begun to harness the next film on the schedule to a much bolder concept, and an artistic ensemble that he believed would free Hammer from the constraints of grind-house exploitation once and for all.

Chapter 3

Diminishing Returns

1960-1962

"I remember a talk that I had with Sir James Carreras many years ago in which we agreed that his company's horror films would avoid mixing sex with horror and would avoid scenes which people could regard as disgusting and revolting."

John Trevelyan
What the Censor Saw (1973)

As the world moved into what social historians would christen the permissive or "swinging" sixties, there was little to indicate that the teenagers who had found their feet in the sneakers of James Dean would blossom and grow into a generation that would overturn the sexual and social mores of the fifties—and even American foreign policy (at least in respect to Southeast Asia) in the process.

To the farsighted, there may have been an indicator or two of what was to come. America was about to elect the youngest president in its 173-year history, and Penguin Books was to test the 1959 Obscene Publications Act (under which a plea of *literary merit* had become an admissable defense in law) and win the most sensational obscenity trial of the century on behalf of D. H. Lawrence and *Lady Chatterley's Lover*, opening the way for the ranker works of Henry Miller, William Burroughs, and Hubert Selby, Junior.

For the nonseers, however, 1960 seemed mostly concerned with matters of unfinished business. Eddie Cochran would follow Buddy Holly into death and legend. Private 53310761 Presley was to complete two years of service in Germany and return, chastened,

to the blander shores of the more acceptable pop career that Colonel
Parker began to orchestrate for him in a series of sanitized teen
movies, such as *GI Blues* (1960) and *Blue Hawaii* (1961). With them,
the last vestiges of rock 'n' roll would fade quietly away, until the
inertia of pop charts compiled entirely of Tin Pan Alley[1] ditties and
stopgap distractions like *The Twist* would once more encourage
buyers to seek out and embrace some grittier alternatives: first, Phil
Spector and his "Wall of Sound"—later, and of more lasting value,
the music of Motown and the Mersey.

On television, 1960 got underway with a repeat of the third and
best of the BBC's Quatermass serials—"Quatermass and the Pit"
— aired in two 90-minute instalments (it had originally aired in the
usual six-episode format in December-January of 1958-9). It was to
be the last great speculative fiction of extraterrestrial life before
Telstar paved the way for the first manned satellite flight. Yuri
Gagarin's orbit of the earth in April 1961 would herald a new dawn
for the science (and science fiction) of space exploration.

Television westerns still held the fort. "Wells Fargo," "Wyatt
Earp," and "Have Gun, Will Travel" had given way to hourlong
series such as "Cheyenne," "Maverick," and "Bronco" which, like
private-eye cult hit "77 Sunset Strip," emanated on the whole from
the studios of Warner Brothers—although "Wagon Train," which
did not, ruled the roost.

In the cinema, however, more conventional fare had begun to
take a backseat to a tentative licentiousness that was soon to
become the norm: *Saturday Night and Sunday Morning* (1960), *Only
Two Can Play* (1961), *A Kind of Loving* (1962). With this in mind,
Michael Carreras had planned a version of *Dr. Jekyll and Mr. Hyde*
that was to reverse the traditional empathies of the piece and
endow Hyde with the same kind of sexual allure that had worked
such wonders for Dracula. "We were pushing the limits," he said.
"I thought it was probably time that we opened up a bit."

Robert Louis Stevenson's novella, *The Strange Case of Dr. Jekyll
and Mr. Hyde,* was published in 1886, and its immediate success led
to a contemporaneous stage adaption by Thomas Russell Sullivan,
designed for American actor Richard Mansfield. By September
1888, this adaption was playing the Lyceum Theatre in London,
concurrent with a series of murders in the Whitechapel area that
legend would eventually come to lay at the door of the pseudony-
mous "Jack the Ripper." The efficacy of Mansfield's performance

in playing *both* roles was such that for a time he was suspected of the actual crimes, and the coincident of art and life forced the premature closure of the production. Since Stevenson's Hyde had *not* been a sexual psychopath but more of a wanton bully in the manner of Dickens's Bill Sikes, this may seem strange, but the Sullivan adaption had altered and simplified the book for the stage, rooting the metaphysical musings of the literary Jekyll in a sexually frustrated courtship, in response to the insurgent teachings of a young Viennese doctor named Freud. With the gamut of popular theories about the killings including the notion of a society doctor frequenting the East End for the purpose of carving out his place in history on the entrails of prostitutes, the libidinous motivation of Sullivan's Hyde was deemed a touch too close for comfort.

So resonant was this reading of the text that its premise stuck, and when Clara Beranger came to script the first major film version of the tale (which was to arrive in 1920 and provide an equally bravura showcase for John Barrymore), not only was the sexual allegory carried over from the play but so was the tenuous connection to the Ripper. The overtone was expanded, and the fiancée was given a doppelgänger in Nita Naldi, whose sultry tart ("Gina— who faced her world alone," as the caption card decorously referred to her) became the object of Jekyll's passion and made the dynamic behind the good doctor's alchemical pursuits unequivocal. This rendition received a more explicit treatment in the 1932 Paramount film starring Fredric March and directed by Rouben Mamoulian (which would climax with Hyde's strangulation of the prostitute, this time played by Miriam Hopkins, while declaiming, "I'll give you a *lover* now—his name is Death!"). But it was in the M-G-M remake of nine years later that the progressive reduction of the narrative reached its nadir.

The unbridled permissiveness of the Mamoulian film (and others) encouraged a backlash that led to the forming of the Catholic-inspired "Legion of Decency" dedicated to the overhaul of the self-regulatory "Hays Code." Such was the influence of this group that within two years, Hollywood invited the Legion-approved Joseph Breen to head the Hays Office. In consequence, the explicit depiction of sex on the screen was no longer acceptable. When Spencer Tracy took on the role in 1941, he was required to exhibit a more subtle Machiavellian guile in Hyde. The paradoxical outcome of Tracy's reticence elevated sexual sadism to the level of art form and turned the sociopath of the story into the psychopath of the modern American *noir* thriller. From this point on, Hyde would never again be recognizable as Stevenson had originally created him—as a "livelier image of the spirit," whose pursuit of evil for evil's sake was nothing more than a dark reflection of what his author had naively decreed to be his "wonderful love of life."

The changes wrought by Sullivan *et al.* went further than the simple ratifying of Jekyll's experiment to the level of psychosexual urge. Stevenson's story had been constructed in the manner of a Chinese puzzle; the fact that Jekyll and Hyde are one and the same was kept as the *dénouement.* In redefining the allegory, the mystery element had been made redundant, so the spectacle was advanced instead, with textual references to Jekyll's "cabinet" (for the keeping of medicines) now elaborated to encompass an actual *booth* (for the changing of personalities, in the style of Superman). This crude piece of incidental stagecraft became central to the tale. The audacious mugging of Mansfield and the increasingly outlandish appliances used to aid the theatrics of Barrymore and March (to the extent that the Hyde of the latter looked more like something that had escaped from the London Zoo than the psyche of a physician) did the rest, entrenching the transformation itself as the *sine qua non* of the story. Tracy strove to reverse the process and achieve both Jekyll *and* Hyde with a minimum of makeup (by Jack Dawn), and the desultory treatment meted out by the critics persisted. They were to give similar succour to Hammer, for the same reason. Paul Massie would find, as Tracy had, that trying to play Hyde as anything other than a demonic primal urge was a thankless task, when it came to an audience weaned on the more simian image of March's lisping bogeyman.

Conscious of the growing need for Hammer to bring something other than a straight Technicolor veneer to each succeeding remake, Michael Carreras had decided that Stevenson's tale of the kindly doctor who transmutes into the evil Mr. Hyde was in need of a more modern metamorphosis. His version contrived to have *Jekyll* the repressed and unattractive half of the indivisible duo. To make the concept tenable, the new Hyde could be no mere brute, whose psychodynamic was to be found hanging between his legs. Instead, he would be the antithesis of the popular stereotype—suave, urbane, debonair.

Such a reading had precedent, though both were of recent vintage. Jean Renoir's *Experiment in Evil (Le Testament du Docteur Cordelier;* 1959) had sought to return Hyde to his literary persona as a spirit of anarchy—faun, rather than satyr—and Hammer had flirted with the theme in the Bernard Bresslaw vehicle of the year before: *The Ugly Duckling.* That there had been a more contemporary *animus* lurking beneath the surface calm of these Jekylls was self-evident, and the new film was to be a logical extension of that same line of thought.

Hammer was to return to the text with a vengeance in one important particular, however. The Hyde of what would appropriately be entitled *The Two Faces of Dr. Jekyll* would be *young.*

> "It appears to be an accelerating of your entire metabolism—as if your life were suddenly burning itself up at a much faster rate..."

> —Litauer
> *The Two Faces of Dr. Jekyll*

To write the film, Michael had turned to Wolf Mankowitz, author, playwright, and one of a new artistic elite currently making its presence felt in all manner of media. Its ranks included Jonathan Miller, Kenneth Tynan, Ned Sherrin, the ubiquitous David Frost, and a bevy of other commentators and humorists. Some of them, such as the *Pythons,* were still perfecting their craft on the sounding boards of Cambridge's *Footlights Review,* but what they had in common was a revolutionary disregard for the conventions of the day. Mankowitz had just won an award for Best British Stage Musical of 1959 for *Make Me An Offer,* but he was no stranger to the Gothic, or the horrors of the Victorian underworld. He would go on to coscript *Casino Royale* (1966), but he would also pen a biography of Edgar Allan Poe and the series "Dickens of London" for television. He had recently scripted *Expresso Bongo* from his own play for Val Guest (which would be nominated for a BFA Award for Best British Screenplay), and it was Guest who had made the introduction.[2] "Michael always tried to make better pictures," said Jimmy Sangster. "He would always try to get better writers, better actors, better budgets." In this instance, Michael was to pay twice Hammer's usual fee to ensure the best. Mankowitz accepted. His country estate lacked a swimming-pool!

Mankowitz was an intellectual of the first water, much given to sermonizing from the increasingly influential pulpit of television. (In a script liberally sprinkled with psychological insights, one can almost hear the writer reflecting when Litauer remarks to Kitty Jekyll, "You are married to a man of very great talents—such men are always difficult to live with.") And he had ideas of his own about how best to reconcile the interests of the arts with those of social commentary—ideas that went far beyond the extravagant caprice of making Edward Hyde a handsome roué: "We were on the edge of a sexual explosion and I wanted to go as far as possible in this film," he said.

It was to be a trifle too far. With a screenplay of astonishing uninhibitedness, Mankowitz drew the unwanted attentions not only of film censor John Trevelyan, but also of the board's recently appointed and far more reactionary president—ex-Labour cabinet minister Herbert Morrison, now Lord Morrison of Lambeth.

Hammer and the Censor

> There is...abundant flouting of the moral code—adultery, two rapes, and the standard shocker genre violence—that make this anything but a kiddie's matinee film.
>
> *Variety* review
> *The Two Faces of Dr. Jekyll*

"At a time of brutal assaults on women, there is danger in this film." So advised a censor's report of 1960 in reference to Michael Powell's *Peeping Tom,* an otherwise sober and meticulous study of the mind and method of a sex killer. The report had been given weight by an atrocious murder committed on December 23, 1959, when Patrick Joseph Byrne decapitated and mutilated the body of Stephanie Baird in a Y.W.C.A. hostel in Birmingham.

John Trevelyan had been with the British Board of Film Censors as a part-time examiner since 1951, becoming its secretary in 1958 when John Nicholls retired. It was a post he would hold until 1971, almost the whole of Hammer's period of operation in the field of horror films. Very much a personality in his own right, Trevelyan was a man of strong principles that he could elucidate with some erudition. He had long sought to create a better climate of cooperation between artist and arbiter and, except for the occasional reaction to backlash, board decisions during Trevelyan's tenure would genuinely attempt to reflect the changes in attitude on matters of sex and violence. Under its former president, Sir Sidney Harris, the BBFC had formulated strict rules about what was and was not acceptable on screen. It was hard on violence and softer on sex, but it was consistently tough on *sexual* violence—rape in particular.

The "X" certificate had now become very big business, especially in its more salacious guise. *Room at the Top*, Fellini's *La Dolce Vita*, and Dassin's *Never On Sunday* (all 1959) had compelled the same sort of queues as *Dracula* and *The Curse of Frankenstein*, and features boasting elements of sex *and* horror were virtually guaranteed at the box office. The first serious contenders to Hammer Horror had come via Anglo-Amalgamated, a distribution outfit founded by Nat Cohen and Stuart Levy in emulation of Exclusive, and home of the *Carry Ons*. Anglo was in the process of handling three films in a row that more than matched the Hammer product in terms of graphic content: *Horrors of the Black Museum, Circus of Horrors*, and *Peeping Tom*. The first had been heavily cut, the second was mildly cut, and the third would be *un*cut (it had been produced in a "continental" version). But *Peeping Tom* deployed the twin sins of sex and horror with such precision that all in the industry would come to feel the sting of Karl Boehm's tripod switch-blade. The film was too much for the establishment of the day and it would be castigated on release like no other, eventually forcing Anglo to withdraw it from circulation. Such a reaction was unprecedented and was to send producer-director Michael Powell's hitherto-illustrious career into a near-terminal decline, from which it would only be rescued, after more than twenty years, through the good offices of Martin Scorsese and Francis Ford Coppola. The BBFC had clearly been prudent in issuing its note of caution, and Hammer was next on the firing line.

> "So we dispense with the unnecessary—good, evil...and love."
>
> —Edward Hyde
> *The Two Faces of Dr. Jekyll*

"Robert Louis Stevenson's story has been turned into a boiling hot script by Wolf Mankowitz. It will be one of Columbia's biggest winners in years," James Carreras promised *Variety*.

In script form, *The Two Faces of Dr. Jekyll* ran the gamut of sexual explicitness, and in its foray into London's vice dens, it even threw in a smattering of taboos for good measure, such as cockfighting and black magic. "The problem presented to the adaptor is the dramatizing of what isn't there—which is to say, the evil life of Mr. Hyde," said Mankowitz. "I tried to utilize the whole of the London scene as described by the contemporary writers."

In October 1959, Trevelyan had warned Michael Carreras of the dangers inherent in this and he continued to do so throughout the production. The result was to be more than a dozen scene and dialog deletions, even though footage for some of these exceptions had been shot. When a fine cut was ready for scrutiny the following February, there was worse to come. "My only fear," Michael advised the board, "is that we have all been a little over-cautious, after the various warnings we received, in translating the script to film, and that our 'by implication' treatment has not proved as successful as our earlier horror treatments." It was a well-founded fear. His accommodating approach may have appeased the secretary, but it was already in danger of sanitizing what had been intended all along as an adult sex film. Notwithstanding, *more* cuts were required. They involved abbreviating the rape of Jekyll's wife, removing shots of an exultant Hyde gloating over dancer Maria's death throes as he strangles her, and fore-shortening the snake dance (as it stood, there was a suggestion of fellatio). "John was very quick at picking up Freudian references," said Mankowitz. Two brief nude-shots of Maria were also excised.

In view of what was to follow twelve months later, Michael Carreras had gotten off lightly. The clever optical "wipes" that had been dictated by Mankowitz's script would partially mask the deficiencies, but *The Two Faces of Dr. Jekyll* would still be the first Hammer horror where large chunks of the action could clearly be seen to be missing.

British film "bad boy" Laurence Harvey had been the original choice for Jekyll and Hyde; Mankowitz had written the part especially for him. As *Room at the Top* had shown, Harvey had the kind of persona that elicited sympathy, in spite of the depths to which the characters he played were required to sink. As Mankowitz was to note, "He could be evil, yet very *sympatico* to the audience." Harvey was keen on the role, but agent and partner Jimmy Wolf would not allow him to accept. Harvey was a *star,* and Hammer salaries never quite reached to the heavens. With this all-important aspect removed from the design of the film, *The Two Faces of Dr. Jekyll* was to be crippled by an internal flaw even before it was assigned a director entirely out of sympathy with its narrative complexity. "With Larry and a halfway-decent director, Hammer would have had *the* most distinguished film they ever made," was Wolf Mankowitz's assessment.

To the surprise of Christopher Lee (who would play Paul Allen), he was never even considered for the role. "I was very disappointed at not being asked to play it; I thought Mankowitz's idea was a very clever one, of the rather wimpish Dr. Jekyll turning into this handsome and malignant Mr. Hyde." Lee approached Michael Carreras on the subject and was turned down, and the same would apply when Hammer announced its intention to make *The Phantom of the Opera.* The reason was simple: "I used to get a bit disenchanted with the continual use of Lee (and Cushing)," Michael later confessed.

When Paul Massie stepped into the breach, he was offered only Hyde, but the young Canadian persuaded Michael that he could manage both roles. Roy Ashton could not, however. His makeup for Jekyll would fail to convince and, on the scope screen, appeared theatrical and crude. (Terence Fisher's clumsy handling of the personality switches was to accord the film a reputation as the one in which Jekyll becomes Hyde by turning his back to camera and pulling his beard off!) The critics would be taken by Massie's performance but not by the cheese paring that it apparently had to surmount—though Hammer was not entirely to blame. Mankowitz had penned no transitions for Jekyll, and his reflection on the lapse is unequivocal: "What I discovered eventually is that the thing that holds the public is the transformation scene, and if you take out the transformation, you take away an essential part of the archetype."

"This is not the Jekyll and Hyde I remember" would be the opinion of Paul Dehn (now at the *News Chronicle*)—once Hammer's staunchest critical ally, but now disenchanted with the affair. As if the cuts were not enough, the Mankowitz script proved to be too clever by half. What Sangster would express in simple language and straightforward construction, this brilliant author would bury in a dense interplay of characters. *The Two Faces of Dr. Jekyll* would turn out to be Jacobean tragedy, and the clinical dissection that Mankowitz had performed on Stevenson's "fine bogey tale" was ultimately to damage the drama.

If the Hyde of the previous versions had been more metaphor than man, it rarely showed; in *The Two Faces of Dr. Jekyll,* it would be only too obvious. Mankowitz had seen him as "an anarchistic force, which needs to be released more often." He never took anything lightly, and his research for this film had been as thoroughgoing and exhaustive as ever. "Jekyll is Victorian bourgeois society—his disorders are not just his personal disorders, they reflect a whole disordered materialism in that society. *My sympathies were with Hyde.*"

In his diatribe against the film, Paul Dehn would write, "It is possible that sequences…concerned with sex and sadism will produce their customary dividends at the box office, in which case Hammer Films will have the satisfaction of knowing that they have butchered R. L. S. for £.s.d [pounds, shillings, and pence]." Mankowitz, on the other hand, declared that he had "written it carefully, so as not to excite the sadistic element." If Dehn was to miss the point, he would not be alone—but then Stevenson himself experienced the same trouble in defending his intent. Time and again, he was moved to decry the extent to which the genital probing of psychoanalysis had reached into and distorted his work. "The harm was in Jekyll because he was a hypocrite, not because he was fond of women," Stevenson wrote.

> "He says so himself; but people are so full of folly and inverted lust, that they can think of nothing but sexuality. The hypocrite let out the beast Hyde—who is no more sensual than another, but who is the essence of cruelty and malice, and selfishness and cowardice: and these are the diabolic in man—not this poor wish to have a woman, that they make such a cry about."

It would do neither any good. Hyde had become a symbol for something else entirely, and Hammer's version of the tale would be seen as merely a more salacious update of the same old sinful story.

> *After a chemical experiment, Dr. Henry Jekyll has freed his "other self"—whom he names Edward Hyde. As Hyde, he visits a night haunt called the Sphinx, where he finds his wife, Kitty, with his best*

friend Paul Allen, a reckless gambler. Allen introduces him to the charms of snake-dancer Maria. Hyde visits Kitty and asks her to be his mistress, but she confesses to loving Paul; the "change" overcomes him and he leaves. Jekyll takes the serum again and, as Hyde, he allows Allen to show him around the vice dens of the London underworld. He offers to cover Allen's debts in exchange for Kitty. Allen refuses. Hyde then invites the two lovers to the Sphinx, where he locks Paul in a room with the python and rapes Kitty. She wakes to find Paul crushed, and falls from the balcony to her death. After making love to Maria, Hyde strangles her. Now aware of Hyde's intention to incriminate him, Jekyll decides to destroy the drug, but Hyde returns and sets fire to the laboratory. When the police arrive, he informs them that Jekyll has committed suicide. After the inquest, Hyde turns back into Jekyll for the last time; now an exhausted man, Jekyll says that he has destroyed Hyde—but he has also destroyed himself in the process.

"How you fall back on the conventional way of thinking, Ernst...I am not concerned with a moral operation."

—Dr. Henry Jekyll
The Two Faces of Dr. Jekyll

Prophetically anticipating the sexual awakening of the sixties, Mankowitz's script used the subtext of the story to comment on the sterile moral conformity of postwar society, so the moral and philosophical implications of the psyche splitting are quickly disposed of in an obligatory exchange between Jekyll and the voice of conscience, as represented by the paternalistic Litauer. "Good—evil—this moral quibbling is useless," the doctor dispenses, as it is revealed that he has already partaken of the drug. By the start of reel 2, Hyde is on-screen for the first time. The thrust of this version is not with Jekyll's experimentation, but with Hyde himself and how he confronts, encircles, and finally obliterates a social infrastructure in decline.

In *The Two Faces of Dr. Jekyll*, Edward Hyde retains the sexual dimension of the preceding films, but Jekyll's *raison d'être* is the exacting of a proxy revenge on his unfaithful wife and disingenuous friend, not self-gratification. "The pattern of justice is complete," Hyde announces when Kitty Jekyll has fallen to her death after discovering the corpse of her erstwhile lover. Justice?—a new ethic for the amoral Hyde, surely? But a natural justice of sorts is

exactly what the character achieves this time round, although he
does not survive to enjoy the fruits of his labors: Jekyll resurfaces
to recant and reveal the truth, thereby destroying them both.

If the previous versions had affirmed the notion of a Victorian
age that was essentially moral, if a little prim when it came to
matters of sex, *The Two Faces of Dr. Jekyll* paints a wholly different
and more authentic picture. Its Jekyll is a man only too aware of
the dual nature of the society in which he functions—a far cry from
the high-minded idealists of March and Tracy—and Hyde becomes
his instrument of revenge on a world whose values are asynchro-
nous to his own. In the Hammer film, *all* the protagonists have two
faces, and the surprise is the remarkable rectitude with which its
Hyde conducts himself in counterweight. He may be conditioned
by his alter ego to commit murder, but some of the lesser brutalities
(the bludgeoning of the thug, the trampling of the wino) were
appended by director Terence Fisher, and Hyde is otherwise a
"perfect gentleman," as the transsexual manager of the Sphinx so
pointedly refers to him. Here it is *Jekyll* who becomes annoyingly
resurgent as the drug wears off, whereas hitherto it had always
been Hyde, who surfaced of his own accord. It is a subtle—perhaps
elusive—distinction, but it is integral to the concept, and Fisher's
hidebound notions of archetype blinded him to the nettle.

The Mankowitz script had plainly been something of a mine
field, and despite an unusual one-day reading for the cast prior to
production, at the insistence of Michael Carreras, it is clear that
writing, playing, and direction are not entirely in accord. It was a
troubled film from the start; it went over budget (finishing at
£146,000) and threatened to go over schedule. Bernard Robinson
asked for more money and was given it; Fisher asked for more time
and was turned down. Fisher sulked and blamed Michael—somewhat unreasonably—although there *was* a case to answer. Mankowitz had written a major oratorio designed to run for two hours,
but Hammer was intent on performing it in a minor key. As a result,
the scope of the piece was compacted (the Sphinx is an amalgam
of *two* locales in the script), and several of its best scenes were
jettisoned to expedite the usual six-week shoot: a *symbolic* transformation, which better explained the conflict in Jekyll; Hyde's return
to the prizefight to take on the Corinthian; and the script's shocking
climax:

In the far distance...we see a man on the gallows. We move in
very fast till we are close to the face of Jekyll. The trap swings away,
the body jerks as the rope tautens. Slowly the body revolves away.
As the body again swings into camera we now see the dead face of
Hyde.

The Two Faces of Dr. Jekyll was Fisher's eighth horror in a row for
Hammer, and repetition was beginning to show itself. He is on
record as having had little sympathy with the material. "You didn't
have a single character...who was worth tuppence ha'penny," he
opined for *Films and Filming*, adding that Hyde "loved every second of his crimes." Wolf Mankowitz saw things differently. "I
couldn't get through to him," he said of Fisher. "He seemed rather
resentful of the whole affair." There was an age gap a generation
wide between them, and the gulf in understanding was wider still.
Mankowitz was neither consulted about the psychology nor ques-
tioned about the motivation. Accordingly, he is uncompromising
over the way Fisher handled the film. "He didn't understand what
the thing was about. He hadn't even read the book. He thought it
was just another Hammer horror story."

Mankowitz's opinion of Fisher is moderated in part by that of
the young actor who played a brief cameo as a pimp in the film.
"He [Fisher] didn't get involved too much. He had a great eye for
the four-wall situation that Hammer was—he knew exactly where
to put the camera, without thinking too much about it," said Oliver
Reed. Fisher had an eye for talent, also. He and current casting
director Stuart Lyons (later to become head of Fox U.K.) saw
potential in Reed and promptly moved to exploit it. "He and Stuart
Lyons tried to put me under contract—a private contract for themselves," Reed remembers. Nothing came of it; Hammer had other
things in store for this particular "extra."

As if to make some sense of the moral quagmire in which he
found himself, Fisher dictated that a line which had been included
as a sop to the puritans should be spoken directly to the camera—
"The death of Dr. Jekyll is a solemn warning to us not to meddle
with the divine pattern of nature," summarizes a coroner. Whatever message was blowing in the wind of the upcoming decade, it
was to be for eyes other than those of Terence Fisher; "Personally,
I would have written it differently," he said of the film.[3] From the
evidence, it appears that he tried to.

Hyde: "Come Mrs. Jekyll, why not sell—what you have so often *given* away?"

Kitty: "I might agree to your preposterous suggestion, Mister Hyde...*were it not for the fact that you utterly repel me!*

—Unscripted addendum
The Two Faces of Dr. Jekyll

No longer available in the form in which it eventually reached the English screen, *The Two Faces of Dr. Jekyll* is not the lost masterpiece of Hammer Horror, but it *is* the Gothic masterwork that Hammer never made. With its abridgments and alterations, what the extant film noticeably lacks is the potency that Mankowitz had breathed into it to begin with. Thanks, in part, to the intervention of the moral purists it had chosen to range itself against, its teeth were pulled before it could bite; it seems they are gone for good. But enough remains to show what should have been. If Hammer's most daring exercise in the genre had not been watered down, and gone comparatively unnoticed as a result—if a film, rather than a *book*, had inaugurated the mood of change that would culminate in the catharsis of the swinging sixties, then *The Two Faces of Dr. Jekyll* would have been that film.

The Two Faces of Dr. Jekyll was to open at the London Pavilion on October 7, 1960. One month later, *Lady Chatterley* would be exonerated in the eyes of the law, and the sexual revolution that film and book *both* had advocated would finally be primed to begin.[4]

—*From Paul Massie:*
"Will you let me go, you filthy witch?"
("Will you let me go, you fourpenny whore?")
"I told you to go to hades, and take that woman with you."
("I told you to go to hell, and take that whore with you.")

—*From Christopher Lee:*
"Darn good chap, Jekyll."
("Damn good chap, Jekyll.")
"Oh, the heck with it."
("Oh, hell.")

—*From Norma Marla:*
"Your friend spoke to me like I was a common witch."

("Your friend spoke to me like I was a common whore.")

—Examples of overdubbing
The Two Faces of Dr. Jekyll

If Hammer found itself on the wrong side of the censor for other than the expected reason with *The Two Faces of Dr. Jekyll*, it was nothing, compared to the problems they were to face when the film was screened for executives at Columbia. Mankowitz's liberal use of mild expletives was greeted with a different kind of horror, and it was requested that they be deleted *en masse*. Michael Carreras had no alternative but to call back the principles and redub throughout, but it was to little avail. When the film eventually reached stateside (in March 1961), it was rated "B" by the Legion of Decency (morally objectionable in part for all), and further cuts were introduced to try to make it acceptable for the preteen mass market that Columbia was aiming at. This failed also. After a delay of more than a year and a disappointing reception to show for it, *Jekyll* would be off-loaded to American-International Pictures, who would announce it as *Jekyll's Inferno* but ultimately cofeature it with *Terror in the Haunted House*, as *House of Fright*.

The Two Faces of Dr. Jekyll had been a pivotal film for Hammer, but now that opportunity was lost for all time. For Michael, it was to be proof positive of the old adage about only being as good as your last success. While those concerned were becoming embroiled in the damage-limitation exercise, *Hell Is a City* enjoyed a gala premier at Manchester's Apollo Theatre on April 10, 1960, and again the plaudits came. Admiring its gritty approach, the *Daily Cinema* was particularly lavish in its praise. "Hammer have made many fine box-office pictures. They have done nothing better than this accomplished piece of craftsmanship, which is as great in entertainment as it is in production value." It was not enough to save the day; in making *The Two Faces of Dr. Jekyll*, Michael was simply considered to have indulged himself. "Within the company it set me back a lot," he notes. "Everybody said, you shouldn't have done it."

"It was just product from a Hammer point-of-view," Wolf Mankowitz concurs, "though not necessarily from Michael's....But of course, he was part of the machinery." Not for much longer. The whole sad experience would go a long way toward convincing Michael Carreras that Gothic horror was not his *métier*.

However unsatisfactory the end result, at least Wolf Mankowitz had identified the topical nature of the beast lurking within the good Dr. Jekyll. Mankowitz's Jekyll had been of the same sociological caste as *Peeping Tom*, but disappointing returns were to ensure that the Hammer formula would resist any further response to this mood. (*Jekyll*'s failure would also preclude the company from making the one film that is missing from their *oeuvre: The Picture Of Dorian Gray.* "Trevelyan said something discouraging, so it disappeared off the schedule," Michael recalls.) By the time Jerry Lewis had turned his attentions to the subject in *The Nutty Professor* (1963), and himself into Dean Martin in the guise of "Buddy Love," even the notion of filming the Stevenson story in its original form would be dealt a mortal blow for a generation or more.[5]

If *The Two Faces of Dr. Jekyll* had experienced more than its share of problems, it did not suffer alone. With Universal pressing for the promised sequel to *Dracula,* Tony Hinds had finally been forced to take the bull by the horns. Sangster was gone, in spirit at least, but behind him lay the script for *The Disciple of Dracula.* Lee had gone in body—to Italy for the appositely titled *Hard Times for Vampires*, with Renato Rascel, back again to Britain for *City of the Dead* and a nonhorror role in *Beat Girl,* then over to Hamburg for *The Treasure of San Theresa,* then off to France for *The Hands of Orlac*—all in search of an international career. In September 1959, while Michael had been sounding out the BBFC's initial response to *Jekyll,* Hinds had asked Peter Bryan (fresh from his success with *The Hound of the Baskervilles*) to rework Sangster's script, with a view to removing Dracula from it altogether!

Bryan did as he was bid, and devised a plague of bats to dispatch the baron at the climax in lieu of the count. He also removed the machinations of Latour (including a neat precredits sequence in which he adopted the guise of a grave digger and impaled a newly interred vampire woman with a shovel through the lid of her coffin; the sequence later made its way intact into *The Kiss of the Vampire*) and reinstated Van Helsing, and he turned the good girl/bad girl concept of the two heroines into a more sensible *one*, named Marianne Danielle. To bridge the gaps, Latour became the Meinsters' manservant (and a token presence in the first reel, as a result), the baron was enabled to turn into a bat (to allow him the freedom of movement that previously had been orchestrated by Margaret), and a new subplot was brought into play, with Marianne and the baron becoming betrothed as the pretext for his visits to the academy. This allowed for a title change to the more marketable *The Brides of Dracula,* in recognition of the sexual element that had been larded onto the original film.

Two years before, Terence Fisher's stated position on such a radical departure from one of the basic tenets of Hammer Horror as a *bat* had been unambiguous. "In the 1931 version of *Dracula,* the count...had a habit of turning himself into a bat. Today's audiences would never accept such antics. They would laugh at them because they would find them unbelievable." Expedience can make a fool out of anyone.

> "They cast no reflection....And *some* have the power to transform themselves into bats."
>
> —Dr. Van Helsing
> *The Brides of Dracula*

Despite Bryan's intentions (or because of them), much of Sangster's original story no longer made sense. The enjoining of the two girls of opposing natures into a single composite heroine had thrown the narrative dynamic to the four winds. The baron was being paraded as a Jekyll-and-Hyde *vampire*—charming by day, and alarming by night—but with the elimination of Margaret, the character of "Marianne" had now to behave in a similarly schizoid manner, and the innocuous activities of the baroness's maid servant had to be made malevolent, to take up the slack. (In Sangster's draft, the servant had become the third *victim.*) Confusion was beginning to reign. But in this version's favor was Bryan's dialog—still a vast improvement on Sangster's—and that, at least, invited a positive reception from Peter Cushing.

Bryan's draft had been forwarded to Cushing at the end of November. It was not enough. "Peter Cushing wouldn't do it," said Hinds, so a *third* attempt was made to give the script a finer polish. "I said I'd get *another* writer; I contacted an agent and they had this chap called Percy on the books. I contacted Peter Cushing and said, do you know Edward Percy? And he had done something....A play of his." The 69-year-old Percy would add a touch of period color but little else, though Cushing was to remain none the wiser.[6] Cushing accepted the role finally, but not without cost to the film.

The rewrites had pushed production past Christmas and into the new year, and the delivery date to Universal was coming dangerously close. With Michael Carreras preoccupied on *The Two Faces of Dr. Jekyll* and Carreras *père* embarked on a monthlong cruise to the West Indies aboard the S. S. *Flandre*, Tony Hinds had chosen not to submit the script of Hammer's second Dracula, with all its attendant problems, to the BBFC prior to shooting. But in light of what was now befalling *Jekyll*, Hinds was forced to step in himself and further moderate the uncompromising edge of the piece even as *re*written, just as the film went onto the floor.

In Hinds's reconstructed version of the Sangster-Bryan-Percy script, Marianne was to be *removed* from the baron's power, made to forget about events at the chateau and, incredibly, fall for the baron's suave charms all over again, to the extent of consenting to become his wife! To make this *volte-face* work, a key sequence had to be altered. Bryan's Marianne had been trapped in the woods by the baron after fleeing the chateau (in Sangster's version, Margaret had been "seduced" at the academy), and it was there that she was to have succumbed to the vampire. Hinds retained the scene but amended the dynamic. The actual entrapment would not take place—though the viewer was still meant to witness the baron befanged in the background—and Marianne was to remain blissfully unaware of his true nature. For the rest, she would simply be required to react with insouciance to the web of evil spinning around her.

The baroness was also to be subject to some revision. The tainted procuress of the Sangster-Bryan draft would become a lonely and embittered old woman. The calculatingly sinister presence and air of inscrutability would now be a bluff—in reality, she is merely the melancholic wet nurse of a son whose condition is primarily of her own doing, touched by maid servant Greta's great loyalty, pleased to have the opportunity of some interesting company, and genuinely upset by Marianne's ultimate betrayal of her trust—a far cry from the monstrous matriarch of Sangster's vision. The doctoring here is light but incisive. The baroness's "I am not hungry—yet" becomes the unambiguously innocent "I have very little appetite." Her reference to the fact that she sleeps "better in the hours of daylight" (from Sangster's "The baroness stays in her room all day") gives way to the promise of a personal escort for Marianne in the *morning*.

Hinds also made ready with the usual contingency. "I would find out very early what our minimum delivery time should be for a feature and I'd divide that by the number of days; if we were getting that amount of screen-time, and we were behind schedule, then obviously we had too much script—so I used to rip the pages out!" The complex laborings over the script of "Dracula II" had brought about just such an eventuality, and during shooting, Hinds would be required to do his page ripping, as well.

When the completed film was appraised by the BBFC in March 1960, Jimmy Sangster again took the brunt of the criticism. "Obviously written by an insane, but very precocious schoolboy" was the assessment, with the examiner adding, ominously, "We have our remedies (with scriptless films)." The board was unconcerned by the intimations of incest and lesbianism but predictably demanded that a closeup of the staking (of Baroness Meinster) be removed. In the absence of John Trevelyan, Hinds decided to chance his arm; he protested that a similar shot had been allowed in the first film. The benefit of the doubt went to Hammer, and the scene was passed. But when correspondence relating to the original was later checked, the examiners discovered their error. The next Hammer Gothic was not to get off so lightly.

The public had expected Lee, and the critics would be quick to point out the omission. At the BBFC, a bemused examiner had commented in reference to the sexual overtones of the film, "What next? Dracula, the *homosexual* vampire?" Ironically, the Sunday tabloids would be just as quick to point out that the sexual preference of his replacement—David Peel—was not entirely in keeping with what was being portrayed on the screen (and still illegal in 1960). In this, they were no doubt helped by an unfortunate remark in the press book: "You know the old saying—whichever way the twig is bent so the tree will grow," offered Hammer's new recruit. "Well, this tree has been thoroughly bent—*bachelor*-wise!" Peel retired from acting soon after (he would die in 1982, at the age of 62) and Hinds was to ensure that his next monster would have his libido pointed indisputably in the right direction.

*Teacher Marianne Danielle is en route to the academy at Bad-
stein. Finding herself stranded at an inn, she is offered shelter by
Baroness Meinster. During the night, Marianne discovers the young
baron held prisoner in the chateau; she frees him. The next morning,
the baroness is found dead and Marianne flees. She is rescued by Van
Helsing, who is investigating an outbreak of vampirism. His search
leads him to Chateau Meinster, where he is attacked by the baron,
who is a vampire. Unaware of his true nature, Marianne has accepted
his proposal of marriage. Meinster kills Gina, one of the students at
the academy, who is laid to rest in the stable to await burial. Gina
becomes a vampire and rises from her coffin to attack Marianne. Van
Helsing intervenes to save her, and follows Gina to a deserted
windmill. There, he is bitten by Meinster, but he cauterizes the
wound. When the baron returns with Marianne, Van Helsing
throws holy water in his face. Meinster sets fire to the mill and flees
into the courtyard. Van Helsing leaps onto the mill sail and traps
him in the shadow of the cross. The baron perishes, and Van Helsing
leads Marianne out to safety.*

"Transylvania—land of dark forests, dread mountains and black,
unfathomed lakes: still the home of magic and devilry as the 19th
century draws to its close....Count Dracula, monarch of all vampires, is dead. But his disciples live on—to spread the cult, and
corrupt the world...."

—Opening narration
The Brides of Dracula

The Brides of Dracula begins at a breakneck pace, offering only
token résumé before pitching its audience into a frantic coach ride
through the wilds of Transylvania. As events build inexorably
toward the first-act climax, Marianne unwittingly frees the vampire from his chain. When she is confronted by what she has done,
she flees....But the anticipated climax never comes, even in its
revised form. The weight of all the addenda and the pressure of a
deadline that demanded shooting be complete before the end of
February had necessitated yet more changes. Along with other
extraneous scenes, the crucial encounter had been struck on the
floor. Removed along with it were some of the linking passages
(Marianne's luggage comes and goes with alarming discontinuity;
it is seen once and it never reappears, yet mention of it persists),
and the much more spectacular original ending, which had the

debilitated baron finished off by the swarm of bats conjured by Van Helsing. (This would also resurface in *The Kiss of the Vampire*, where it *would* form the climax.) It had been too late to include a revised synopsis in publicity material, which would draw on the *Bryan* scenario, and these additional excisions only added to the resulting insolubles.

In the cutting room, Hinds had been able to revert the construction of the film to the tried-and-tested lines of its enormously successful forerunner. The costly and time-consuming sequence in the woods (which had featured a clutch of "extras") had been replaced by the quicker, cheaper alternative of a "soliloquy" from Greta to her dead mistress—a process fade bringing the proceedings to a close, after she has flung back the curtain to reveal the baron's coffin.[7] Thus the film's first appearance of Meinster in vampire form now comes with him confronting Van Helsing in the great hall of the chateau (another substitution requiring the principals alone), emulating the library scene between the count and Harker in *Dracula.* But lost in the translation was how Marianne had come to be in the position to free the baron in the first place, when Greta could easily have done it for her.

In his attempt to plug this hole in the plot, Hinds had inadvertently compounded the *faux pas.* The dialog he had written to explain it away had reprised the original script. Sangster's pragmatism had dictated that the baron would have required *nourishment*, and the "heroine" was to have provided *that*, not just the means of escape.

> "You've done what you could for him. Keeping him here…a prisoner. *Bringing these young girls to him—keeping him alive with their blood.*"

> —Greta
> *The Brides of Dracula*

The attempt to soft-pedal Sangster's wild Freudian fantasy was, of necessity, cosmetic. The revisions may have been sufficient to erode Marianne's complicity in the affair, but her subsequent actions were to stay bewilderingly *similar*, and residual from the changes can be detected throughout the film. Marianne can plainly be seen struggling with some conflicting emotions. She reacts with surprise when Meinster tells Frau Lang of his mother's death, yet she had seen the body for herself. She opens the window in Gina's room on a pretext and, on exiting, in flaps the baron to feast on her erstwhile companion. She appears consistently to be distracted, as if in possession of some secret knowledge just beyond the reach of memory....Much is resolved by coincidence: Marianne's presence in the stable when Gina rises from her coffin (in Bryan's draft, *she* was to have released the locks). But the baron's emergent ability to turn into a bat skillfully pastes over the joins. Of the anomalies that remain, only Marianne's naive acceptance of the baron's proposal of marriage is ultimately untenable. Hinds's surgical strike had been effective enough, but it was not without casualties and was to leave some lasting scars on the landscape of the story.

In spite of everything, *The Brides of Dracula* is replete with some of the most bravura imagery in the history of the horror film: David Peel's modish designer Dracula (all blond Aryan good looks, grey opera cloak, and immaculate Oxbridge diction); Peter Cushing's modernist, man-for-all-contingencies vampire killer who, having been bitten by the bad baron, retains the presence of mind to burn out the virulence with a branding iron and cauterize the wound with a salve of holy water.

Peel's autocratic vampire is unique in the cinema. With his quintessential English manners and faculty for ice-cold sadism, he adds a chill streak to the old-world charm and underlying guile of the archetype as formulated by Lee, as adept in using a chain for a *garotte* as he is in delivering *bon-mots* to the tenants on his estate.

Paid scant regard by critics in general, due to its conception as a commercially motivated successor to the original film (long before sequels became fashionable), *The Brides of Dracula* is nevertheless the one Hammer horror that genuinely *looks* as though it had all the resources of a big Hollywood studio behind it. It is immaculately dressed, superbly mounted, and for the most part, flawlessly acted and directed. There are minor irritants in the form of some of the subordinate playing, one or two ill-conceived effects, and an anticlimax that would not have passed muster with a major, but they are blemishes on a canvas whose sheer pictorial sweep is a staggering achievement. Later Hammers would construct an entire narrative around sets equivalent in size to the coaching inn in *Brides*, yet here, in addition, are Robinson and Thomas Goswell's most grandiose chateau interiors (a triumvirate of flying gryphons gracing the great hall to further disguise the famous balcony), a graveyard, a stable-cum-crypt, the whole of the Lang Academy, and an entire mill precinct. These are further complemented by integrated miniatures (the chateau and the mill) and matte shots, all designed to make it wholly credible that the audaciously named village of Badstein is surely a long, long way from Water Oakley in Berkshire.

For once, the characters have an entire *milieu* to inhabit. Badstein is a locality extant in gloom: a twilight land of devils and angels, where vampires scrabble to escape their graves at dusk, huge bats soar overhead, and Disneyesque windmills reside on dark hilltops, bathed only in the glow of the odd, incongruous brazier. Fisher conducts much of the action in this half-light. Despite Hammer's growing notoriety for splurging on color, *Brides* is strictly a film of shadow play. It thrives on darkness. Unlike *Dracula*, where the warrior sun ultimately interceded to extinguish the terror by night, *The Brides of Dracula* comes to a close without the purifying ingress of daybreak.

Hammer was continuing to attract notable talent to its films. Martita Hunt, a grande dame of the English theater and most fondly remembered as Miss Havisham in David Lean's *Great Expectations* (1948), attacks the part of Baroness Meinster with an intimidating gusto. She is imposingly sinister, and her commanding presence makes the most of some excellent lines: "We pray for death, he and I—at least I hope *he* does." Hunt died nine years later, but her role here is a standout in the glossary of tortured souls. The ever-dependable Miles Malleson contributes the very best of his comedic interludes as a hypochondriac doctor, afflicted with more ailments and cures than all his patients put together. Mona Washbourne (who three years later was to supply the head to occupy Albert Finney's hat box in Karel Reisz's film of Emlyn Williams's *Night Must Fall*) pitches in with the bumbling but essentially well-meaning eccentric aunt, the like of whom no self-respecting fairy tale could be without. And Freda Jackson's Greta—a cross between Mrs. Danvers and Rochester's wife—has a line of mad laughter that is the very stuff of the night. (Jackson and Hunt generated tension on-screen *and* off, and the film is the better for their upstaging antics.)

On a print in pristine condition, the lushness of Jack Asher's vivid Technicolor photography defies description. The very hues

are alive with a sensuality all their own. Yet this brilliant cinematographer would light no more Gothics for Hammer. Asher was
"not a well man," Peter Cushing observed of the spinal problem
that was to slow him down, but having already collected a number
of awards, Asher's independent streak and virtuoso pursuit of
excellence was to put him in conflict with Hinds's desire keep
within budget at all cost. Asher had been in the business since 1930
(he had become a lighting cameraman in 1947, after completing his
training at Gainsborough), and his departure would remove a
range of expression from Hammer's palette that it would never
quite be able to replace. Asher could have photographed a blank
wall and given it the texture of an Old Master. He would return to
Hammer twice more—for *The Scarlet Blade* (1963) and *The Secret of
Blood Island* (1964)—but Jack Asher's career, like that of several
others involved in the film, was to peak with *The Brides of Dracula*.

Terence Fisher would never direct better, fatigue and the stultifying effects of repetition had not yet begun to afflict Bernard
Robinson, and Cushing would take his Van Helsing from here to
film immortality. All that is lacking is the musical vision of James
Bernard, though late substitute Malcolm Williamson (who was
soon to become Master of the Queen's Musick) rarely lets the side
down.

On a purely technical level, the changes in the script cause the
plot to come apart at the seams, yet they also bring about an
astonishing transformation. In the ensuing impenetrability of the
events, the dream state that Bryan had sought to create is actually
heightened, and what emerges is a work of considerable persuasive power. With her conversion from willing acolyte to wide-eyed
innocent in the thrall of unholy terrors, Marianne becomes a
Grimm's heroine, with the baron standing in for the whole gamut
of evil guardians. This fairy-tale quality was unintentional, but it
works like a charm and it would never be repeated.

The genesis of *The Brides of Dracula* may have been more luck
than judgment, but the film is the archetype of Hammer Gothic. It
is *Brides*, more than any of the rest, that typifies the style, the
content, the look, the plotting, the production values, and the
players—all at the peak of performance. It is the high point of
Hammer Horror. It confounded audience expectation; it found
itself the center of a mild controversy; it suffers from being both
forward-looking, yet somehow curiously dated; it is exquisite to

behold—bloody and bold—yet it disappoints as a whole. But it functions in a universe that is entirely of its own making, separated from the mechanics of its creation. Like all good fairy tales, it is rooted in a reality of sorts, yet elements of it stay in the mind long after, garish and redolent as a dream. *The Brides of Dracula* is Hammer's flawed masterpiece. There would be no other.

> Van Helsing: "Have you heard of the Cult of the Undead?
> Marianne: "The Undead?"
> Van Helsing: "It is most prevalent in Transylvania and the lower Danube."
> Marianne: "And... could it spread?"
> Van Helsing: "Unless it is stamped out...."

> —*The Brides of Dracula*

With *The Brides of Dracula*, Hammer was on the verge of creating mythic archetypes to replace the venerated models from Universal Studios, and had Jimmy Sangster stayed with the Gothic, that is just what would have happened. But Sangster had moved on to new areas of interest, and his vast storehouse of original ideas had moved with him. Sangster would be irreplaceable, as Hammer was soon to find out.

The Brides of Dracula was to go on general release in America with homegrown Universal offering *The Leech Woman*. Odious by comparison, it would prove beyond the shadow of a doubt that the British were now the undisputed masters of the art of the horror film.

Sadly, it would not be so for much longer.

The next stop on the line would be in the Far East and involve a brace of action thrillers that were intended to feed off a common design, one of which would be another attempt at a TV pilot. *Visa to Canton* had even assumed contemporary relevance after the U-2 incident, as *Variety* was to point out. "Hammer Films fortuitously is first in the field with a film depicting the shooting down of Western planes over Red territory." By the time Gary Powers was domiciled in a Soviet prison camp, that relevance had faded into memory, and when the film failed to sire the proposed series, it was consigned as support to the upcoming *Sword of Sherwood Forest*.

Visa to Canton was disposable, however. It was only the icing on a cake whose main component was to be a second stab at a historical horror in the style of *The Stranglers of Bombay*, but with the added benefit of color. Tony Keys had nominated fellow Rank veteran Anthony Bushell to direct, and the net was trawled over the preceding feature to furnish some of the headliners in the cast. Since her accent had not seemed out of place in Transylvania, it was held to be credible in China too, and Yvonne Monlaur—*The Brides of Dracula's* Marianne and France's "newest sex-kitten"—was rushed into what had provisionally been titled *Terror of the Hatchet-Men*. The film would give Christopher Lee star billing (or at least grant him pole position for a change) and, in its story of one man's struggle against the acolytes of an evil and all-powerful enemy, it was a Hammer Gothic in all but place and time: Hong Kong at the turn of the century, under threat from what was to commence shooting on April 18, 1960, as *The Terror of the Tongs*.

> *Hong Kong, 1910. A secret sect, the Red Dragon Tong, murders the daughter of British merchant skipper Jackson Sale. Sale sets out to crush the Tong. After rescuing Lee, a Tong bond slave, he is captured and tortured but he escapes. Tong head Chung King decrees that Sale must die in a ceremonial killing on the wharf. In trying to warn him, Lee falls victim to the executioner's hatchet instead; her last words implicate an East India Company official as a Tong member. Sale and other agency men encourage a revolt on the waterfront to break the power of the Red Dragon. Chung King chooses death by stabbing at the hands of one of his men.*

Jimmy Sangster had written the film for Ken Hyman, so he could earn his producer's spurs—but director Anthony Bushell had earned his long before, as an associate to Olivier on *Hamlet* (1948). Oxford-educated and an ex-Guards officer, Bushell's sidesteps into direction had been few and far between (he was best known for his acting stints on the small-screen, notably as Colonel Breen in the BBC's "Quatermass and the Pit") and his work here is flat and functional, though Dr. Fu Chow's death by hypodermic is as effectively staged as anything in Hammer Horror. It is left to the script to deliver the requisite moments of shock and suspense, and this it does in a tightly plotted tale of revenge conducted along the lines of *The Stranglers*.

Lee's inscrutable Chung King is magisterially menacing in his black silk, though Sangster's aversion to research makes the Tong head's prediliction for peppering his threats with Confucius-like proverbs a more all-embracing affair than might otherwise have been the case. But whether quoting the *Rubaiyat* or, more anachronistically, Lord Hewart (or merely enquiring of Sale, "Have you ever had your bones *scraped*, Captain?"), Lee essays the role with deadpan relish, and it would serve as a dry-run for the series of *Fu Manchu* films on which he was later to embark for producer Harry Alan Towers.

The Terror of the Tongs takes every opportunity to deploy its arsenal of knives, hatchets, and billhooks—though the actual depiction of blood was kept to a minimum, and while scripted excesses (such as a decapitation and the lopping-off of a pair of hands) were toned down in the shooting, an excruciating torture scene had to be shortened for American release. Both the film's opening shot (of the Hong Kong to Macao ferry) and its nominal heavy, wrestler Milton Reid, had seen service in Rank's *Ferry to Hong Kong* (1959). Reid—the executioner in *The Camp on Blood Island* and epitome of the evil oriental thug—would repeat his one-note performance in the following year's *Captain Clegg*. The standing set would subsequently do likewise for Michael Carreras and *Visa to Canton*.

At the time, Ken Hyman was also overseeing the U.K. operation of 7-Arts from offices at 24 Berkeley Square, and a conflict of interest was inevitable. It came when Hyman jetted off to Paris to finalize arrangements for *Gigot* during the filming of *The Terror of the Tongs*. The resulting contretemps with Michael sped the end of his direct involvement with Hammer and led him to concentrate his energies on independent production for 7-Arts, instead—*The Small World of Sammy Lee* (produced by Frank Godwin; 1961); *The Hill* (1964).

The Brides of Dracula opened at the Odeon, Marble Arch, on July 4. Tony Hinds's next job was to have been an *alternative* companion piece to *The Stranglers* (from his *own* script this time), which had been announced to the trades as *The Black Hole of Calcutta*. With the poor reception accorded its predecessor, any notion of a further feature with an Indian location had given way to Ken Hyman's idea of a variant set in Hong Kong. Hinds turned his attention to another Gothic from Universal's archives that he had pencilled in under the simple generic of *The Werewolf*, instead. But like the character in the story, things had now begun to change.

A young Hollywood producer-director named Roger Corman had decided to take a leaf out of Hammer's book and abandon the mad-monster quickies that he had been churning out for the drive-in market in favor of rekindling the Gothic flame via the short stories of Edgar Allan Poe. Before filming was sanctioned on his new version of *The Fall of the House of Usher*, Corman explained the absence of any composite fiend in the tale by declaring to his backers—American-International—that the house *itself* was the monster. That was good enough. Poe had reached the screen, and through the writing talent of Richard Matheson (and Vincent Price's studied portrayal of inherited evil), the metaphorical monsters of the subconscious were made flesh—the madness was made *human*. This crossbreeding of the demons of folklore with the extrapolated fantasies of a disordered psyche was to produce a more current idiom for the pathological obsessions of postanalytical man and create a rough-beast of ambiguity that would pave the way for the purely psychological horror film to come. As the New England Gothic of Poe's mist-shrouded landscapes fused with the California Gothic and sun-drenched secret dreams of *Psycho*'s "Bates Motel," a new generation of terrors was slouching toward the light, to be born.

A Star is Born

"To think of the *Werewolf*—I was 22. And to *see* this young fellow strutting down the road, whistling...and throwing stones. Black hair—lean body. You never grow old when you've got that...."

Oliver Reed
talking about *The Curse of the Werewolf*

Impressed by his screenplay of *Yesterday's Enemy*, Michael had set Peter Newman to work on what was to become *The Rape of Sabena*, a psychological thriller set in the Spain of 1560, in which a *Torquemada*-like Papal Inquisitor exploits the undercurrents in a small town to foster a climate of fear among its citizens. Although similar in style to *Yesterday's Enemy* (and in treatment to Tigon's later *Witchfinder General*), *The Rape of Sabena* was a more melodramatic affair, while still managing to harness its thrills to a typically Newmanesque tirade against intolerance and the abuse of power. Newman had also been allocated the task of scripting Hammer's first western, a project Michael had embarked on unilaterally, in order to fulfil a cherished childhood ambition.[8] By the summer of 1960, an entire Spanish-Mexican townscape had been authorized for construction on the Bray lot, to accommodate them. As building got underway, Tony Hinds was handed the property that was to serve as the basis for his werewolf saga—Guy Endore's novel *The Werewolf of Paris*, to which Universal owned the screen rights.

In the absence of Sangster—and after the trouble he had experienced on *The Brides of Dracula*—Hinds decided to script this one himself also. All the horrors for Universal were effectively subcontractual (inasmuch as they were being made to a fixed price) and *Brides*, at a little over £125,000, had come near to eating into Hammer's slim profit margin. Hinds was looking for economies on his *Werewolf* and not employing a screenwriter merely compensated for a payment against the book. The next logical step was to use existing sets, but a square of sun-bleached haciendas was hardly to be mistaken for the Parisian *bas quartier*. There was only one solution: the script was duly completed with a corresponding change of location, and both *The Rape of Sabena* and *The Curse of the Werewolf* were submitted to the BBFC in the usual way.

While all this was going on, Hammer began to cast around for a monster, and one young actor in particular had been brought to the attention of Tony Keys. His success in the part was to be the springboard to international stardom and, increasingly, Hammer was to search out new faces for its films because it was cheaper than employing established talent. Hammer would acquire a reputation as a star builder in the process. With such considerations very much to the fore (and the fact that his smoldering looks exactly fitted Roy Ashton's bill), the roisterous, swaggering, playboy nephew of film director Sir Carol Reed had been asked to undergo his one and only screen test for the role of the beast-man in *The Curse of the Werewolf*.

Oliver Reed had no formal training. He had smooth talked his way into films by claiming to have worked in repertory in South Africa and Australia, countries beyond the ken of agents and casting directors of the time. A bout of national service, followed by a clutch of uninspiring jobs, had led him to act as master of

ceremonies in a clip-joint in St. Anne's Court, off Wardour Street.
He had come to the notice of Stuart Lyons and was offered a BBC
serial—"The Golden Spur"—and work as an extra in several features, before being required by Hammer to mimic his former
occupation as minder to a coterie of strippers in *The Two Faces of Dr.
Jekyll.* "I just wore louder clothes in the film," Reed was to observe
wryly.

Another cameo followed. In *Sword of Sherwood Forest*, he had
assassinated Peter Cushing's Sheriff of Nottingham. This put him
in the running for *The Curse of the Werewolf* and, by then, he had
become something of a regular at Bray. "The bread-and-butter
pudding, I remember, was *superb!*" Reed had been courteous,
efficient, willing—but above all, keen to learn. "I'd been in the
crowd, so I knew what a mark was and I knew what a key light
was and I knew what cameras were, and I knew what lenses were,
because I had *listened.* So I simply crossed my fingers and kissed
the girls."

His enthusiasm had not gone unnoticed. "He was a marvellous
chap with us," acknowledged Tony Hinds. "You'd say to him, 'can
you drive a car?' And he'd say 'yes,' and he'd go off and *learn*—and
learn to do it brilliantly." (With brother David acting as instructor
while they drove to the studio, in this instance.) But most important
of all, he was cheap. *The Curse of the Werewolf* was to be four weeks
work at £120 per week! "I could pay the rent and have a beer," said
Reed.

The film would afford the aspiring actor much more than that.
Given the nature of its business, this was not the first time Hammer
had stumbled upon a sibling talent. James Carreras had tried to
persuade Bob Lippert to put a young Diana Dors under contract
following *The Last Page*, and Michael's tenure as casting director
had launched Diane Cilento on her film career with a role in *Wings
of Danger* and put the ill-fated Belinda Lee into *Murder By Proxy*.
But Oliver Reed was to benefit from a concerted campaign *intended*
to groom him for stardom. *The Curse of the Werewolf* was to make
him a name and remove him from Bray's egalitarian canteen, once
and for all. "After *Werewolf*, I was asked to dine with the directors,"
he recollects. "Then you *knew* you'd made it, because that's where
Christopher and Peter were."

By now, the BBFC was beginning to react with draconian ruth-lessness against what it perceived to be the excesses of horror-film producers. The pendulum had swung too far, and the rule book was still being rewritten in the light of the furor that had erupted following the May 16 release of *Peeping Tom*.[9] By observing diplo-matic niceties, including the novelty of an annual lunch, James Carreras hoped to bend the censor to his way of thinking. But John Trevelyan was not a man to be bought, and with the sea change in what was considered acceptable on screen, he had now decided that Hammer should stop making horror films altogether.

Accordingly, the scripts for *The Rape of Sabena* and *The Curse of the Werewolf* were returned on August 22—two weeks before shoot-ing was due to commence on the former—with extensive revisions requested on both films.[10]

As if to dispel any lingering doubt, Trevelyan had returned the script of *The Curse of the Werewolf* with a letter to Hinds, singling it out for the strongest condemnation yet deployed against a Ham-mer production. Referring to the forced degradation of the beggar and his subsequent rape of the servant girl, he warned, "In our view these two incidents are deplorable and go beyond what is legitimate in a horror film. *Such scenes could only run into serious censorship trouble.*"

Michael had already become reconciled to this conflict of inter-est. "If we hadn't *known* the censors—hadn't entertained them and so forth—I think we would have got away with a lot more," he said. But that was not his father's style. "He used to always give way—take the easy way," claimed Hinds. "Take the money and spend it." True to form, James Carreras took it upon himself to reply, saying that he agreed "entirely" with all the reservations that had been expressed and that he had discussed the situation with Michael and Tony. He finished by assuring the secretary that by the end of 1960/61, "subjects, *as per* the two above, will have been deleted from our programme." With the matter thus laid to rest, John Trevelyan left on one of his increasingly frequent fact-finding trips to the U.S.

There had been *no* meeting, but while Carreras may have had his tongue firmly in his cheek when he penned his response, son Michael took the change of heart seriously enough to announce Hammer's new "dual" policy to the trades. The company was to concentrate on "serious but popular films, exploitable melodramas and comedies"—with one, possibly two horror films included in the schedule. Among the contenders would be *One More River, The Amorous Prawn* (from the West End stage hit), and his western, *The San Siado Killings,* intended to star Stanley Baker. In addition to a remake of *The Phantom of the Opera,* there was now to be a third Dracula.

Still smarting over the fiasco of *Jekyll,* Columbia gave the steamy contemporary drama *One More River* the thumbs down. Undaunted, Michael plowed ahead with *The Rape of Sabena,* now retitled *The Inquisitor.* But that was not to be, either. As Michael recalls, "I suddenly got a call from my father, and he said, 'I'm stopping the picture.' It was the rarest occasion of all—the only time that Hammer ever stopped a film that was in production. I think a flash of light went before his Catholic conscience."

The "flash of light" was actually more secular in origin: Hammer's relationship with Columbia was becoming decidedly frosty, and the decision had been made that Michael was to be reined in. At Columbia's "suggestion," there were to be no more comedies like *The Ugly Duckling,* and no more items of "limited appeal" on the future Hammer slate. "All production is being slanted from now on in for acceptance in the important American market. Mike Frankovich watches the daily rushes of the Hammer output and pencils out the overly British material," an unusually deferential James Carreras informed *Variety,* before pulling the plug on *The Inquisitor.*[11]

This was alright as far as it went, but things had gone too far already. When he realized that much time and money had been spent on *The Inquisitor* (sets had been built and John Gilling had been slated to direct), James Carreras began to have second thoughts. Instead, he sanctioned a compromise: Hind's *Werewolf* would be brought forward to fill the gap (since it was intended to share its design with *The Inquisitor,* in any event), Gilling would be written into the package being assembled as Hammer's contribution toward the ACT-backed BHP production *The Shadow of the Cat,*[12] and the assurances to the censor would be quietly forgotten.

> "There are...werewolves that have but one body, in which the soul of man and of beast are at war. Then whatever weakens the human soul, either sin or darkness, solitude or cold, brings the wolf to the fore. And whatever weakens the beastly soul, either virtue or

daylight, warmth or the companionship of man, raises up the human soul. For it is known that the Wolf shrinks from that which invites the man....These great truths are now forgotten...."

—From Guy Endore's
The Werewolf of Paris

Or, to put it another way...

"A werewolf is a body where the soul and the spirit are constantly at war. The spirit is that of a wolf...and whatever weakens the human soul—vice, greed, hatred, solitude; especially during the cycle of the full moon when the forces of evil are at their strongest—these bring the spirit of the wolf to the fore....And in turn, whatever weakens the spirit of the beast—warmth, fellowship, love—raise the human soul...."

—The Priest
The Curse of the Werewolf

This maxim, originated in the Guy Endore novel and central to the film that was now to be adapted from it, epitomized the conflict between the forces of light and the powers of darkness—the self-proclaimed quintessential of the Hammer horror films of Terence Fisher. It restates the basic tenets of the Gothic: good and evil, love and death, terror and ecstasy. And in the romantic agony of Leon the werewolf,[13] it was to encapsulate an eternal truth. Under the pen name of John Elder—a corruption of James Elder Wills, the ex-Hammer art (and company) director—Tony Hinds would translate it intact for the screen. Fisher was to adore the concept, shoot it as a fatal love story, and end with a film that would set the tide to turn against Hammer and be instrumental in bringing the Gothic cycle of the previous four years to a premature close.

The Werewolf of Paris had been published in 1934, one year before Dennis Wheatley's *The Devil Rides Out*. The background for its convoluted tale of lycanthropy is the Franco-Prussian war, and much of the action takes place during the Siege of Paris in 1871. The book purports to be historical fact and is written in a style that disregards many of the normal conventions of dramatic fiction in pursuit of a more biographical approach.

In condensing the sprawling canvas of this awesome work,
"Elder" preserved most of the primary elements of the wolfman's
life: the conception through rape; the birth on Christmas Eve and
its related superstitious misgivings; the preying on the lambs; the
attack on the prostitute; the uncle-father figure. The suicide of the
wolfman was retained in the spirit, if not the letter, of the adaption.
There were two changes: the aforementioned displacing of the
action to Spain, and the moving of the period to 1760. But while
Endore's polemic (which puts the werewolf's nocturnal proclivi-
ties in perspective amid a slaughter that allows them to go undetected) was reduced to the level of rudimentary melodrama, his
strict linear construct would be adhered to. Thus the plot of *The
Curse of the Werewolf* can be broken down into three distinct and
separate "acts," in the manner of a theatrical adaption, and if the
film that it produced was static and slow moving, it was largely
due to the stage-bound nature of this structure.

When Terence Fisher was brought onto the project, he was
unaware that the original had been set against a background of the
Paris Commune. Removed from this historical frame of reference,
the mythic properties of the tale came to the fore. Devotees of the
film find favor in its purity of narrative and rejoice in the fact that
the work sacrifices some dramatic tension for the sake of its alle-
gorical priorities. Its detractors point to that selfsame lack of pace
as its greatest weakness. But it was this aspect that held particular
appeal for Fisher, whose stated preoccupation with the battle between good and evil had led him to accentuate the abstraction in
previous films whenever opportunity allowed. With *The Curse of
the Werewolf*, opportunity was to allow on the grand scale.

The end result would be poorly received by press and public
alike, partly because of what was felt to be its lack of sophistication.
It has since found itself a band of admirers for whom critical
admonition is mere grist to the mill when it comes to bestowing
cause celèbre status, and the intervening decades have shown it to
be as close as Hammer ever came to making a "cult movie." It even
possessed the cachet of "lost" footage due to censorship. To ensure
it pride of place in the bosoms of the faithful, *The Curse of the
Werewolf* lost money, as well.

> *Spain. A servant girl is raped by a beggar who has been impris-
> oned in the dungeon of an evil marques. She gives birth to a boy, then*

dies. The child is adopted by Don Alfredo, but a series of occurrences convince him that young Leon is half wolf. When he is grown, Leon leaves his foster home to work at a vineyard where he falls in love with Cristina, daughter of the owner. One night, he and José visit a local taverna. In the company of a prostitute, Leon becomes a werewolf and kills both the girl and José. On discovering the truth, Leon is nursed through the next night of the full moon by Cristina, but before they can elope and marry, the police arrest Leon for murder; the Alcalde refuses to believe that he is a werewolf and puts him in a cell. That night, Leon transforms again and kills a fellow prisoner. He breaks free of the jail and makes for the rooftops. Don Alfredo loads his musket with a silver bullet and climbs to the bell tower where Leon has been cornered. He fires—and Leon falls dying. Alfredo covers the body with his coat; the curse of the werewolf is at an end.

The Curse of the Werewolf was a full-blown monster yarn in the old Universal tradition: a one-dimensional fable of original sin, devoid of the intellectual nuance of a Frankenstein or a Dracula. In quality, the film is far from Hammer's best, in spite of it enjoying the identical virtues of a regular crew and well-entrenched teamwork behind the scenes. Excellence was being spread a little too thinly by the pressure of runaway success, and with *The Curse of the Werewolf*, the veneer had begun to peel. For once, Robinson's masterful economy of design failed him, and production values too often descend to the level of the downright shoddy. (A few authentic Spanish accoutrements and a pleasing adobe conurbation originally intended to serve the intentionally frugal design of the town of *Sabena* provide scant backdrop in this context.) But most jarring of all is the *casting*.

"Strange things are abroad—things that should not be spoken of..."

—Old Soaker
The Curse of the Werewolf

The roster is filled with able and familiar talent—Ripper, Woodbridge, de Wolff—but the trouble is their essential *Englishness*. Where previous Gothics had paraded the likes of Cushing, Lee, Gough, and Peel through a Germanic *mittel* Europe with only the authority of the English Theater tradition to aid them, the same cannot be said of *The Curse of the Werewolf*. The perception of the British character as cool and austere is in keeping with the Teutonic mold, but it is hardly a match for the fierier temperament of Pyreneesian peasants. This lapse is compounded by incidental roles that are also filled by British support actors. If more were needed to underpin the inadequacy, Elder's dialog is always on hand to fling anachronistic colloquialism in the face of actor and audience alike, with such native quotes as " 'Ere—wot's all this then?" (Pepé) and "You alright, dear?" (Vera) offered up at the drop of every 'aitch.

That *The Curse of the Werewolf* was designed in disregard of the increasing sophistication of genre films and audiences can also be witnessed in the names of the protagonists: "The sinister Marquis," "The beggar," "The servant girl," and so forth. One need only add "The ingenue" and "The wise man" to substitute for Cristina and Don Alfredo to make it abundantly clear at what level the story is pitched. (From this point on, a similar lethargy would begin to afflict character *names* in Hammer Gothics, as well as characterizations: "Fritz" would interchange with "Franz," and soon, hardly a film would go by that did not include at least one "Hans" in the cast roller.)

While its catalog of imperfections might single out *The Curse of the Werewolf* for more than its fair share of criticism, weighing in against it is the sheer power of the myth that the film embodies. The myth is the loser ultimately, but not before it produces a climax of lasting excitement. In his rage, the werewolf uses the rooftops to encircle the town, and Fisher uses every available angle on the restricted sets to capture a sequence that more than matches the climax of *Dracula* and still holds as one of the great monster chases in fantasy history. As the beast man throws off the shackles of body and jail, he liberates *The Curse of the Werewolf* from the stultifying effect of much of what has gone before. Like the pounding score that simultaneously bursts from the bounds of a string section that hitherto has been trapped in romantic cliché, a new momentum infects the film. Freed from the plodding contrivances of the screenplay and the dead weight of his own philosophical outpourings, Terence Fisher showed that he could direct high-action drama with the best of them.

The werewolf's dance of death atop the haciendas of Santa Vera finally captures the epic sweep of mythic ritual being played out, and it is on a level far more attuned to the emotional subconscious that the film has apparently been aiming for than all the pallid, mock-religious interplay that precedes it. This one sequence serves as testament to the fact that if only the scenario had been different—if only Hammer's werewolf had been given its head of yak hair throughout, instead of for a mere six minutes—if only a writer of Sangster's narrative ability or Matheson's subtlety at delineating character could have mapped out its protagonist's nocturnal wanderings, then *The Curse of the Werewolf* could have been the greatest Hammer horror of them all.

> "Pepe's silver bullet—so it's come to that at last..."

> —Teresa
> *The Curse of the Werewolf*

If the moral universe of the film was a simplistic one, it reflected the conceptual fundamentalism of the duo who had fashioned it. In the case of Hinds, it was to be the start of more fatuous things to come. He was soon to reduce Frankenstein and Dracula to the same base icon, similarly cursed to wend their predestined ways through increasingly pointless ritual. As a product of the religious overtone in *The Curse of the Werewolf,* John Elder would continue to pit his monsters against Christianity's front-line troops, be they priest, monk, or bishop. It would be a characteristic of his scripts. In consequence, the conviction scientist would depart with Sangster, and future films would be the poorer for it. From here on in, they would all be parodies of biblical parables; trite morality plays, with the bad guys wearing black and the good guys wearing cassocks, and the triumph of good over evil just a matter of running time. With Jimmy Sangster, it was never so easy or so assured; he knew the virtue of uncertainty. In the fictional worlds of Anthony Hinds, such uncertainty held no sway. *The Curse of the Werewolf* began Hammer Horror's inexorable descent into formula. As for Fisher, having been afforded the opportunity to translate the Gothic archetypes into the language of his own ideological precepts, he had merely managed to show how dated they were becoming in the face of the more iconoclastic horror films of the sixties.

Hammer might have been content to continue ferreting around the musty corpses in the vaults of Universal City toward the end of 1960, but for the sleeper success of Hitchcock's *Psycho*. The shattering impact of this Oedipal "old dark house" shocker— which was little more than Jekyll and Hyde for a postmodern audience—had made the demand for a reply in kind irresistible, and Sigmund Freud was now considered to be high on the mandate of requisite ingredients, if the fare in which Hammer specialized was to continue to find favor with the paying public.

Jimmy Sangster had already tired of the Gothic. In three years, he had penned almost as many period thrillers for other companies as for Hammer, and he had long since begun to feel that he had exhausted the form. His penchant for black humor and structural complexity had striven for supremacy since *The Curse of Franken-stein*, which (with a few minor adjustments) could easily have been constructed as a plot by Elizabeth and Paul Krempe to frame Victor for murders committed by *them!* A script he had sold to Sidney Box remained unmade, and with *The Curse of the Werewolf* underway at Bray, Sangster now bought it back and offered it to Hammer, on condition that he produce it himself. The psychological murder mystery was originally titled *Hell Hath No Fury*, but in the wake of *Psycho*, it was revised and retitled *Taste of Fear*, and it headed for Nice on October 24.

> Penny Appleby is wheelchair bound. She has not seen her father for ten years, and decides to visit his villa on the French Riviera. Her stepmother, Jane, explains that he has been called away on urgent business. That night, Penny thinks she sees his body in the summer-house. Only Bob the chauffeur believes her, and after similar appa-ritions, Penny begins to doubt her sanity. The body is eventually discovered in the swimming pool, and Penny and Bob agree to go for the police. En route, Penny is trapped in the car, and it hurtles toward the edge of a cliff. It transpires that Bob and Jane had plotted her death in order to claim the inheritance. But Penny is not dead. Jane is accidentally killed by Bob, and he is arrested; it is then revealed that "Penny" was an imposter all along, out to avenge the death of the real heir.

Sangster used his position as producer to jettison the usual flotilla of Hammer back-room boys in favor of a different combi-nation of talents. The film was expertly directed by ex-Ealing editor

Seth Holt, evocatively lit in luminous chiaroscuro by Desmond Dickinson (who had photographed *Hamlet*), tensely orchestrated by Clifton Parker (who had composed a memorable score for *Night of the Demon*), and nicely underplayed by a cast headed by 22-year-old Susan Strasberg (daughter of Lee and fresh from the Broadway stage) and Ronald Lewis (fresh from a thriller called *The Full Treatment*, which had been partly financed by Hammer). It delivered its mixed bag of chills with professional grace.

There were some hidden novelties. The twist ending is actually revealed in the prologue (a sleight-of-hand ploy that would subsequently be refined by slasher director Dario Argento), and the Christopher Lee character has the same name (Dr. Gerrard) as the one he played in *The Man Who Could Cheat Death*. A clever ad campaign was designed to resonate of *Psycho*, but in concept, mood, and construction, *Taste of Fear* was more of a kissing cousin to *Les Diaboliques*. "Exactly—that's what it was," its author cheerfully admits. Divested of the grotesquery normally associated with Hammer Horror, it employed the repertoire of the *schauerromane* instead, to memorable effect. Once again, Sangster had shown the way. The film would do well at the box office and be equally well received by a critical fraternity relieved to be spared the usual visceral assault on its sensibilities.

Taste of Fear would see Hammer commence on a whole subcycle of "psycho-thrillers" (as they were to become known) and next up would be the much-postponed film version of Josephine Tey's *Brat Farrar*.[14] But only *Maniac* (of *Paranoiac, Nightmare, Hysteria, Fanatic,* and *Crescendo*—which was to reprise the Riviera setting and swimming-pool set piece of the Holt film) would be accorded anything like the polish and expertise that had been lavished on *Taste of Fear*, and the series soon descended into second-rate fare of uniformly undistinguished repetitiveness. *Taste of Fear* is unique in capturing the stark mood of *noir* horror that was to reach its zenith two years later in the camp *grand guignol* of Robert Aldrich's *Whatever Happened to Baby Jane*. It remains a classic of its kind: one of the only films to take on *Psycho* on its own terms and come perilously close to toppling Hitchcock's masterpiece from its perch of precision-engineered shock.

Taste of Fear was shot at Elstree. While the unit was on location in Nice, a fire had broken out at Bray, and despite the swift arrival of the fire brigade, the house (with its integral stage) had suffered widespread damage. Much of the first floor had been destroyed, and lost in the blaze were costumes, props, and promotional materials from Hammer's "Golden Age," as well as a library of 16mm prints, and furniture and other personal items belonging to Michael Carreras (who was resident at Oakley Court at the time, having just sold his house at Boulter's Lock). In true Gothic fashion, a *deus ex machina* had intervened to erase many of the familiar *motifs* of the cinema's first horror renaissance. It was not without its significance, and for Michael, at least, it was to be portent enough. But for Hammer and Tony Hinds, more bad news was in the making.

A completed print of *The Curse of the Werewolf* had now been seen by the BBFC. The film had opened on a pair of demonic eyes, shedding tears behind the credits. On release, that one glimpse of the title creature would have to be made the most of. When the long-awaited transformation from man into wolf *did* eventually arrive, it was curtailed in a flurry of censorial activity.

The cuts were legion. Incensed at the changes forced on him by the BBFC prior to production, Hinds had jettisoned them and given Fisher his *original* to shoot—"for foreign versions," according to the producer. The outcome could hardly have been worse. Trevelyan had demanded "acceptable" alternatives to the brutalization of the beggar and the rape (which in the script had been watched by the marques), and had asked for the murder of the marques—"The girl plunges the sconce deep into his chest, raises it, then plunges the now-bloody weapon again and again"—to be revised, so that the blow could be struck off-screen. He had also insisted that shots of the werewolf "should not be too unpleasant or terrifying." Various compromises had been agreed upon, yet the monochrome print submitted to the board at the end of November 1960 contained these and more, just as if nothing whatever had transpired in the interim.

Hinds expressed shock at the long list of excisions that resulted from his action, protested them in detail, and again essayed the ploy that he would have to score, dub, and edit the complete version, in view of the fact that it had been accepted without cuts in the U.S. He suggested resubmitting the film in color when the postproduction work was complete. On February 2, 1961, the board screened the film again.

This time, Trevelyan was having none of it. He had insisted on no contact between the parties during the rape; the scene was to be conveyed by suggestion alone. What was merely "The beggar springs . . . " in the script had been filmed with the beggar leaping onto the girl from behind, wresting her hands from the bars, then forcing her to the ground out of camera range. To make sure that the point is taken, a subsequent shot showed lacerations to her face and breasts. ("These were not visible in the black-and-white version," noted Trevelyan.[15]) "The way I shot it, you never saw them make contact," Fisher was later quoted as saying, "but there was a strong suggestion."

The uncensored print makes it all too obvious that exactly the opposite was the case and that it was Fisher's *handling* of this sequence that caused the problem. "I have always strenuously tried to avoid being blatant; wherever possible, I have used the camera to show things happening by implication," he was to assert. In this instance, "implication" seemed to have been satisfied by a teasing shot of Yvonne Romain (pretty in pink in her dungeon hellhole and lit with so many fill-ins by Arthur Grant that she might have been posing for a *Playboy* centerspread) seeking to shield her ample bosom from the old-fashioned look that she has seen in the beggar's eyes. If this was Terence Fisher's idea of it, then it was certainly not the BBFC's; the entire episode was to be expunged: "The scene in the dungeon must stop as soon as the girl is thrown in the cell...and the scene can only resume with the shot of her being released."

From here on in, the cuts came thick and fast. The stabbing of the marques was also removed in its entirety, despite the quoting of *Psycho* in precedent. "After seeing a recent 'X' film in which a young pervert stabs a naked girl to death in the bath to satisfy some queer lust of his own, I felt that we were reasonably safe in showing a normal, healthy girl protecting her honor by stabbing her would-be seducer," offered Hinds. That was Hitchcock and this is Hammer, was the implicit riposte, and *The Curse of the Werewolf* lost both of its first-act climaxes.

With the addition of color, earlier objections to the baptism scene (with its foaming font and gargoyle reflection) were waived, but not those to hair on the palm of the young Leon, which was deleted. Now the examiners had arrived at reel 7 and the first appearance of the werewolf.

Elder ought to have known better. He had contrived to have his hero turn bestial in the boudoir of a prostitute and added injury to insult by having him nip her on the bosom in full view. The symbolism was unmistakable, and Hinds had been instructed, in no uncertain terms, that to have his man metamorphose into a wolf in a whore's bedroom would be out of the question. "We do not want 'brutal lovemaking' combined with a sadistic treatment of the girl, as the script suggests," Trevelyan had advised. But Fisher's camera had been unwavering in its devotion to the full-effrontery of horror *by implication*, and the protracted sequence (which culminates in the murder of the tart) was to be resolved in a welter of cuts as, true to his promise, the censor reduced it to a meaningless jumble. With it would go the single most graphic shot that Hammer had yet seen fit to film, as a shock cut to a broken and blood-spattered mirror tilts up to the body of the girl, lying with her throat ripped out. (The board agreed to consider a substitute for this shot at Hinds's request, with the proviso that "anything approaching" it would be "quite impossible." As it happened, no alternative had been filmed.)

The killing of José had followed, but he was luckier. His demise had already been tempered in accordance with the wishes of the board. (He is, after all, a man, and thus is merely strangled and thrown in the bushes.) But the murder of the "old soaker" in the jail was shorn of Reed's blood-caked visage, as Trevelyan dictated the *specifics* of what could remain to convey what had occurred. From here to the end of the film, all shots of the gore-stained features of the werewolf were to be removed, including a climactic final close-up, in which a tear forms in the corner of his eye. These were in addition to a variety of "minor" trims, one of which Fisher invariably quoted in interviews as an example of the *nominal* censorship problems he encountered—a syphilitic marques scratching at his diseased nose.

There were to be fourteen cuts in all (two of them, whole sequences) totalling almost five minutes of film: a vivid illustration of the reality of Hammer's "good relations" with the British censor. So complete was the destruction wrought on the film that Trevelyan felt a word of explanation might be in order. *The Curse of the Werewolf* was the first of Hammer's Gothics to mix the "dangerous cocktail" of horror and sex, Hinds was informed. Commenting on the recent adverse criticism that had been directed at the industry on the release of *Peeping Tom*, Trevelyan confessed a reluctance to pass the film at all—"even in a heavily censored version"—and closed with the thinly veiled threat that if the cuts were not complied with in full, the film would be banned for exhibition in Britain.

Hinds was aghast, but he made one final appeal for clemency with regard to the close-up of the dying werewolf. "We have a bad enough ending as it is, but without this shot we have no ending at all," he wrote. John Trevelyan required the BBFC to be defensible (as he had just found out, it had become increasingly necessary to defend it) and a hardening of attitude was the order of the day. The answer was still no.

Tony Hinds resigned himself to his fate. "I was always fighting the censor; Jim Carreras didn't back me at all on that," he said. But he had tired of the argument, and now he would begin to cast around for less contentious subjects to film. "We were running out of ideas," Michael reflected. "The butchering wasn't the reason, but it may have compounded our own thinking at the time. Even Tony was getting disenchanted." Hinds was not to forget the iniquities rained down on the film. Years later, he would still quote *The Curse of the Werewolf* in respect to his dealings with the censor. "It's got particularly difficult since Lord Morrison took over. We always submit the script, but we get back a *three*-page letter of things they're not prepared to pass…" "We were rather hard on this one," John Trevelyan was subsequently said to have admitted.

The Curse of the Werewolf began production on September 12, 1960 but, typically, it was not to be released until July 1961. When it opened, what remained of Hammer's film found itself up against American-International's first excursion into big-budget Gothic: Roger Corman's wide-screen version of *The Fall of the House of Usher*. Word of mouth had it that the *Poe*-pourri was a sophisticated shocker, and audiences were not about to visit two horrors in a single week. *Usher* won hands down.

The slower, more dated *Werewolf* held little appeal against the miasma of Eastmancolor madness that marked AIP's coming-of-age, and Hammer's exalted position as the uncrowned kings of horror now came under serious threat—initially, from the continuing series of Poe adaptions built on *Usher*'s success (*Pit and the Pendulum, The Premature Burial, et al.*[16]) and later, from the stylistically similar productions of Amicus.

By the standards of the previous Hammers, the film would be considered a failure by Universal. It was also to be a turning point, though few would recognize it as such at the time. Its poor showing would see to it that there would be no more werewolf films. It was to entrench critics in their view of Fisher as a pedestrian director; dull, long-winded, and prone to theatricality—the same qualities that endeared him to his fans. It is unlike any other Hammer horror, and it would pay the price for that: *The Curse of the Werewolf* took in a bare one-tenth of the money that had accrued from *Dracula* or *The Curse of Frankenstein.*

The bubble was bursting. The heyday of Hammer Horror was coming to a close. In a few short years, Hammer—indeed, the world—would be marching to the beat of a different drum. "It was a depressing period," said Michael Carreras. "I think they had lost their spirit—all of them—by that time." Even before *The Phantom of the Opera* was to end Hammer's hold on the affections of the faithful, *The Curse of the Werewolf* had started the ball rolling imperceptibly away.

> "Señor, I beseech you—don't make me stay here…"
>
> —Leon
> *The Curse of the Werewolf*

Oliver Reed would appear in six more Hammers after this, from *The Damned* to *The Brigand of Kandahar* ("The worst film I made in my life") before a call from director Michael Winner prospected the lead in *West 11* (1963) opposite Julie Christie. The film's producer had other ideas, and neither of them would make it. "Danny Angel said Christie was a B-picture artist and I was a *nothing*—but Danny Angel couldn't walk, so I couldn't knock him over," said Reed. The role went to Alfred Lynch, but Winner persisted. His next project would be *The System* (1964), and this time, Reed *did* get the part. It was to be the road to bigger and better things, until a nightclub brawl left the famous features permanently scarred and the actor reduced to mini-cabbing to pay his way. Enter Ken Russell, making *his* name with a series of musical bio-pics for the BBC's art digest, "Omnibus." "What about the scars?" Reed asked. "What scars?" Russell replied, and "The Debussy Film" would follow, along with two others in the same vein. "People began to accept me—not just as a werewolf, but as someone who made art films," Reed acknowledges. These were to launch him into another, more lucrative spree with Winner, culminating in *The Jokers* (1966). By that time, Hammer would be left far behind, but their young star was not to forget them. "They gave me exposure in America"—for which he would be eternally grateful. As Reed puts it, "Michael [Winner] gave me my money, and Russell gave me my art. But *Hammer* gave me my technique."

After the successes of *Hell Is a City* and *Yesterday's Enemy*, both of which starred Stanley Baker, Michael Carreras wanted to repeat the performance. He offered Baker a Jimmy Sangster script called *The Criminal*, but Baker wanted Joe Losey to direct, and Losey hated the Sangster screenplay. Consequently, the film was rewritten by Alun Owen and produced elsewhere. On completion of *The Criminal*, and after another period of isolation for Losey, Columbia asked Tony Hinds to hire him for the science-fiction film that Hinds had proposed as a less-contentious offering from Hammer after the trauma of *The Curse of the Werewolf*, based on the H. L. Lawrence novel *The Children of Light*. Hinds had worked with Losey on *A Man on the Beach*, also at Columbia's request, and the occasion had not been an unpleasant one. He was delighted—though not for long. Losey's career prior to *The Criminal* had included highlights such as directing a promotional film for the new Ford Anglia—"I thought I was doing him a favor," Hinds said. "*He* thought he was doing me one."

> "I've seen you before. You're the man who knows all about violence, aren't you?—You're the man who knows all the answers, aren't you? Why are you doing this?—What's it all for...?
>
> —Simon Wells
> *The Damned*

With cold war tensions on the increase as a result of the shooting down of the U2 spy plane, and work beginning on the construction of the Berlin Wall, this fable of strategic planning for the aftermath of an atomic holocaust seemed like a good bet, though Hammer added security in the form of box-office attractions Shirley Anne

Field and Oliver Reed. "All I was doing was riding around on motorcycles," said the latter.

When the unit decamped to Weymouth in Dorset in May 1961 (scene of some location shooting for *Four Sided Triangle*), Losey's first action was to scrap the script that Columbia had approved—written by his one-time collaborator Ben Barzman—and start again with scenarist Evan Jones. Tony Hinds was horrified and, true to form, he promptly disappeared from the scene. "Tony couldn't take things like that—he couldn't take temperamental blackmail," said Michael, who had to pick up the reins of the production and see through the remainder, though no one except Losey and Jones now knew what the film was actually to be about.

The Damned (or "The Brink" as Losey preferred) was to be about a group of irradiated (and therefore radiation-proof) children, kept under lock and key by a government planning for the postnuclear rebirth of the world. Given that the film was pretty much "written on the hoof," it is rarely less than interesting, often electrifying, and sometimes quite brilliant. More than once, Evan Jones's script echoes of *Things To Come*, with the roles reversed. The artist is now the visionary, and the scientist (in the guise of the bureaucrats of *Quatermass II*), the unthinking, unfeeling ideologue. "My children are the buried seeds of life," Bernard, the all-powerful civil servant, explains. "When that time comes, the thing itself will open up the door—and my children will go out, to inherit the Earth." The sculptress, Freya, his lover and philosophical counterweight, is appalled. "*What Earth*, Bernard?—What Earth will you leave them? After all that man has made, and still has to make…Is this the extent of your dream?—To set nine ice-cold children free in the ashes of the universe?"

The Damned was an elegant and elegaic discourse on the Big Question of the day, and by the time of the Cuban Missile Crisis, it would begin to look remarkably prophetic, but its conclusions (in both senses) were somber and depressing, and Columbia's Mike Frankovich took the whole affair personally and refused the film a release. What Raymond Durgnat would consider "undoubtedly one of the most important British films of the year, even, perhaps, of the '60s" would eventually be sneaked out in May 1963 on the lower half of a double-bill with *Maniac*—a film the same critic would refer to as one whose "macabre ideas are worked out in a style as creative as the operation of a meat-grinder." It was to be an unhappy pairing, and it would do little to advance the company's aspirations to legitimacy, but *The Damned* is probably the finest film that Hammer ever produced.

Losey may have brought an unruly and undisciplined approach to the shooting—at least by Hammer's standards—but it is doubtful if any of the company's house directors, whatever their individual merits or technical skills, could have supplied the intellectual weight that suffuses the piece. *The Damned* would go on to win the "Golden Asteroid" at the International Festival of Science Fiction Films in Trieste in 1964, but like *The Two Faces of Dr. Jekyll*, the cohesion of the original is now impossible to gauge. The film was cut in distribution from 96 to 87 minutes (and to 77 in the U.S.).

Losey was grateful to Michael, but he never worked for Hammer again, despite the latter's ongoing attempts to encourage him. "The man who rescued the situation for me then was Michael Carreras," Losey would tell Michel Ciment.[17] "Michael...has been trying to get me to do another picture with him, and I think he is a good producer. But he always gives me things that have so much overt violence in them that I just can't bring myself to consider them seriously."

If only *Hammer* had paired Baker and Losey—or Bogarde and Losey—but then, what price glory?

"...Evidence which you cannot refute has been brought against you!"

—Perez, the Inquisitor
The Rape of Sabena

Michael still had the yen to diversify the Hammer product into other areas, but the failure of *Jekyll* had irrevocably damaged his standing in the company. None of his films since then—*Visa to Canton* (his second abortive TV pilot), *Cash on Demand* (a second-feature adaption of a television play)—amounted to anything like the box-office winners Gothics continued to be, as his father was often quick to point out through a comparison of the "take" between *his* films and those of Hinds. In the past, Hammer's strategy had always been dictated by prior success, but now there was tension in the air over the direction in which the company was going. There were increasing disagreements—a sense that an irresistible force had at last come in sight of an immovable object. Michael continued to develop different projects for Hammer (including a plan to turn *Hell Is a City* into a TV series), but much of this was a sop to his artistic pretensions, rather than any serious attempt to find something new. New thinking was not only not encouraged, it was fiscally frowned upon. James Carreras knew the virtue of a successful formula, and he had no intention whatever of deviating from it.

While Hammer's program of horrors had been wending its bloody way, the ailing Italian film industry—spurred by the huge international success of *Ben Hur* in 1959 (much of which had been shot at Cinecitta in Rome) and the surprise hit that Joseph E. Levine had nurtured from the low-budget *Hercules*—had embarked on a cycle of historical-mythological spectaculars that were proving surprisingly popular with audiences on both sides of the Atlantic. Epics were suddenly in, and exploitation companies had been quick to realize it. The cycle of so-called epics offered the opportunity of an alternative line of supply for Hammer and, since the type of film it embraced invariably slotted into the "U" bracket, it also promised to reopen a market that had been all but closed off in the company's dedicated pursuit of more adult material. AIP and others had contented themselves by buying original Italian product and redubbing it, relying on saturation advertising to do the rest. Conscious of Trevelyan's recent remarks, James Carreras decided that Hammer should make some spectaculars of its own.

Sword of Sherwood Forest had already hinted at the potential in this area, although that had been more the result of the traditional policy of spinning-off a successful television series than responding to a mood. (The film had been coproduced by TV "Robin Hood" Richard Greene and filmed at Ardmore Studios in Ireland.) But the box-office returns were good, and Hammer was now to go the route again. "This is the day of the colossal spectacle and the gimmick picture," Carreras heralded. "Straight routine productions no longer attract audiences." Steve "Hercules" Reeves had starred as *Morgan the Pirate* the year before, so the usual crew was rounded up. With half a galleon and the services of Christopher Lee, *The Pirates of Blood River* set sail on July 3, 1961.

"I have to travel where no one has ever been before...I want to lift the curtain of life, and see what lies beyond..."

—Georges Bonner
The Man Who Could Cheat Death

Sensing a new trend, Carreras further proposed to add a second pirate adventure to the roster for good measure—this one trading on the equally familiar attributes of Peter Cushing. For Michael, it was to be the last straw. His disillusionment with Hammer and the strictures that were imposed by the need to guarantee success was complete. "We forced too many ill-prepared projects onto the floor," he would note in later years. "If we'd been more sparing, the company would *still* be going." By the end of the following year, that opinion would seem only too valid—although not permanently damaging at this stage. But it was a lesson that Hammer— and James Carreras—would never learn. Having finished *The Damned*, and served his term before the mast on *The Pirates of Blood River*, Michael cleared his desk and left the company. The previous December, after *The Inquisitor* had followed *One More River* into oblivion, he had formed the astrologically apt Capricorn Productions in contingency; he was 33 years old. Unlike his father, Michael was a gambler, and he was now to gamble on making his fortune, his musical, *and* his western far from the rigid confines of Bray.

Jimmy Sangster provided the storyline for *The Pirates of Blood River*, though even as scripted by John Gilling—a veteran of such *Boy's Own* yarns—the film was considered "X" certificate material by the BBFC. Alterations were made, and Hammer agreed to content itself with an "A." In the interim, the opportunity had arisen for *Pirates* to cofeature with surefire Columbia winner *Mysterious Island*, and the film was sent back to the board for further pasteurization.

John Trevelyan takes up the story himself in his biography, *What The Censor Saw*.[18] "We looked at it again, asked for further cuts and put it into the U category. This is the only film I can remember that started as an X film and went out as a U film." He gives an example of the distinction between the three versions.

In the early part of the film a young girl, escaping from a villain, plunged into a river and set out to swim to the other bank. In the X version a shoal of pirhana fish rushed through the water and attacked the girl who struggled and was apparently dragged under the water which then became tinged with blood; in the A version the pirhana fish rushed through the water but the scene stopped as they reached the girl; in the U version the pirhana fish never appeared at all.

The Pirates of Blood River might have been emasculated for the greater good, but what was originally meant to have cofeatured with it, and star Peter Cushing, was now to go begging for a running-mate, as a result.

This was to be a remake of Russell Thorndyke's *Dr. Syn*, an idea brought to Hammer by John Temple-Smith and his Major Productions. No sooner did the company announce its intention than the Walt Disney Organization slapped an injunction on the use of the title. (Disney was lining up its own version.) With Michael gone, Tony Hinds had taken on the wages of *Syn*, and discovering that the Disney copyright extended only to the name, he did the obvious. The character was changed to Dr. *Blyss*, and the film lensed at the end of September under the working title of *The Curse of Captain Clegg* (Syn's piratical alter ego).

Romney Marshes....Many legends have come from this corner of England—but none so widely believed or widely feared—as the legend of the marsh phantoms—who rode the land on dark misty nights, and struck fear into the hearts of all who crossed their paths...

—Screen caption
Captain Clegg

While not a horror film in the conventional sense, *Captain Clegg* was nevertheless sold as Hammer Horror. Certainly it is closer in spirit to the Thorndyke novel than the bland version of the tale that would be made a year later by Disney. *Dr. Syn: A Tale of Romney Marsh* is pure Gothic horror, for which we have the word of Russell's more famous acting sister, Dame Sybil, in testimony. It had been inspired by the two witnessing a murder in Spaltenburg, Carolina, during a theatrical tour, when an irate stepfather had shot his stepson dead on the steps of their hotel. The body had been left on the sidewalk for several hours, to await the arrival of the authorities, and the gruesome sight had been the catalyst for the idea of the smuggler-parson. Subsequently, Sybil wrote, "That dreadful night we piled horror upon horror's head, and after each new horror was invented, we took another squint at the corpse to encourage us."

There were seven *Dr. Syn* novels in all (not including a posthumous contribution by William Buchanan), but their hero had been killed off at the end of the first, so the following six had to be written as retrospective adventures. When Gainsborough tackled the subject with George Arliss in 1937 (the script that Temple-Smith originally brought to Hinds had been taken virtually word-for-word from this film), rumor was that Thorndyke had sold the rights for a mere £20 which, being something of a *bon vivant*, he had promptly disposed of in a single night, wining and dining at the Pier Hotel in Chelsea.

> *1792—Captain Collier and his men arrive in Dymchurch to investigate smuggling in the village. With them is a mulatto rescued from marooning at the hands of pirate, Captain Clegg, who had since been hanged. When the mulatto sees Dr. Blyss, the parson, he attacks him. Collier becomes suspicious. The smugglers are led by Blyss, and disguise themselves as the "Marsh Phantoms" to divert attention away from their illegal activities. Eventually, the mulatto breaks open Clegg's grave and finds it empty. Collier accuses Blyss of being Clegg. Blyss denies it, but the mark of the hangman's rope tells its own story. The villagers rally to save him from capture, but he is killed by the mulatto, who is then shot by bosun Mipps. Clegg's body is finally laid to rest in the grave that he had eluded all those years before.*

The contretemps with Disney was apt. Certainly, it seemed to inspire director Peter Graham Scott to steer a new course for Hammer Horror. The film opens like a live-action version of *The Legend of Sleepy Hollow*, with its ghostly vision of the "Marsh Phantoms" in full flight against dark, overcast skies, to the accompaniment of mock-eerie music. This curtain raiser is superbly atmospheric and comes close to capturing that spirit of "magic and devilry" that the *mise en scène* of *The Brides of Dracula* had conjured so vividly.

The belated Disney production was to be called *Dr. Syn, alias The Scarecrow*. In a sly dig in the ribs to Disney, the "scarecrow" figures prominently in *Captain Clegg,* from the credit titles onward, and it is always perfectly clear from what text the film had sprung. Thorndyke's wonderfully Melvillian monickers are all in evidence, bar *one*—Mipps, Rash, Clegg, Ketch, and Wurzel—and Hammer's stock troupe turned out in force to give them form: Ripper, Reed (Oliver), Romain, and Reid (Milton).

Peter Cushing's playing in *Captain Clegg* provides his single best performance for Hammer. When Blyss is finally unmasked as one of the skeletal smuggling band and revealed to be Clegg himself, it is to Cushing's credit that an element of surprise still pertains, despite the fact that this *dénouement* has been guessed long before. Cushing "loved" the film, read Thorndyke as a precursor to taking on the role (it was he who suggested to Roy Ashton that Blyss should be adorned with the literary Syn's Ahab-like shock of white hair), and his natural athleticism was used to the full in a realistic bruising with Milton Reid and another Fairbanks-style leap from a chandelier (performed by Cushing's long-time stunt double, Barry du Boulay).

Hammer newcomer Scott brings a spritely television clip to the proceedings and, given the quality of Peter Cushing's performance in the dual role of ironman Clegg and his clerical counterpart, Dr. Blyss, it is the more surprising that he and Scott did not get on during the filming. Scott had his own clear ideas about how things should be done, which were eventually to draw the chastening response from Cushing to cameraman Len Harris—"Take no notice, Len. We've done enough of these now to know what we're doing." But despite occasional evidence of an unsteady hand on the tiller, Scott does bring a new eye and fresh approach to the piece, though his awareness that this was a *Hammer* production clearly encouraged him to treat the story's violent content with a relish for detail that the censor would find impossible to subdue to a "U."

Captain Clegg provides many good moments of shock and suspense, and manages some quite delicious *frissons* into the bargain. While the "Marsh Phantoms" may be a highly volatile lot (the process photography is distinctly variable), Cushing's expression, as it twists from the fear and loathing that has been prompted by his fight with the mulatto into the rictus grin that erupts into silent laughter when he realizes that the King's men have fallen for his ruse, is the single most hideous apparition of this or any other Hammer horror film of the sixties.

> "No man can stand upon the gallows without coming face to face with his soul.... Now on that day, truly, the old Clegg died..."
>
> —Dr. Blyss
> *Captain Clegg*

Clegg has something that no other Hammer horror is possessed of: heart. It is what marks it. In an extraordinarily moving finale, Michael Ripper's bosun Mipps carries the dead Clegg to the grave that he should have occupied sixteen years before. The slab is put in place over Cushing's ashen face, and the end titles fill the screen. Had it but known it, Hammer was burying its own immediate past, as well. Mipps' tears flow not only for a fallen comrade but for Hammer's "Golden Age." For reasons that were just becoming clear at the time, it was now at an end. For Clegg—and for Hammer Horror—the game was up.

In 1958, Christopher Lee had remarked that his ambition in horror films was "to star in a remake of *The Phantom of the Opera.* This film would give me a chance to prove that I can sing." Just such a remake had first been touted only one year later, and Lee had made his approach. "I felt I should have played the Phantom," he said. "I did speak to Michael about that." Michael, however, had long-since stopped listening, and now that the time had finally come, Lee was making ready to leave the country, with new wife Birgit, for a villa in Vaud and a view over the northern slopes of Lake Geneva. This time, he intended it to be on a more permanent basis.

By spring 1962, Lee would be domiciled in Switzerland. The villa overlooking the valley of the Rhone was to be his base of operations for two years, during which time he would commence his autobiography, avoid what he had described as Britain's "vicious and crippling tax system," and pursue his quest for international stardom by accepting every offer that came his way. "I could only hope that they would serve some purpose, and that perhaps a reputation might come in the same way as a coral formation, which is made up of a deposit of countless tiny corpses," he would write. Not that his departure made any difference. For *The Phantom of the Opera*, Hammer had in mind a bigger fish from the very beginning.

The Fall of the House of Usher had ridden to glory on the back of a major Hollywood star, and the opportunity had arisen for Hammer to do the same thing with the last of Universal's monster classics to remain unfilmed. *The Phantom of the Opera* had been mounted in deference to an approach by—of all people—Cary Grant, who had expressed interest in appearing in a Hammer film during his sojourn in England for Stanley Donen's *The Grass Is Greener* (1960). With a star of Grant's stature knocking at Bray's door, Tony Hinds had been instructed to write the film especially for him. Hinds was unconvinced, but he went through the motions. "It worked for *him* because it was all very lighthearted and humorous," he said. But not lighthearted enough, apparently. Grant's agent turned it down flat, and the notion of attracting a major star promptly collapsed with it.

> Maria: "I saw him, I tell you…Standing just over here—just here. Black—all over…Black…And his eye—staring at me—"
> Harry: "His eye—?"
> Maria: "Eye!—One eye…in the middle of his forehead. And his face, Harry—it was horrible!"
>
> —*The Phantom of the Opera*

In touting *The Phantom of the Opera* as its major release for 1962, Hammer was going right back to where Tony Hinds thought it belonged. In common with most of the previous "remakes," *The Phantom* had sprung from a literary source. Gaston Leroux's 1911 novel was not well known, and in the wake of the first film version of it (which had starred Lon Chaney), was all but forgotten. In consequence, the tale is perceived as a product of the Hollywood machine, and any prospective remake has had to take this earlier adaption very much into account. *The Phantom of the Opera* had been the silent screen's most spectacular horror fantasy.

The original 1925 Universal production had been remarkably faithful to Leroux, whose "Phantom" was a criminal lunatic, disfigured from birth, who used his civil engineering prowess to construct himself a subterranean home in the depths of the Paris Opera House, slept in a coffin ("It keeps me reminded of that other dreamless sleep that cures all ills—forever!"), and was oddly disposed to litter his strange abode with all manner of booby-traps and devices of torture. In the film, as in the book, Gounod's *Faust* was the opera in question.

The same company's respectful Technicolor remake of 1943 removed the serialistic melodrama of the original and simplified the Phantom's genesis by recasting him as violinist Erique Claudin, a frustrated (rather than mad) composer who is disfigured by acid while attempting to save his concerto from the clutches of a plagiarist. The relationship between Phantom and singer (not fully explained in the novel and ignored altogether in the silent version) now became implicitly paternal, and *Faust* was sidestepped for the more popular melodics of Tchaikovsky's "Fourth Symphony" and Flotow's *Martha*, in keeping with the fact that the film had been designed as a vehicle for Nelson Eddy and Susanna Foster. Universal had been aware that they could not hope to top the Chaney Phantom's unmasking—arguably the single most frightening scene in the history of the horror film—so the fall of the great chandelier (a minor highlight in the original) was moved to center stage instead.

Not only had the Rupert Julian, Edward Sedgewick, and Lon Chaney directed original benefited from a cast of thousands, it had also been the recipient of some massive sets left over from Chaney's *The Hunchback of Notre Dame* (1923), such as the Cathedral. And Hammer was remaking a film that had already been remade in (exquisite) color, so it could hardly score there, either. In addition, the story is a starring role for the monster, and with Cary Grant having been persuaded to withdraw, Hammer's monster was now packing his bags for the continent. Nevertheless, with the company committed to the production, James Carreras saw *The Phantom of the Opera* as his big opportunity to backpedal on the gore and move Hammer's product more substantially into the mainstream.

Under these circumstances, and with the limited resources available at Bray, *The Phantom of the Opera* was full of pitfalls. Hammer's success had been built on outdoing the originals it chose to remake. With the crude theatrics and dated appeal of Universal's other horror properties, that task had been relatively easy, but *The Phantom* contained two legendary sequences. The fall of the chandelier and the unmasking *would* be included, but by reducing the remainder of the narrative to the mandatory half-dozen characters,

Hinds/Elder could only retain the bare bones of the previous films. The Parisian locale devolved into the more prosaic backwater of London's Wimbledon Theatre—a move that raised critical hackles even before *The Phantom* was released. To simplify the musical proceedings, the opera and the stolen composition became one and the same, so Edwin Astley had to depart from Gounod and engineer an original music score of his own for the new version.

In July 1962, the BBFC had advised Hinds about the production on the basis that he would be aiming for the usual "X" certificate. "The script as it stands has quite a bit of 'X' stuff," said the reader's report. "Probably they want this category anyway." Even so, there had been a proviso from John Trevelyan. "Criticism of the 'X' category horror films has increased in the last two years. In the circumstances I must ask you to take special care in the shooting of all shock sequences." Hinds altered the film's first shock shot. In the script, the murdered scene shifter in the opening sequence is described as hanging *upside-down*. But the rest would be as had been mutually agreed, and shooting began on November 20, immediately after the close of production on *Captain Clegg*.

Hammer's *Phantom* was hyped as its most expensive Gothic to date, at some £400,000. "The most costly and spectacular thriller of its kind ever filmed in Britain," said the press book. Since little of this was to be apparent on-screen, the publicists must have decided to use inflation to their own advantage—or they simply thought of a number and doubled it. "We cut the budget down, and it didn't quite work," Hinds understated.

> The year is 1900, and the first night of a new opera by Lord Ambrose D'Arcy at the Albany Theatre ends with the death of a stagehand. The prima donna refuses to go on, and producer Harry Hunter auditions for a singer to replace her. He sees a promising alternative in Christine and, at her lodgings, discovers evidence that the opera was stolen from a Professor Petrie, who had been killed in a fire. They subsequently learn that Petrie survived the blaze but was disfigured by acid. Back in her room, Christine is confronted by a hideous dwarf and carried off to an underground lair below the Opera House, where a figure plays at the organ—the "Phantom" intends to train her to be a great singer. Hunter finds the lair and exposes the Phantom as Petrie. The Phantom explains how D'Arcy stole his music, and begs Hunter to let him finish the task in hand. Hunter agrees and the opera is staged with Christine singing the lead.

> *During the performance, the dwarf is spotted in the eaves and chased;*
> *he jumps to a chandelier, but his weight snaps the rope. The Phantom*
> *spots the danger and leaps onto the stage, throwing Christine*
> *aside—but he is too late to save himself: the chandelier falls, crushing*
> *him to death.*

With Grant out of the picture, Hinds thought to salvage the project with Herbert Lom. Lom hailed originally from Prague and had made a career out of playing sleazy gangsters of mid-European or Mediterranean origin. In 1959, he had been a pimp in Alvin Rakoff's *Passport to Shame*. Lom was also intent on changing his image. In *Mysterious Island*, he had played Nemo, and he was soon to become the memorable Inspector Dreyfus in *A Shot in the Dark* (1964). Lom was known to Hinds as an actor of repute, but in Fisher's hands, Lom's Phantom becomes an ineffectual absent-minded professor inhabiting a grotesquely unreal Eastmancolor grotto filled with idiosynchratic delights, not to mention a music-loving dwarf! So insipid is he that his self-sacrificing leap onto the stage at the climax seems more like a last act in a life of accident-proneness than the *grande geste* it is intended to be.

In addition, the script is dramatically unstable and morally confused. In line with the notion that a star like Grant would not have played the part unless an element of audience empathy existed, Lord D'Arcy is nominated to be the actual villain of the piece, with the sympathetic Phantom subordinated to a supporting role. But D'Arcy does not get his comeuppance (unless you count being unexpectedly confronted by a sight that may have caused a measure of hysteria in Mary Philbin in 1925, but barely produced a shudder in Susanna Foster in 1943), yet the dwarf and Petrie do—a case of two wrongs, clearly.

Elder's dialogue is more rounded than in *The Curse of the Werewolf*, but there are still *longeurs*, and much of it simply directs and dictates the action. Fisher is obliging in this and has people walk aimlessly around to fill in the blanks. "I think there is something evil in this theater, Christine," says Harry, at which point an innocent rat catcher is stabbed in the eye by the opera-loving dwarf in a last-minute attempt to spice up the proceedings. It was not enough to save an ill-conceived production, and the scene was to end up among the BBFC's outtakes, anyway.

Like *The Curse of the Werewolf, The Phantom* has its advocates, but no amount of apology can alter the fact that the story is puerile, the staging crass, the production overlit, the drama bogus, and the poverty of ideas apparent. Against that, *The Phantom of the Opera* is *beautiful* to look at, Heather Sears and Edward de Souza as heroine and hero are both excellent, Astley's opera is particularly fine (especially at the climax), and one or two of the supporting players—such as Thorley Walters—are worth the price of a ticket by themselves. But after a rousing opening reel, it is downhill all the way.

"There are forces of evil at large in the Opera tonight..."

—Professor Petrie (the Phantom)
The Phantom of the Opera

Despite its customary surface gloss and token injection of gore, *The Phantom of the Opera* turned out to be an old-fashioned melodrama, ill-constructed and executed, and ultimately disappointing on almost every level. But not all its failings could be laid at the feet of Terence Fisher. The cardinal sin was a genuine sin of omission: on his British release, Hammer's Phantom was not unmasked *at all!*

By April 1962, with the final figures on his desk, James Carreras began to have misgivings about the scale of Hammer's investment in *The Phantom of the Opera.* The film had come in at a little under £171,000, even with Tony Hinds taking only a nominal £200 for providing the script, and the expected U.K. gross (which went direct to Hammer) was no longer looking so good, in the more restricted market available to the "X" certificate.

With its catalog of torture, brutality, murder, grave robbing, and attempted rape, *Captain Clegg* had been sold to Universal as Hammer Horror (under a new title of *Night Creatures*), which meant pairing it with *The Phantom.* Since the reader's report of the previous July had offered, "I think the makers should be told that they could make it in an 'A' way if they liked," Carreras and Rank decided to ask for *The Phantom of the Opera* to be cut to an "A" to match *Clegg* and increase the appeal of both. Consequently, the film paid another *two* visits to the BBFC in May, each one leaving it more bereft than the one before. Out went the hanged scene shifter swinging into the camera. Out went the stabbing of the rat catcher from where the dwarf raises the knife. Out went closeups of the Phantom with the mask on. But most critically—in spite of Trevelyan opining, "I do not think that further cutting will damage the film"—out went the Phantom tearing the mask *off* to reveal his "hideously scarred face."

On release, one critic—under a headline heralding a "funny" phantom, commented, "Keep it dark, but something's gone sadly wrong with *The Phantom of the Opera*." That something had been the decision to broaden the acceptability of Gothic horror by diluting its very essence. Rank had been instrumental in putting the squeeze on, and Hammer had dutifully obliged. Michael Carreras was dismissive—"It was a half-speed film." But director Terence Fisher sought to justify the farrago in later interviews:

> "I've never isolated the monster from the world around, or tried to avoid showing him. The *exception* is *Phantom*; there was no reason to show his face there; you'd seen the acid go into his face, you knew how pitifully he was in agony all the time.

No reason? Hammer Horror was breathing its last and *The Phantom of the Opera* was to be its death rattle. It was certainly not about to compete with the likes of *From Russia With Love* and what *Sight and Sound* would call "the new brutalism" at the box office. *Phantom* was no fairy tale for adults; it was a fable for children, as the "A" certificate and its superior cofeature seemed to testify. Hammer had lost its way. The archproponent of screen horror had become respectable, to the disdain of audiences and the hypocritical ire of the critics.

The August 28 opening of *The Phantom of the Opera* had done Hammer no favors, and so evident was the disappointing reception accorded the film that the company felt obliged to comment. It would correct its mistake and "include" an unmasking scene for America, even though American audiences would see the unmasking, anyway! By the time *The Phantom of the Opera* and *Captain Clegg* went out through Rank during September, *The Pirates of Blood River* and *Mysterious Island* would already have opened on the ABC circuit, backed by a television campaign that not only helped put them into the "Top Ten" for the year, but unwittingly hanged Fisher's lame-duck *Phantom* in the process.

In the meanwhile, the last drop of blood was being wrung out of the remaining cadavers in the corridors of Bray. *Brat Farrar* was jolted back into life as *Paranoiac* for Oliver Reed, and schlock-king William Castle was encouraged to pool his talents with Hammer for a spoof remake of *The Old Dark House* after Castle's *Homicidal*— another *Psycho* variant—had been successfully paired with *The Terror of the Tongs*. Both would end up back in the freezer, however, where they would be followed by *Nightmare,* when Jimmy Sangster tapped into the same empty vein. Sangster's ongoing *affaire* with France had seen him set his follow-up to *Taste of Fear* there. While *Maniac* was being produced in the Camargue, Tony Hinds was pressing ahead with his stumbling program of Gothic horrors. "We shall continue to make them as long as we can find subjects," Hinds said, "but it's getting a bit difficult now."

"Ladies and gentlemen. May I introduce a new disciple?"

—Doctor Ravna
The Kiss of the Vampire

"*Brides of Dracula* is taking a packet in the USA…which makes me think that we can start another one for Universal sometime in 1962," James Carreras had advised Hinds in a memo two years earlier. Universal now wanted that other Dracula to compensate for the lackluster performance of *The Curse of the Werewolf.* To appease them, Hinds had concocted a lukewarm mystery with supernatural overtones from the familiar intrigue of *So Long at the Fair* (1951) and a sauce of ingredients left over from *The Disciple of Dracula,* in a further attempt to find a formula that would substitute for the current unavailability of Lee. But he was not without reservations and requested a meeting to discuss future policy. "I was thinking in terms of beer and sandwiches," Hinds recalls, "but the meeting is at one of the best restaurants in London; there was just Brian Lawrence, Jim and myself, and there was the three of us and *six* waiters! That was the *only* policy meeting we had—and we talked about nothing. Nothing."

In the crisis days of 1955, Hammer had found itself with a log-jam of unwanted features. Now it was in danger of creating that situation over again. Nevertheless, the third Dracula was to go into production as planned on September 17, 1962. Hinds had decided on his own that an injection of fresh blood *behind* the lens might make Hammer Horror more current, and he had already called upon the newfound directorial talent of cinematographer Freddie Francis to helm *Paranoiac*. Since Fisher had been nominated to take the fall over *The Phantom of the Opera*, second-feature director Don Sharp was assigned to what would become *The Kiss of the Vampire*.

The cinema's monsters of terror had now shaken off the manacles of the creature and the silver chain of the vampire, however. The brute-man had taken on the form of Max Cady in *Cape Fear* (1961), while phantoms in the night came in the shape of the asthmatic Red Lynch in *The Grip of Fear* (aka *Experiment in Terror*; also 1961). *The Kiss of the Vampire* was to be Don Sharp's debut in main features, but it would be more than a year before he would hear the applause. The last Gothic of the old school was to open to a more positive critical reception, but by then, it would seem to belong to a different era altogether.

> *While honeymooning in Bavaria, Gerald Harcourt and his wife, Marianne, are invited to a ball at the chateau of Dr. Ravna. During the festivities, Gerald is drugged and Marianne abducted. When he comes to, Ravna informs him that he arrived alone, and he is thrown out. When he can find no trace of Marianne, Gerald is distraught, but he is eventually consoled by Professor Zimmer, who reveals that Marianne has fallen into the clutches of a cult of vampires; Zimmer's own daughter had been one of Ravna's victims. Gerald returns to the chateau and is captured, but with Zimmer's help, he frees Marianne and they both escape. As Zimmer performs a magic ritual to invoke the powers of darkness, Marianne again succumbs to Ravna's hypnotic influence. A swarm of bats invades the chateau and destroys the cult. With Ravna's death, the spell is broken and the couple are reunited.*

The Kiss of the Vampire turned the clock back to the days before *The Curse of Frankenstein*. Under Sharp's eclectic direction (except for the befanged appearance of Tania in a mist-laden graveyard), its first hour is more like the horror-by-suggestion thrillers of RKO's Val Lewton. The film's small scale aids the impression, as does Sharp's predilection for swinging shutters and swaying trees. He had come to *The Kiss of the Vampire* unfamiliar with the house style of Hammer Horror, and much of the film harks back to an earlier age. It is not so much a continuation of Hammer Gothic as an *hommage* to it.

For the most part, the pace is leisurely. The action is constantly punctuated by fades or dissolves. But throughout, Sharp's grip on the narrative is faultless. Unlike Fisher, he is clearly aware that there is more to atmosphere than decor alone. Sharp's mastery at evoking *mise-en-scéne* is exhibited to good effect in an early sequence in a forest, when an anxious Marianne waits in the *de Dion Bouton* while her husband goes foraging for gas. (This unsettling episode was filmed in fern-carpeted Black Park at Pinewood, a location that would now be used with increasing frequency in Hammer Horror.)

The plot is of the spider-and-fly variety, spun out as a mystery. The vampires in the film are very low key, and a dinner scene where Doctor Ravna explains his unusual circumstances was revised to incorporate an extra sequence more in keeping with the Hammer that Universal had been led to expect—Tania, the hoteliers' "missing" daughter, inflicting the *kiss* of the vampire on Professor Zimmer.[19] Having drawn inspiration from the plot device of *So Long at the Fair* and *The Lady Vanishes*—where the contrived disappearance of a character is later shown to be part of an elaborate deceit— Hinds had originally invested his film with the air of a whodunnit. But in so doing, he had been hoist by his own *pétard*. Tania was intended to remain an enigma, until her appearance at the *bal masque* in the chateau revealed the truth about Ravna and acted as a catalyst for the disappearance of Marianne. But the whole concept of Hammer Horror was so indelible in the public mind by this time that the villains in *The Kiss of the Vampire* are never in doubt, so the conceit of such a "surprise" was a *non sequitur* to begin with ("Welcome to my house," says *Herr Doktor* in true Dracula fashion). In its first draft, the screenplay had been more subtle but, without the added scene in the graveyard, the film might have looked *decades* out of date, rather than years.

To Universal, it looked that way, anyway. While *The Fall of the House of Usher* and other AIP Poe films were regularly formatted in both color and scope, Hammer had chosen to stay with the Academy ratio. *The Kiss of the Vampire* had many virtues, yet it was a portrait in miniature, and its old-fashioned style (and BBFC-fearing reticence) would tarnish it with a curious ambiguity that *Films and Filming* would refer to as "the appearance of being done tongue-in-cheek." Almost without realizing it, Hammer had conceded defeat in the battle of the Gothics. Roger Corman had won.

By the time *Nightmare* was added to the quota in December, Hammer would have six films piled up awaiting release. Only two of them (*Maniac* and *The Damned*) would make it into theaters before 1964. The company was staring retrenchment in the face. Money from overseas sales had been slow in coming in, and British film production had gone into one of its habitual declines following the inflationary boom of 1959-60. The promises about the future prospects of Bray Studios took on a hollow ring. "When Phase Two has been completed, we can go on developing," Michael Carreras had been projecting only three years earlier. "There is ample room—should the need arise—for continued expansion." As Phase Two had *not* been completed, the need was unlikely to arise. Of the two new stages originally proposed, only one had been built, and the new workshops got no further than the drawing board. With production being eased into a lower gear, work would begin on the long-awaited repairs that had been necessitated by the fire, and existing facilities could be upgraded, instead.

Rationalization was the order of the day, and economies were sought. Lighting cameraman Jack Asher would be the first sacrificial lamb on the altar of expediency—but not the last. The shooting of *The Phantom of the Opera* had been beset by rumor and a vague sense of unease. New coproduction deals with Robert B. Radnitz and, more recently, Roberto Dandi (for *The Kiss of the Vampire*) had gone by the wayside. The permanent staff at Bray were assembled and informed of the worst: their numbers were to be cut until the situation showed signs of improvement, advised general manager Tony Keys.

What Hammer had to do was to cut its cloth in line with the tastes of a new generation of buyers, and predominantly American buyers at that, since two-thirds of the potential box office was now being accounted for by foreign markets (as opposed to only 20 percent, ten years previously). But what were those tastes to be?

James Bond had already shown the way, although it would be some years before the message sank in. Sixties cinema was to be escapist in tone and iconographic in tenor. The cult of personality, whether fact or fancy, would be the in thing. The parochial English horror film would soon be required to transmogrify into the international fantasy epic, where substance became subjugated to spectacle and story mattered less than special effects.

An ambivalence was creeping into Hammer's films. Some, like *The Kiss of the Vampire*, would surface to find the mark again, while others would go wider still. Things had come a long way from the days when British films unfolded to the spring-fresh strains of Walton, Elgar, or Vaughan Williams. The new dawn was marching to the modern jazz of Henry Mancini or the strident brass of John Barry. The thrills in *The Phantom of the Opera* were sparse compared with the rough-and-tumble catharsis of James Bond. Times were changing, and Hammer had signally failed to notice. Now it would be forced to.

As the year drew to a close, the outlook was bleak. With Trevelyan's warnings still ringing in its ears, Hammer's career as a purveyor of top quality horror films seemed to have run its course. When it was eventually over for real, Jimmy Sangster would say of the company's cinematic reign of terror, "Hammer were just very, very lucky for a long time." By the close of 1962, that luck seemed to have run out. Hammer's first glorious, golden summer was at an end.

Brigadier Chichester-Cooke with Major James Carreras at Rye, Sussex, 1944.

Anthony and William Hinds, circa 1952.

Michael Carreras, circa 1952.

Gilston Park Country Club, Grays, Essex.

Vera St. John Carreras, Constance Smith, Enrique Carreras, and Mrs. D. J. (Violet) Goodlatte on the set of *Room To Let*.

Alan Wheatley, Francis Searle, Jimmy Sangster, and Richard Carlson on night location in Windsor for *Whispering Smith Hits London.*

SHADOWS AND NIGHT: *Whispering Smith Hits London*—(actually Goswell Hill in Windsor: 1951).

Exclusive Sales Conference of 1952. L to R: Michael Carreras, James Carreras, William Hinds, Anthony Hinds, Brian Lawrence.

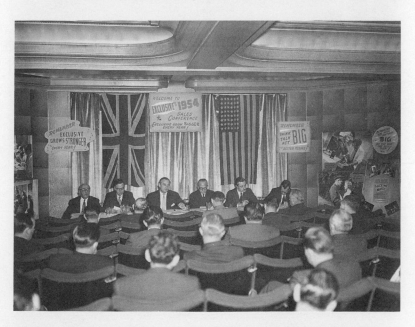

The viewing theatre at Hammer House, during Exclusive's Sales Conference of 1954. L to R at table: Harry Bernow, James Dawson, James Carreras, William Hinds, Michael Carreras, Brian Lawrence.

MAD LAB MAYHEM: *Four-sided Triangle*—Stephen Murray (1952).

Bandleader Cyril Stapleton with Michael Carreras lining up a shot in Cinemascope for *Cyril Stapleton and the Showband*.

Bray Studios, during shooting of *Dick Turpin—Highwayman* (Down Place in background).

Left: Robert L.Lippert—Right: Eliot Hyman.

Peter Cushing as the baron—Christopher Lee as the creature (*The Curse of Frankenstein*, 1956).

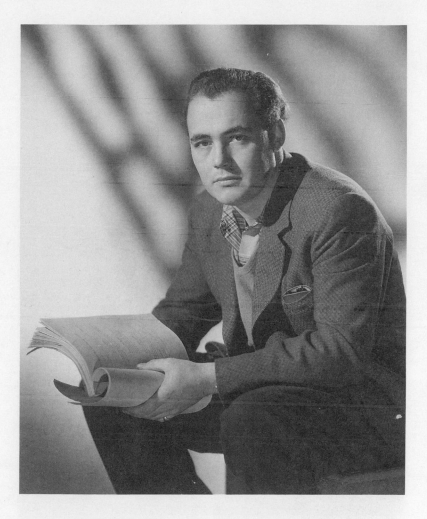

Jimmy Sangster holding his script for *The Curse of Frankenstein*.

HISTORY IS MADE AT NIGHT: Scene 1, Take 1 of *The Curse of Franken-stein*. "Two careers were launched that night—Peter Cushing's and Terence Fisher's," was the opinion of camera operator Len Harris. Jock Easton is on the gibbet, while Peter Cushing looks on.

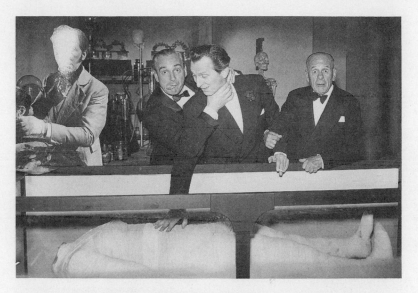

James Carreras, Peter Cushing, and William Hinds at the British premire of *The Curse of Frankenstein*.

Michael Carreras and editor James Needs.

Exclusive luncheon for branch managers and head office staff. (Michael and James Carreras and Brian Lawrence head the table and among those in attendance are Morris Young (London circuits), Harry Bland (South Coast), Joe Cohen (London), Ralph Shaw (Birmingham), Sam Greene (Nottinghamshire), Bernard Newrick (Liverpool), George Cowan (Newcastle), Tom Hanlon (Dublin), Jack Tiktin (Cardiff) and Horace Coxall (Scotland).

Jack L.Warner, James Carreras, Nat Cohen, and Mike Frankovich, attend a Variety Club function.

JONATHAN HARKER'S BEDROOM—CASTLE DRACULA: One of
Bernard Robinson's set designs for *Dracula*.

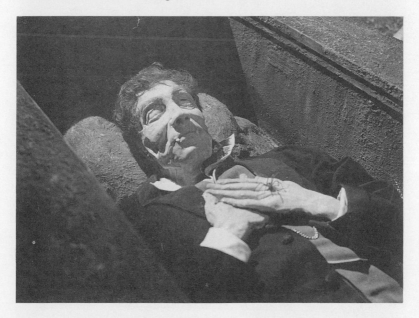

"Shots of Jonathan's dead face should not be too horrible . . . " — John
Trevelyan: Dummy corpse constructed for *Dracula* but abandoned on
advice from the BBFC.

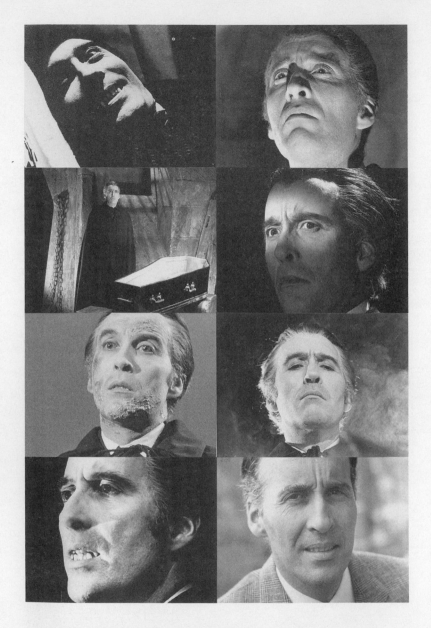

THE 7 FACES OF DRACULA: *Dracula* (1957), *Dracula—Prince of Darkness* (1965), *Dracula Has Risen From the Grave* (1968), *Taste the Blood of Dracula* (1969), *Scars of Dracula* (1970), *Dracula AD 1972* (1971), The Satanic Rites of Dracula (1972)—and Christopher Lee.

Exterior set for *The Camp on Blood Island,* erected on the Bray Studios back lot.

STREET GIRL: "All right, cheri?—Same time next week?"
LITTLE MAN: "I must be getting along. I've a long way to go…"
Scene eliminated from the prologue of *The Man Who Could Cheat Death*—
Middleton Woods, Gerda Larsen (1958).

MAD MONSTER MAYHEM: *The Mummy*—Christopher Lee (1959).

Chapter 4

The House of Horror

1963-1969

"Michael had one great characteristic, and it was that if he put the talent together, he never messed with it. He never tried to control it or manipulate it—he just directed it, very gently. And he could have done that very well if it hadn't been for the 'old man' up there, and the remorseless mills of Hammer."

Wolf Mankowitz
talking about Michael Carreras

Hammer's search for new worlds to conquer had proved to be singularly uninspiring. *The Damned* and *The Old Dark House* had both ended up on the Columbia shelf, and by 1963, the company was appealing to trade and public alike for help: "Got an idea you think would make a good film? One with an exciting title to match? If you have, contact James Carreras. Because good, compulsive selling ideas with the right titles are what Hammer are looking for right now." The exhortation in *The Daily Cinema* was repeated in the classified columns of selected national newspapers, with the same predictable result: more monsters. To those who responded, the name of Hammer remained linked inextricably with horror, so Carreras bowed to the inevitable and in August, he announced six films, the first of which was to commence at Bray on August 17: *The Devil Ship Pirates*. The next four were *Quatermass and the Pit* (to be directed by Freddie Francis), *She, Blood of the Foreign Legion*, and *Brainstorm*—of these, only *Blood of the Foreign Legion* would fail to reach the screen. But it was the sixth that would remove any doubt about the direction in which Hammer's ship was now to sail.

"Hammer...are back in the horror business," trumpeted studio publicist Dennison Thornton, in fanfare for a feature that was originally to have been produced by Jimmy Sangster. "After a two-year interlude devoted largely to straight thrillers and swash-buckling adventure films, they have brought back to the screen that notorious gothic scientist and monster maker—Baron Franken-stein." Well, not quite. With Herbert Morrison still presiding over the BBFC, the horror content was to be proscribed and the baron rehabilitated. Accordingly, the publicity became even more frantic. "One of the most horrific films even Hammer has ever made," screamed the advance blurb as the press was judiciously barred from the set of *The Evil of Frankenstein*.

> Bernard: "We don't yet know how to repeat the exact conditions that produced these children—"
> Freya: "You mean you would if you could?"
> Bernard: "Certainly."
>
> —*The Damned*

After an excursion to Germany to codirect Christopher Lee in *Sherlock Holmes and the Deadly Necklace*, Terence Fisher had con-tracted to do a brace of films for Bob Lippert, so when *Quatermass and the Pit* was postponed (again), Tony Hinds nominated the younger Freddie Francis to helm the baron's overdue revival. "Hammer didn't want to get involved in anything important, or anything there could be any discussion about," said Francis, who, in his former capacity as a lighting cameraman, had photographed *Never Take Sweets From a Stranger*. Peter Cushing was welcomed back with open arms, and the film went before the cameras in October.

In the summer of 1964, Lord Morrison was to retire from the BBFC due to ill health (he would die in 1965) and he was replaced by the less intimidating Lord Harlech. By then, *The Kiss of the Vampire* and *The Evil of Frankenstein* would both have rung the bell, and Hammer would be back in the horror business for good.

> *Baron Frankenstein is forced to return to his ancestral home at Karlstaad with his assistant, Hans. Finding the castle ransacked, they follow a young beggar girl to a cave in the mountains, where they discover the creature the baron created, encased in a block of ice.*

> *They thaw it out, but its brain remains dormant, and Frankenstein*
> *enlists the aid of a fairground mesmerist to awaken it. With the*
> *creature in his power, the scheming Zoltan determines to use it as a*
> *weapon of revenge—he sends it to murder the burgomaster and the*
> *chief of police. When Frankenstein learns of the subterfuge, he throws*
> *Zoltan out, but the mesmerist incites the creature to kill the baron*
> *also. During a struggle, Zoltan is speared to death instead. Franken-*
> *stein is imprisoned for the murder of the burgomaster, but he escapes*
> *from jail and races back to the castle. In the meanwhile, the creature*
> *mistakenly drinks from a bottle of chloroform. Enraged with pain, it*
> *sets fire to the laboratory, trapping Frankenstein inside. Hans and*
> *the girl flee to safety and the castle explodes, burying its occupants*
> *in the rubble.*

In common with Italian cinematographer turned director Mario Bava, Freddie Francis showed himself to be more concerned with style than content. He admitted to having no particular affinity with the Gothic, and his foray into Fisher's territory was the result of friendship with Hinds rather than a feeling for the genre. In *The Evil of Frankenstein*, the spectacle is all, and the director invested a large part of his frugal budget on a laboratory for the baron. There are some beautiful compositional effects in the film—more color, light, and life in every frame. The apparatus that galvanises the monster into action is eye-catchingly extravagant, and the creation sequence is lavish enough to more than make up for the fact that the previous episodes in the series had skimped on it. There is also a splendid fiery climax. But while there is thunder, there is precious little blood.

In this first *Frankenstein* by John Elder, the baron is unashamedly transformed into a persecuted victim of circumstance. "Why can't they leave me alone? Why can't they *ever* leave me alone?" Any pretext of a connection to *Revenge* is dispensed with in a brazen display of contempt for continuity. A flashback creates a prior history that is wholly unrelated to the dictates of the last Sangster script and is plundered from the plot of Universal's *Frankenstein Meets the Wolfman*. If Frankenstein remains recognizable, the credit must go to Cushing, who rewrote "quite a bit here and there" to keep him "basically the same chap." He was fighting a losing battle. "We are putting more compassion into our horror films," said Hinds at the time. But as Elder's baron cut himself adrift from his own history, so Hammer was severing the links with its own Gothic past.

The most telling sequence in *The Evil of Frankenstein* (tentatively titled *The Fear of Frankenstein* at an earlier stage) is the prologue. A little girl witnesses a body snatcher spiriting away a corpse in the dead of night and flees in terror. In the woods, she is confronted by Baron Frankenstein. He sneers in mild rebuke, momentarily distracted from his task, and proceeds on his way (to perform a perfectly timed heart removal behind the credit titles). Since these events are perceived from the girl's point of view, the impression that the bad baron has been reduced, in the interval between *Revenge* and *Evil*, to the level of a bogeyman in a child's nightmare is inescapable.

With Universal's blessing, the monster is unequivocally of the bolts-and-all variety, in caricature makeup and the automaton form of wrestler Kiwi Kingston. The story is a retread of another Universal product—*The Son of Frankenstein*—with Zoltan and his mesmerism replacing Ygor and his pied pipes. There are some nice lines: "There isn't a man born of woman that I can't put under," brags the mesmerist, unaware that his next subject has been *stitched* together—"Then this experiment should prove very interesting," observes Frankenstein, tartly. And the climax, if somewhat contrived, is a scorcher. "In the end, Kiwi and I had to shout, *That's enough!*" Cushing remembers. "They didn't realize the enormous heat that was building up." But in the final analysis, *The Evil of Frankenstein* is no more than a respectable Gothic thriller, at best.

Behind the scenes, there were more comings and goings at Hammer. Musical director John Hollingsworth died while working on the film and was replaced by Philip Martell, and a young production accountant named Roy Skeggs enrolled for a three-week stint and stayed to inherit the company. Baron Frankenstein may have condemned himself to a life outside society, but Hammer Horror was now part of the establishment, and so it would remain for the duration.

"They beat him after all…"

—Hans
The Evil of Frankenstein

On completion of *The Evil of Frankenstein*—nominally his fiftieth film as a producer—Tony Hinds, at 41, was accorded the honor of an elaborate celebration dinner at the Savoy Hotel on Wednesday, November 13, 1963. It was a timely tribute: he would produce only three more films for the company.

Hinds was the quiet man of Hammer. Before the war, he had spent a year at film school, with the intention of becoming a cameraman. After serving with the R.A.F., he had been persuaded to join Exclusive by his father: "He knew that if I was in the firm, his money would be secure." When he convinced Carreras to return to Down Place in 1951 on a permanent basis, Hinds never wanted to leave it again. "I was always for keeping us small," he said. "I didn't want to get big. I was probably frightened." (Hinds "knew his limitations"—and those of Hammer—in the opinion of Hugh Harlow.) When he returned to Hammer as producer (on *The Glass Cage*) after failing in his attempt to get union recognition, Hinds had been surprised to discover that his colleagues in the industry considered him to be among the most successful producers in the land (well before the company hit the big time). He was just as surprised to find them turned out in force to honor him at a dinner whose cost "exceeded my average picture budget!"[1]

Will Hinds had died in 1959 as a result of a freak cycling accident, and his will had virtually disinherited the rest of his family in favor of his youngest son, making Tony a man of "independent means" from that point on. While the flamboyant James Carreras put an increasingly public face on the company's activities, Hinds remained steadfastly in the background, inspiring, cajoling, and maintaining consistency in the product that his partner could sell so well. If Carreras was the showman, Anthony Hinds was exactly the opposite: introverted—insecure, even—modest to a fault. Like his father, he had little time for the clamor of show business. Unlike his partner, he had no time at all for the Variety Club and involved himself in its affairs "as little as possible." Always a very private individual, with interests far removed from the world of films, Hinds was well known and equally well respected. He was the power behind the throne, and *his* was the creative philosophy that Hammer had enshrined: to make films economically and effectively, only the *best* people were good enough. But all that was about to change.

Before James Carreras elected to reestablish Hammer's Gothic credentials through the dependable channel of *The Evil of Franken-stein* in the summer of 1963, Tony Hinds had sought inspiration from the mail that had arrived after the company's public plea for help.

One submission had shown promise, and when Hinds was diverted to Hammer's third Frankenstein instead, he had asked its author, John Llewellyn Devine, to flesh out his story in script form. He then engaged John Gilling, who was fresh from writing a new costume romp, *The Scarlet Blade*, to give the screenplay a more professional glaze. The Gilling draft made extensive changes in characterization and construction, though most of the essential action remained the same. It also opted to call the piece by another name: *Supernatural*. With one eye on an already-squeezed budget, Hinds was less than impressed with the result, and under the baleful influence of John Elder, he reverted the Gilling script to the shape and title of Devine's original for the film that was to follow *The Evil of Frankenstein* into Bray. Gilling kept his credit, but he vehemently disowned any responsibility for the only Hammer horror ever to reach the screen via such a route—*The Gorgon*.

> "Overshadowing the village of Vandorf stands the Castle Borski. From the turn of the century a monster from an ancient age of history came to live here, no living thing survived and the specter of death hovered in waiting for her next victim."
>
> —Screen caption
> *The Gorgon*

This imbroglio over *The Gorgon* would inadvertently turn out to be the last act of Tony Hinds's stewardship of Hammer Horror, as the executive gap left by Michael's departure became an increasing irritation in James Carreras's busy schedule. From this film on, Tony Nelson Keys would take over the producer's chair, and Hinds would effectively retire from studio life to take up the very desk job that he had declined almost ten years before. It would be the end of an era, both for Hammer and for Hinds, but he had set the standard that others would now be required to follow, and his influence would be enduring. The vision of the tremulous damsel, bosom heaving expectantly as she waits in the warning shadows of the baroque baronial hall hung with "yards and yards of red plush" (in Ken Hyman's words), would be the legacy of Anthony Hinds to the cinema of the macabre. "I set the *tone* for the Gothic Hammers—Jimmy Sangster and I," is Hinds's own appraisal of his contribution. "There was nobody else involved. Nobody else had anything to do with it."

Tony Keys was a first-class pupil, however. He had been in the business from way back, along with his brothers Basil Keys (an occasional associate producer for Hammer) and director-screen-writer-artist-novelist John Paddy Carstairs. Tony himself had worked on *Pandora and the Flying Dutchman* (1951), *Albert R.N.* (1953), and *The Sea Shall Not Have Them* (1954), among others, and he had breezed in and out of Hammer on an irregular basis before being persuaded to join the company full-time in 1957. Smooth and unflappable, he was epitomized by Dennison Thornton in one of his "potted" biographies: "Sandy-haired, fast-talking and immaculately *Saville-Rowed*"—although a more acid judgment was delivered by John Gilling: "He was an efficient hatchet-man." Tony Keys had exerted considerable influence at Hammer (his hand had been there to steady the tiller on Michael's second accredited film as producer, *Never Look Back*), and it was he who had brought Bernard Robinson and Jack Asher into the fold. He ran Bray Studios with thoroughgoing professionalism, but he had still found time to personally produce Hammer's excursions onto the high seas and into the English Civil War (two of which had been with Gilling as director). His slick diplomacy in the field was now to ensure that the remainder of Gilling's work for the company would be a good deal more trouble free than his participation in *The Gorgon* had been.

When his son is the latest in a long line of victims to be discovered dead near Castle Borski, Professor Heitz decides to investigate. He visits the castle, only to find himself staring into the face of the Gorgon—Megaera. Heitz manages to send for his other son, Paul, before turning to stone. Paul asks for help from Professor Meister, who suspects Professor Namaroff and his assistant, Carla, of complicity in the deaths. Paul becomes attracted to Carla, but she seems strangely troubled and is watched over by Namaroff, who believes that the spirit of the Gorgon possesses her on nights of the full moon. Against Meister's advice, Paul ventures to the castle to learn the truth. He is confronted by Namaroff, sword in hand, and they duel. Suddenly, the Gorgon appears and Namaroff is petrified by her gaze.

*Paul catches sight of the monster, just before Meister decapitates her.
As Paul also turns to stone, he watches Megaera's features become
those of Carla once more.*

With *The Earth Dies Screaming* and *The Horror of It All* happily
behind him, *The Gorgon* had been Terence Fisher's welcome back
to Hammer Horror. And with Peter Cushing and Christopher Lee
joining him on the floor at Bray to complete the lineup, it was much
like old times. Too much like old times, as it transpired.

The attraction of the original story for Hinds had been the
narrow confine in which the action was required to unfold. His
distaste of Gilling's script was for exactly the opposite reason. But
Gilling was a natural filmmaker, and he had expanded the original
to make it more *cinematic*. Devine's script, while able, had betrayed
an amateur disregard for montage—a trait it shared with the
screenwritings of John Elder; Hinds the writer could never quite
escape the clutches of Hinds the producer, and his screenplays
were invariably written with the twin dictates of speed and efficiency very much in mind. With *The Gorgon* would come the first
signs that this approach was growing staid and repetitive.

Previously, the films had always convinced by design that more
money had been expended on them than was ever the case. Now
the opposite seemed to be true. Though it would be released less
than five months after *The Evil of Frankenstein*, *The Gorgon* opens on
a glass shot that had just done service in its predecessor (an
economy already dangerously reminiscent of the overuse of stock
shots in Corman's Poe series), exteriors are self-evidently *interiors*,
and the action is typically restricted to interchanges between sundry village habitats and the weird castle on the hill.[2]

The Gorgon was a brave attempt at an original monster in the
tradition of Baron Meinster, Massie's Hyde, or Doctor Ravna, but
in its tale of a pagan demon pitted against Christian science, none
of the obvious possibilities are explored. The film as a whole is stiff,
slow, and devoid of any excitement (bar the final *Prisoner of Zenda*-
style confrontation between Namaroff and Paul Heitz), and the
banality of entrapping the Gorgon Megaera within the constraints
of a flat, one-dimensional melodrama quite saps the potential. It is
The Curse of the Werewolf in drag, since the plot requires nothing
more of its protagonist than that her spirit should reside in Barbara
Shelley at times of the full moon; in a further confusion, this

intrigue of possession is played as a mystery, but since there is only one female among the leading members of the cast, guessing whodunnit is hardly a challenge.

Shelley is majestic—even serene at times—but she completely lacks the enigmatic quality required of the role. She is too modern a miss, and yet Alfred Shaugnessy had extracted just such an ethereal air of other-worldliness from her in his *Cat Girl* (1957). As her serpentine alter ego, Prudence Hyman (an extra in *The Two Faces of Dr. Jekyll*) comes on more like Kiwi Kingston in the preceding opus.

The sort of budgetary concerns that were exemplified by the treatment meted out to Gilling's script were never so misplaced as in the attitude taken to the monster in this film. On the use of *two* actresses to play the role of the Gorgon, Tony Keys was diplomatic. "No matter how well Barbara Shelley was made up, she might still have been recognizable."[3] The truth was simpler: it was a saving in *time*. (With the two, scenes could be shot concurrently.) But cost-effectiveness did not stop there. The Gorgon head is a construct of stupefying ineptitude. Roy Ashton's mask (with help from Richard Mills on this occasion) contributes little enough to the mood, but the wig is worse than useless, showing all too clearly exactly what it was composed of: toy snakes. Effects artist Syd Pearson was quoted in *Kine Weekly* during production as saying, "I'm going to use artificial snakes and they're going to writhe, spit, and strike; they will be remotely controlled."

Against this, Michael Reed's color photography is exemplary, indistinguishable from the best work of Jack Asher, and the production design is similarly excellent. The project undoubtedly looked good on paper, but it is a static tableau in the flesh. And not only the characters were calcifying. *The Gorgon* was a tale of the supernatural as Gilling had decreed, yet in Fisher's uninvolving and prosaic style, not a modicum of imagination is in play in scenes that attempt to depict the unearthly. The thrill was gone. By this time, Hammer's horrors were widely perceived to be rooted in a reality of sorts; it was not Cushing and Lee (as villain and hero here) who were playing against type, it was Terence Fisher. Ironically, it would fall to John Gilling to reverse the trend to mortification that so imbued *The Gorgon* and fan the Gothic flame into life again entirely on his own account.

"Herbert Spencer once said that every myth and legend known to mankind is not without its authentic foundation."

—Dr. Namaroff
The Gorgon

Myths and legends were precisely what Hammer now had in mind, and this time, neither Terence Fisher nor Tony Hinds were to figure prominently in the strategy.

Michael Carreras's absence had turned out to be coincident with a period of treading water for the company. When production on *The Gorgon* was complete in January 1964, Bray closed its doors for another bout of overdue renovation, but in the eighteen months that had passed between the release of *The Phantom of the Opera* and that of *The Kiss of the Vampire*, a new teenage audience had burst onto the scene that was turning out by the tens of thousands for a first U.K. tour by a group who called themselves The Rolling Stones. *The Kiss of the Vampire* (which would open on January 17, the week after Robert Wise's much-vaunted but fundamentally unsound *The Haunting*, from Shirley Jackson's *The Haunting Of Hill House*) was to benefit from the fallout, but over at Capricorn, it was what had created this explosion in the first place that would be of more interest.

Prodigal Productions

Dad's gone down the dog-track,
Muvver's playing bingo,
Grannie's boozin' up the corner,
You wanna see the gin go,
No one seems to notice me,
Isn't it a sin,
What a crazy world we're living in…

Alan Klein
"What a Crazy World"

The project that *was* to have inaugurated Capricorn Productions was originally purchased for Hammer. Michael Carreras had bought *The Whites Grew Pale* (a drama of racial intolerance set in the Dutch East Indies) from first-time author Hugo Lous, with the intention that Peter Newman should turn it into a play, a novel, and ultimately a film, in the fashion of *Yesterday's Enemy*. Michael's growing awareness that he would never be allowed to produce such a story at Hammer had persuaded him to transfer the rights to his own company in December 1960. But fears over the existing relationship between Hammer and Columbia Pictures had inspired the tyro outfit to adopt a more cautious policy of producing only "short and second feature films" initially, and although Newman had written his play, neither novel nor film were to make it off the drawing board.

Michael's defection to Capricorn had lasted for just over two years. First, he directed *El Tierra Brutale (The San Siado Killings)* under the umbrella of a Spanish coproduction partly financed through Lawrence Bachmann, author of *The Phoenix* but now an executive at M-G-M. Then he cowrote, produced, and directed a street musical based on Alan Klein's stage play *What a Crazy World* on a meager budget of £98,000 (through the good offices of ABC's Bill Cartlidge, whose son occasionally acted as an assistant director for Hammer). The western had been shot in Almeria, Spain, with Richard Basehart and Alex Nicol, and Metro's participation had necessitated a British producer in addition to José G. ("Pepé") Maesso, owner of the coproduction company, Tecisa. Michael had nominated Jimmy Sangster (now also a director of Capricorn) for the job, and Sangster had returned the favor by suggesting that Michael direct the psycho-thriller he had been preparing for Hammer: *Maniac*. Since Michael was in the general vicinity, his father had agreed—it saved on the air-fare. *El Tierra Brutale* was later retitled *The Savage Guns* by M-G-M and cobilled with the Steve Reeves starrer *The Thief of Baghdad*. A second western—*A Good Day For a Hanging*—was not even that lucky, and after eventually mounting *What a Crazy World*, Michael was out of options.

An approach to Anglo's Nat Cohen had drawn a blank for fear of offending friend and fellow Variety Clubber James Carreras, and a sex comedy called *Love in Smokey Regions*, announced for a December 1962 start, had also gone the way of all flesh. In its place had come the opportunity to spend a year in Kenya on preproduction of a 36-part series for Screen Gems: *The Last Frontier*. The project had initially promised much, but that, too, was stillborn, and by December 1963, Michael had found himself in the shadow of Hammer again, contemplating an uncertain dawn.

"You can't run away from the curse of the mummy's tomb. We're all doomed to die for this act of desecration."

—Hashmi
The Curse of the Mummy's Tomb

Michael's thirty months in the wilderness had produced one film disposed of as a second feature, another awaiting release, and *Maniac*—a hand-me-down that had been used to lay a ghost from Columbia's past: *The Damned* collected some critical kudos, but the pairing failed to pay its way—*Maniac*'s thunder (though there was precious little of it) had been stolen by the earlier release of the much-hyped *Whatever Happened to Baby Jane*, produced by Ken Hyman at 7-Arts. But the bottom, in any event, had begun to drop out of so-called realistic horror in favor of what the pundits at *Films and Filming* were calling the "tuppence-colored variety," which now seemed to them to be "catching its second wind." Michael decided to be pragmatic. Having been invited to do so by Tony Hinds, he renewed his reluctant association with Hammer by agreeing to direct, produce, *and* write another *Mummy* (with a little help from director Alvin Rakoff), to provide a backup feature for *The Gorgon*.

As 1964 got underway, Hammer appended the following to its roster for future production: *Hysteria*, *The Fanatic*, *Disciple of Dracula*, *Secret of Blood Island*, and now Michael's *Curse of the Mummy's Tomb*. (For 1965, there was to be *The Zombie* and *The Reptiles*, as well.)

While associate producer Bill Hill consented to undertake the actual production in return for a bonus payment and a crate of champagne, Michael concentrated on cowriting a tongue-in-cheek reprise of old-style Hammer Horror. Unable to resist at least a token display of defiance, he gnawed playfully at the hand that had fed him by fulfilling the task under the pen name of Henry *Younger*, a thinly veiled pastiche of Hinds's own pen name. When the film went onto the floor at Elstree on February 24, another teen musical was shooting at Pinewood under the quirky direction of Richard Lester: *Beatlemania*. On release, its title would be changed to *A Hard Day's Night*, which is just what Michael Carreras had experienced in his fleeting pursuit of independence.

> *An archaeological expedition has uncovered the sarcophagus of*
> *Ra-Antef, which American showman Alexander King intends to put*
> *on exhibition to a paying public. On the opening night, the mum-*
> *miform coffin is found to be empty. Soon, those involved start to fall*
> *victim to the vengeance of a living mummy, who appears to be*
> *enacting the curse of the pharaohs in search of the pieces of a*
> *medallion inscribed with the secrets of life and death. The mysterious*
> *Adam Beauchamp is also after the medallion, and it transpires that*
> *he is actually Be, brother of the mummy and himself cursed to eternal*
> *life. Having restored the medallion, Adam kidnaps Annette Dubois,*
> *daughter of one of the archaeologists; he intends that she should share*
> *his immortality. The mummy will not strike the fatal blow, however,*
> *and when Adam makes for the sewers with Annette, Ra-Antef brings*
> *the roof down on himself and his brother, and Annette is enabled to*
> *escape into the arms of her fiancé.*

The mixture of laughs and thrills that stamps *The Curse of the Mummy's Tomb* may be an uneasy coalition, but at least it attempted to keep pace with recent changes in taste, and the film seemed to have its finger more firmly on the pulse than did *The Gorgon*. "Hand it to Hammer...They've got this kind of scarey hokum down to a grisly art," praised *The Daily Cinema*. "The blood looks redder, the decor weirder, the cobwebs older, the corners darker, the screams sound richer in a Hammer job." As with *Maniac*, Michael's direction is assured, if not particularly distinctive. His was a hand versed in cinema, and there are some neat Hitchcockian touches in the film, though the surprise climax is telegraphed to a degree by the casting of Terence Morgan, an actor best known for his role as the sadistic stepfather in *The Scamp* (1957). Morgan's career was in decline and he was grateful for the opportunity, but Burmese-born female lead Jeanne Roland, who had already suffered the indignity of a change of name from her own Jean Rollins, was to find herself revoiced as well, before production was complete (as had Rhode-sian-born Norma Marla in *The Two Faces of Dr. Jekyll*).

Even with the now-familiar Carreras use of Techniscope, the restrictions imposed by a budget of £103,000 (as opposed to the £190,000 allocated to the Beatles' film, for instance) gave *The Curse of the Mummy's Tomb* a certain disposable air, and not simply because of Dickie Owen's patched-up mummy suit. The reuse of Franz Reizenstein's score from the first film had been decided on to save commissioning a new one, rather than to foster any notions of series identity. But if it appeared to be a lightweight piece, a more heavyweight version *had* been intended.

Michael had received the censor's instructions via Tony Hinds. Despite the relatively innocuous nature of the material, there were still three pages of comments. Strong objections had been raised to all scenes depicting the severing of hands, and much that had previously been allowed in Hammer's horrors was called into question now, such as the graphic throttling of King and the breaking of Sir Giles Dalrymple's back (softened to a bludgeoning in the film). This was recognized as par for the course, though Hinds's attitude remained little changed. Eight minor deletions were advised, but as to the rest, "I should take a chance, if I were you," Hinds suggested.

"If money is the yardstick, then I fear for the future…"

—Sir Giles Dalrymple
The Curse of the Mummy's Tomb

Michael's reappearance on Hammer stages did not mean the end of Capricorn, as reviews for *What a Crazy World* (which had also opened in January 1964) were to ensure. "One of the best British teenage musicals yet" was typical, and even Peter Cushing was moved to send a missive of congratulation to the man behind the film. "If you'd been given the budget to make it in color, it would have beaten *West Side Story*," Cushing enthused (*West Side Story* had gone on general release the same month). Another Klein idea, *Grab Me a Gondola*, was planned in the afterburn, this time with the Venice Film Festival acting as a backdrop, but that went adrift. With *The Whites Grew Pale* and other key projects also abandoned due to a lack of interest, Michael finally capitulated and constructed a horror of his own: *The Werewolf of Moravia*.

Begun as *Lady Bathory* (from a folk tale that Hammer itself would embrace in 1971), and again intended as a Spanish coproduction venture, the project was offered to James Carreras for Hammer to produce. Carreras turned it down and the idea came to nought, though three more years would be expended in the attempt to turn it into celluloid. (Peter Cushing had agreed to participate, provided the film could be shot in Wales. "Wales is not in Spain," Michael had to inform him.) Not that Capricorn was to forget about The

Rolling Stones, either. *No One...No where...Nothing* was written especially for them in June 1965, but by February of the following year, Stones' agent Tito Burns would turn that down, also.

The prospect of bringing Peter O'Donnell's cartoon heroine *Modesty Blaise* to the screen, announced on completion of *The Curse of the Mummy's Tomb*, was to prove similarly elusive (the film would eventually be made by Joseph Losey). And by the summer of 1964, Michael was in the arms of Hammer once more, consoling himself with a new blue Maserati 305GT Berlinetta and pleased to be tossed the first of what were to be two tasty morsels from Ken Hyman's table at 7-Arts: *She.*

Originally intended for Universal, *She* had landed on Tony Hinds's desk the previous year with the promise of 7-Arts participation if Hammer decided to proceed. Hinds had assigned both the scriptwriting and producing duties to John Temple-Smith, in the hope of an epic adventure with broad appeal. But Temple-Smith's script (which was dark, violent, and true to the Rider Haggard novel) had left Universal cold. They preferred the long-overdue sequel to *The Camp on Blood Island*, if anything[4]. Hinds tried again with crime writer Berkely Mather, but with a similar result, and promptly caught the same chill in sympathy. The project was then passed on to Michael, who turned to David Chantler. (Chantler had coscripted *Cash on Demand*.) This time, adventure would be to the fore and M-G-M would be to the back of it, courtesy of an existing arrangement with 7-Arts—and smack in the middle was the *Honey*ed allure of Ursula Andress, fresh from the clutches of *Dr. No.*

Hammer had made its last film for Universal, but Metro's involvement would bring about a tripling of the customary budget and, at £312,000, *She* would become the company's most expensive production ever. *She* moved into M-G-M-Elstree Studios on September 7, 1964, after two weeks of location filming in Israel. For Hammer, about to shut Bray for yet another extensive period of renovation, it was to be the beginning of a whole new ball game.

By 1965, ABC was having difficulty placing all the "X" films waiting for release, and producers were looking for gimmick subjects—preferably with international appeal. The newly formed Amicus Productions of Rosenberg and Subotsky had already found one in *Dr. Terror's House of Horrors*, a palliative portmanteau piece that had harnessed the talents of Cushing, Lee, Francis, and others so effectively that its success at the box office inspired the company to repeat the formula (not to mention the actors and technicians), almost without variation, for many years to come.

Hammer's most recent offering, on the other hand, had been *Fanatic*, a half-hearted exercise in camp *guignol* (from Anne Blaisdell's novel *Nightmare*) that had been designed to bring silent star Tallulah Bankhead out of an 11-year retirement. As *Fanatic* went into release on March 21, Seth Holt took charge of Bette Davis for *The Nanny*, in another attempt to revive the flagging psycho-thriller sub-genre. But it was to no better effect. "The characters and atmosphere are as lifeless as the corpse in the bathwater," Allen Eyles would comment.

During Hammer's eighteen-month absence from the field, the Gothic gap had been plugged by imitators many and various. In addition to AIP's Poe series (and in answer to *Psycho*), there had been the more psychologically based Italian sex-and-sadism romps of Bava and Riccardo Freda (*The Terror of Dr. Hichcock* [aka *The Horrible Dr. Hichcock*; 1962], *Night Is the Phantom* [aka *What!*; 1963]), Compton's *The Black Torment* (1963), and an American outing, *Curse of the Living Corpse* (1963). Amicus had now established itself as a potential rival, and Tigon was about to follow. And both would produce films with so many of the same faces on *both* sides of the camera that they would soon become indistinguishable from the Hammer product.

In the meantime, Christopher Lee's flirtation with the Swiss Alps had turned out to be not quite the idyll that he had imagined. "The mountains got closer every day...It could be quite claustrophobic, beautiful as it was." After three years in solitary, during which time, only the occasional excursion to appear in *The Devil Ship Pirates*, *The Gorgon*, or *She* could be countenanced under British tax law, he decided that the price of income-tax avoidance was too high. His return from self-imposed exile opened a window of opportunity for Hammer to combat the increasing threat from competition, and the prospect of a fourth Dracula—one that would actually feature the count himself—was now not only possible, but *vital*.

"I had misgivings about it, because of the screenplay," Lee said of the offer for him to reprise the role. But with the assurance of a second, more substantial, star part included in the package to help offset any suggestion of a reversion to type, he agreed to revisit the scene of his greatest triumph in what was to become *Dracula— Prince of Darkness*—"although this will probably be the last time," he told *Films and Filming*'s Robin Bean. Hammer now required a vehicle of sufficient *gravitas* to honor their commitment to Lee, and an idea that had been put forward to Tony Hinds by actor George Woodbridge was pressed into service. Prince Felix Yusoupoff's *I Killed Rasputin* would form the basis of the supplementary film and, despite the specter of litigation that had plagued an earlier version of the same story, *The Mad Monk* was also sanctioned for production.

> "After a reign of hideous terror spanning more than a century, the King of the Undead was finally traced to his lair, high in the Carpathian mountains.
> "Thousands had been enslaved by the obscene cult of vampirism—now, the fountainhead himself perished. Only the memory remained—the memory of the most evil and terrible creature who ever set his seal on civilization..."

—Opening narration
Dracula—Prince of Darkness

When Bray reopened in April 1965, Hammer had four features crammed into a mid-summer start. At the suggestion of Tony Keys, it was decided to shoot them all back-to-back in two pairs of two, using many of the same cast and crew for each individual pair, and the same producer—Keys—for all four. Apart from helping to make up for lost time, there were considerable economies to be had. The films would be designed to benefit as much as possible from their commonalities, and participants on both sides of the camera would be hired for a single twelve-week stint.

The lion's share of the budget was to be allocated to the first of the four—*Dracula—Prince of Darkness*—where new sets would be constructed that could then be redressed to accommodate *The Mad Monk*. The principle would apply equally to the two supporting features: *The Zombie(s)* and *The Reptiles*. The main features were to be shot in scope by way of compensating for their thinner veneer, and all would ride on the back of the largest advertising campaign in the company's history.

With the delay in production of *Prince of Darkness* caused by the refurbishment, Peter Cushing was no longer available to reprise the character of Van Helsing, as originally planned. The role was rewritten as Father Sandor and given to Andrew Keir, with Cushing's appearance limited to a precredits replay of the finale from *Dracula*. The clip was released to television for promotional purposes, which helped imply that Cushing was actually in the film, and although the actor had waived any residual payment for his contribution, a grateful Hammer nevertheless picked up the check on some urgent repairs to his cottage at Whitstable.

Confusingly, *Prince of Darkness* had been announced to the trades as *The Disciple of Dracula*—the title of Jimmy Sangster's draft for *Brides*. In reality, it was the outline for *The Revenge of Dracula* (which had been intended as the sequel to the *original* film) that had been dusted down to act as a vehicle for Lee's encore as the count. This was overhauled by Hinds to accommodate Cushing's absence before being handed to Sangster to develop and bring up to a more appropriate length for the mid-sixties, but final screenplay credit would go to "John Sansom," the pseudonym that Sangster had already devised for just such jobbing work.

The Nanny had been the first of six films to be produced as part of a fourway concordat between Hammer, old ally 7-Arts, 20th Century Fox, and ABPC—which was to handle U.K. rights through its distribution affiliate, Warner-Pathé (Warners held 37.5 percent of ABPC). The quartet that was to begin on April 26, 1965, with *Dracula—Prince of Darkness* would now form the next four.

With Fox/7-Arts had come a harder-sell approach to advertising and the notion of corporate-identity marketing. From this point on, Hammer was literally to become the "House of Horror," as a first step toward product merchandising (soon to be more fully explored in two "horror omnibuses" published in association with Pan Books). The filming of *Prince of Darkness* would be something of a "media event," as a result. Interested parties (and there were many) were welcomed to Bray, to watch the shoot and tour the sets, with Tony Keys acting as genial host. No stranger to the virtue of publicity, Hammer now courted it as never before on behalf of a film that it confidently expected would be one of its biggest money-spinners since the original feature.

> *1895. On a trip to the Carpathians, two English couples find themselves stranded at an eerie castle, where they are greeted by Klove and offered shelter. In the night, Alan Kent investigates the activities of the mysterious manservant and is stabbed to death by Klove. Klove suspends the body above a coffin and slits Alan's throat; the blood spills on the ashes within, and reconstitutes Count Dracula! The next day, Charles Kent and his wife, Diana, go in search of the others. Charles finds Alan's dismembered body and Diana is confronted by Alan's wife, Helen, who is now a vampire. Charles is attacked by Dracula, but he manages to outwit the count and escape with Diana to a nearby monastery. Klove arrives, bringing Dracula and Helen. Helen is captured and put to the stake by Father Sandor, but Dracula kidnaps Diana and is driven back to the castle by Klove. Charles and Sandor set off in pursuit. Klove is shot, and Dracula's coffin slips from the carriage onto the icy moat; he awakes and seizes Charles. Sandor fires at the ice, cracking it. Charles is freed as the ice gives way, and the count is consigned to the moat—destroyed by running water.*

The best thing about *Dracula—Prince of Darkness* is the prologue, which is merely a replay of the climax of the first film, enclosed in a swirling mist to mask its different aspect ratio on the scope screen.[5] Be that as it may, there *were* some shudders in store. And even a graphic decapitation in its running mate was not sufficient to prepare the unsuspecting viewer for what was to follow from the main feature, as Klove first murders Alan Kent, then suspends him upside-down over Dracula's coffin before slashing his throat open with a knife, to shower the contents with his blood!

This ritual slaying was considered shocking enough in critical circles for it to prompt echoes of the outrage that had greeted *Dracula*, and Hammer was duly condemned for pandering to the worst possible taste, despite the censor having reduced the flow of blood by the removal of some intermediate shots. But audiences would think otherwise—as far as they were concerned, Dracula's resurrection amid a welter of gore was thoroughly appropriate.

Close on fifty minutes of *Dracula—Prince of Darkness* elapse before the count makes his appearance, and when he does—his hand scuttling, spider-like, from out of a seething mass of reconstituting flesh—it is in a significantly altered form. Entirely deprived of the power of speech (at Hinds's insistence, after complaints from Lee over the quality of Dracula's dialog), and subject to a depend-ence on the ministrations of his manservant, Dracula is no longer a man, but merely the *shell* of his earlier self. With all trace of his erstwhile humanity having apparently been lost somewhere on the floor of the throne room after the close of the first film, he is little more than an animate corpse, completely in the thrall of the devil within. Here, the count is the very personification of evil—an "abhuman entity" (in Lee's words), more spirit than substance, though still capable of bouts of "tigerish ferocity" when the blood lust is upon him. It was a signal change for Hammer's archmonster, and it was not to last.

The attempt to reconstruct the count is only partially successful. Any proper metaphysical interpretation would have required to lean in part on sympathetic special effects, and Hammer's aversion to expensive opticals is instrumental in undercutting the concept. Lee's Dracula is too clearly a man (as Hammer precedent intended), and his lack of speech diminishes rather than enhances the strength of his portrayal. It was a valiant effort, nonetheless, and it was aided by whatever means Fisher could put at its disposal: Dracula's entrance is unexpectedly low key, his gaunt face alone appearing in shot, framed in a sea of shadows. Cinematographer Michael Reed does his bit, altering the lighting in the main hall during the count's more explosive second entrance, to bathe everything in a deep red glow. Anachronistic it may be, but it adds a modicum of crude atmosphere and helps lessen the culture shock of the pantomimic red lining that Hammer now saw fit to include in the cape of its demon-king.

Had Dracula's encore taken place as intended, some eighteen months after his first bow, it might have had a more meaningful appeal. All the familiar ingredients are in place. Unwary travelers arrive at the castle to be confronted by the vampire; on home ground, the "family" is subjected to a sustained assault; a *savant* steps in to save the day by pursuing the count to his lair and destroying him. Even *motifs* from the first film are reintroduced to satisfy the expectations of an audience keen to sup of the same wine for a second time: Dracula's ferocious appearance on the balcony and his attack on Charles; his stride across the castle drawbridge; the staking of Helen; the hot-pursuit chase at the climax. There is some evident padding for length (as when Charles and Diana, having failed to find their companions, inexplicably leave the castle—only to return to it some minutes later to continue the search). But in all other respects, *Dracula—Prince of Darkness* is the archetypal cloned sequel.

With the intervention of the best part of a decade between the two films, what once might have been *superior* to the original now seemed to be a poor imitation of it. The breadth of imagination that had been brought to Hammer's first sequel—*The Revenge of Frankenstein*—can still be sensed, but in paring down the film to its bare essentials for economy's sake and filming it out of time, it emerged as a pale shadow of its former self. Had it been produced seven years earlier, *Dracula—Prince of Darkness* would have been powerful, indeed; now, it was just a colorful confetti of memories.

> "If you wish to see the destruction of the horror spawned by Count Dracula, come with me.... But I warn you—it is not a sight for the squeamish!"
>
> — Father Sandor
> *Dracula—Prince of Darkness*

Apparently it was. A cut eliminated the close-up of the stake being driven home, which was covered by a reaction shot, as per the original film. But it did not end there. Most of the intended violence had been softened up at the script stage—the *decapitation* of Alan and the subsequent casting aside of his head refused "on grounds of disgust" by the BBFC—but Hinds had gone back to Stoker for a later scene: "With that he pulled open his shirt, and with his long sharp nails opened a vein in his breast. When the blood began to spurt out, he took my hands in one of his, holding them tight, and with the other seized my neck and pressed my mouth to the wound, so that I must suffocate or swallow some of the—Oh, my God, my God!—what have I done?" Committed a symbolic act of fellatio, according to the Freudians. The British print stopped short of making it overt, though Fisher's direction and Lee's expression as he draws Suzan Farmer to within a nose of the drawn blood see to it that the implication is unmistakable. Trevelyan had seen to it that the action was truncated before Dracula so much as laid his hands on the girl's shoulders.

The sex *was* overt in *The Mad Monk*, but it was also less effective. Barbara Shelley's cool detachment clung to her stubbornly, even though her ermine robe did not, thanks to the rough-house attentions of the charismatic holy man from Tobolsk province, and

Suzan Farmer's wide-eyed vulnerability was never even threatened on this occasion, symbolically or otherwise.

"Look deep into my eyes...and think only of me."
— Rasputin
Rasputin—The Mad Monk

Rasputin was Lee's prize for agreeing to reprise the role of the count (additional to the small percentage of the producers' gross that he had secured from both—"two or three thousand pounds," he would calculate). While Fox/7-Arts were looking the other way, *Dracula*'s sets were quickly redressed to represent the avenues and alleyways of Tsarist Russia, stomping ground of *The Mad Monk.*

For the first time in five years, Hammer was taking on a subject with literary pedigree *and* a cinematic antecedent—M-G-M's *Rasputin and the Empress*, which had been made in 1932 as a vehicle for the Barrymores, and was released in Britain as *Rasputin—The Mad Monk.* The original production had been a lengthy and detailed affair, but since this new version was to be Hammer Horror, the spectacle was waived in favor of "some incidents" from Rasputin's life, intended to act as a preamble to the *raison d'être* of the piece— the protracted murder of said "monk" at the climax.

Rasputin and the Empress had been landed with a $1 million lawsuit (which it lost) as a result of the liberties that it had taken with the historical record, but Hinds had been careful to avoid any repeat performance. "We had to get the okay from Rasputin's murderer," he explained. Yusoupoff personally sanctioned the script by signing each and every page! Just to make sure that they were all in the clear, both Lee and *The Mad Monk's* director, Don Sharp, were at pains to point out in interviews that Hammer's film was really nothing more than "an entertainment."

Apologies were in order. As a biography of Rasputin's rise to power and influence in the Russia of the Romanoffs, the film was certainly nothing more than a retread of a saucy Italian romp called *The Nights of Rasputin* (1962), which had starred Edmund Purdom and been co-billed three years previously with *Corridors of Blood* (aka *The Doctor of Seven Dials*). This spin-off from the cycle of epics that had enjoyed brief popularity in the years following *Hercules Unchained* had featured a larger cast, more sexual shennanigans, and depicted its set piece murder with as much brutality as the Hammer film—but so did M-G-M's version, thirty years before it.

> Renegade monk Grigori Rasputin arrives at St. Petersburg and inveigles himself into the court of the Tsarina via an affair with Sonia, her lady-in-waiting. Sonia helps in contriving an accident to the young Tsarevitch in order that Rasputin can restore the boy to health; in return, the Tsarina ensures him wealth and power. Now tiring of Sonia, Rasputin wills her to kill herself. She does. In revenge, Sonia's brother Peter determines to kill Rasputin, but a fight between the two ends with Peter disfigured by acid. Peter's friend, Ivan, now conspires with Dr. Zargo to assassinate the monk. On the promise of a night with Ivan's sister, Rasputin arrives at the palace, where he is fed poisoned chocolates. When this fails, the doctor plunges a hypodermic syringe into him. The monk refuses to submit and stabs Zargo; he then attacks Ivan. Dying, Zargo topples Rasputin from the parapet and he falls to his death on the frozen river below.

The Mad Monk is a thoroughly functional piece, devised to serve a single end. John Elder's script supplies much incident but little thrill, and whatever sense of period it attempts to evoke is swamped by garish Technicolor and exposed by threadbare set design and the clear need for the occasional stock shot. Direction and playing are wholly without subtlety, and only a single lap dissolve sequence of Rasputin staring out over St. Petersburg (a simple diorama of rooftops) from a snow-speckled window contrives to show what might have been. With even the murder scene deprived of some of its action to meet the running-time requirements and bring the ill-considered proceedings to an abrupt end, the sole attraction of what was also released as *Rasputin—The Mad Monk* would be Christopher Lee's virtuoso performance in a role that had been designed specifically for him and which he unsurprisingly heralded as "probably my best screen part to date."

"Someone in this village is practising witchcraft..."

— Sir James Forbes
The Plague of the Zombies

While Rasputin lay dying on the same ice-floe that had just put an end to Dracula, the back lot at Bray had been magically transformed into a Cornish Everytown for the next set of features, now refined as *The Plague of the Zombies* and *The Reptile*.

If the first two films had belonged to Christopher Lee, the second two were to belong to John Gilling. The 53-year-old writer-director had done competent journeyman work for Hammer since the very beginning, including *Room to Let*. He was never allocated much of substance, outside of all-action costume dramas, and his career had peaked in the early sixties, with *Fury at Smugglers Bay* (which had starred Peter Cushing) and Hammer's own *The Pirates of Blood River* (both 1961). He was a robust character and much feared for his abrasive approach on the set. First assistant Douglas Hermes had walked off *The Scarlet Blade* because of a row with him, and on *The Pirates of Blood River*, he had fired a whole stunt crew for refusing to perform a particular fall. Gilling was renowned for having a "short fuse" and made few friends in the ranks, but Michael Ripper was one of them, as was Oliver Reed. "People loathed John, because they said he was a bully," Reed explains. "He was brash—gruff....But I liked him."

John Gilling did *not* like Tony Hinds, however—or his "abysmal" screenplays. "I don't think he was a very subscriptional member of the triad," he said of him, in relation to James and Michael Carreras. (Hinds had made the mistake of joking at the director's expense, to the effect that he would "shoot himself into a corner" from which "John Elder" invariably had to provide the means of escape. Unfortunately, Gilling had no sense of humor.) But he *did* profess a liking for Michael (though he would change his mind. "He was wounded rather savagely in the forehead during the war," Reed adds—which might have had something to do with it), and he had a healthy regard for the "salesmanship, showmanship and drive" of James Carreras and the *ad hoc* nature of the Hammer set-up generally, so the idea of shooting "back-to-back" appealed to his inprovisational nature. Being offered *The Reptile* also appealed to his Liverpudlian sense of natural justice.

Gilling had accepted the Cornish duo, provided he could rewrite the scripts as he pleased. *The Plague of the Zombies* was filmed almost word for word from a Peter Bryan screenplay, but John Elder's *The Reptile* was considerably revised on the floor—*The Gorgon* was avenged!

> *A call for help finds Sir James Forbes and his daughter Sylvia*
> *visiting Peter Tompson in a Cornish village. The doctor explains that*
> *the village is plagued by inexplicable deaths. Forbes suggests that*
> *they disinter a body for examination, but the grave is empty. When*
> *Tompson's wife is found dead, Forbes suspects witchcraft. As they*
> *watch over the grave, she rises from her coffin: a zombie! Forbes*
> *decapitates her. The other graves are empty, too. Forbes discovers*
> *that the village Squire has spent time in Haiti. He breaks into Squire*
> *Hamilton's house, but is caught; during the struggle, he sets the*
> *house on fire. In an altar room deep inside an old mineshaft, Hamil-*
> *ton is now preparing to sacrifice Sylvia. As their waxen effigies are*
> *consumed by the fire, the zombies burst into flames and begin to run*
> *amok. Forbes and Tompson rescue Sylvia, and all three flee the blaze*
> *as the squire falls victim to the enraged zombies.*

In *The Plague of the Zombies,* Gilling confined his alterations to
the staging. True to form, he enlarged on the *dynamic* of a number
of scenes—the dislodging of the coffin into the riverbed; the fight
between Forbes and Denver in the Hamilton house; the casting
down of Alice's body by the zombie; the attack on the vicar. But he
would so embellish a nominal "nightmare-sequence" in the script
(an idea pinched from Corman) that it has since become a classic
in its own right.

The central set piece of *The Plague of the Zombies* is a model of its
kind. Gilling builds superbly from a midnight exhumation to the
slow dissolve transformation of Alice's disinterred corpse into
ravening zombie; the walking dead girl is then dispatched by
having her head lopped off with a shovel (in a sequence that would
give the film "a deserved X" according to *Films and Filming*) and
her husband collapses in a faint. But there is more to come. Another
dissolve turns the screen a sickly green, and as James Bernard's
insistent rhythms intrude on the soundtrack, the graves open, one
by one, to give up their dead...Tompson awakes in shock cut, and
with a shriek of terror. So startling was the imagery of this sequence—and so all-embracing the iconography—that it was entirely to submerge the base theatrics of the melodrama that had
inspired it (despite its impact being muted by release to television
for promotional play). Not only was it to give *The Plague of the
Zombies* the stamp of a cult-classic—as well as anticipating the
seminal *Night of the Living Dead*—but it was to serve as a symbol of
Hammer Horror throughout the rest of the sixties, all by itself.

By such bravura tactics, *The Plague of the Zombies* manages to surmount a supporting cast that seems to have wandered in from the Windsor amateur dramatic society. Brook Williams consistently plays to the gallery (a failing made all the more conspicuous by the wry performance of André Morell), while Diane Clare might have been better hung from one, so ill-at-ease is she in a period role. Clare had come from the Fox-Lippert quickie *Witchcraft* (1964), and Don Sharp had coaxed a more natural performance out of her in modern dress (as well as using her own voice).

For reasons of cachet, Lee's (horror) star status, and the timely provision of Techniscope, *Dracula—Prince of Darkness* was made the A-side of the double bill with *Zombies*. It endowed the pair with a sense of anticlimax (though Hammer had the good sense to reverse polarity on the allocation of the aspect ratios, this time round—which it had not done with *The Gorgon* and *The Curse of the Mummy's Tomb*). *The Plague of the Zombies* was the better film— pacier, more exciting, more seat gripping in every way. Only a certain shoddiness in its execution resulting from the haste of its production subdued enthusiasm. Nevertheless, it contained enough of the stuff of nightmare to become a paragon of horror cinema—and in a film that was *not* directed by Fisher, written by Elder, or entrusted to Cushing or Lee. It was the work of most of Hammer's other talents, however, and proved beyond doubt that Hammer Horror was the product of *all* the people who functioned at Bray, not just a select few of them.[6]

If *The Plague of the Zombies* was a perfect example of synchronisity, *The Reptile* would smack a little too much of close harmony.

The Reptile was an unconscious borrowing from Bram Stoker's *The Lair Of The White Worm*, and once again, the cast would consist of friendly faces: Noel Willman and Jennifer Daniel, reunited from *The Kiss of the Vampire*, were to be joined by Jacqueline Pearce from *The Plague of the Zombies*, in addition to regulars like Ripper, Marne Maitland, George Woodbridge, and Charles Lloyd Pack—this in a film whose co-feature had included four of the leading players from *Dracula—Prince of Darkness* among *its* leading players! Even Oakley Court was becoming as familiar to audiences as to the actors who paraded its grounds. All might have been well, or at least better, were not greed to urge *all* four films onto an unsuspecting public within the same quarter of 1966.

The Reptile would be one Gothic too many. Hammer Horror was becoming as predictable as the *Carry On* comedies. But what can often be a virtue in comedy, is always a vice in more serious fare. Things were becoming *too* recognizable now, and if Hammer's films of the sixties were to be guilty of one thing above all else, then it would be the complete absence of any remaining element of surprise.

> *Harry Spalding[7] inherits a Cornish cottage on the sudden death of his brother. When local eccentric Mad Peter is attacked and killed nearby, Spalding and publican Tom Bailey disinter the bodies and find fang marks. Harry responds to a call for help from Anna, the daughter of a neighbor, Dr. Franklyn. On entering the house, Harry is attacked by a reptilian creature in the form of Anna, but with the face of a snake. He manages to stagger home and his wife, Valerie, lances the bite. While Harry is recovering, Valerie enters the house and sees Dr. Franklyn kill his Malay servant. An oil lamp is overturned, and the house catches fire. Franklyn seizes Valerie; he explains how Anna had been cursed by a Borneo snake cult and now turns into a reptile at periodic intervals. Anna appears and strikes down her father. As she closes on Valerie, Harry and Tom arrive and break a window; the cold has a fatal effect on the reptile, and Valerie is rescued from the inferno.*

With *The Reptile*, Gilling was not so fortunate. If the script for *The Plague of the Zombies* provided ample scope for visual invention, that of its companion piece offered the opposite. Hinds thought in theatrical mode, whereas Gilling's flair was fundamentally *filmic*. He was an instinctive director, and he worked best with a minimum of dialogue. The Elder script was verbose and undramatic, and Gilling had to cut a swathe through it. The climax in particular was tightened up. In its original form, *Harry* had thrown the Malay into the sulphur stream (only to see him pop out of it again later), and Franklyn had indulged in a longer explanation of Anna's predicament before leaving *both* the Spaldings locked in the house while he organized their demise. Gilling had Franklyn fight the Malay instead of Harry (who was left out of the action at this juncture) and added a fire to tie up the loose ends. But even reduced to its required 90 minutes, *The Reptile* seemed unduly labored, and had too many elements in common with the preceding film: midnight grave robbing, peculiar goings-on at the manor house, a

single sympathetic local (Ripper, in both cases), and the usual blaze
to usher in the *Kia-Ora*. The whole Cornish-village-harbors-a-dark-
secret scenario proved incapable of suspending audience disbelief
for a second time, and Keys's four-card trick was exposed as a
fraud. The Cornish duo had turned into the King's New Clothes.

What had begun as an economic master stroke was to end in
disenchantment for many of those involved. Bernard Robinson's
skill at disguising sets had been laid bare for all to see, and Roy
Ashton's expertise in the makeup chair had been unable to conceal
the ragged edge of corner cutting. "People with real talent will only
work at their best for so long," said Michael Carreras. "Here you
had people with real talent working for a man who was really
asking them just to work for the money." Hinds's opinion of the
exercise was much the same, however: "Sordid," he said later.

> "When I came here—ten—fifteen—was it twenty years ago?—it
> was a good place. People were kind and gentle...Then *they* came,
> bringing their vileness with them."

> —Mad Peter
> *The Reptile*

"In any business, there are artists and there are craftsmen. There
were more *artists* at Hammer than in any other film company that
I ever worked for," Michael Ripper considered. But there are limits
to what artists can do when accountants think they know better,
and by the middle of the sixties, the industry was already in the
hands of its accountants. The four films had been budgeted at
£402,000 in total, but as with all the best-laid schemes, the first two
had gone over by £21,000, despite cuts being implemented in *The
Mad Monk* to try to reduce the ongoing deficit. John Gilling had
ended up with the light side of the balance sheet, in any event, but
the second of *each* of the pairs had suffered disproportionalely as a
result—with *The Reptile* suffering the most. While it might be
obvious that the graveyard that divested itself of its dead in *The
Plague of the Zombies* also played host to the victims of *The Reptile*,
nothing could disguise the fact that the Winter Palace in *The Mad
Monk* had once been Castle Dracula either. In the Cornish duo, there
is evidence of a hastier shoot, but in *The Reptile* in particular, there
is a poorer script and some perfunctory makeup. It would be Roy

Ashton's last regular assignment for the company. Asked to maintain the speed of output and join the crew of Hammer's next flesh-and-fantasy epic immediately on completion of the Gilling film, Ashton bowed out, effectively putting the brakes on the increasingly hectic pace of his Hammer career.

Taking a leaf out of Joe Levine's book, the extensive campaign that was mounted to promote the first two Hammer releases of 1966 majored on peak-time television slots (with a specially shot "teaser"), bus fronts, and full-page newspaper ads. The gamble paid off. The pairing of *Dracula—Prince of Darkness* and *The Plague of the Zombies* was hugely successful. Anything that *Rasputin—the Mad Monk* and *The Reptile* brought in would only be icing on the cake. The money was to come in handy. Hammer was now in production with its so-called one-hundreth film, which at a cost of nearly half-a-million pounds all-in was proving to be its most expensive ever: *One Million Years BC*.

The first features to be produced at Bray since it had closed for refurbishment eleven months earlier were seen as a real return to form, a fact borne out by the eventual inclusion of *Dracula—Prince of Darkness* and *The Plague of the Zombies* in the Top 15 money-earners of 1966. The hype had done the trick, and their stablemates were in ABC cinemas less than two months later. In the advertising for *Rasputin—The Mad Monk* and *The Reptile*, the company would be referred to as "The House of Horror" for the first time. The House of Hammer had achieved official recognition, at last, but its days of being situated on the banks of the Thames were numbered.

> "I dreamed I saw the dead rise—all the graves in the churchyard opened, and the dead came out…"
>
> —Dr. Peter Tompson
> *The Plague of the Zombies*

The press screening for *Dracula—Prince of Darkness* had been followed by a luncheon to celebrate "Ten Years of Horror." The *Daily Worker's* Nina Hibbin—who had been so scathing about the merits of the original film, attended. "It was a sad occasion," she would note solemnly. "Saddest of all was the contemplation of the Hammer company's spectacular rise to power and prosperity

through ten years of trading in morbidity, putrefaction and pain."
Toward the end of 1965, when all in the garden was still looking
rosy, thanks to the continuing influx of American finance, Michael
Carreras had been prompted to sound a note of caution about
rising costs and its knock-on effect within the industry. "The high
tide of American investment is prompting the unions to reach out
for new demands and, for the first time, we are getting close to the
edge of disaster. Eventually the Americans will back away and we
will be left to cope with a tremendous salary bill."

The euphoria of the mid-sixties would see the industry remain
buoyant for some time to come, but by the end of the decade,
Lyndon Johnson would cut back tax benefits on American investment overseas to fund the escalating costs of the Vietnam War, and
Michael's words would return to haunt him—the Americans
would do exactly as he had predicted, and the nightmare would
become a reality.

Hammer had begun to faction after the relative commercial
failures of both *The Curse of the Werewolf* and *The Phantom of the
Opera.* Due to the nature of the arrangement with Universal, where
the films were made to a price for outright sale, Hammer lost no
money, but neither did Universal make any, so they lost interest.
At the same time, the five-year pact struck with Columbia in 1959
also reached its end. With the demise of these two agreements,
American willingness to accept the traditional Hammer product
was greatly reduced, and Hammer was now entirely in the hands
of Fox/7-Arts. While Tony Hinds found himself occupied by tedious executive duties, James Carreras's instinct was still to go where
the money was, and the money was now in whatever Fox, 7-Arts,
or British partners ABPC felt the box office would buy.

"M-G-M has come up with one of the most potently exploitable
films of the year," the *Independent Film Review* had said of *She,*
correctly predicting a performance that had given ABC's collective
spirit a much needed boost. Now hot on Andress's heels was the
promise of an even more stunning anatomical attraction in Hammer's next venture. In the interim, Ken Hyman had decided that
the box office would buy a remake of the Hal Roach saga of
prehistoric life, *One Million BC* (aka *Man and his Mate;* 1940), in
which the Carole Landis role would be recreated by a young actress
whose best assets had so far been hidden beneath a constricting

rubber suit in *Fantastic Voyage* (1965). When the talent of Raquel Welch was liberated by an antediluvian bikini and displayed amid the sun baked plains of Lanzarote for photographer Pierre Luigi, the picture that resulted would go around the world, and "Hammer Glamor" would arrive with just as much of a bang as Hammer Horror.

Initially unaware that beauty, rather than beasts, would sell the film, Michael Carreras had covered his bets by engaging stop-motion expert Ray Harryhausen to oversee the prehistoric menagerie. Harryhausen was the acknowledged leader in the field, but he had already done his best work. His recent offerings had been indulgent exercises in virtuoso technique, set on some mysterious island or similarly exotic location that could best showcase his matte paintings and monsters. *One Million Years BC* held to the formula. The island was Earth at the dawn of (pre)history, the mattes were fewer (it was mainly filmed in Las Canadas, Teneriffe), but the mayhem was of much the same variety as *The Animal World* (1954) and the plethora of giant monster fantasies that had followed it. Here, the difference was Welch. Earning $25,000, she was also half the price of Andress, and by the time the Harryhausen pterodactyl had carried her to the heights, Hammer's six-picture deal with Fox would have become an *eleven*-picture deal.

Already on the schedule for the spring of 1966 was a property that had been brought to Hammer by Hollywood diva Joan Fontaine. *The Devil's Own* was a novel by Nora Lofts, writing as "Peter Curtis," and Nigel Kneale had been brought in to add spice to the otherwise tepid brew of a psychologically disturbed schoolteacher who finds herself embroiled in pagan goings-on in an English village. The film had been intended as a star vehicle from the outset, and nothing could be included that might upset Fontaine's carefully coiffeured demeanor. Kneale could write a supernatural yarn *par excellence* when the mood took him, but the witchery in *The Devil's Own* was too sedate by half. The fact that a narrative with little shock value and even fewer shock effects still managed to earn an "X" certificate (at Hammer's insistence) did nothing to relieve the disappointment. Despite its British release title, *The Witches* would fail to cast the appropriate spell.

One Million Years BC was weaving a different kind of magic. Spurred by the most tremendous surge of prepublicity that it had ever experienced, Hammer decided to embrace more subjects in which female flesh was predominant. *She, Goddess of Love* had already been touted—as *Ayesha, Daughter of She,* and originally intended for Andress—and *Prehistoric Women* (aka *Slave Girls*) had been put onto the floor to use standing sets from *One Million Years BC.* But into production went *The Viking Queen,* and now that the time was finally right, *Frankenstein Created Woman.*

> *Baron Frankenstein is experimenting to trap the soul at the time of death. After a fracas in a café with three youths, his assistant, Hans, is arrested for the murder of the owner. He is executed by guillotine and his distraught girlfriend, Christina, throws herself into the river. Frankenstein arranges for Hans's torso to be brought to his laboratory where he has conceived the idea of transferring Hans's soul to the body of the dead girl. The experiment is a success, but Hans's spirit seeks revenge on the three youths who were responsible for his execution. Christina/Hans lures two of the youths to their deaths. Frankenstein tries to avert the killing of the third, but he is too late. Realizing what she has been made to do, Christina throws herself into the river again as Frankenstein looks on, his experiment now a failure.*

Austrian model Susan Denberg, whose main claim to fame had been her elevation to Miss August in *Playboy* magazine after a feature role in the Fox potboiler *See You in Hell, Darling* (aka *An American Dream*), was cast opposite Cushing. "Hammer Glamor" prepublicity for *Frankenstein Created Woman* showed Miss Denberg in a bikini against a backdrop of laboratory equipment from *Evil.* For once, a film looked set to fulfill the promise of its title, but this was to be no *Bride of Frankenstein.* A feeble script stripped the story of a creation scene, and the bulk of the action is restricted to a single café environ. Some cursory location sequences helped to spread the load, but the overall effect was not dissimilar to that of a stage play that had simply been "opened out" for the screen.

Metaphysics is the name of the game on this occasion, and the baron is an earnest academic in search of the philosopher's stone, as willing to lay down his own life as those of others in the cause of research. Cushing is thawed out to announce to the understandably bewildered Thorley Walters, "*Dead* for one hour, yet my soul did not leave my body. Why?" A ludicrous experiment at best, if you think about it. The film was another attempt by John Elder to canonise a character who had left more corpses littered around the hamlets of Europe than Bluebeard, and inconsistencies are wholesale. Subordinated to a juvenile drama of revenge, Baron Frankenstein could just as easily have been someone else altogether, and thanks to the labotomy performed on him by Elder, he is reduced to the level of the contrivance through which the real plot is allowed to unfold.

In an effort to enliven the show, Fisher pinched a trick from the then-popular TV series, "The Man from Uncle" and conducted a fight scene with a hand-held camera. The result was merely intrusive. He also reorganized the climactic suicide to have the girl leap into a fast-flowing river, whereas the script had called for a perfunctory bout of *hara-kiri*. This was not so inappropriate. With Andress occupied elsewhere, Susan Denberg had been booked for the sequel to *She* (now *The Return of She*), and by April 1967, she would once more be gracing the pages of *Playboy*. But a whirlwind descent into the West Coast drug scene was to blow her mind—and any further chance of stardom.

> "I had the feeling that...if I spoke the words, I would be animating some...horrible thing..."
>
> —Claire de Sangre
> *The Mummy's Shroud*

As a sign of how Hammer's faith in its policy of "t and a" was being kindled, its NFFC-funded contribution toward the four horrors that had been made back-to-back had been a mere £40,000 apiece, whereas £85,000 had been requested in advance of *One Million Years BC*, and a similar amount again for the return of *She*, rising to £125,000 by the time of *The Lost Continent* and *Moon Zero Two*. Of course, part of this was being dictated by the very inflationary factors that Michael Carreras had warned of, but as further proof of the way things were moving, the last film on the slate had been mentioned almost in throwaway—*Shroud of the Mummy*. It had been intended merely as padding for Hammer's latest Frankenstein saga (in place of *Slave Girls*) and went into production on September 12, 1966—but the grant requested stayed strictly at a 1965 level: £40,000.

*1920, and on a dig financed by businessman Stanley Preston,
archaeologist Sir Basil Waldon has discovered the tomb of boy
Pharaoh Kah-to-Bey. But the tomb has a guardian, and using the
sacred shroud, Hasmid calls the mummy of Prem to life, to destroy
the members of the expedition. One by one, they meet a horrifying
end at the hands of the mummy, until only two remain: Paul Preston
and Claire. Suspecting who is behind the deaths, Claire investigates
but finds herself trapped in a museum with the mummy. When Paul
and Inspector Barrani arrive, Prem attacks. He is impervious to
bullets and a blow from a fire axe. Barrani shoots Hasmid. With his
death, the mummy of Prem crumbles to dust.*

"Tedious and embarrassing," was the eventual verdict of the
Financial Times. "Incongruously pretty," said *Punch.* "A stilted re-
hash," noted the *Monthly Film Bulletin.* "Static and stodgy," observed another, typical of the rest. Roundly condemned by all
(including director John Gilling: "One of my worst," he subsequently declared), *The Mummy's Shroud* is nevertheless a bravura
exercise in technique. With little but the obligatory series of set-
piece murders to build upon, Gilling stages each of them with
stunning visual invention: the mummy's appearances are pre-
saged by a variety of perceptive tricks, in the manner of literary
master M. R. James—he is evidenced in a trail of eons-old dust,
spotted as a shadow on an alley wall, shown reflected in a crystal
ball or in a tray of developing solution, or even as a *blur* in the
myopic vision of Michael Ripper's Longbarrow. The killings are
staged with equal aplomb. Sir Basil's skull is cracked open like an
egg in a giant's hands; Stanley Preston's is smashed against a wall,
to leave its imprint in blood; the photographer, Barrett, is baptized
in acid and fire; the mild-mannered Longbarrow is hurled from an
upstairs window—his body shattering against the side of an orna-
mental pool, to stain the waters scarlet.

As exercises in montage, these sequences are a delight, but there
are other sweetmeats. The spear scene in *The Mummy* is topped by
that of Barrett thrusting a heavy-duty photographer's tripod
through the reanimated body of Prem. The disintegration in
Dracula is matched by the clever effects work of a crumbling
mummy tearing *himself* apart as he implodes into dust. All this was
a far cry from the red paint and tokenism that had passed for horror
in *Frankenstein Created Woman*!

If *The Mummy's Shroud* was "embarrassing," it was in the one-dimensional banality of the characters as written, and in the case of ex-debutante Maggie Kimberley, *played*, as well. But even here, there was to be a plus: Michael Ripper's Longbarrow was translated from script to screen "with a pathos rarely achieved in the impersonal and well-nigh inhuman world of horror cinema," opined Cecil Wilson.

In Hammer's Cornish duo, the versatile and largely underused Ripper had been given the opportunity to show what he was capable of. Ripper had been a long-time friend of Tony Hinds and had acted in Hammer films as far back as *The Dark Road* and *A Case for P.C.49*, when he was picked at audition by James Carreras himself. Hinds admired his ability to convince in the sparest of parts and often created character roles with the diminutive actor in mind. Invariably called upon to provide the requisite comic relief, Ripper was a clown who had genuinely played Hamlet (in his younger days in the theater, before the throat operation that gave him the voice and persona for which he is best known). A complex and serious artist, he "wasn't what was ordered," in his own words, preferring drama class to ordinary schooling by the age of fifteen.

A thirty-year veteran of the film industry at this stage, Ripper was also highly regarded by John Gilling. In *The Mummy's Shroud*, he was given his head, and he very nearly stole the show from the bandaged cadaver and an equally daunting clutch of seasoned fellow professionals. He is part of the fabric of Hammer, and he would appear in fifteen of their horrors, as well as sundry others along the way—sometimes as nothing more than an afterthought, yet always with a presence that would belie his stature and ensure him a place in the more selective cast roster of memory.

With *The Mummy's Shroud* in the can, and production now tied exclusively to the majors (and their corresponding desire to see their own stages used by affiliates), Hammer finally vacated Bray Studios on November 18, 1966, for the greyer pastures of ABPC Elstree—already a dispute-riddled corporate dinosaur, plagued with strikes and typified by perfunctory staging and poor craftsmanship.[8]

The connection with Fox/7-Arts/ABPC had resulted in the production of a record eleven features in eighteen months by September 1966, and James Carreras was quick to announce a new batch of titles, reporting as he did that "the first pictures under the deal are already in profit." *Quatermass and the Pit* was to spearhead another five, with *She—The Avenger* (eventually to lens in July 1967 as *The Vengeance of She,* with Olinka Berova in the title role), *The Devil Rides Out,* from the "classic" novel by Dennis Wheatley, *Robin Hood's Challenge* and *The Bride of Newgate Gaol* (from a story by John Dickson Carr, and budgeted at £325,000) to follow, to make sixteen in all.

The halls of Hammer were now bedecked with giant-sized pinups of Welch, Andress, and others, in place of the traditional "quads" advertising forthcoming attractions. The fun palace had moved to Wardour Street and notched up a gear. Hammer was no longer synonymous with horror. For the remainder of the sixties, the new flesh was to be much more pneumatic, and it had considerably more potential as a sales aid.

James Carreras was now well and truly established as a doyen of the business—a man whom "everyone wanted to rub shoulders with," and who "took advantage of it," in the opinion of Brian Lawrence. Carreras would verbalize his business philosophy in a variety of homilies confided to intimates as if they had been set in tablet of stone and handed down from the Great Entrepreneur in the sky. "Never deal with a man who can only say 'no,'" was one such, to take account of the fact that he viewed the U.K. heads of American companies as mere "branch managers." And Lawrence was invariably on hand to drink in every word, considering his mentor "the most amazing man I ever met." Amazing, he certainly was, as well as amiable, affable, and always available for lunch. *Jimmy* had become a commodity in himself—sought out, sought after, and prized—as friend, consort, or colleague. He was larger than life. He had a chameleon ability to be all things to all men. He was, in short, almost too good to be true.

To all intents and purposes, Hammer House had become an adjunct of Variety Club and a virtual luncheon club for the rich and powerful—Earl Mountbatten was a frequent visitor. Its "wine cellar" was permanently stocked with the best vintages, its cigars were Havana, and its decor was enhanced by the ranks of the eager young starlets who were now falling over each other to be in the running for the title of Hammer's latest glamor girl. "We were the most colorful company in Wardour Street," Lawrence was to reflect. It had once been the color of blood. Now it was the color of money.

The December 30, 1966, opening of *One Million Years BC,* after nine months spent on special effects, broke the all-time record of the ABC circuit in North London. The desire of audiences everywhere to witness those much-publicized breasts on the big screen would lead to the film becoming Hammer's biggest financial success: $8 million worldwide (though at a final cost of £425,000, it was not the most profitable in percentage terms). It was also the ultimate international film. In *Prince of Darkness,* Dracula may have uttered not a word of English, but *One Million Years BC* had *no* dialogue at all, except for the Jurassic Esperanto that Michael Carreras had concocted for it during shooting.

Hammer's euphoria was to be short-lived, however. Returns from the U.S. soon began to reveal a significant fall-off, with none of the rest of Hammer's releases for 1967 managing to break even. This tale of woe was to continue without relief until 1969, by which time *The Vengeance of She, The Lost Continent,* and *The Devil Rides Out* (in spite of a good domestic performance) would barely register at the American box office. It would be the result of a classic series of managerial misunderstandings. The Fox executives who ordered the films would forget to inform those on the sharp end that they were coming, but more critically, there would be no one at Hammer to remind them—James Carreras was now to spend a good deal of both 1967 *and* 1968 fundraising on behalf of the Variety Club.

The year 1967 was the heyday of flower-power. Fashions were changing fast, attitudes faster. But if this was to be the decade of change, then Hammer was slow to notice. With the release, in June, of *Frankenstein Created Woman* and *The Mummy's Shroud,* one critic would sound the warning bell, though there were others who could hear the chimes at midnight. "Time has stopped at Bray Studios and they're still making 'B' pictures for a market that was willing to queue in the rain for Stewart Grainger and Patricia Roc." If Frankenstein was nearing the end of the road by 1967, then the mummy had reached it, but the bent for retrospective thinking was now indelible at Hammer, and no one thought of curtailing the February production of a project that had been hanging around on the schedule from as far back as 1960—*Quatermass and the Pit.*

> *Workmen building an extension to the London Underground at Hobbs End discover a skull. Archaeologist Dr. Roney is called to the site, and further digging uncovers what appears to be a huge bomb. The army asks Quatermass in to help. He suspects that the bomb is really an ancient spacecraft. When the device is opened, long-dead creatures are discovered inside. The craft itself still seems to be active, and Quatermass tries to prevent further tampering, but he is over-ruled. Colonel Breen orders the site to be reopened. Quatermass establishes that the craft has come from Mars, millions of years before, and that its purpose had been to conduct genetic experimentation on man. The craft is activated, and those descended from the Martians start to run amok in an attempt to purge impure elements. Breen is killed in the holocaust. Quatermass realizes that this power must be drained to earth. Roney climbs a scaffolding crane to direct it at an airborne vision of the Martian consciousness. There is an explosion, and Roney perishes—leaving Quatermass alone amid the rubble of London.*

Advertised as "The most terrifying science-fiction film ever made," *Quatermass and the Pit* was a Technicolor travesty of the best and most exciting of the three television serials. Kneale's notional science-fiction writings were rooted in their time; they were a response to *immediate* events, not a generalized muse on the nature of things, possible or otherwise. As such, *Quatermass and the Pit* did not travel well.

The television version of *The Pit* had been a cold war commentary on the self-destructive nature of the violent impulse—an intricate and carefully worked-out thesis on the condition of man, cleverly embracing every aspect of superstition and demonism. But where the teleplay had been a cohesive and original whole trading on a prevalent perception, if not a specific anxiety (Erich von Daniken's contemporaneous theory about "ancient astronauts"), the film condensation is a potpourri of miscellaneous ingredients melded into a mishmash of monstrousness. And the Lovecraftian revelation of altered reality that Nigel Kneale had buried with the demonic horde that is inadvertently allowed to spew forth from a spacecraft of yesteryear quite loses its *tenor* in the translation.

To contain the budget, if not the marauding Martians, the action is transposed from the building site of the original to a Subway extension, and Roney's last-ditch stand with chain and muscle power in the serial is writ impossibly large as he single-handedly topples a giant crane onto the naked face of the electromagnetic nucleus. But these apart, nothing new was added to the eight-year-old thrills. Despite the supposed benefit of Technicolor, it had all been done better by the BBC, and its mechanical staging at Elstree was exemplified by the crude improvisations of the special effects department. *Quatermass and the Pit* lacked the currency that both of the earlier films had traded on: the notion that this could be happening *now.* Four years after the advent of "Doctor Who," the third of Nigel Kneale's illustrious Quatermass serials seemed like merely another colorful frolic into the realms of science fantasy.

Just as *The Quatermass Experiment* had acted as a barometer for the advent of the new dynamic that was to be Hammer Horror, so *The Pit* signalled the expending of that energy. Where Hammer had led the field in 1955, it now seemed to be lagging significantly behind, and *Films and Filming* continued to document the decline in standards. "*Quatermass and the Pit* fails to carry one tenth of the unnerving credibility of the Quatermass predecessors," wrote Richard Davis.

Of Hammer's announced productions for 1967, the Jimmy Sangster scripted *The Bride of Newgate Gaol* would now be abandoned. *The Bride* had originated toward the end of 1965, in the wake of *Tom Jones* (1963) and *Moll Flanders* (1965), and Restoration sex romps had since gone largely by the way. A second Sangster subject, *The Claw* (formerly *Brainstorm*), and written to advance the line of psycho-thrillers, was put on hold for the time being due to the move away from Bray, for which it had been specifically designed.

Essentially another reworking of the *Taste of Fear / Les Diaboliques* scenario, where a murder plot is masked by an elaborate deceit, *The Claw* had been planned as a second feature in the manner of *Nightmare.* Characterless and contrived, bleak and downbeat, and in its present form containing a *dénouement* that was implausible if not completely illogical, it had been conceived and written quickly, with intended Oakley Court/Thames-side riverboat locations. These factors no longer applied, but Sangster was starting to repeat himself, and he knew it. As can be evidenced in the script of *The Claw,* the next step forward was already surfacing between the jaded lines: his thoughts were turning to direction.

In place of these, Sangster was offered the chance to script and produce *The Anniversary*, an adaption of a stage play (by Bill MacIlwraith) intended to showcase the awesome presence of Bette Davis—whose daughter, Bea, was now married into the Hyman family. Davis's salary, of $200,000 on this occasion, accounted for 20 percent of the film's total budget (as it had with *The Nanny*, where she was also accorded 9 percent of the gross). Within a week of shooting, director Alvin Rakoff had crossed swords with the great lady once too often, and Michael Carreras—who, effectively, was once more exercising executive duties at Hammer—was nominated to break the news. Rakoff was replaced by the more empathic Roy Ward Baker, who was known to the actress from a previous sojourn in Hollywood. But it was to be the beginning of an unfortunate trend.

By this time, Michael had been asked to choose one of the several other works by best-selling author and occult expert Dennis Yates Wheatley that were now under option to Hammer, thanks to the good offices of Tony Keys. He picked *Uncharted Seas*—a seafaring yarn that Wheatley could not even remember writing. Michael then signed Leslie Norman to direct what was to lens under a title snatched from an old Lippert programmer—*The Lost Continent*. Before principal photography began in earnest on September 11 (but after he had undertaken preproduction work and shot some of the second-unit footage), a divergence of approach led to Norman's departure, with Michael picking up the reins. The end result was to be an epic and enthralling adventure in the *King Kong* mold, with the Michael "Nash" (Carreras) script making the most of its shipfull of misfits stranded among the lost souls and carnivorous crustaceans of the Sargasso Sea.

Hollywood effects specialist Robert A. Mattey had also been brought in, primarily to oversee the welter of "blue-backing" required for the visuals, but he would stay to construct the spectacular monsters. These creatures are some time coming, but when they do appear, they are pure Lovecraft: a giant octopus with a single, unblinking eye; an outsize scorpion; a mutant mollusk; a dislocated, human-devouring orifice in the hull of a stranded galleon. All are splendidly fantastical creations, frightening enough to earn the film an "X" certificate in Britain (though Hammer itself had wanted an "A"). The mix of adult drama and juvenile giant monster hokum was not altogether successful, although a superb pyrotechnical finale more than made up for any shortcomings. "Hammer have done it again…A feast of excitement and vicarious terror for the fans," one trade critic was to applaud. But along with all the other coproductions in this third batch of five for Fox, no one in America interested enough to want to come and see it for themselves would find it available for view.

While shooting on *The Lost Continent* was being rescheduled in the light of Norman's departure, and with the hippie cult turning its attentions to ever more esoteric religious outgrowths as The Beatles embraced the teachings of the Maharishi Mahesh Yogi, Hammer commenced production on *The Devil Rides Out*.

> "You fool!—I'd rather see you dead than meddling with black magic—"

> —Duc de Richleau
> *The Devil Rides Out*

The second of Hammer's ventures into the forbidden territory of thriller writer Dennis Wheatley was in a more traditional vein. *The Devil Rides Out* was one of several black magic novels in which the Duc de Richleau and his companions battled the legions of evil in all their diabolical forms. A slackening of censorship restrictions (as well as the personal prompting of Tony Keys) had persuaded Tony Hinds to back a screen version of this most famous of Wheatley's books. With Hinds on board, the call had gone out to Terence Fisher.

The failure of its first incursion into the fictional wilds of rural English witchcraft should have made Hammer pause for thought before it was agreed to sanction the occult thriller for which *The Witches* was to have been the dry run. But confidence in the pulling-power of Wheatley's name was high—his books had been reprinted in over fifty languages. Wheatley's black magic novels, in particular, were known for their graphic depiction of the horrors of satanism. Under the pretext of alerting his readers to the dangers inherent in such practices, the author would vent his purient descriptive powers on the minutiae of the obscenities involved. Hammer's full-frontal style made it the perfect choice in principle to bring his no-holds-barred approach to the screen. But unlike the book, the film was to shy away from transcribing the details of devil worship. [9]

If *The Devil Rides Out* ultimately embodied a sense of *déja vu,* it was Hammer's and Fisher's reticence that caused the problem. Even producer Tony Keys would come to have reservations about how *little* was shown. Had its quota of horrors been made more explicit, its Black Mass been made more authentically licentious, then this film could have been as ground breaking as some of its forerunners, instead of just the skilfully crafted nostalgic delight that it actually turned out to be.

> *The Duc de Richleau and Rex Van Ryn discover that their protégé, Simon, is in the hands of a band of Satanists, led by Mocata. When Simon disappears, Rex tries to find him through a young initiate, Tanith; she and Simon are to be baptized by Mocata at a Black Mass. During the ceremony, he and Richleau rescue the pair and take them to their friends, the Eatons—but Mocata vows to get them back. Richleau constructs a pentacle on the floor of the Eaton library to protect them against the powers of darkness. The group assembles within it, and throughout the night, are assaulted by visions, culminating in a visit from the Angel of Death. During the onslaught, Tanith dies and the Eatons' daughter is kidnapped. When it is over, Richleau and the others find Mocata's lair just as he is about to sacrifice the girl to the Devil. Using ritual magic, Richleau destroys the Satanists and rescues the child. With Mocata dead, Tanith is restored to life and Richleau thanks God for their salvation.*

From the graphic design of its title cards (based on the famous etching of the Horned God of the Witches by French magus Eliphas Levy) to the grand design of its moral universe, *The Devil Rides Out* is resoundingly faithful to the Wheatley tale. The action careers along at a frantic pace, and the extended sequence inside the pentacle generates considerable tension. For once, Hammer's budget-driven distaste of elaborate special effects paid dividends. The novel's demonic conjurations—the *black man* in the tower room; the Goat of Mendes at the Sabbat—are given an unnerving *solidity* and are the better for it. The supernatural beings of this film are the real stuff of nightmare, viable manifestations of an alternate universe capable of intruding on our own at the drop of an invocation. Only a giant tarantula (unhappily inherited from Richard Matheson's otherwise excellent script, which had replaced an original draft by John Hunter) and a *Mélièsian* puff of smoke as the Devil is vanquished with holy water spoil a convincing air of unreality.[10]

With a nevertheless generous budget of £285,000, the period is evoked with similar care. Vintage Rolls-Royces and Bentleys juggle for pride of place in the tranquil English countryside, and their presence effortlessly sets the action between the wars, as Albion's demi-paradise slumbers unaware of the forces of discord and anarchy that are gathering without. Oddly, Terence Fisher professed himself unmoved by this most clear-cut example of the cosmic battle between good and evil. His only declaration of concern about *The Devil Rides Out* was over the script's underdevelopment of the *love* interest.

In many ways, Fisher's film was a brilliant comeback for Hammer Horror. Its opening in the summer of 1968 would restore the faith of the fans, hint that a renaissance was in the wind, and show that the company could return to the splendor of the Golden Age glory days any time that it chose to do so. (The New Victoria first-night audience, Wheatley enthusiasts all, would sit through the screening in silent rapture.) Michael Armstrong, writing in *Films and Filming,* epitomised the mood of anticipation that had been felt in the run-up to release: "With *The Anniversary* came a new hope and now, with *The Devil Rides Out,* Hammer has returned to its original standard, for here is a film where time, money and serious effort have been spent in trying to produce a good piece of thrilling entertainment, and the end product has certainly paid off." Despite the euphoria in the ranks, however, *The Devil Rides Out* was a film out of time.

Hammer's black magic opus was to be followed into release by Michael Reeves's *Witchfinder General*—advertised as "the year's most violent film" by an unrepentant Tigon. *The Devil Rides Out* would seem curiously dated by comparison, as if it was harking back to a style of romantic melodrama that was all but gone. Its values were the values of yesteryear, and not just in terms of its plot. It had disappointingly refused to shock, outrage, or downright disgust, as the Tigon offering most certainly did. When it was also trotted out in the U.S. (as *The Devil's Bride*) with the same terminal lack of enthusiasm as *The Lost Continent,* any notion that the collected works of Dennis Wheatley might sire a new series for Hammer would fall at the first fence.

"I shall not be back—but *something* will...Tonight. Something will come for Simon and Tanith."

—Mocata
The Devil Rides Out

In his seminal study of the genre, *Horror Movies—An Illustrated Survey*,[11] Carlos Clarens wrote, "Hammer does not intend to change the formula, or experiment with a new one, unless public taste changes first. This may be sooner than expected." If Fisher's style was beginning to seem dated by 1968, so too was that of Hinds/Elder. Public taste had already begun to change, yet Hammer remained unaware of the need for new brooms. It was not to be long before fate would intervene to provide them.

As the bad news of dwindling returns from overseas started to filter through to Hammer House, sterling was devalued, and Hammer's response to the prospect of more lucrative foreign markets was typically unequivocal: James Carreras decided to rush a new Dracula into production on the vacant stages of Pinewood.

Dracula Has Risen From the Grave was dropped into the schedule for April. "After doing the second one, I didn't want ever to play it again," said Christopher Lee. "And I did it five more times." On this occasion, the decision was taken out of his hands. Unknown to him, he was now a statutory part of the package. "What do you do when someone says to you, we've already sold this picture on the basis of you being in it?" asked the incredulous actor.

The Queen's Award

"It was the best of times, it was the worst of times. It was the season of Light, it was the season of Darkness."

Charles Dickens
A Tale of Two Cities (1859)

On October 9, 1967, with *The Lost Continent* in its final weeks of shooting at Elstree, *The Devil Rides Out* in postproduction, and *Quatermass and the Pit* about to go into distribution, Brian Lawrence had persuaded James Carreras to file an application for Hammer to be considered for the prestigious Queen's Award to Industry. Between October 1964 and September 1967, Hammer Films had generated export earnings to the value of £2,742,797, or 70 percent of a total income of almost £4 million (though given the way that Hammer financed its productions, how much of this was actually received into the British treasury is another matter. "A con trick," said Hinds.) On April 10, 1968, when a £100 lunch for Fox executives had secured for Hammer the biggest overseas contract in the history of the company—the production of 17 television films for a series called "Journey to the Unknown," the application was officially approved.

The announcement that Hammer was to receive a 1968 Queen's Award to Industry (the first film company to be so honored) was released to the press on Thursday, April 18, four days before work was to commence on *Dracula Has Risen From the Grave*. The news hit all the nationals by the Saturday morning and made a front-page headline in the *Daily Sketch*: "Dracula And Co. Win Queen's Award." Interviews on Radio 4 and BBC 2 followed quickly, with Colonel James Carreras presiding over his stock-in-trade. In reply to a question on "The World This Weekend" about the so-called different versions of Hammer's horror films, he explained,

> "They differed because of censorship. In Great Britain, we're only allowed to show a person placing a stake on Dracula's heart and raising the mallet. In America, they used to allow the mallet to hit the stake. In Japan, they not only wanted the mallet to hit the stake, but they wanted to see the fellow...sort of leap up and try and pull it out. That really was quite terrifying so we stopped doing that, and now we make them all the same."

After ten years, it was still a good story, even if on this occasion it had been embellished from the script of a film that was to go on the floor a day later!

The award ceremony was arranged for Wednesday, May 29, and Carreras first suggested Hammer House as the ideal venue, but this was soon amended to Pinewood Studios, where *Risen From the Grave* would be nearing completion. The particular nature of the award encouraged Carreras to downplay Hammer's history of horrors, especially in light of an early letter of congratulation from Earl Mountbatten that intimated the possibility of a higher honor still. "Most of our pictures are of the Hitchcock type," Carreras wrote to Brigadier Sir Henry Floyd, the Lord Lieutenant of the County of Buckinghamshire, who would be making the presentation. He added, "Of course, we have had great successes with our horror films." The Brigadier took the hint (expanded upon in a preparatory lunch with Carreras and Tony Hinds on the Friday prior), as his speech was to testify on the day. "I know that you have had great success with what are termed 'horror films'," he told the assembled cast and crew of *Dracula Has Risen From the Grave*, "but I was glad to learn from your Chairman that the word 'horror' does not include scenes of actual personal violence, and that in this respect your company feels you have a responsibility towards the viewing public."

Since they had just spent that very morning watching Christopher Lee being bloodily impaled on a large crucifix, this took some swallowing. Not so what followed. Construction manager Arthur Banks dutifully received the Award on behalf of Hammer, and all those present were treated to a luncheon of melon, salmon, strawberries, and *Veuve Clicquot*.

Mountbatten's letter was only one of a great many to come in the wake of the news. Everyone who was anyone in the industry rushed to pay tribute to Hammer and James Carreras. There were the expected notices of appreciation from Anthony Crosland at the Board of Trade, the British Export Council, and Fred Pontin on behalf of the Variety Club, but perhaps the most telling was the telegram from comedian Charlie Drake, which advised, "I'm afraid we're going to have to knock you six shots."

Hammer's fifth Dracula would be more custom-made than its predecessor. The typical audience was now seen as being predominantly in the 18-to-30 age group, and the heroes and heroines of the tales were to be brought into line. This meant, in effect, that the *savant* would make way for an embarrassing string of sweet young things, dabbling with sex, and almost incidentally defeating an adversary whom Van Helsing had previously required all of his prowess to tackle. The resulting film would be the first of Hammer's Gothics in which it would be obvious that the company was pandering to preconceived taste—the first in which it was pointedly to ignore the demands of the dress circle and direct its remarks to the gallery, instead. ("Your fly's undone," one character advises another amid ribald laughter.)

Dracula Has Risen From the Grave would start a fad for exclamatory titles. It would be joined by *Destroy All Monsters* (1968), *It's Alive, The Beast Must Die* (both 1972), and *I Don't Want to be Born* (aka *The Monster*; 1975), to name a few. Not everyone approved—Lee preferred the more prosaic "Dracula Arisen"—but it was appropriately antitraditionalist. Terence Fisher had been slated to direct, but he was forced to withdraw when he broke his leg in a road accident, so Tony Hinds turned to the man who had replaced him on *The Evil of Frankenstein.* In the interim, Freddie Francis had been much influenced by the more fantastical worlds that he had been creating for rival, Amicus, and, with his peculiar pictorial style now in full flood, he brought the same phantasmagorical approach to *Risen From the Grave.* The result was to be a kaleidoscope of visual trickery, designed to numb the senses rather than stimulate them.

The sex would be tacky and the violence would be tacked-on, but on this occasion, it would work. *Dracula Has Risen From the Grave* was also to become one of the highest grossers in the company's history.

> *Monsignor Muller is persuaded to perform an exorcism of Castle Dracula, but the hapless priest who helps him unwittingly revives the count in the frozen moat. Dracula vows revenge on the Monsignor and his niece, Maria. The priest installs the vampire in the cellar of a café and directs him to Maria's room. Muller notices the mark of the vampire on Maria and lies in wait, thwarting Dracula—but he is attacked by the priest and he dies. Maria's boyfriend, Paul, is now alert to the danger and forces the errant priest to take him to the count's resting place. There, he drives a stake through the vampire's heart—but the priest is unable to complete the ritual prayer, and the count escapes. Dracula wills Maria to join him, and the three set off for the castle with Paul in hot pursuit. During the struggle that follows, Paul topples the count over the precipice and onto the crucifix that Maria has hurled into the valley below. The priest utters the prayer and dies, and Count Dracula turns to dust.*

To say that *Dracula Has Risen From the Grave* is the most vivid of Hammer's Gothic horrors would be an understatement. From its psychedelic opening titles to its closing shot of the Wicked Warlock of the East melting into a mound of bright red *Plaka*, it is a cartoon caper: Hammer Horror meets pop art. The film was Bram Stoker through the mesh of a Warhol screen print, and it caught the mood of an increasingly cynical hip-culture that wanted either "serious" art or comic-book fantasy—but nothing much in-between.

Under Freddie Francis's weird but gaudily vibrant sense of decor, two priests journey through the mist-shrouded landscapes of Peter Melrose's glass paintings in search of Siege Perilous, a looming Magic Castle on Bald Mountain; towering, expressionist roofscapes rise from the Hansel and Gretel village square as the fairy princess is summoned by the demon king; the vampire's every move is enveloped in an amber vignette, while a fish-eye lens bloats his features into the gargoyle corpulence of the Wicked Coachman in *Pinocchio*. Impressive as he could be, Lee is rarely more than a green-faced Doctor Doom here, pitted against the less than Fantastic Four of Maria, Paul, the priest, and the monsignor.

In his attempt to ring the changes in the formula, Elder had revised all the rules of the game, but without the skill that Sangster had shown in being able to substitute something just as potent in their place. The count can drain his victims, but not turn them into vampires as a result, and even the traditional stake is no longer enough. Not only does it need to be accompanied by the appropriate prayer, but the supplicant has to be *devout,* as well—otherwise Dracula can simply pull out the offending article and magically heal, like many an alien from *I Married a Monster From Outer Space* onward. The goalposts were not just being shifted; they were being removed from the field altogether.

Since the films seemed to be turning into a serial rather than a series, escape clauses abound, as do images more fanciful than grotesque: an early victim is discovered hanging upside-down in a church *bell*; when Dracula expires on a huge cross, he dies weeping tears of *blood*. *Dracula Has Risen From the Grave* would be sold in the U.S. under tongue-in-cheek slogans such as "You can't keep a good man down," but with more than half a million American combat troops now committed to the killing fields of Southeast Asia and student protests against the war increasing by the day, no one was in the mood to take such things seriously, in any event. If it had been the intention to spoof the film, then Warners would find an audience in tune. Nothing was sacred, and that was to be the appeal.

With the lull in production that had followed *The Devil Rides Out,* Tony Nelson Keys had taken a leave of absence to work on a film version of the Mermaid Theatre's Restoration comedy romp, *Lock Up Your Daughters*. With Keys in Kilkenny, Southern Ireland, production of *Dracula Has Risen From the Grave* had been put in the hands of Aida Young. Young was one of only a handful of women producers in the industry, and this was her first Gothic. She had been involved in the Unity Theatre before cutting her cinematic teeth on documentaries and short films, which she then abandoned in favor of commercial free-lancing; after her stint at Bray in the early fifties, she had worked her way up to first assistant, production manager, and eventually associate producer. "I was the only woman doing my kind of job anywhere in the feature industry. I was the first third [assistant director], the first second...If you were a woman, you had to do continuity, or you were a secretary, or you were wardrobe, makeup and hair—that was it." In the capacity of associate producer, Young had assisted Michael Carreras on *What a Crazy World*, and when *he* had returned to Hammer, she had accompanied him, to fulfil the same function on *She* and *One Million Years BC*. She had asked Tony Hinds if she could produce the sequel to the former by herself. Hinds had agreed, and *The Vengeance of She* was her only other producer credit.

During the making of *Dracula Has Risen From the Grave*, Aida Young referred to some of Peter Melrose's matte paintings as "Gibbs' castles"—an allusion to a picture on a popular brand of toothpaste. The series that had benefited from them was becoming just as disposable.

In his original application for the Queen's Award, James Carreras had stated, "Our production programme has been completely geared to overseas markets and in particular to the United States." With the respite provided by the award celebrations at an end, and the blue flag flying in triumph over Hammer House, that program was now to resume in earnest. Warming to his newfound theme of respectability, Carreras told the *Financial Times*, "I suppose you could call us junior Hitchcocks. We specialise not so much in horror films as in thrillers." Over at the *Express*, Christopher Lee was pointing out, not for the first time, that of the ninety-one films *he* had made, only fifteen had been in the horror vein.

Gothic horror was becoming a thing of the past, as far as Hammer was concerned—the Hammer of James Carreras and Brian Lawrence (now a director of the company), at any rate. As far as

Michael was concerned, it had been a thing of the past for many years. By July 1968, *The Lost Continent* had followed *The Devil Rides Out* into release and Val Guest had prepared a script for *When Dinosaurs Ruled the Earth*, a sequel of sorts to *One Million Years BC*. About to go into preproduction were *Moon Zero Two* and *Crescendo*, and on the horizon were titles like *In The Sun* and *The Day the Earth Cracked Open*—which left only *Frankenstein Must Be Destroyed* and yet another outing for Count Dracula. It was a Hammer that Tony Hinds no longer recognized—a Hammer whose two main series characters seemed ready to degenerate into nothing more than sub-Bond ciphers, destined to ride a merry-go-round of ever more repetitive adventures until the public tired of them. And if all that were not enough, there was "Journey to the Unknown."

With a budget of $3 million in a three-way deal between Fox, ABC-TV, and Hammer, and a looming dateline of September 23 for the completion of the seventeen hours of television, it was now imperative that the treadmill which had been set in motion on May 24 be brought up to speed. A lot was riding on "Journey to the Unknown" and, as a token of Hammer's commitment, Carreras had chosen to second his codirector to the line producer who had been allocated to the show by Fox. It was a decision that was to deal Hammer the biggest blow of its twenty-year existence.

In June 1967, Eliot Hyman's 7-Arts had taken control of Warner Brothers in a $125 million buy out that had been underway since the previous November. By September 1968, Carreras was launching a major program of production at ABPC's Elstree Studios in advance of signing a *new* five-picture deal for Warners with his old partner. And on October 11, he hosted a luncheon at the Savoy in honor of Ken Hyman, now Vice President of Worldwide Production for Warner/7-Arts. Present were the cast and crew of *Dracula Has Risen From the Grave* and *When Dinosaurs Ruled the Earth*, as well as regular industry notables such as Goodlatte, Cartlidge, Columbia's Bill Graf, Nat Cohen, and Bernard Delfont. "When Jim Carreras shows us a poster with a title on it, we know the script probably has not been written yet—but that we shall have a marvellous, profitable picture delivered to us in due course. I wish that more people could function in the same way," Hyman enthused. But Hammer's relations with the Hymans had already reached their peak, and a second takeover within a year would see Warners controlled by the Kinney Corporation, whose Ted Ashley would not be the pushover for Carreras's title, poster, and promise routine that Eliot (and Ken) Hyman had been.

If Ashley was the Ghost of Christmas Future for Hammer, his presence was undetected as yet. The Ghost of Christmas Present came in the guise of the ACTT, and among the assembled guests, it was Tony Hinds who was being haunted by the specter at the feast. Even with "Journey to the Unknown" now complete, there was little for him to celebrate.

> "Why can't I make a lot of 'polite' conversation, like everybody else?—What do I have to take things so seriously for?"
>
> —Paul
> *Dracula Has Risen From the Grave*

The dichotomy that existed in the British Film Industry—with its monopoly distribution—was the conflict between art and commerce. As Michael Carreras had observed, "The cinema in this country is up against the establishment mind." This was reflected in a stark light at Hammer. His various assertions about how the company functioned marked James Carreras as an archetypal Thatcherite businessman (before the term was ever invented). Yet the commodity he sold was not a product of automation and the conveyor-belt, but of groups of individually talented men and women—artists in many cases, craftspersons in all. Tony Hinds stood between these two conflicting philosophies, and it fell to him to translate the wishes and desires of the one into the language and *modus* of the other.

The contradictions of Hammer were thus embodied in the personalities of the two men who had built it. One was reserved, urbane, and passive; the other was active, extroverted, entrepreneurial. They could be complementary types, but when the market garden turned into a factory farm, these divisions had surfaced, and each man had gravitated instinctively toward his natural environment. In the case of Carreras, it had been kindred spirits among the bigger fish of the film industry. "He preferred wining and dining executives in London's best restaurants, at which he was very good," was Hinds's opinion of that aspect of the business—one that was anathema to himself and, to some degree, to Michael Carreras as well: "Tony was never a man for mixing with those sort of people; he had nothing to communicate with them."

Since 1965, the two had drifted apart in ideology. Hinds had tired of the type of film that Hammer had begun to make and had contented himself with fulfilling the executive duties required of him. He travelled to and from Soho by train, rarely leaving the confines of his office and seeing only those who desired to see him. Carreras, on the other hand, still followed the teachings of Onward and Upward—a doctine that took little account of who had helped to build the ladder in the first place.

Over the years, Hinds had absorbed a series of personal set-backs. The critical assault on *Never Take Sweets From a Stranger* had hurt. The ACT's refusal to grant him a ticket that would have enabled him to work for Balcon had hurt more. The executive duties had taken their toll on his enthusiasm, and what he thought of as being "hired out" to line producers Joan Harrison and Jack Fleischman on "Journey to the Unknown" had taken what remained of his self-respect.

But there had been no arguing with James Carreras. "He saw me as part of the package," Hinds said, and all his wily partner's persuasive powers had been brought to bear to ensure compliance. "ABC in America decided that as I'd had no experience in television, they ought to send over a representative...She was very nice—we got on very well. But I hated that; I hated being demoted...I didn't think I would—but I did." The Carreras charm was impossible to resist, as Christopher Lee would also discover, and Hinds was an honorable man. "I had to do it, and I had to stay with it all the way through, hating nearly every minute of it." On the last week of the 26-week contract, while shooting on location, the union had refused to sanction any overtime. Hinds had been so incensed at this that he had resigned from the ACTT immediately on close of production. It was to end his career as a producer.

"He was a changed man," Michael considered. Always mercurial, rarely assertive—the Hammer hierarchy was known as father, son, and "holy ghost"—Hinds had been in the financial position to retire since the death of his father in 1959. The 26 weeks of postproduction chores on "Journey to the Unknown" would keep him occupied until the spring of 1969. But by then, with *Frankenstein Must Be Destroyed* ready for its West End opening at the very same

Warner theater that had hosted *The Curse of Frankenstein* less than twelve years before, Tony Hinds would find the pressure to retire irresistible.

> "I fancy...that *I* am the spider, and you...are the fly, Franken-stein..."
>
> —Professor Brandt
> *Frankenstein Must Be Destroyed*

The most striking aspect of Hammer's fifth Frankenstein is that it was *not* shot at Bray, written by John Elder, or even produced by Anthony Hinds, yet Hinds's presence is stamped all over it. The production that was to commence on January 13, 1969, would be the last *true* Hammer horror—the last film with the feel, the style, the look of the Golden Age greats; Terence Fisher knew the score, but Tony Nelson Keys had learned the music well. Sadly, it was to be *his* curtain call, also.

Frankenstein Must Be Destroyed was to be aided by a good script. This was all the more surprising, since it was a first for long-time assistant director Bert Batt and was continuously rewritten to add new scenes and stretch its running time as it was shot. Here, the baron is his old self, "a dangerous medical adventurer" who commits the "crime of the century" as the story begins. After lopping off a convenient head with a sickle, he surprises an intruder in his laboratory and a fight ensues, during which the lab is comprehensively wrecked and his hat box falls open to reveal this latest in an accumulation of spare parts—just like Danny's in *Night Must Fall*. Frankenstein was back. And he was mean.

> *When a burglar stumbles upon Frankenstein's laboratory, the police are called to investigate. The baron escapes and takes up residence at a boarding house run by Anna Spengler. He blackmails Anna and her boyfriend Karl into helping him free brain specialist Dr Brandt from an insane asylum, to obtain his formula for transplantation. But the doctor suffers a heart attack, and the baron is forced to transplant his brain into a new body: that of Professor Richter. A visit from the police arouses the suspicions of Brandt's wife and she recognizes Frankenstein; he reassures her about his intentions, but makes ready to leave. Brandt awakes in Richter's body, but is accidentally wounded by Anna. Enraged by her stupidity, Frankenstein kills her. Brandt goes to see his wife for the last*

time. After bidding her farewell, he sets a trap for Frankenstein. He lures the baron to the house and blocks the exits by hurling oil lamps at them. In the melee, Karl is shot. The baron tries to flee the inferno, but Brandt carries him back into the burning building.

The film is more than usually alert to the dramatic benefits of narrative crosscutting, as the new experiment is interwoven with a police investigation into the old (much of which was added later). There are some original touches: Frankenstein is said to be a native of Bohemia, for one. There is the occasional line that smacks of Cushing—"Doctor Knox had Burke and Hare to assist him; think what they did for surgery—I have *you*," he informs his young hostages to fortune. There is also some effective incidental humor. Observing Karl, paint-brush in hand, "decorating" the Spengler house to distract the police's attention away from the nefarious activities within, the sergeant remarks, "I hope he's a better doctor than he is a painter." And one eloquent and poignant scene has Frau Brandt confronted by her erstwhile husband in the body of another man. But depth is largely dispensed with for the sake of pace, and although it slackens off toward the end, Fisher still maintains it at a high level.

At the climax, the onus is snatched away from the baron and given over to the man monster he has created, and it is *he* who orchestrates the exciting and original conclusion in the house—the best of the entire series. First he flings oil lamps at the various exits and then, when Frankenstein still manages to escape by hurling himself through the French windows, Brandt carries him, kicking and screaming, into the flames of a new age of random horror. But despite the lacing of gore and a spurt of sex, the savage brutality that was now starting to imbue the horror films of the American underground was nowhere to be found in *Frankenstein Must Be Destroyed*. Hammer Horror had begun to take on an antique charm. To audiences becoming inured to outrage through daily news bulletins from Vietnam, the self-serving barbarism of Baron Frankenstein was starting to look like mere expediency.

With his last two films for Hammer, the 65-year-old Fisher seemed to have caught a second wind. But his failure to offset some of the gratuitous sadism nevertheless confirms the journeyman nature of his talent. Hinds's opinion of Fisher was pragmatic. "Terry used to come into script readings, but he would be just as happy not to; he didn't think that was his job. His attitude was 'give me the script, and I'll give you as good a job as I can give you'." Not that it mattered—none of it was good enough, now. *Franken-stein Must Be Destroyed* was castigated by a correspondent to *Films and Filming* for "not having *enough*...horrific scenes."

> "I have become the victim of everything Frankenstein and I ever advocated...My brain...is in someone else's body!"
>
> —Professor Brandt
> *Frankenstein Must Be Destroyed*

This was the end of the line for Frankenstein. Two more films would be produced, but the notion of a continuing series was to finish here.

Hammer had put other projects on the floor in the meanwhile. The first was the ill-timed space opera, *Moon Zero Two,* and the second was from a script by Alfred Shaughnessy and Michael Reeves, which had been revised by Jimmy Sangster following Reeves's drug-related death in February 1969 at the age of 24; Christopher Lee had expressed a desire to star in *Crescendo,* but Warners had "wanted an American," so James Olsen had stepped in from *Moon Zero Two,* instead.

Having fulfilled his obligations on "Journey to the Unknown" and written a screenplay for one more Dracula, Anthony Hinds ceased to play any further role in the affairs of the company. With typical humility, he subsequently began to feel that he had "deserted the sinking ship," and offered his half-share in Hammer to James Carreras. Carreras offered him the nominal sum of £5000 (and the retention of his company car) in return, ostensibly to compensate him for "loss of office." The Hinds family connection having effectively been ended, secretary James Dawson—whom William Hinds had brought to Hammer with him—also resigned, and on April 14, he was replaced by the 35-year-old Roy Skeggs.

The certainties of the sixties were evaporating in the cold light of the austerity to come. The teen scene that had begun with *Going To a Go-Go* was ending with a plea to *Gimme Shelter.* What remained of the hippie dream was turning sour in an excess of drugs and despair, and on August 9, 1969, it was to be wiped out for good at

the point of a knife with the atrocity perpetrated in the Hollywood
Hills by Charles Manson and his "dune-buggy attack battalion."[12]

The *now* generation had been finding other forms of escapism
to that provided by the cinema. In the course of the decade, the
number of halls in the U.K. had fallen by 50 percent, but attendance
figures had declined by 75 percent. At Hammer, trade screamers
were readied for the winter of 1969. *In the Sun, Disaster in Space, The
Reluctant Virgin (The Bride of Newgate Gaol), When the World Cracked
Open, The Haunting of Toby Jugg,* and *The Claw*—all were trumpeted,
but only one would ever see the light of day.

With Warners now in the hands of Ted Ashley, a tighter budgetary regime was to be imposed on all future coproductions with
Hammer. Further renewals would be more dependent on past
results. In line with this new corporate thinking, the quota of films
was to be reduced to one a year. "You can forget Frankenstein,"
James Carreras immediately advised the trades. "It's Dracula the
kids are interested in."

For Anthony Hinds, the Hammer days were at an end. With the
completion of *Frankenstein Must Be Destroyed,* Anthony Nelson
Keys would follow on into the wasteland. Hinds would perform
some writing assignments on a free-lance basis before eventually
going to live in Majorca, then subsequently returning to England
and the world of amateur dramatics in rural Gloucestershire. Keys
would form the short-lived Charlemagne Productions with Christopher Lee before his eventual retirement to the golf course.

James Carreras had never considered that Tony Hinds, at only
46, might unilaterally decide to call it a day—much less that his
impulsive departure would be the first step along the road toward
the disintegration of the company. But Hinds had gone, and unlike
Michael, he did *not* intend to come back. The House that was
Hammer had begun to fall.

Chapter 5

Last Rites

1970-1979

"I can't say that I greeted them with any particular enthusiasm because I felt that the Hammer genre was coming to the end of its natural life, and, indeed, the box office receipts of these films reflected this."

Bryan Forbes
on Hammer's "Elstree" films

"I think they went wrong when Tony Hinds left...I don't think anyone else had the same sympathy, the same feeling for quality. To me, Tony Hinds *was* Hammer," Don Sharp would inform an interviewer from the BBC. Of the talents who had helped Hammer Films become a legend in its own time, few now remained. With the passing of the decade, so went Asher, Ashton, Francis, John Gilling (to cinematic exile in Spain), editor James Needs (after what was termed a "professional disagreement" over the editing shop he had persuaded Tony Hinds to let him run), and Bernard Robinson.[1] The best of the Hammer years were gone with them.

In addition, Bray was about to be sold. And Hammer House, also. All the great creative ties were to be severed between past and present. Terence Fisher, returning to his beloved Holly Cottage in Twickenham after directing *Frankenstein Must Be Destroyed*, walked in front of another car at Richmond station, breaking his leg for a second time. This would put him out of action until autumn 1972.

Hammer's budgets had doubled over the past decade; the average cost of each production had now risen to £200,000. The men in suits were to have their day at last: never mind the quality—feel the cost-efficiency. If the speed and proficiency of each new Hammer production was still to be admired, the skill and flair that had given them their striking individuality in the past had vanished. The craftsmen whom James Carreras had often deployed as objects of disdain when asked the secret of Hammer's success were no more. In their place were crude factory economics and the cynical concept of film as commodity. The man who took pride in declaring, "We are a purely commercial company. We know straight away when there's a slight fall-off, and then we just tear up scripts," was in sole charge.[2]

Despite the outward show of equanimity, Hinds's departure was followed by an unseemly rush to the protection of the Transylvanian barricades. Hinds had supplied another Dracula script, and Carreras quickly seized upon it as a means of keeping things afloat until a newer program could be found. First, there was the usual hurdle to be crossed: Christopher Lee. After some wrangling, Hammer was able to negotiate around him and make it to the other side, and the unsavory-sounding *Taste the Blood of Dracula* started at Elstree in the last week of October 1969. But this fifth episode in the saga took care of Hammer's Warner allocation for 1970, and even the ever-confident James Carreras was now less than certain of what the future was to hold.

"With each successive screenplay that I read, it was quite obvious that they'd written the general story first, and then started asking themselves how they were going to fit the character of Dracula into the story," Lee would subsequently comment in relation to the declining values of the series as a whole. It was an astute observation, and *Taste the Blood of Dracula* was to be the film on which he would base it.

> *Hargood, Paxton, and Secker all live double lives. When they meet with the depraved Lord Courtley at a brothel, he persuades them to join him in a black magic ceremony to raise the spirit of Count Dracula. During the rite, Courtley drinks the blood of Dracula and is infected with a dreadful madness; he is killed by the others. Dracula comes to life again in the body of the dead aristocrat, and swears revenge on the three. His instrument will be their children. Hargood is killed by his daughter, wielding a shovel; Paxton has a wooden stake driven through his heart; Secker is stabbed to death by his son. Paxton's son, Paul, resolves to exorcise the evil. He pursues the count to a desanctified chapel, and in a battle of wills, Dracula is overcome*

by the holy power. He falls to his death on the altar—and all that
remains is red ash...

Taste the Blood of Dracula was originally intended to be a Dracula
film in name only. While Carreras was persuading Lee to reappear,
an exasperated Brian Lawrence had encouraged Hinds to write the
next opus *without* the count, in the style of *Brides*. Hinds was
unaware of what was going on behind the scenes. "I was asked to
write a script that didn't need Lee because I was told he had become
too expensive," he said. Lawrence felt that Hammer's one remaining ace should not forsake the allegiance that had helped forge his
career in the first place—especially at a time of greatest need: "too
expensive" referred to the doubling of Lee's usual fee, after his
recent appearance in Billy Wilder's *The Private Life of Sherlock
Holmes*. (Lee's fee had already risen from £5000 to £8000 between
Prince of Darkness and *Risen From the Grave*.)

Lee saw things differently. "I've never denied the debt I owe
you," he told Lawrence. "I've never denied the obligations, the
responsibilities. But I long ago discharged that debt and all those
obligations. I don't owe you anything—not now."

For his part, Lawrence had been content to argue the point, but
not so Warners. A new vampire named Lord Courtley held little
appeal for them, and Lawrence had been forced to relent while
Carreras turned on the big guns. "It was a great performance he
put on, I may say," Lee recollects. "He called me at home, because
I was a personal friend—which put me in an impossible situation.
The operative phrase he used to use was, 'you *must* do these films
because we've already got a deal with Warners—If you don't do
this film, think of the people you will put out of work'." Lee
thought, and came to the conclusion that humility was the better
part of valor. A new draft of the script inserted the count in place
of Courtley (after the *latter* was meant to have become a vampire
in the original story). This encouraged a legion of trendy critics to
note symbolic significance in Dracula's quasimetaphorical incur-
sions into the narrative and sanction the cut-and-paste expedience
as serious "art."

The choice of Peter Sasdy, whose visual style was fresh from the
faster pulse of television, to direct *Taste the Blood of Dracula* was
further testament to the company's willingness to remove itself
from the rigid corporate approach of the past in the search for

alternative ideas. Even the advertising was given a slicker glaze. Pinching the concept of the American ads for *Risen From the Grave*, the new film would be plugged with the slogan "Drink a Pint of Blood a Day," in pastiche of a recent campaign on behalf of the Milk Marketing Board. But the film had been "pepped up" in other ways too. An episode in a bordello was extended to include some topless tarts. These scenes found their way into a special sex-and-horror edition of *EXciting Cinema* magazine, but not onto American screens.

Taste the Blood of Dracula was the bells-and-whistles salute of the partygoer who refuses to acknowledge that the revelry has stopped. And yet, in a way, Hammer got it right. If the end result was tiresome—all hand-held cameras, murky photography, throbbing zooms, and frenetic pacing—it matched the jaded palettes of the post-sixties youth who waited gloomily for the inevitable anticlimax of the next decade. If the tone was deadbeat, with nowhere to go, it was perfect fodder for minds heading inexorably towards the end of their tether. These were downer days, and *Taste the Blood of Dracula* was Hammer's unwitting contribution to the general malaise.

> "And now he's out of the way, your own star can shine more brightly, can't it? Three cheers for Preston! Give him a knighthood!"
>
> —Paul Preston
> *The Mummy's Shroud*

The Sweet Ride may have gone on its *helter-skelter* way, but for the man who had escorted Prince Philip and Earl Mountbatten on two phenomenally successful fund-raising tours of the U.S. and Canada only two years before (that together, had raised more than £790,000 for charity), there was still the Variety Club, with its royal patronage.

The chairman and managing director of Hammer Films became *Sir* James Carreras in the New Year Honors List of 1969. It was the fulfilment of a lifelong ambition, and it finally set the seal on Hammer's quest for respectability. "His life was Variety Club—charities. He mixed with royalty—he was always frightened of sullying his reputation," Michael observed. But with Hinds gone in all but name on the letterhead (which would be rectified in May

1970, when he was finally to resign his directorship), desperation had begun to creep in, and the panic expressed by the insertion of a gratuitous rape scene into *Frankenstein Must Be Destroyed* was still calling the tune.[3]

By now, the word on the street was that the system of classifying films for exhibition in Britain (which the BBFC had operated virtually unchanged since 1951) was to be completely revised. The liberalizing of attitudes had radically redefined what was acceptable on the screen. In conjunction with this, there was consternation both inside and outside the industry about what was perceived to be a lack of family entertainment. At this point, some 55 percent of all films were being classified "X." It was clear that something had to be done, and a new category, the "AA" (with a reduced age restriction of 14) was to be introduced, allowing the age of the "X" to be raised and the numbers of films necessitating it to be lowered, as borderline cases became "AA" instead. With an 18-X, a new market of possibility opened up to Hammer: horror *and* sex.

With the more liberal censorship, which was soon to sanction Ken Russell's *The Devils,* Stanley Kubrick's *A Clockwork Orange,* and Sam Peckinpah's *The Straw Dogs,* the once-dangerous cocktail of horror and sex was suddenly viable. "In an increasingly permissive age, we modified our attitude to the introduction of sex. Nudity became quite common in these films and by 1970, we even had lesbian vampires," wrote John Trevelyan. But they were not to arrive before the BBFC had put up what was now becoming a token display of resistance.

In October 1969, Carreras had been approached with the idea of filming the 1871 novella *Carmilla* (written by Irish Gothicist Joseph Sheridan Le Fanu) by the trio of Harry Fine, Michael Style, and Tudor Gates, operating under a collective of Fantale Films. Using his friendship with James H. Nicholson of AIP, a typical poster rendering of the theme was commissioned, and Carreras struck a coproduction agreement with American-International to finance the film. In the deal signed on November 25, production was to be subcontracted to Fantale, under the aegis of Hammer.

Fine was known to Carreras from his acting days in *To Have and To Hold* (1950) before he had moved to a varied career on the other side of the camera. Louis M. "Deke" Heyward, with a string of British horror productions behind him, was to be executive producer on AIP's behalf. Terence Fisher was still out of active service, so Roy Ward Baker was assigned to direct. Peter Cushing agreed to add his weight to the piece—which left only Carmilla to cast. A new Hammer glamor-girl, Polish-born Ingrid Pitt, was to ingratiate herself sufficiently with Sir James for him not only to offer her the role but to herald her as "the first exciting new star of the new decade." To back her up, the usual sterling cross section of British acting talent was assembled, and *Vampire Lovers* went into Elstree on January 19, 1970.

The idea of basing the film on *Carmilla* was Harry Fine's, but it was left to Tudor Gates to fully exploit the sex angle. When the BBFC saw that (*The*) *Vampire Lovers* were of the Sapphic bent, John Trevelyan wrote to Fine listing twenty-three objections and, mindful of the problems that his board had encountered over the lesbianism in Robert Aldrich's *The Killing of Sister George*, added the warning that if his concerns were not taken seriously, the resulting film could not be passed for exhibition. Fine responded by disowning the script's "lurid and graphic stage directions," but reminded Trevelyan that the lesbianism in the story was Le Fanu's, and not Gates's.

Trevelyan's dictate was received a week into the shooting, but Baker was nevertheless requested to downplay the lesbian element. By then it was too late; in Baker's words, "The boat had already sailed."[4] The film would be awarded an "X" certificate, without cuts, in any event.

> In the province of Styria, Baron Hartog seeks out the Karnstein vampires and destroys them. One grave escapes the baron's frenzied work: that of a young girl—Carmilla Karnstein. Years pass, and Carmilla is reintroduced into society as Marcilla, the daughter of a countess. She is invited to stay with General Spielsdorf. When the general's daughter dies of anemia, Carmilla vanishes...Some time later, at the house of Roger Morton, Carmilla preys on daughter Emma and her governess. The butler suspects and calls in a doctor, who diagnoses vampirism. Both are killed by Carmilla. Morton sends for Baron Hartog. He arrives in the company of the general and Carl. Together they trace Carmilla Karnstein's ancestral grave, and Carl returns to the house in time to save Emma. The baron orders the grave disinterred; inside is the body of Carmilla. She is put to the stake and decapitated. A man in black watches silently, then turns and rides away...

Adapting *Carmilla* for the screen was neither novel nor original. Carl Dreyer's *Vampyr* (1931) is credited as having been sourced from it (although the link ends there); Roger Vadim's *Et Mourir de Plaisir* (*Blood and Roses* in the U.K.; 1960) was a "contemporary" reading; even Christopher Lee, during a sojourn in Italy, had trod the path of the "Karnsteins" (*Crypt of Horror*; 1963). What *was* novel and original was making explicit the lesbian undertone in the Le Fanu story. For "explicit," read crass and embarrassing in the Hammer version, however. Much soft-porn, full-frontal female caressing (bosoms exposed, if not directly fondled) substitutes for the veiled eroticism of the Vadim film. And with the vampire's bite moved from neck to bosom, any narrative requirement for exposure of the wound serves a dual purpose. Nevertheless, the film supplied a demand, and did so with a certain crude style. Considering her *ingenue* status and the occasional awkwardnesses of a persistent accent, Ingrid Pitt acquits herself surprisingly well, and conveys the plight and passion of her vampiric entrapment with a depth of skill that would elude Yutte Stensgaard when she was to take over the role in *Lust for a Vampire*. And whatever else may be said about *The Vampire Lovers*, its reverence to Le Fanu cannot be faulted, so faithfully adhered to are all the basic tenets of the story.

> "The enemies I sought were no ordinary mortals—they were murderers from beyond the grave. For this ruined castle, where I laid in wait, had once been the home of the Karnstein family...and at certain times, their evil spirits thrust out from their mouldering tombs and took a kind of...human shape—to roam the countryside, and seek for victims to satisfy their need, their passion, their thirst...for blood!
>
> "Sometimes to court its victim, savoring its enjoyment, and other times—to strangle and exhaust at a single feast..."
>
> —Baron Hartog
> *The Vampire Lovers*

Not only does this discourse—part of a lengthy precredits sequence—set the tone of the upcoming story, but it also set out to establish the new rules by which Hammer's vampires were to operate in the decade ahead. Although the concept of the vampire that could kill or savor as it chose is wholly Le Fanu's, the redefining of the myth helped counter one of the anomalies that had crept into the Dracula series, where some victims would become vampires while others would simply expire in an instant of bloodlust. Of course, new anomalies present themselves in the process. Le Fanu's *Carmilla* could walk abroad in shaded sunlight. She could remain absent from her tomb for an inordinate length of time. She is fundamentally of supernatural origin, yet she could eat, love, feel, like any ordinary mortal. In *The Vampire Lovers*, these aspects of the tale are dealt with less satisfactorily.

The narrative follows its source exactly. Carmilla inveigles herself into one household, then, at greater length, into a second, from whence she is dispatched. Baker declared himself unhappy with this construction, reasoning that the first vampiric excursion into the Spielsdorf home gave the game away. Le Fanu was interested in other effects, and in terms of *The Vampire Lovers* breaking the mold of previous Hammer bloodsuckers, the film survives the flaw if the original assault is seen, like Hartog's soliloquy, as merely laying down the ground rules for what is to follow. But when Carmilla returns to her grave at the climax—having faded from Carl's view as though she were a ghost—in order that she can be staked by the waiting contingent of outraged patriarchs, there is the appearance of contrivance. Similarly, the vampire's attacks are mainly conveyed in dream imagery, with Carmilla in the form of a cat (as per the novella). No one seems to be entirely sure as to whether they are making a story of the supernatural or a vampire yarn in the old Hammer tradition, where such creatures of the night are firmly rooted in flesh and blood.

The limitations of Hammer's tight budgets were becoming as transparent as Carmilla herself in the finale of *The Vampire Lovers*. In the view of Christopher Lee, "Production values were deteriorating—stories were deteriorating—and you didn't have to be a genius to know the reason: you were given a time and you were given an amount, and that was it. Not a penny more and not a day more." Here, the budget had demanded a minimum of sets, and, unusually for a Hammer horror (though the practice was soon to become the norm), much use was made of location shooting. Moor Park Golf Club stood in for General Spielsdorf's imposing residence, and Wallhall College in Aldenham was the Morton house. In addition to these is a small-scale (though effective) castle interior and an obligatory graveyard, whose limited confines and workaday painted backdrop are barely disguised by an overabundance of mist and low-key photography. But the period design is nice, the whole is authentically dressed, and Baker and his cast manage some lasting effects: Spielsdorf's heartfelt howl of entreaty to Carmilla at the death of his daughter, its echo plowing the empty house in a vain search for the departed vampire; Moray Grant's restless camera prowling around the gravestones in search of Carmilla's tomb; the dawning of understanding between the principals of the horror in their midst, when each recognizes in the other's tale of woe the mirror-image of his own—"Only now, do I see the evil in her eyes," Morton acknowledges to the portrait of Carmilla, as it, rather than the corpse of the vampire, ages and decays before his eyes, in the style of Wilde's *Dorian Gray*.

Not that horror was absent. Graphic stakings maintained the state of the art, and a stunning decapitation got the proceedings underway in the grand manner. The lesbian intrigues, despite voyeuristic handling, did provide a viable alternative reading of the real nature of the "infection" that was posited to be running through these repressed households. But the most striking thing about *The Vampire Lovers* was the marked deterioration in the quality of the product in the twelve months that had elapsed since *Frankenstein Must Be Destroyed*.

> "Thus ends my account of the fearsome Karnsteins. Before God, may we be spared from these supernatural happenings again...."
>
> —Baron Hartog
> *The Vampire Lovers*

Not likely. With *The Vampire Lovers* presold, work started immediately on a follow-up, again under the auspices of Fantale, announced as *To Love a Vampire*. On its American release, *The Vampire Lovers* received an R (Restricted) MPAA rating, although it had already been cut by AIP. More worrying for Carreras was the fact that a deal for further coproductions was summarily abandoned; the company could not be trusted to deliver in the way that its erstwhile partner had been led to expect. "Hammer was like a ship without a rudder," Deke Heyward observed of the short-lived liaison:

"There was a feeling of carelessness, which extended from the casting to the overseeing of the money. There was no backup to anything—no substance. It was like being part of a fairy tale; for all of Jimmy Carreras's smiling, I didn't know who the Wicked Witch was, and I should've liked to have known. I didn't know who was running the company."

The sequel went into the works, regardless, but from this point on, Hammer Horror had to be entirely home-produced.

With *The Vampire Lovers* failing to deliver a transatlantic alliance that would have helped replace the effective loss of Warners, it was just as well that the head of Hammer had seen fit to hedge his bets. The time had come to call in some favors, and a bit of arm-twisting at the Club enabled him to mount a double bill of his main attractions, Dracula and Frankenstein, through ABPC (soon to be subsumed into music giant EMI and renamed ABC-EMI[5]) and its Chairman Bernard Delfont—and with all-British finance, for a change.

There was a fundamental difference in the structure of this arrangement, however. As with other ABP production, overseas sales were to be negotiated *after* completion of the films. For the first time since the 1950s, Hammer had no distribution guarantee. But in the original compact between Hammer and Warner/7-Arts, Warners had been given legal right of first refusal on Dracula subjects, and that had worked in Hammer's favor to secure the deal with ABPC.

Christopher Lee was once more begged and cajoled to play the count. "Jimmy made it a personal thing on the basis of our friendship," Lee recalls. "It was wrong, there's no question about it." Lee suggested to his agent, John Redway, that he should try to secure him a percentage deal to agree. Redway had already tried and advised against it, and Lee agreed anyway. He would do so twice more. Jimmy Sangster was begged and cajoled to rewrite a thinly disguised treatment of Hammer's first Frankenstein that had been submitted by Jeremy Burnham. He was further enticed with an offer to *direct* the film, as well as produce. He agreed also, but on better terms. The result was a lame and exhausted pairing of *Scars of Dracula* with *The Horror of Frankenstein*. One of them was a comedy, but audiences would be hard pressed to decide which one.

> *With the death of his father, young Victor Frankenstein inherits both an estate and the desire to create life. Helped by two grave robbers, he pieces together a body. But he is sold a damaged brain. He goes ahead with the experiment, anyway, and the creature is brought to life; it immediately escapes and kills a workman, but is seen by a little girl. Since Frankenstein, by now, has already killed his friend, his mistress, and sundry associates, he has aroused the suspicion of the police, in any event. They arrive at the castle with their eye-witness, and the baron hides his handiwork in an acid tank. When his back is turned, the little girl releases the acid. Frankenstein sighs—back to the drawing board. . . .*

"Prepare yourself for a new Frankenstein—a *young* Frankenstein!—The most evil genius of all time," promised the American trailer. By all accounts, it was fun to make, but that was where the entertainment ended. (The sole item of interest is the schoolroom scene at the beginning, which apes a similar one that was shot for *The Curse of Frankenstein* but deleted to reduce the running time.) The film was notable only for a second entrée by Jon Finch—the one actor from the ranks of Hammer who came close to reaching the height of international stardom attained by Oliver Reed.[6]

If *The Horror of Frankenstein* evidenced the dearth of ideas at Hammer, Sir James Carreras appeared content to try to make a virtue of it, at least until something better came along. He asked the newly exiled Tony Hinds if he could write another Mummy. As Hinds went to work, it became clear that interest in such a project was now nil. In the meantime, something better *had* come along, in the shape of a story idea called *Murders at the Folies Bergere*—a transvestite psycho-thriller that was to become *Terror in the Moulin Rouge* when it was passed to Harry Fine for a brief period of development (before it, and Fantale, were to part company with the company).

The Horror of Frankenstein may have been a watercolor rendition of an original oil, but *Scars of Dracula* was merely a sketch in John Elder's notebook—a couple of charcoal lines daubed at random in a vain attempt to capture a fleeting thought. Having been set aside in the debacle over *Taste the Blood of Dracula,* the earlier script had now been resurrected, just as it was originally written, without any concessions to the intermediate episode in the saga. Since it was also to be married to the briefest of schedules, Roy Ward Baker made much of it up as he went along, to compensate for the pages of dialog that had to be ditched. The expeditious assembly had the count running around his castle after the latest in nubile young things like a proverbial old-time villain in a silent film. "Dracula doesn't open doors; doors *open*, and Dracula walks through. They have them in all the supermarkets," Baker later quipped about the *mise-en-scène* he had been forced to create to keep things moving. Lee failed to appreciate the joke, or the fact that he had become a commodity to be reconstituted whenever the need arose. Remarking on the reverence with which he thought audiences still greeted his portrayals of Dracula, he said in an interview, "They never laugh at me to my knowledge." Evidently he had not attended a screening of *Scars of Dracula*.

> *After a series of misadventures, Paul finds himself at Castle Dracula, where he sees the count murder a vampire woman. Sarah and Paul's brother, Simon, set out to look for him. They are forced to take refuge at the castle, where Simon finds a locket owned by Paul. Seeking help at a local village, Simon is tutored in the ways of the vampire by a priest. Returning to the castle once more, he persuades Klove to reveal Dracula's crypt and enters armed with a stake. He finds Paul impaled on a meat hook. Dracula escapes and dispatches a giant bat to the church to kill the priest; he now has Sarah captive. As Simon and the count come face-to-face on the battlements, Dracula is struck by a bolt of lightning. He is enveloped in flames, and topples to his death in the valley below.*

An irredeemably tacky endeavor, *Scars of Dracula* is composed entirely of wooden characters, cardboard sets, and paper-thin plot. For two reels, the dialogue is never more than perfunctory, designed solely to move the story toward its predictable end. There are numerous exchanges of the most banal kind, culminating in a serving wench who responds to an inquiry about why the hero should stay away from Castle Dracula at night, by saying, "I don't know. I'm new here." Nothing else was. The infusions of gore give the film a certain charnel-house abandon, in the manner of the "penny dreadfuls," but if Dracula's modus operandi is inexplicable (he simply mopes around his castle—when it is not being razed to the ground—waiting for the occasional unwary visitor on which to feed), it merely exemplified Hinds's disillusion. In the rush to production, any notion of a continuing series had been forsaken. The giant bat that was to have fed the count's ashes with blood after his climactic disintegration in *Risen From the Grave* was now an extraneous element supplementing the diet of a Dracula who is clearly capable of fending for himself. The despondency that had infected the shooting is plain. "It was the beginning of the end and everybody knew it," was the opinion of producer Aida Young.

Immune to the fallout, Hinds would admit to having discovered that "nobody gave a damn" anyway. Dislodged from a continuity of context, the plot of the film was juvenile, at best, and contemptuous of the audience, at worst. Lee's pronouncements on what was now the continuing saga of "will he or won't he" play the role again remained more or less sanguine. "If Dracula subjects are successful in cinemas all over the world and the public want to see me in that part, I will play it—I will stop when audiences don't want to see me playing it anymore." With that, he signed up for his *sixth* outing as the count.

In the case of the American audience, Warners made that decision for them; it immediately turned both films down. Next time, Hammer was going to have to think of something *new*.

> "Out—both of you—you're not wanted here!"
>
> —Landlord
> *Scars of Dracula*

The concerted effort that had been taking place to revitalize flagging British film production and ease the rapidly worsening state of the industry had been concentrated on the Elstree Studios operations of M-G-M-EMI, now in the charge of actor, author, screenwriter, and newly appointed head of production, Bryan Forbes.

To the world at large, Hammer was now part and parcel of Elstree, and Bernard Delfont had picked up where AIP had left off and appended *To Love a Vampire* to his growing roster of Hammer product. The pact was soon to be extended to include another six pictures over the next three years with an option for nine more, and Hammer was perceived as central to Anglo-EMI's assault on the world market. The reality was not quite like that. The "hidden agenda" agreement between Hammer and EMI/ABP was eating into a production budget for the studio that had provisionally been earmarked for things other than Hammer's horror films. "The decision to make them was very much an 'old pals act' between

Delfont and Jimmy Carreras," Forbes was to note. "The cost of these films came out of the very slender resources at my disposal and meant that I had to cancel other films which I would have preferred and which, I think, might have more materially contributed to the commercial success of my program."

By June 1970, Carreras had also encouraged Rank to back three horrors in a similar vein. Hammer was precluded from using Dracula and Frankenstein, which were to remain exclusive to Anglo-EMI (and the ABC circuit), but a way had been found to combine both Carmilla *and* the count, that would redeploy the budding talents of Ingrid Pitt at the same time: *Countess Dracula*. To provide a safety net, "Jimmy will presell them in America," said Fred Thomas, joint managing director of RFD. Carreras would need more luck than the foreign sales division of EMI. After being turned down by Warners, Hammer's first three for EMI were to go out in the U.S. through Continental—an independent distributor which would find itself out of business immediately after their release.

In *To Love a Vampire*, the Karnstein films were to show the same disregard for consistency that had begun to plague Hammer's latterday Draculas. In *The Vampire Lovers*, Carmilla's birth-death dates are given as 1775-1794; in *Love*, they become 1688-1710. The film takes place in 1830, "*Forty* years to the day since they [the Karnsteins] were last seen," according to an innkeeper. In an exchange with her tutor, Carmilla is asked to name some contemporary 19th-century novelists. She replies, "I don't know any, but I have read a lot of 18th-century work." Difficult for someone who died in 1710. The reason for these anomalies is that, in the interim, Gates had concocted a novel ploy designed to extract the maximum mileage out of the whole Karnstein concept. The innkeeper actually goes on to say, "and before that, forty years *again*," thus creating an entirely new myth structure of cyclical reincarnation, whereby ensuing episodes could be set either backward or forward in time as their writers so chose. The original script for *To Love a Vampire* placed the action in 1870, not 1830, but this was revised with the prospect of a third, even a fourth Karnstein epic: *Vampire Hunters*.

"O, Lord of Darkness, Prince of Hell—hear this, thy servant's plea. Send—from thy black realm—the power that we may do thy

will on earth. Recreate this dust of centuries…that in thy service, the
dead may join with the Undead!"

—Count Karnstein
Lust For a Vampire

With Ingrid Pitt now precluded from reprising her role as Carmilla in the sequel—*Countess Dracula* was due to go before the
cameras at Pinewood within weeks of the commencement of principal photography on *Love*—new Hammer discovery Yutte Stensgaard, wife of Amicus art director Tony Curtis, was elevated to the
pivotal role. It had also been intended that the film should benefit
from the experienced hand of Terence Fisher and the pulling power
of Peter Cushing. Neither of them were to make it, either. Fisher's
injuries prevented him from undertaking the location work that
economy demanded, and Cushing would be forced to withdraw
from the role of Giles Barton after a sudden deterioration in his
wife's poor health. Jimmy Sangster, who was editing *The Horror of
Frankenstein* at the time, was asked to step into the directorial
breach. He, in turn, persuaded Ralph Bates to take on the role of
Barton, the two men having become friends during the shooting of
the earlier film. If the end result gave the appearance of haste, it
could hardly have come as a surprise. Now entitled *Lust For a
Vampire* (at the suggestion of Bernard Delfont), the sequel wrapped
as *The Vampire Lovers* opened to unexpectedly brisk business. *Lust
For a Vampire* was on release less than four months later. The public
tired quickly. The series was to spawn only one more episode
before it would peter out as an aberration.

> *A girl is sacrificed at a Black Mass and her blood poured onto the
> ashes in a coffin…. Writer Richard Lestrange tricks his way into a
> teaching post at a finishing school near Castle Karnstein, and falls
> in love with Mircalla. Giles Barton, joint owner of the school and a
> student of the occult, suspects one of the pupils of being a vampire,
> though he is unsure as to which one. A clandestine meeting with
> Mircalla to discuss his theory leaves him dead—the mark of the
> vampire on his throat. More deaths follow, not only among the pupils
> but also in the nearby village. Lestrange begins to suspect Mircalla;
> the villagers eventually decide to burn the castle, and she reveals
> herself to be Carmilla Karnstein, reincarnated from the ashes. She
> begs Lestrange to join her as one of the Undead. A fiery stake from
> the burning roof impales itself in her heart and she dies. Lestrange*

*escapes, but the Count and Countess Karnstein remain behind,
trapped in the flames.*

In a flagrant attempt by Gates and company to have their cake
and eat it, the first film's "Man in Black" (who had hovered on the
very edges of the narrative like a medeval figure of Death) was
elaborated in *Lust For a Vampire* into fully fledged vampire Count
Karnstein, in the manner of Dracula. Though with Carmilla constantly in tow, and minus fangs, the effect was more Svengali than
Undead.

The count was played by Mike Raven on this outing, who in
stature and saturnine looks (if not acting ability), was to be Hammer's first real alternative to Christopher Lee. The one-time "pirate" radio deejay had been introduced to producers Fine and Style
by glamor photographer and would-be agent Philip Stearns. Raven's contribution to the film included the devising of Count
Karnstein's curtain-raising black magic incantation—a quasi-
authentic confection of Hebrew and dog-Latin that he had culled
from A. E. Waite's *Book of Ceremonial Magic,* to improve on the one
that Gates had improvised: "I sewed several spells together, so we
wouldn't get any unwanted additions to the cast on the set!" By
September, Raven was starring alongside Cushing and Lee in the
ill-fated Amicus 3-D version of Jekyll and Hyde—*I, Monster.* He
subsequently gave up his day job for a career in films. But he was
to find himself revoiced in *Lust For a Vampire* (by Valentine Dyall),
and his unhappiness at the result helped bring his brief foray into
horror to an impromptu end.

"Agla, Adonai, Magister Mundi...Te adoro et te invoco. Venite,
venite—Lucifer!"

—Count Karnstein
Lust For a Vampire

Revoicing an actor or actress to achieve a more acceptable effect
or tonal resonance (or to eliminate the vagaries of regional accents)
is a commonplace in films, and Hammer had long since come to
approve of the practice in respect to the American market. Australian Leon Greene was revoiced (by Patrick Allen) in *The Devil Rides
Out.* Margia Dean was treated likewise in *The Quatermass Experiment.* Similar lip-service was paid to Lelia Goldoni in *Hysteria,*

Diane Clare in *The Plague of the Zombies,* and Susan Denberg in *Frankenstein Created Woman.* Ewan Hooper and sundry villagers were dubbed in *Dracula Has Risen From the Grave,* as were Maddy Smith in *The Vampire Lovers* and Jenny Hanley in *Scars of Dracula.* Still to come would be Ingrid Pitt in *Countess Dracula,* Valerie Leon in *Blood From the Mummy's Tomb,* the Collinson twins in *Twins of Evil,* Robert Tayman in *Vampire Circus,* John Forbes Robertson in *The Legend of the 7 Golden Vampires,* and Nastassja Kinski in *To the Devil—A Daughter.* Any decision on whether or not to opt for remedial action of this kind lay with a producer, subject to contract, but few actors in Hammer's films ever had the muscle to circumvent such an eventuality. In Raven's case, the fact that he made his living with his voice exacerbated the indignity. To add insult, close-ups of Lee's bloodshot eyes (from *Dracula Has Risen From the Grave*) had been spliced into the proceedings in place of his own. Raven broke with Hammer as a result, and his career thereafter was short-lived.[7]

After its barnstorming opening, the remainder of *Lust For a Vampire* is tediously conventional. It is *The Vampire Lovers* crossed with *The Brides of Dracula,* for the most part, its best sequence swamped by the catchpenny accompaniment of a pop song—"Strange Love"—also included at the instigation of Harry Fine. It may be the most identifiably Hammeresque of the three Karnsteins but curiously, there is little violence (two graphic stakings being about all that could conceivably be categorized as Hammer Horror), and canine teeth are conspicuous by their absence until the final reel.

Sangster's direction is much less assured than in *The Horror of Frankenstein* (which he also produced), as witness the overplaying of some of the support and the underplaying of most of the rest. Bates and Stensgaard are seriously miscast, and only Helen Christie, as Miss Simpson, comes out of the affair with any honor. There are one or two striking sequences—the revelatory flashback to Carmilla's resurrection as she kills Barton, and a slow-motion plunge down the shaft of a dried-up well—but these owe more to the cutting than to anything done on the floor. There is the usual fiery climax, and some evocative final moments with Raven as he walks the battlements of the castle while awaiting his inevitable demise. And there is the occasional original touch: Lestrange is a Gothic novelist, though without a frame of reference to add depth.

(Gates *had* seen fit to provide one, but it was deleted.) There is even the pictorial distraction of another Corman-inspired dream sequence. But the film as a whole looks tired and jaded, and by now, even the audiences were catching on.

While *Lust For a Vampire* shot at Elstree, *Countess Dracula* took to the floor at Pinewood, and Rank's Frank Poole trumpeted the news that a fourth horror was to be added to *his* quota: *Hands of the Ripper*. Not one to stop at a surfeit, Carreras promptly leafed through his list of stock titles and announced that Hammer would be making *The Picture of Dorian Gray*. "We are preparing a very exciting screenplay," he enthused. Harry Alan Towers had already prepared one, so that idea was quietly abandoned.

> *Through an accident, the aged Countess Nadasdy has discovered that blood has rejuvenative power, but the effect is temporary and more is needed to maintain her refreshed appearance. Her servants keep her supplied. In her new youthful persona, the countess pretends to be her own daughter and falls for Imre Toth, a young army officer. They become betrothed, and she orders her daughter kidnapped to aid the deception. When the villagers stumble on the bodies of her victims, Toth confronts the countess and catches her bathing in blood! He breaks off the engagement, but she blackmails him into going through with the wedding. She now intends to kill her daughter and use her blood also. During the ceremony, the countess suddenly reverts to her true age in front of the assembled guests. In her madness, she attacks her daughter. Toth intervenes and is killed. The countess is arrested and thrown into a dungeon to await execution...as "Countess Dracula!"*

Countess Dracula is another curiosity in Hammer's crypt. What should have been a straightforward historical horror recounting the legend of "bloody countess" Elizabeth Bathory was turned into an admixture of Jekyll and Hyde and *The Queen of Spades*. This time, director Peter Sasdy's pretensions had included styling his film after Eisenstein's *Ivan the Terrible*—an exercise that was patently lost on *Films and Filming*'s Richard Weaver, who considered it a "lethargic piece of story-telling." Turgid and slow moving it certainly is, and some splendid sets and nice color design are wasted on a storyline in which the countess's perverse obsession is subordinated to predictable castle intrigues and a series of budget transformation scenes. The makings of a good script are buried beneath the precipitate haste of the production and the desire to inject naked flesh at every available opportunity. The result is a tedious cross between romantic period thriller and crude sexploitation piece: "They'll make a fine pair," Captain Balogh remarks of the impending marriage between Toth and the countess. "But not as fine a pair as these, eh?" suggests the local whore, thrusting her bolstered breasts under Toth's nose—"The lady has a sizzling wit," replies the latter in bored acknowledgment, as if two entirely different films had just found themselves thrown together on the same set.

Composer Harry Robinson adds to this impression by scoring the love scenes between Toth and the countess as though they were between Hercules and Omphale in *Hercules Unchained*, or any number of similarly saccharine Italian epics. (Robinson would provide the following year's *Twins of Evil* with a pastiche Ennio Morricone "spaghetti western" score.) And any connection to Dracula beyond title and hype is so tenuous as to be nonexistent.

The expectations of Rank's London managers were to be dashed to disbelief when they were presented with their first Hammer horror film since 1962. The nudity that formed much of the *raison d'être* was to be excised from American prints, and with that gone, a feeble climactic collapse from youthful beauty to decrepit old age was insufficiently tantalizing to persuade audiences to stay what remained of the course. In almost all respects, *Countess Dracula* was strictly from Hungary (Sasdy and producer Alex Paal were both Hungarian émigrés).[8]

With the tacit guarantee of long-term funding from both EMI and Rank, any writer or producer with a likely story and an eye for a market trend was finding that it was open house at Hammer. 113 Wardour Street was one of the few places in town where there was money to spend, and a line began to form among those who felt they had something worth spending it on. Carreras himself may have been professionally unaffected by Hinds's departure, but Hammer was not. The loss had left a vaccuum in terms of production acumen that could not be filled for long by the self-serving interests of independent producers alone—or reliance on the TV spin-off. (*On the Buses* was to revive the practice at a meager £89,000, and at the instigation of Brian Lawrence.) As the year drew to its close, James Carreras sent for his son.

Michael's luck in trying to finance other projects had not improved greatly in the meantime. Universal had recently turned down *Mistress of the Seas* (about the life and times of pirate-girl Anne Bonney, designed for Raquel Welch), and while still at his office on Warner Boulevard in Burbank, California, Ken Hyman had also declined an invitation to participate in Capricorn's latest venture, *The Mad Motorists*, due to Warners' own disastrous excursion into the same territory with *The Great Race* in 1965. On his return from the Namib Desert in Southwest Africa, where he had been on location for a third romp through prehistory, *Creatures the World Forgot*, Michael decided that he had nothing to lose by listening to what his father had to say. The role of executive producer was offered, and turned down—if he was to return to Hammer on a permanent basis, then it would be on *his* terms and in a position where he could influence the direction in which the company was now to go. To Michael's surprise, Sir James agreed.

On January 4, 1971, Michael Carreras returned in triumph as the managing director of Hammer Films. His first official act was to appoint Roy Skeggs as production supervisor to oversee the growing list of features that had accumulated in his absence. But as luck would have it, the production that was scheduled to inaugurate the new regime would prove to be the most ill-fated in the company's history.

The growing list of would-be horror film producers who had been bending the ear of James Carreras had included press agent Howard Brandy, who had sold Hammer the idea of a film based on Bram Stoker's *The Jewel of the Seven Stars* on the strength of its *female* mummy, and a treatment by AIP writer in residence Christopher Wicking. "This is a happy, up-beat time for horror," Brandy gleefully informed the trades. On January 11, *Blood From the Mummy's Tomb* started shooting with Peter Cushing in the central role of archaeologist Julian Fuchs. Before the day was out, Cushing's devoted wife, Helen, was rushed to the hospital, where she died three days later, and the forlorn star had no alternative but to pull out of the film. Cushing was replaced by Andrew Keir, and *Blood From the Mummy's Tomb* started from scratch the following day. But the "Jewel of the Seven Stars" was a stone that clearly had a curse upon it.

> *Professor Fuchs has discovered the burial tomb of Tera, Queen of Darkness—her mummified body flesh, her right hand severed at the wrist. On the hand is a ruby ring: the Jewel of the Seven Stars. And in the tomb are other strange objects: the statue of a snake, a mummified cat, and the skull of a jackal. The artifacts are brought to England and divided among the members of the expedition, who each go their separate ways. Fuchs enshrines Tera's body in the cellar of his home and gives the ruby ring to his daughter Margaret. When she wears it, she feels a psychic affinity with the dead queen, for whom she is the living double. The other three members of the team suddenly fall victim to some supernatural force. In the meanwhile, Margaret has come under the influence of Corbeck, an evil schemer who has designs on the power trapped in Tera's tomb: Corbeck plans to conjure Tera's spirit in Margaret's body. As he reads from the scroll, Fuchs tries to intervene. A struggle ensues, and in the confusion, Margaret plunges a dagger into Tera's heart. The vault collapses in on them all, and Margaret alone survives. Or does she? As she lies swathed in bandages, only the eyes are visible....*

The film had been forced onto the floor two months earlier than originally planned and Brandy and Wicking's agents had already fallen out, with Wicking being barred from the set. ("I was *persona non grata* for Howard Brandy. I wasn't allowed to talk to anybody. It was quite silly," he said.) That apart, filming had proceeded more or less as normal until mid-February. But the *auteur* approach of director Seth Holt (who had not worked for two years prior to being offered *Blood From the Mummy's Tomb*) meant that he had kept the cutting plan for the film to himself—even to the exclusion of his editors. At the close of the fifth week, Holt, at 47, died suddenly of a heart attack.

It fell to Michael Carreras to pick up the pieces. Having organized a day or two's shooting for cinematographer Arthur Grant, he soon realized that *Blood From the Mummy's Tomb* was in a "terrible, terrible mess." Next, he fired editor Oswald Hafenrichter (replacing him with Peter Weatherley), and began to cast around for another director. But Holt inspired fierce loyalty in his crew, and resignations were now to follow his untimely demise. Michael struggled to keep production going through what should have been the film's sixth and final week and offered the director's chair to Don Sharp, with the option that he could start over again, if he decided to accept. Sharp turned it down, and by week seven,

Michael was left with no other choice but to finish the shoot himself and try to make sense of the chaotic assemblage.

Blood From the Mummy's Tomb would ultimately go into release as a *second* feature because of the uncertainties over the final cut. The critics were unusually kind, but one sensed a deference to Holt's memory in the reticence of their reviews. The tone of the film is one of sustained frenzy, and the always-uncertain continuity finally comes apart under the sheer volume of murder and mayhem that is force-fed into the last two reels. The perceptible note of hysteria and confusion that had been discovered among the jumble of footage in the cutting-room said something about the state of Seth Holt's mind during his last days on the film, but the fact that so much remained in the patchwork that subsequently surfaced said just as much about the state of dissension in the ranks of those who completed it for him.[9]

> 1st Nurse: "Is there no information?"
> 2nd Nurse: "Nothing. She's the same as she was when they brought her in—naked, and more dead than alive."
> —*Blood From the Mummy's Tomb*

Blood From the Mummy's Tomb had turned into a baptism of fire for its fledgling producer, and he was not to come out of it unsinged. Brandy attempted to float a second Stoker-oriented vehicle—*Victim of His Imagination*—but Hammer's enthusiasm was short-lived. Projects that were *not* to reach the screen would now be in the majority.

Michael was more than usually afflicted with episodes of this sort. He had stood in for Don Taylor on *Visa to Canton*, had done the same for Leslie Norman on *The Lost Continent*, and he would be forced to fire Monte Hellman from *Shatter*. After the debacle of *Blood From the Mummy's Tomb*, he opted to cut Hammer's tie with Fantale, cancel a fourth prehistoric outing, and curtail anything scheduled on nothing more than a nod from Sir James.

Next in line was *Hands of the Ripper*. This would turn out to be a more sober and effective yarn than many of its predecessors, thanks to the steadying influence of Aida Young—now Hammer's most experienced house producer and a lady especially associated with its various romps through ancient history, particularly those she referred to as her "silly dinosaur ones." But her relegation in the ranks caused by the recent flirtations with outside producers typified the "neglect" that she already considered herself to be suffering at Hammer's hands. When Young was done with *Hands of the Ripper,* she, too, was to withdraw from the company, to seek more rewarding employment at EMI.

> *A young girl watches, trance-like, as her father murders her mother: he is Jack the Ripper. Years later, Anna is now working for a medium. When she kills the woman in a fit of madness, Doctor Pritchard is a witness and takes her under his wing; a psychoanalyst, he intends to cure her dementia. Despite his precautions, Anna murders again—first a maid, then a prostitute, finally, the royal medium during a seance. But these killings have revealed the truth about the girl, and Pritchard senses that he is on the edge of understanding at last. In a moment of distraction, he kisses her—inadvertently sparking the schizoid trauma—and Anna impales him with a sword. Fleeing, she is spotted by Pritchard's daughter, Laura, and taken to St. Paul's Cathedral. Pritchard sets off in agonized pursuit. High in the Whispering Gallery, the spirit of the Ripper overtakes her once more, but before she can harm Laura, Pritchard arrives below and beseeches her to join him. Anna throws herself from the balcony, and they both lie still in death.*

Hands of the Ripper is in the classic mold of Hammer Horror: stylish and superior, and containing the best work that director Peter Sasdy would do for the company. That it had been produced by an "old hand" at Hammer's game is evident throughout, and while Aida Young had given the impression of being overtaken by the all-embracing banality of the last two Draculas (and the discouraging process of working at Elstree), her star had risen again with the budget and the class acts that were mustered around her on the last truly original idea that Hammer was to commit to film in the name of horror. The daughter of Jack the Ripper is haunted by repressed childhood memories of murder and blood, and when she is made the subject of the new discipline of psychoanalysis, her nightmares drive her to kill. Not only was the plot well worked out, but it had the added benefit of operating on the murder-every-fifteen-minutes principle that was later to become the *sine qua non* of the "splatter" film.

Unfortunately, *Hands of the Ripper* is let down in the last reel. When the murderous Anna's unconscious ire is turned against the doctor at the climax, he finds himself skewered on a saber. With a Van Helsing-like presence of mind, he pops a couple of aspirins and promptly rids himself of the offending implement by hooking it on a door-knob and kicking himself free, before rushing off to apprehend the culprit! The fine line between horror and humor is irretrievably crossed. The first-night audience would find itself in stitches (unlike Dr. Pritchard). Not even Anna's elegantly filmed slow-motion dive from the dizzy heights of the (front-projected) Whispering Gallery in St. Paul's could save things, after that.

Until its ill-fated final minutes, the film displayed a nice sense of period and delivered its quota of thrills with enthusiasm, if a little too much clarity on occasion. (A throat-slashing with a broken mirror-glass was to be deprived of a more graphic *second* stab by the BBFC.) *Hands of the Ripper* would be relegated to playing the lower half of a double bill with the upcoming *Twins of Evil*, which would display the full-frontal charms of the Collinson twins. While neither film could realistically be considered first-feature material at this juncture, the billing would make it plain that the sleaze factor had now conquered all.

Following through the door would be Brian Clemens and Albert Fennell, a writer-producer combo whose joint credits had been restricted to undemanding television drama series (though Fennell had dabbled in horror previously with *Night of the Eagle* [aka *Burn Witch Burn*] in 1961). Their new idea was *Dr. Jekyll and Mistress Hyde*, who was to transform into *Sister Hyde* when she eventually slunk into Elstree in the sultry shape of Martine Beswick.

Dr. Jekyll and Sister Hyde would effectively shoot back-to-back with *Blood From the Mummy's Tomb* and therefore begin only three weeks after *Hands of the Ripper* had gone onto the floor at Pinewood. The two concurrent productions made an interesting comparison. Both films were set ostensibly in late Victorian London and within a dozen or so years of each other. Whatever else it might have lacked, *Hands of the Ripper* was steeped in period and rich in typical Rank production values. *Sister Hyde*, on the other hand, could not even offer up atmosphere. It was fast becoming clear that Bryan Forbes, EMI, *and* Hammer all faced an increasingly uphill climb when it came to pitching Elstree's wares in the international marketplace.

> *In his search for the Elixir of Life, Dr. Jekyll formulates a drug using female hormones. When he tries it on himself, he discovers that it changes him into a woman: Sister Hyde. Denied a supply of corpses for his further experiments when body snatchers Burke and Hare are put out of business by a mob, Jekyll stalks the streets as Hyde, in search of victims. Complications ensue as a result of the dual personality and Professor Robertson becomes suspicious; he is killed by Hyde. Eventually, the net closes in and, chased by the police, Jekyll falls to his death from the rooftops. When the onlookers examine the body, they find it a mixture of man and woman.*

"Actually, it's not a horror film at all, really," said Clemens. "More a thriller." True, inasmuch as most of the thrills were voyeuristic in nature and designed to be engendered by the sight of Beswick cat walking in and out of a variety of Victorian corselettes. The sex-change concept also allowed for a variety of sniggering permutations to be intimated of the otherwise coy liaisons, as Jekyll's orientation becomes confused. But the film translates its homoerotic gender-bending theme into the stuff of smutty jokes, conducted in a London of perpetual fog and half a dozen streets, where tarts advise each other not to go talking to "strange men," and Sister Hyde delivers such soporific one-liners of her alter ego as, "He's not been feeling himself."

This Jekyll is looking for the Elixir of Life, employs the body-snatching services of Burke and Hare (sixty years out of time), and becomes Jack the Ripper. *Dr. Jekyll and Sister Hyde* certainly tried to cover all the angles. But it would turn out to be Hammer's second Ripper film in almost as many weeks in release, and final proof that the genre was no longer capable of sustaining thematic credibility.

As if to reflect the poverty of imagination, Clemens's script had Dr. Jekyll living in a ground-floor flat instead of a town house. The monsters were in retreat, and Hammer House would soon be scaled down to match. *Dr. Jekyll and Sister Hyde* was originally intended for the Rank circuit but was switched to ABC. In its place, the nation's Odeons were to receive their first visit from the Karnsteins.

"The Devil has sent me...twins of evil!"

—Gustav Weil
Twins of Evil

The last installment of the saga that was intended as a series jettisoned the concept of cyclical rebirth that *Lust For a Vampire* had tried to graft onto Carmilla in its attempt to find a formula, and chose to concentrate on developing the Dracula-in-waiting character of Count Karnstein, instead. Originally titled *Vampire Virgins*, the third part of the so-called Karnstein Trilogy was to benefit from the improvement in production values to be afforded at Pinewood through becoming one of Hammer's four films for Rank, though *fin de siècle* desperation was never far from the surface in the film that lensed on March 22 as the less contentious *Twins of Evil*.

> *Twins Maria and Frieda arrive at Karnstein to stay with their uncle, Gustav Weil, leader of The Brotherhood—a fanatical puritan sect. Frieda is fascinated by Weil's archenemy, Count Karnstein. In his castle, Karnstein sacrifices a young girl and reincarnates his ancestor, Countess Mircalla; she transforms him into one of the Undead. Through Karnstein, Frieda becomes a vampire also. After claiming several victims, she is caught in the act and jailed to await death by burning. Karnstein switches the twins—Maria is to die in Frieda's stead. Anton realizes the truth and rescues Maria. The Brotherhood converges on Karnstein Castle, and in the battle that ensues, Frieda is decapitated. Maria is captured by the count, who kills Weil. But his triumph is short-lived: Anton's lance pierces his heart.*

Twins of Evil marked Peter Cushing's return to Hammer after the anguish of his wife's death. The actor had been inconsolable; he would burst into tears in the company of friends and colleagues and, by his own admission, had actively contemplated suicide. But good sense had prevailed, and he had come to the view that continuing his career would be the best therapy. "I knew the only way to keep going was to keep busy," he reflected. "It didn't matter what they offered—I just kept working; it was the only thing that saved my reason."

Cushing's grief would endure for years, yet so consummate a professional was he that no trace of his loss is allowed to surface in *Twins of Evil*. As the puritan witch-hunter Weil, his entrance in the film is understated. He comes upon a young girl accused of consorting with the Devil, and in no more than a fleeting glance, his expression betrays satisfaction, resignation, determination. The tone is set immediately—both for the character and for the dynamic of the piece—for Cushing could convey as much by a look as many of his contemporaries were able to communicate through pages of dialog, and it is *his* presence alone that saves *Twins of Evil* from becoming the travesty of genre bending and exploitational excess that its producers had evidently decreed was the only way to secure a reasonable return in an increasingly unsafe financial environment.

Twins of Evil was Hammer's most blatant example of pop horror to date, and it was entirely unabashed in the contempt it showed for the audience it should have been seeking to cultivate. Every time the pace slackens, another villager is arbitrarily torched or some secondary character is casually fanged. This was to be the third Karnstein adventure to reach the screen in just over a year, and the motivation behind them had become obvious to all but the most ardent fan: Hammer's interest in such subjects went no further than the balance sheet. The Hammer name, which had always stood for a certain quality in Gothic horror, was being capitalized on by a company whose only concern seemed to be to make hay while the last rays of the dying sun still shone.

In the film's favor is some powerful and engaging work by the principals (especially in the initial tense confrontation between Cushing's sanctimonious puritan and his adversary, the count), a strong sense of *mise-en-scène*, and the fact that, unlike its forebears, it was to be the top half of a marketable double bill. (The previous Karnsteins had been paired with *Angels From Hell* and *The Losers*, respectively—both abysmal AIP biker schlock.) There might have been little in the way of extra money, but here it is clearly expended to better effect. Dick Bush's lighting and Roy Stannard's art direction show a marked improvement over their counterparts in the previous two installments, despite Don Mingaye's participation in *Lust*. John Hough's direction is smooth and professional, if undistinguished. He has an eye for composition and constantly fills his frame with movement, keeping faith with the notion of an audience whose threshold of boredom was next to nonexistent— though it surprises how even a director of evident worth can fall foul of exploitative sex scenes: an actress stroking the shaft of a burning candle during a passionate embrace is likely to arouse only laughter in the average viewer. If nothing else, the film offers a partial return to full-scale Hammer blood and thunder. The climax is a veritable splatterfest, for 1971, with an eye gouging by firebrand, a staking, two ax murders (one of which shows a man's head split open with a meat cleaver), and a decapitation—all within a few minutes of one another.

But against these are characters who are thinly sketched at best, moral battle lines that are clichéd and simplistic to the point of fable, and set pieces that come across as straining for effect. Blighting the entire Karnstein series was the haste apparent in the rush to release, the perfunctory nature of many of the (uncredited) effects, and the triteness of the writing. In *Twins of Evil*, Damien Thomas's count is in a direct line of descendancy from the decadent noblemen that Hammer had created for *The Hound of the Baskervilles* and *The Curse of the Werewolf*. The actor is up to the role, but his dialogue is distinctly precocious and the characterization lacks even the refined sadism of the public-school bully. Tudor Gates and his producers had sat through four of Hammer's earlier horrors "to get the feel of them," according to Fine. They got an *impression*, certainly, which accounts for the hybrid quality of the Karnstein films, and Fine had also worked out some spurious construct on "curves of excitement," which he purportedly used when organizing his plots. But in trying to be all things to all men, *Twins of Evil* merely pointed up the flaw that had been inherent in the concept from the start: it is a medley for differing tastes, and like the proverbial Chinese meal, once it is over, the desire for something more substantial returns with a vengeance.

Twins of Evil must remain fundamentally a frolic—fun while it lasts, but instantly forgettable. Yet because of the intensity of Cushing's performance, it never quite collapses into self-parody; neither does it simply honor the past. Despite the shortcomings of lightweight support, a banal script, and the catchpenny nature of the whole production, it holds on by the fingertips to what had now become the remnants of a greater glory. In it can still be detected a vestige of the indefinable quality that was Hammer Horror, but this was to be the last time that the screen would make its acquaintance.

The explosion of horror product in the second half of 1971 was saturating the market and heading the genre to the very brink of a self-inflicted hiatus. *Twins of Evil* had been a calculated and cynical attempt to wrest every last penny out of a commodity now perceived to be in terminal decline. In what was destined to herald the end of the series, the character of Carmilla had been relegated to no more than the device by which the now-familiar merry-go-round of ecstasy and exorcism was set in motion.

Three months later, *Vampire Circus* would give new meaning to the words desperation and excess. Devoid of stars, the film was to pitch a welter of lesser talents into an orgy of substandard gore effects and soft-core sex. It finally stripped the pretense as naked as Frau Mueller would become within a minute of the opening reel. What in other circumstances might have served as the plot-line for a typical Hammer horror by itself was enacted in microcosm (almost in pastiche) for a prolonged precredits sequence. A young girl is delivered into the clutches of vampire Count Mitterhouse by the wife of a village schoolmaster, herself a sex slave to the monster. The village elders storm the castle, destroy the count, and burn the place down. As Mitterhouse expires, he vows to return; the village is purified—for now.

This prologue was little more than a pretext for a succession of sex and "splatter" scenes that confirmed what many had long suspected: that Hammer's films were becoming just as cheap and nasty as all the rest.

> *1810. In the village of Schtettel, a group of elders kill vampire Count Mitterhouse, who curses them before dying. Fifteen years pass and a strange circus arrives. It is peopled with the disciples of the vampire, and its purpose is to avenge Mitterhouse and use the blood of the villagers to restore him to life. Much death ensues before the villagers realize the truth. They eventually set fire to the caravans and storm the castle again. In the battle that follows, the count revives—only to be decapitated, and the castle is put to the torch. A pair of young lovers, alone, survive the melee.*

Announced as *Village of the Vampires*, the film was not without pedigree. The story was by George Baxt, who was responsible for *Circus of Horrors* and *The Shadow of the Cat*, but apart from pinching its one good idea from Ray Bradbury (the "Circus of Nights," which bears more than a passing resemblance to the Dark Carnival of *Something Wicked This Way Comes*), Baxt seemed content to let events unfold in the time-honored tradition of death and revenge. Hammer's new recruits for the occasion were producer Wilbur Stark and writer Judson Kinberg (neither of whom had any prior experience with horror), but when their saturation tactics went over schedule, Michael Carreras pulled the plug on the production.

He probably saved a few more villagers from messy extermination, in the process. Singer David Essex had been turned down in favor of Anthony Corlan for the role of Emil, but John Moulder-Brown had passed the audition. His somnolent performance is reminiscent of the inattentive schoolboy whose mind seems forever to be on other things, a trait that no doubt endeared him to Jerzy Skolimowski when he cast the part of the daydreaming bathhouse attendant in *Deep End* (1970).

Vampire Circus climaxed with a more exuberant bout of overkill than it began, and by the closing credits, the castle crypt was littered with enough dead bodies to do justice to the average Mexican or Spanish junk film. It was one surfeit too many, however. While *Vampire Circus* marked the end of Hammer's deal with Rank, so *Blood Will Have Blood* (produced concurrently at Elstree) was effectively marking the end of its deal with EMI. The first would receive only limited distribution, and the second would be relegated to the status of supporting feature for the product of another company (*Tower of Evil*, aka *The Horror of Snape Island*). The days of Hammer Horror were finally coming to a close.

> "Blood will have blood, they say. Well, there must be *no more* blood on our souls…"
>
> —Count Zorn
> *Demons of the Mind*

"It was in the north-eastern province of Bavaria, where the Böhmerwald mountains define the borders of Bohemia, that the legend of *Blutlust* originated in the seventeenth century…"

So ran the first lines of a self-penned mythology that composer and occasional film producer Frank Godwin pretended to have "discovered" in a museum in Stuttgart. It had been used to sell James Carreras on the drama of lycanthropy that Godwin and cowriter Christopher Wicking (whose fingers were currently in a number of pies) had dreamed up, and the ruse had resulted in *Blood Will Have Blood* finding a place on Hammer's schedule, with an original starting date of April 12.

The recasting of the lead roles postponed production until August, but after a trouble-free shoot, nothing much else about what was subsequently retitled *Demons of the Mind* would match the ease with which the film had come into being in the first place.

> *1830. Bavaria. Count Zorn is obsessed with the notion of heredi-tary evil and keeps his children imprisoned in his castle. He disposes of the bodies of girls murdered by his son, Emil, in a nearby lake. Falkenberg, a psychiatrist, is conducting an experiment to try to get to the root of Emil's disorder—which Zorn believes to be caused by centuries of inbreeding. The experiment ends in the death of yet another village girl. Zorn disposes of the body, but this time, he is seen by the villagers. When Emil kills again, Zorn goes berserk and first murders Falkenberg, then Emil. Before he can kill his daughter, the villagers arrive in force and their priest plunges a fiery cross into the count's heart. The evil has been exorcised, but Zorn's daughter now seems to be possessed....*

In the course of the film's stop-and-start launch, Eric Porter was snatched away from the role of Zorn by Aida Young (to appear in *Hands of the Ripper*) and neither Paul Scofield nor James Mason could be prevailed upon to substitute, and Marianne Faithfull was dropped at the last minute in favor of Hammer newcomer Gillian Hills. *Blood Will Have Blood* eventually set sail on August 16 on the tranquil waters of a first-rate cast, a stereo sound track, and the "loving attention to detail" (in Godwin's words) that was to be evidenced in every frame—only to flounder within reach of the shore and sink without trace in the impenetrable deeps of EMI corporate thinking.

"We didn't want it to be just another Hammer film, so we didn't want to use Cushing and Lee," Frank Godwin explains. Robert Hardy and Patrick Magee were to represent unusual alternatives, but more unusual still was the fact that the film had been afforded a week's location shooting within the obligatory six (though not in Bavaria, but at Wykehurst Park in Bolney, East Sussex) and cine-matographer Arthur Grant had lost no opportunity to exploit the late summer sun, turning in his best work for the genre.

But not all was sweetness and light. Director Peter Sykes is never less than masterful at evoking the *mise-en-scène*, and the shadow of the Gothic hanging over the idyllic lake setting is highly resonant, but writer Christopher Wicking is equally ardent at wringing every psychosexual complexity from an otherwise routine plot, and the dramatic landscape is unnecessarily clouded by a fog of pseudopsychological preoccupations. The Zorn family is a veritable Freudian case history: an impotent sadist of a father, a virgin aunt, an incestuous son, and a neurotic daughter—all in a single household. With such a congestion of trauma, it is hardly surprising that the script has more than its fair share of half-finished sentences and half-formed ideas. The latter part of the film devolves into Roderick Usher on the analyst's couch, and the weight of its guilt-ridden sexual obsessions ultimately submerges interest. "The world will be a better place without me—and it won't even know that you died," says a resigned Zorn before blasting the psychiatrist spectacularly to kingdom come in the film's best-staged sequence. And not before time.

The token concession to Hammer Horror comes at the climax, when a priest lops off Zorn's hand at the wrist before ramming a fiery cross through his stomach to the appreciative cheers of the villagers. It is a parody by repetition—in the way that many of Universal's horror films had become by the 1940s—though in a sly tilt at Elder, Wicking had made his priest a deranged eccentric, even more psychotically inclined than the demonic urge that he is at pains to root out in the name of the Almighty.

In the revisions that took place between April and August, the werewolf motif was much reduced, at Hammer's request, as were explanatory shots of Zorn releasing his son from captivity so that he could act out the count's savage impulses à la *Forbidden Planet*. This was to have been no ordinary horror film, but a psychological *roman noir* untarnished by concessions to Hammer traditionalists. So much for the theory. What resulted was simply impenetrable, but more damaging still would be the fact that those traditionalists included EMI.

When the advertising designs commissioned by Frank Godwin were rejected as unsuitable, the producer sought Michael's backing. "At a time when the ordinary horror movie is not on the upgrade, it seems a great mistake…to put it over as if it was exactly the same as all the others." EMI thought not and exercised its right of veto by producing a poster of its own. But Michael agreed with Godwin and, incensed that his authority was being undermined, he wrote a letter to his father voicing his support and spelling out his concerns about the stalemate that seemed to have arisen between them in the matter of who runs Hammer. "I…was neither consulted, invited to comment, shown any artwork or advised of when and where it could have been viewed. There is obviously something very wrong with our liaison on these matters and I suggest we quickly lay down a pattern which will not allow this to happen again."

The plea fell on deaf ears. James Carreras was not about to do anything to offend his only remaining ally, as he would make plain. "They...submitted artwork which they thought more suitable, and I must admit that Brian Lawrence and I agreed with them." He had little choice; EMI hated the film and had already decided against giving it a West End opening or even a trade screening. With its chances of success severely curtailed as a consequence, Godwin retired from the fray and switched his attention to other, more profitable, pursuits. But such incidents were only adding fuel to the fires of speculation that all was not well at Hammer House, as *Variety* was later to corroborate. "There was recurrent film row scuttlebutt of frequent personality (and policy) clashes between the two [Carrerases]."

While *Variety* was busy forecasting the slump, reporting that "International markets have never been more volatile," Michael Carreras, from atop a record pile of films completed, in production, or planned, was continuing to make reassuring noises in spite of a 30 percent drop in Hammer's returns from U.S. outlets due to the rise in increasingly desperate competitor product. Sir James was similarly confident. "With our sort of picture you can't lose," he reassured *Variety*. That might have been true in the past, but it was not to be so for much longer.

Behind the smiles, it was a very different story. According to Bryan Forbes, none of the latter-day Hammer horrors did well at the box office. In some instances, they would take up to twenty years to recoup their production costs alone. Hammer was over-producing. But it was of no more than passing interest to Sir James Carreras. The "old pals act" that had been set in motion two years before had been engineered for a purpose other than the mere plundering of Forbes's Elstree budget. A buyer had been sought for the whole House of Hammer.

If anything, Carreras had proven himself to be too good a salesman. Through fifteen years of squeezing the golden goose for all it was worth, he had inadvertently wrung its neck. Hammer had made too many films for too many people, and now there was nowhere left to go. No one left to go to. "Mentally, he had left the film business," Michael would say of his father at this point in time. "He used Hammer to fund his other life; he had a 'different life'." That other life, ostensibly as elder statesman of the industry, had taken precedence, with two more consultancy posts beckoning to add to the roster of Sir James's ambassadorial pursuits.

> "The year 1872, and the nightmare legend of Count Dracula extends its terror far beyond the mountains of Carpathia to the Victorian metropolis of London..."

> —Opening narration
> *Dracula AD 1972*

Hammer's dwindling fortunes had inexorably come to depend on the eventual fate of Count Dracula, but since 1969, alienation thrillers such as *Night of the Living Dead* had literally pumped new blood into the genre. The cinema of "splatter" had been surfacing in a number of diverse films made fast and furiously (in ironic mimicry of Hammer's own early beginnings), and on the kind of budgets where even the few that failed were able to cover their costs and still have enough money to try again. In the face of these young turks—George Romero, Wes Craven, Dario Argento— Hammer trotted out *Dracula AD 1972*, in which the count was not only a stranger in a strange land, but also an outdated metaphor whose time, like his image in the glass, was fading fast.

"Every single time I turned it down, I got a telephone call from James Carreras," Lee would explain. "And it was always along the same lines: 'You can't say no; I'm in my sixties and I can't cope with this kind of strain and pressure indefinitely...I beg you to do this film—this film—this film'..." Such was his justification for once more donning the leaden cape for a hybrid that was rooted in the *sixties* in style and content. Like its predecessor, *Dracula AD 1972* would make no attempt to integrate with others in the series. The discontinuities would only serve to confuse the audience and confirm suspicions of careless exploitation. Hammer philosophy had always been to give the paying customers what they wanted. With the latest Dracula, it seemed to be giving them what *it* wanted to give them.

By the time *Dracula AD 1972* opened (in October 1972), a work-manlike little hard-core-turned-mainstream monster movie called *Count Yorga—Vampire* would have transposed *its* vampire protagonist into contemporary Los Angeles, been moderately successful, spawned a sequel (*The Return of Count Yorga*), and exhausted the idea. Where Hammer once had led, now it could only follow.

> *London—the present. Johnny Alucard has inherited the artifacts of Count Dracula. With a group of friends, he performs a black magic ritual in a desanctified church, where he conjures the spirit of Dracula. The count kills one of the girls. The police call in Lorrimer Van Helsing and he suspects that vampirism is abroad. A second death in the group confirms Van Helsing in his view and he realizes that Alucard is an anagram. Van Helsing's niece, Jessica, is lured into a trap, but Van Helsing kills Alucard by immersing him in a bath of water. He follows Dracula to the church, where Jessica is held captive. A fight ensues, and Van Helsing defeats the count by impaling him on a stake. The evil of Dracula is vanquished once more.*

What was originally *Dracula Today*, then *Dracula—Chelsea 1971*, is not all bad. It has a tremendous opening and an equally tremendous finale. The problem is the section in-between. The film's one innovation is in returning Peter Cushing to the role of the vampire hunter, here cloaked in the guise of grandson Lorrimer. As ever, Cushing gives the proceedings his all, if a touch more arthritically than in 1958. An actor of tremendous dynamic, it is Cushing's scenes that breathe what life there is into a script that, like its farcical Chelsea vampires, should never have seen the light of day.

The swinging sixties had already inspired a spate of films inflecting on the age, which had invariably ended up looking gauche and affected as they tried to depict the attitudes and mannerisms of the "turn-on, tune-in" generation. That ought to have been sufficient warning to the makers of yet another opus hoping to highlight the lowlife of a gang of Kings Road "trendies," but Hammer was wilfully blind to the signs and portents.

While the latest in a long line of overtheatrical juvenile leads was paraded center stage as "Johnny Alucard" (Christopher Neame), a more vigorous specimen was also introduced to the ranks of the protagonists, in the form of Inspector Murray (Michael Coles). With Dracula restricted to the confines of a church, the film concerns itself as much with the antics of the inspector and Alucard as it does with those of Van Helsing and the count. There was method in it, as the next episode would make clear, but *Dracula AD 1972* merely looks like Hammer Horror as performed by the National Youth Theatre (literally, in this instance: Philip Miller, son of fifties crooner Gary Miller—and Bob in the film—was an old Alleynian and graduate of the "Young Vic," like *Frankenstein Must Be Destroyed*'s Simon Ward.[10])

Unlike the previous Dracula, *AD 1972* had been accepted by Warners as part of the continuing program set up between Sir James Carreras and Ted Ashley. The invitation to BBC "Come Dancing" producer Josephine Douglas to oversee the proceedings had also been at the whim of Sir James, though Michael had decided that they should bring Dracula into the modern world, metaphorically *and* literally. *Dracula AD 1972* was not completely devoid of good ideas, but it failed to realize the possibilities inherent in the concept. Dracula's cape could have billowed unnoticed in the Chelsea streets and his "biographer," Bram Stoker, had actually penned the tale while resident in the same area. Instead, Dracula was consigned to lurking in a ruined church, looking for all the world as if he had budged not an inch from his Transylvanian pile and making a mockery of the entire period switch, in the process. It was half-cocked and half-hearted, and it signified a clear display of timidity on Hammer's part. The paradoxical nature of the material is never fully exploited, and the film was to fail where Robert Quarry's streetwise *Yorga* had succeeded with such bravura—"masquerading" as himself at a fancy dress party, and watching Hammer's *The Vampire Lovers* in his off-duty hours!

The obligatory pop group (Stoneground) had been recruited for the film and foisted onto it at Warner's behest, in the hope of some residual record sales. They were not to be. Neither was the sentiment expressed in the inscription on which *Dracula AD 1972* saw fit to close: "Rest In Final Peace."

> "Dracula. There is a legend that he was buried in Chelsea—probably by one of his disciples...Possibly at St. Bartolph's, in some desanctified corner."
>
> —Lorrimer Van Helsing
> *Dracula AD 1972*

When Lee had done with *AD 1972*, he went into *Nothing But the Night*—the first and last feature from his Charlemagne Productions, the company he had formed with Anthony Nelson Keys. Several Hammer regulars went along for the ride: Les Bowie, Eddie Knight, Doreen Dearnaley, and Tom Sachs. Malcolm Williamson, who had contributed so memorable a score to *The Brides of Dracula*, was assigned to the music, and Peter Sasdy was nominated to direct. But in its tale of possession and supernatural revenge among a group of orphaned children on a remote Hebridean island, the film was ponderous and ultimately unsatisfactory. Rank was unsure of what it had and looked for approval by screening it before a contingent of its own staff in the embarrassed presence of Lee and Keys. *Nothing But the Night* received a thumbs-down, a reluctant release at the very end of the cycle, and flopped as a result. Charlemagne promptly followed suit. The day was coming when Christopher Lee would set his sights further across the water than the Western Isles.

The more "adult" material that Hammer had been introducing into its horror films to tempt customers was now being expunged in its biggest foreign market. The typical American audience was *under* 18, with the result that the films had become increasingly troublesome to their dwindling band of U.S. bookers and increasingly disjointed as censor and distributor alike did their worst. This confirmed the view held by Warners that the basic product had become second-rate, and the accusation "draggy, boring, and completely unprofessional" was finding echo. "Jimmy would get very defensive about the quality of the pictures," Paul Lazarus notes, "even though he had little or nothing to do with the making of them." It was a no-win situation, and James Carreras knew it. With doubts about the efficacy of Hammer multiplying on both sides of the Atlantic, the time to get out was now at hand.

Having severed the company's informal link with Fantale, Michael began the search for more fresh-thinking policies, with one eye to the longer term. As four of the most recent Hammer horrors—*Hands of the Ripper, Twins of Evil, Dr. Jekyll and Sister Hyde,* and *Blood From the Mummy's Tomb*—opened almost simultaneously on both circuits across London in October/November 1971 ("The stupidest exploitation I'd ever seen—complete saturation," said Christopher Wicking), two more went into production: *Straight on*

Till Morning and *Fear in the Night*, both of them at least partial attempts to ring the changes in the formula.

The double bill traded under the slogan, "Women in Terror!" *Fear in the Night* was *The Claw*, finally making it onto celluloid. Despite a dusting-down with Technicolor, it was Sangster of old— twist and double twist, and nothing quite as it seems to be—but *Straight on Till Morning* was the dark and inexplicable underside of the kitchen-sink: a bizarre excursion into the "social realism" that had been turned out all-too-regularly by filmmakers who subsequently wondered why no one came to view. If a particular type of film helped hurtle the industry into the decline of the seventies, then this was it: the pointless slice-of-life tale of the sad and seedy, rooted in the fevered imaginings of suburban pseudointellectuals. That Hammer and Michael Carreras allowed this maudlin burlesque past the script stage—let alone tried to sell it as a thriller— was an indicator of just how bad things had become.

With funds running low, there was nothing else to do but sell the family silver. The big three Hammer Gothic horrors—*The Curse of Frankenstein*, *Dracula*, and *The Mummy*—were sold to ITV for £75,000 apiece. And television, in the form of Brian Clemens again, was to return the favor early in 1972, and sell Hammer another series idea intended to pick up the reins from where the Karnsteins had left off: *Kronos*.

> *Wandering adventurer Kronos and his hunchbacked aide, Grost, are sent for by Dr. Marcus to help solve the mysterious deaths of several girls. Vampirism is suspected, and Marcus himself falls victim. He has to be destroyed by Kronos, but his death reveals how the scourge can be defeated. The culprit is found to be Lady Durward, who has been draining the villagers of their blood in order to raise Lord Durward from the dead. Kronos kills her henchmen, then, using his mistress as bait, he seeks out and destroys the vampire couple. He and Grost ride off once more to continue the fight against evil.*

Kronos was a belated attempt to suck from the same vein of pop horror that had been tapped into by *Twins of Evil*, and Brian Clemens's desire to overturn Hammer conventions is manifested in the film's set piece: Kronos is ignorant of how to kill a vampire, and he has to try out several methods on poor Dr. Marcus before he settles on a dubious revision that is merely contrived to enable him to *sword fight* them to death! Much of *Kronos* is shot outdoors, and the paucity of what set design there is can be seen in a castle interior whose brightly painted walls mask the absence of any period detail, and a cabin whose door opens to reveal an "exterior" composed of a single picket fence. The net result is thoroughly bland and, with Clemens directing as well as writing on this occasion, it is devoid of a single saving grace.

Driven by the desire to create the conditions that would allow its horror-comic heroes to be spun-off into further adventures, the retitled *Captain Kronos—Vampire Hunter* was little more than a pilot film. Much time is spent on trying to develop a rapport between its curious principals, while much less is devoted to the now-familiar vampiric activities that they have been summoned to investigate. A singular combination of talents might have made it work, but the teaming of Horst Janson, Caroline Munro, and John Cator was singular only in its collective lack of charisma. Typical of Clemens, a dash of mystery had been added to the usual mix of ingredients to enrich the bouquet, but there was no horror to speak of, no sex that had not already been exploited by Ms. Munro's widespread exposure on behalf of *Lamb's Navy Rum,* and no humor beyond the unintentional.

Clemens was known for his work on the cult TV series "The Avengers," the best episodes of which had been directed by Robert Fuest. Fuest had also moved into features, and he was currently enjoying a huge hit with an "Avengers"-style pastiche about the exploits of a mad doctor. *The Abominable Dr. Phibes* had benefited from the camp casting of Vincent Price in its quest to mock the genre, and it would sire a sequel of even higher camp but significantly lower returns. Lacking both the visual flair of Fuest and the self-deprecating presence of Price, *Captain Kronos* was cut to the quick before he had even set out with his hunchbacked Sancho Panza.

Clemens and Fennell had traded on past affiliation to produce a spurious pseudohorror sanctioned in a moment of weakness and made without even the security of Hammer personnel to at least ensure it some adhesion to corporate values. But what was afoot would leave the good captain languishing on the shelf indefinitely.

Next in the lists for 1972 was *That's Your Funeral,* another insipid meander through the backwaters of television sit-com land. Michael Carreras had undertaken to produce this one himself, and it would feature the crew (including he and Skeggs) in cameo, dressed as pallbearers behind the credit titles. Given what was now taking place behind the scenes at Hammer, the irony could not have been lost on any of them.

As had been predicted, escalating costs within the industry (on top of the withdrawal of overseas finance) were helping to drive home the purgative stake. And not only for Hammer. For some time, James Carreras had been in negotiations with Peter Lorne of Studio Film Laboratories (a utilities supplier that was also in financial difficulties) over the possible merger of the two. This was to have led to Sir James becoming chairman of a holding company, with Hammer and SFL as operating subsidiaries. While discussions had been going on, SFL had found another source of capital, and the plan had been put on hold. But Studio Film Labs had not been the only suitor to come calling.

Michael's relationship with his father had reached an all-time low—a situation that had not been helped by the attitude that EMI had adopted in respect to *Demons of the Mind.* By 1971, Hemdale's Laurie Marsh had taken charge of Tony Tenser's Tigon Films, and the restructured Tigon Group had become the lessee of a suite of offices in Hammer House formerly occupied by Grand National Pictures. In May, the new Tigon Chairman had intimated to trade journalists that in keeping with the Group's aim of going public, he was negotiating for a couple of companies described as "compatible with his plans for expansion in the leisure market." No more had come of this in the intervening twelve months, but when the deal between Hammer and SFL began to waver, Carreras turned to Marsh. The two soon reached an agreement in principle whereby Hammer would be subsumed into the newly floated Tigon Group (soon to become the Laurie Marsh Group), of which Tenser was now an executive director.

The pact was to be sealed over lunch at *Les Ambassadeurs*, but when Lawrence and Edwin Davis came to pore over the small print, it became apparent that because the deal was performance related, Sir James was not to be as richly rewarded in the short term as he had thought. The bad news was conveyed, but the meeting went ahead as if all was well, with Carreras putting a brave face on his disappointment for the assembled executives from Tigon. "It was the saddest lunch I've ever attended," Lawrence recalled. Even before the *hors d'oevres*, the absorption of Hammer by its archrival had become a nonevent, and SFL was back at pole position in the exit stakes.

Michael had been party to the negotiations with Studio Film Labs, but not to those with Tigon. With the SFL merger temporarily halted, he called a meeting to discuss what to do if Hammer was to be forced to continue on alone. Sir James was now on a cruise, and attending were Lawrence, Skeggs, company secretary Harry Hopkins, and Edwin Davis. The program that had been set in motion by Sir James was due to end with the next Dracula film for Warners, funds were scarce, the market for horror was on the wane, and ideas were in short supply. Michael was looking for a way to break the deadlock. As he addressed his concerns, it was Davis who intemperately dropped the bombshell. "You won't have to worry about any of that," Michael was assured. "Your father is *selling* the company."

Brian Lawrence, who *had* been privy to the negotiations, was pressed for an explanation. He conceded that the prospective buyer had been Tigon, and the offer was in the region of £300,000. But he pointed out that nothing had been signed, let alone delivered.

Assuming that neither he nor anyone else had been included in whatever arrangement Sir James had come to with Tigon, Michael phoned Tenser. The news was greeted with surprise and the reply that there had been a tacit understanding. Tenser offered to meet and talk. Michael was in no mood to discuss it; he had been persuaded to take up the reins at Hammer so his father could enjoy *la dolce vita*, and had just endured the latest in a long line of bitter battles over how the business was being run. Michael replaced the receiver and never spoke to Tenser again. As far as he was concerned, he was now faced with a stark choice: shrug his shoulders and let things take their course, or try to beat the Tigon offer. Unfortunately for him, he would choose to do the latter. [11]

Pandora's Box

"I went to America to renew contacts and reestablish that Hammer would in no way be changing except to expand and go forward.

I see no reason why Hammer should not continue its expansion for the next 25 years—or 250 if there are still people on this earth."

Michael Carreras
Cinema TV Today
December 1972

With the revelation that the Tigon/Laurie Marsh Group was ostensibly to become the new owner of Hammer, events gathered momentum. The fact that the deal was effectively going nowhere was of no consequence. Michael decided to launch a counterbid to take over the company himself, with the idea that if *he* bought out his father, Hammer and its key personnel would be safer in the long term. While Sir James was still out of the country, Michael reapproached former suitor Studio Film Labs to fund the purchase of his father's portfolio and thereby secure itself a stake in the company. SFL agreed, and contracts were drawn up. But at the same time, Brian Lawrence had thought to go one better. The pension fund subsidiary of industrial giant ICI (Imperial Chemical Industries) was investing in all manner of venture capital areas, including film production. Lawrence submitted a business plan to PFS (Pension Funds Securities) that was more advantageous in the short term (on the assumption that the development deal with EMI would ensure the longer term), and it was accepted with no strings attached for the required loan of £400,000, with another £200,000 for two features. At the eleventh hour, despite incurring a five-figure penalty with Studio Film Labs for failing to honor its contract, Michael decided to go with PFS.

When the ship carrying Sir James and Lady Carreras returned to Southampton, Michael's offer to buy Hammer was waiting to meet it at the dock. A week of silence followed. Finally, word was sent to Michael that the offer was acceptable: Hammer was to be his. The acceptance letter was couched in an expression of surprise; Sir James had apparently been unaware of his son's interest in acquiring the company. "I knew what *he* wanted to do, and watched him do it—superbly—all my life," Michael observed. "But he never asked me what *I* wanted to do—*ever*."

Hammer Films passed from father to son in a brief formal ceremony in the dining room of Hammer House. Sir James and Lady Vera Carreras resigned their directorships, effective January

31, 1973. The company was now in the hands of Michael Carreras, safe for another generation of the family to inherit.

It was not long before Sir James requested that he be allowed to keep the company Rolls and be paid a consultancy retainer. It was the first that Michael knew of a Hammer Rolls-Royce, and he refused. Soon after, EMI support for future production (the development deal that was to have ensured Hammer's business continuity) was withdrawn. The reason was simple: all cooperation between EMI and Hammer had been on a personal basis, and as far as Bernard Delfont was concerned, Michael was *not* his father. Suddenly, the *réal gothique* of Hammer had begun to come hideously alive. [12]

Hammer had been purchased in haste and pretty much on trust. The upshot of what Michael Carreras would soon come to think of as "the most stupid decision I ever made" was to be a series of shocks that would signal the beginning of an inexorable descent toward ultimate disaster. EMI had rescinded the deal for another nine films, and interest in the Hammer product among the American majors was now entirely nonexistent. But in addition to these, because of the way Sir James had done business, the rights to most of Hammer's films were owned by the companies that had financed them. The value of the remaining residuals amounted to little more than £200,000. "80 percent of what I thought was there wasn't there at all," Michael discovered.

Only now did Michael realize what Brian Lawrence had always known about Sir James's intentions: "He quit while the going was good; he had exhausted the supply of cash," Lawrence said. "I think he was utterly brilliant at gauging the time," Michael was to reflect—"He really got out when the reputation was gone and the coffers were empty." Hammer had been left high and dry, with barely enough money in the bank to produce more than a handful of films and without the safety net that EMI development funding would have provided. The priority was to buy the company some time. Once again, product merchandising was explored—books, records, magazines—anything that held out the prospect of generating income in the short term. "I tried to diversify—I tried to use the *name*," Michael explains. "It was about all I'd got left." But first, he was able to wrest $280,000 out of a reluctant Paramount for a *seventh* Frankenstein film that he would cobble together from a script by Tony Hinds, offer to Peter Cushing and Terence Fisher, and rush onto the stages of Elstree in late September 1972.

The result was to be *Frankenstein and the Monster From Hell*—the last will and testament of Elder, Cushing, and Fisher, all working under the company banner. Tony Hinds was content to turn out an occasional script, but he would refuse an invitation from Michael to return to Hammer on a full-time basis.

Long before the close of 1972, horror had been elbowed out of the more expansive surroundings of Elstree and Pinewood and into the backwaters of smaller studios that were normally designated for television production and other workaday fare, and a third Phibes—*The Bride of Phibes*—had been abandoned as a lost cause in the rush to the lifeboats.[13] Even as it was being written, the final Frankenstein had been left with nothing new to say: the legacy of Hammer was already settled.

> *Dr. Simon Helder is committed to the asylum at Carlsbad. After being tortured by the warders, he is taken to the prison doctor, whom he recognizes as Baron Frankenstein—whose work he has been trying to emulate. "Dr Victor" allows Helder to become his assistant. Helder stumbles upon a hidden laboratory, where Frankenstein has constructed a huge creature, its body covered in bandages. The baron reveals that he has rebuilt the body of a grotesque neanderthal of a man who had fallen from a cell window. An inmate called the "Professor" dies, and Frankenstein acquires the final item: a brain. When the creature attacks Helder with a broken bottle, it begins to look as though the old body has triumphed over the new mind! In Frankenstein's absence, the creature escapes and goes on a rampage. The enraged lunatics attack it and tear it limb from limb. Frankenstein returns in time to witness the destruction, and muses idly that he will have to begin again...*

Frankenstein and the Monster From Hell was Michael Carreras pressing the panic-button. The script was much revised, even in its final draft. The input ranged from wholesale deletions to token dialogue alterations, and the broth was in danger of being spoiled before the show went onto the floor. For economic reasons, the story was divested of some minor characters and a neat inflection to its predecessor (bar one) when a magistrate talked of having sent the baron down in '68, which was changed to "some time ago." In addition to this, a complex, wordy, and character-laden tale was afforded the tiniest budget of any recent Hammer horror film, and the shortest schedule since the company's earliest days.

The asylum setting was a bright and original idea, but it is plain that Hinds's way with the Gothic had not changed radically or improved much since *Risen From the Grave*. *Frankenstein and the Monster From Hell* was *intended* as a throwback, but the increasingly graphic content of other genre offerings should have been addressed with more potency than a transparently fake brain removal and the wanton destruction of the monster in the final moments. The film was doomed to failure, and it would be overshadowed in release by the blasphemous cavortings of the demonically possessed twelve-year-old in William Friedkin's *The Exorcist*.

The Exorcist did not finish Hammer Horror off. The process was already underway by the time of *Monster From Hell*'s spotty release in 1974. But it showed quite clearly that there was no road back.

By the seventies, Fisher's prosaic way with horror had become distinctly passé and as rooted in the theatrical manner of yesteryear as that of the Universal films which he had updated so vigorously in the fifties. *Frankenstein and the Monster From Hell* was a noble last act—a valiant encore for Fisher, Cushing, Charles Lloyd Pack, *et al.*—the final flourish of what had become a great tradition. But it was a film for the collector, not the mass market. There would be no return to the Golden Age of Hammer Gothic, nor should there have been any attempt at one. Like the participants, it had been of its time, and its time was past.[14]

> "We must get this place tidied up, so that we can start afresh. Now we shall need new material, naturally..."

> —Baron Frankenstein
> *Frankenstein and the Monster From Hell*

While the baron took his last curtain call, the count waited in the wings to do the same. Hammer's eighth Dracula had represented the last act of Sir James Carreras before *his* departure from the scene. It had been announced to an incredulous world under the trite title of *Dracula Is Dead...And Well and Living in London*. The nadir of what Christopher Lee was to christen his "graveyard period" would be reached with a film that was ominously lined up to go before the cameras on November 13, 1972, as *The Satanic Rites of Dracula.*

> *The police and S.I.7 are investigating reports of black magic rites involving prominent people. Visiting Pelham House, Inspector Murray finds motorcycle bodyguards and a clutch of vampire girls chained in the cellar. He escapes, but an S.I.7 agent is killed. Van Helsing discovers that one of the participants has been cultivating a plague virus. When the scientist is murdered, he traces the phial to the industrial conglomerate of D. D. Denham. He confronts Denham, and the magnate is none other than Count Dracula! The count adds Van Helsing to his roster of captives at the house, which now includes Murray and Van Helsing's daughter. The inspector frees himself and turns on the sprinklers, destroying the vampires in the cellar. In the altar room, Dracula reveals his plan: he intends to destroy humanity—and himself in the process, for want of blood. The phial is smashed but Van Helsing topples a burning brazier onto the bacteria and escapes as the house erupts in flame. He is pursued by Dracula, who becomes trapped in a hawthorn bush. Van Helsing drives a stake through his heart, and the world is saved.*

From Transylvania With Love might have been just as appropriate for what would turn out to be a secret-agent thriller, in which Van Helsing and Inspector Murray from *AD 1972* are called in by S.I.7 to investigate some subversive goings-on in a multinational conglomerate run by the mysterious D. D. Denham. The plot was an outright steal from the previous year's Bond film, *Diamonds Are Forever*, with Dracula replacing Ernst Stavro Blofeld. But the film was lively and inventive and acted with conviction by a better cast than its predecessor (Freddie Jones, Richard Vernon, William Franklyn, Patrick Barr, and Lockwood West).

Most of the uncertainties that had been allowed to plague the count's previous return to (contemporary) life are ironed out in *The Satanic Rites of Dracula,* and his liberation from a twilight existence in St. Bartolph's leaves him free to function more fully in the modern world and transform himself into a super villain whose purpose is to destroy society. Dracula's castle is now a fog-shrouded skyscraper in the heart of London, where he presides over the fate of the human race in a penthouse suite of red pile, while sporting a mock Lugosi accent. Christopher Lee cuts an elegant dash as the count in modern dress, and the change of tack was to serve as a dry run for his impending role as *real* Bond villain Scaramanga in the following year's *The Man With the Golden Gun.*

It was a good idea, and it was worked through with some flair in Don Houghton's script. There are *frissons* worthy of Nigel Kneale himself: the skyscraper risen from the ruins of the church; the photograph that shows only a door where "D. D. Denham" was seen standing; the title sequence, where the shadow of Dracula gradually encroaches on the London skyline. There is also a better use of the London locations, and "Kojak"'s John Cacavas orchestrates a more engaging score than *AD 1972*'s Michael Vickers, with a novel variant on James Bernard's familiar three-note-theme tune. But if it ultimately fails to gel—and it does—the fault lies with the direction.

Alan Gibson's brash directorial style is gimmick ridden and opportunistic, and even less attuned to his material here than it was in *Dracula AD 1972.* He constantly seeks unusual setups, only to find irritating ones instead, and the frequent focus pulling merely encourages regret at the passing of fixed-focus lenses. In what should have been the film's best sequence (when a bevy of vampire girls is discovered in a cellar underneath Pelham House), Gibson's technique for engendering suspense is to have his protagonist turn the lights *on* before the action starts. But he does furnish an exciting and spectacular finale, which is only diminished by the climactic intrusion of yet another identikit Les Bowie disintegration scene.

As had been predicated in *AD 1972,* the grooming of Inspector Murray to take the lead in the ongoing fight against the vampire horde besetting modern London continued apace in *The Satanic Rites of Dracula.* Hammer had found an original creative talent in Australian Don Houghton, and the film ends on a tantalizing freeze-frame of a pensive Van Helsing clutching Dracula's signet ring. It is intriguing to speculate on what Houghton might have come up with had this line of inquiry been allowed to develop.

Hammer could no longer do anything right for its American distributors but insisted on doing it. Since *The Vampire Lovers,* many of the more graphic horror sequences in Hammer's films had been cut to ensure a MPAA rating compatible with the traditional target audience. The story was much the same for the increasingly explicit sexual content. The depths that were being plumbed by the mavericks remained largely unacceptable in the mainstream, and Hammer continued to be perceived as a mass-market producer. *The*

Satanic Rites of Dracula may have marginalized the horror, but there was the usual quota of sex—a sacrificial victim is displayed with full-frontal nudity on the altar, and stakes are rammed home between *naked* breasts. It would all prove too much for Warners, and although they had already agreed to take the film, it would promptly be shelved, surfacing only briefly as *Count Dracula and His Vampire Bride*. But just as ignominious would be the nature of its patchy release in the U.K. more than a year after production, when mention of the fact that it was a Hammer film was to be removed from theatrical advertising. Even the company *name* would matter little by then.

> "Perhaps—deep in his subconscious—that is what he really wants. An *end* to it all…"

> —Lorrimer Van Helsing
> *The Satanic Rites of Dracula*

With *The Satanic Rites of Dracula,* Christopher Lee finally foreswore playing the count. Sir James Carreras having retired from the scene, there was no one else at Hammer able to persuade him otherwise, and he knew that he could divest himself of the role with impunity. In the final installment of the saga, Count Dracula was to be played by "The Man in Black" from *The Vampire Lovers*: John Forbes Robertson.

The era was almost at an end; Hammer was no longer a force to be reckoned with. The time that remained was to be filled by more excursions into the transient territory of television farce—*Love Thy Neighbour, Holiday On the Buses*—and television drama—*Man at the Top*. The optimism of two years before faded like a dream, and the pace slowed to a standstill. Much was still forecast, but even the promise of a sequel to 1972's *Nearest and Dearest* would remain unfulfilled.

By the end of 1973, in the wake of power strikes, the international oil crisis brought on by the Yom Kippur war, the declaration of a State of Emergency, and the imposition of a three-day working week, the British Film Industry was once more falling flat on its collective face. There was still some time to go before *Jaws, Star Wars,* and *Close Encounters of the Third Kind* were to change the face of cinema forever, and the promise of sanctuary came from some very strange quarters. With the aid of Don Houghton's Chinese wife, Pik Sen, Michael was introduced to Run Run Shaw, oriental movie mogul extraordinaire and coowner of Shaw Studios, the biggest film factory in Southeast Asia. It was an unlikely alliance, at best, but it raised the possibility that the dissipating fad for martial-arts movies could be used to prop up another adventure for the only name that still meant anything: Dracula.

The new film was originally intended for Avco-Embassy, which had released *Frankenstein and the Monster From Hell*, but Warners again exercised its right of veto on the strength of the success it had nurtured with Bruce Lee's *Enter the Dragon* (1973). Warner's pact with Hammer was not open-ended, however, and Ashley and company were happy to see it concluded on a permanent basis by the time they were presented with *Dracula...and the Legend of the 7 Golden Vampires.*

> *Transylvania, 1804. Dracula's spirit enters the body of Chinese warlord, Kah. One hundred years later, Lawrence Van Helsing is in Chung King searching for the 7 Golden Vampires. After a series of harrowing adventures, where he and his intrepid band encounter a veritable horde of the living dead, the vampires are vanquished. The quest ends in a temple in Ping Kuei, when Kah reveals himself to be Count Dracula. There is a brief struggle, and Dracula falls on Van Helsing's spear and crumbles to dust; the legend is finally laid to rest.*

The Legend of the 7 Golden Vampires was an unmitigated mish-mash on the level of Toho's *Godzilla* series. In the tradition of many television detective shows featuring an old hand, Van Helsing now required a young companion to bear the weight of the action—time waits for no man, and his days of table-hopping to tackle vampires were long over. The film still required Peter Cushing's name to bear the weight of publicity, though, and what a dead weight it had to carry. Dracula is a garish pantomimic caricature, parenthetically tacked onto the story to better distribute the differing strands of the production. The business in hand is primarily conducted between David Chiang of "The Water Margin"and a Zulu-stomping army of the living dead. It is curiously watchable for its sheer verve (not to say nerve) in attempting to crossbreed the European myth of the vampire with the outlandishness of Chinese martial-arts action, but even Don Houghton's bold strokes with Hammer's pen were hard pushed to make something workable out of Dracula in the orient.[15] (Since Houghton had also produced the film—a task for which he was eminently unsuited—the blame came twice over. When Houghton left Hong Kong, he left Hammer, also.)

Michael Carreras maximized mileage on the trip to the Far East by shooting *7 Golden Vampires* back-to-back with *Shatter*, a cut-rate thriller starring Stuart Whitman, with Cushing in support. Anton Diffring phoned his role in. *The Legend of the 7 Golden Vampires* was to be Cushing's last excursion into Hammer Horror. "Michael thought that twenty years of that kind of film was enough," he said, "but of course, it was like people wanting a box of chocolates still to have their favorite assortment in it; they didn't want anything *new* out of the Hammer stable."

Michael thought he had bought a film company. He had not—he had bought a corporate identity for a very specific product, and anything that deviated from that went against the expectations of the public and of any prospective financiers. Hammer Films had been turned into a Frankenstein monster of its own making, and when returns began to percolate through from the releases of the last three Gothic horrors, it soon became clear that not only did the public not want anything new from Hammer, they did not seem to want anything *at all*.

In the first months of 1974, Hammer found itself unable to fund anything more promising than another television spin-off, as Richard O'Sullivan, Paula Wilcox, and Sally Thomsett descended on Elstree for the familiar routines of *Man About the House*. For some years, Michael Carreras had been one of a select few to be invited to the birthday lunches of author Dennis Wheatley. With no new ideas on the table, he used the opportunity to pick up on two of the eight Wheatley stories that were still optioned to the now-defunct Charlemagne: *To the Devil—A Daughter* and *The Haunting of Toby Jugg*. By June, he had secured the services of Lee and Tony Keys (as producer) by offering each of them a percentage, and with EMI prepared to go along for the ride into preproduction at least, *To the Devil—A Daughter* was announced for filming. The deal was elaborated to include a short-story series for television under the nominal heading of Wheatley's factual study on demonology—*The Devil and All His Works*.

In the meanwhile, the youthful talents of Christopher Wicking had reappeared on Hammer's doorstep—this time in the company of new collaborator Adrian Reid and pitching a psychic detective film-cum-television series called "The Sensitive." But the attractions of a feature that could be spun off into a series for American TV were thought to be more realizable with the adventures of Allan Quartermain, the hero of Rider Haggard's *King Solomon's Mines*, whose potential was being explored by both parties independently. In their shared vision of a new direction for the company, the two formed a rapport. "Michael and I discovered that we had all sorts of things in common," said Wicking. "A liking for good jazz, food, drink, and films," Michael clarifies. Wicking was set to work, and *Allan Quartermain Esq: His Quest for the Holy Flower* was added to the list of possibles in urgent need of a backer. But long before *The Holy Flower* would fail to blossom, the ills that were about to afflict *To the Devil—A Daughter* were already taking root.

The film could hardly have endured a harder journey to the screen. There were ongoing problems with the finance, the script, and the casting. John Peacock had provided the first draft, but an apathetic Nat Cohen was soon exhibiting reluctance to advance the small amount considered necessary to get it into better shape. A start date of August 4 came and went, and with little progress to speak of, Michael began to get desperate. Memos to EMI urging action became more frequent and increasingly impersonal, and by October, Cohen had grudgingly consented to contribute 50 percent of the cost, provided that Hammer fund the other 50 percent. Since the coffers were now empty, this could only be done in conjunction with a coproducer, and finding one rested on the quality of the script.

AIP had been Michael's first choice, but they had been forthright about the Peacock draft, decrying it for being "silly" and "written in a confusing style," and concluding that it needed "a tremendous amount of work." Chris Wicking, who had now adopted the mantle of Hammer's script editor, was allocated the task of plugging the holes in the screenplay, in the hope that his efforts might shed some light on the obscurities that Peacock had managed to instill into Wheatley's occult thriller. The next task was to find a director.

Front-runners Jack Gold and Douglas Hickox had already made their excuses and declined. October saw Don Sharp provisionally accept the job, in spite of similar misgivings about the basic story.

Within three months, he was gone, bowing out with "It just isn't for me." Ken Hughes was nominated and available, but he was vetoed by Nat Cohen personally, as was Ken Russell. Terence Fisher was also available, but he was not even considered, though almost every other director working in England was. It had now become a matter of finding somebody acceptable to both parties, and one name remained: *Demons of the Mind*'s Peter Sykes. In April 1975, Sykes signed up to do the film. But it was on the express understanding that he was *not* to tamper with the script.

The agreement with EMI meant that if *To the Devil—A Daughter* was not ready to go by June 30, 1975, funds advanced to it were to be reimbursed. AIP had passed as a potential coproducer, and Warners, Avco-Embassy, and Universal had followed suit, but contacts that Michael had cultivated through Capricorn finally came good, and he found a partner in Constantin-Film of Munich. No sooner was that deal done than it was undone, however, as internal wrangling sent Constantin into a sudden tailspin. A second-string company by the name of Terra Filmkunst GMBH of Berlin stepped into the breach, but even by June 16, with the deal firmed up at last, Hammer's troubles were still not at an end.

Casting the lead had been the same problem over again. The need for an international star soon spread the quest to every well-known name working in England *and* America. Stacy Keach and Orson Welles had been among the first in the ring, but only the former was ever a serious contender—until he saw the size of the pay-check. Michael (along with Wicking and Sykes) tried to persuade Cliff Robertson to participate in the venture, but to no avail. With the June deadline almost upon him, he offered the role of Verney to Richard Dreyfuss, Beau Bridges, and Peter Fonda *simultaneously*, in the hope that one of them would bite. Seven days later, Michael Sarrazin was added to the list of potentials. There were to be no takers. A name that had been floating around since October 1974 resurfaced in a new light, his original asking price of $130,000 now looking much more attractive, and by July 1975, Richard Widmark had joined Lee on board. But there still remained the pivotal role of Catherine Beddows.

With Widmark's participation effectively doubling the cost of his character, it was necessary to restore some equilibrium to the budget. Consequently, newcomer Nastassja Kinski displaced all thought of Twiggy, Olivia Newton-John, or any of the dozen other names previously in the running. In the process, Anthony Valentine substituted for David Warner and Michael Goodliffe did likewise for Jeremy Kemp—in both cases, literally days before *To the Devil—A Daughter* was due to go onto the floor.

To finance its part of the deal, Hammer had been forced to borrow an additional $250,000 on the open market, but further conditions were imposed by EMI. The company's share of the joint profit was to be much less than in past years, and half of its overhead was to be deferred. Another formal missive was fired off to Cohen. "It has taken over twelve months to mount this production," Michael wrote, "and on its most basic level, we need all of this fee to ease our current cash-flow position." By now, Hammer stood to benefit to the tune of a mere 17.5 percent of the gross (allowing for deductions, the percentages due to both Lee and Wheatley, and the 5 percent that was earmarked to go straight to PFS), and a further 10 percent of *that* was owed to Tony Nelson Keys, who had now to forfeit his role as producer for the sake of economy, and return, disappointed, to his beloved Richmond and Twickenham Golf Club.

EMI was intent on taking its pound of flesh, and Hammer could ill-afford to spare it. Brian Lawrence had already been forced to relinquish his directorship and take his salary in "fees" for the collection of Hammer residuals through his own Tintern Productions, and at the end of 1974, company secretary Ken Gordon had followed him out of the door. Since January 1975, Roy Skeggs had been acting as production supervisor *and* a director of Hammer in Lawrence's stead, and with the departure of Keys, he had to take charge of *To the Devil—A Daughter,* as well.

With Hammer reduced to a handful of executives and a few office staff, Michael Carreras was caught between the *Devil* and the deep-blue sea of corporate collapse. But for Chris Wicking, it still appeared to be business as usual.

> "The unspoken relationship we had was that as and when some funding turned up, I would be put in charge of a second-string, low-budget department, developing people—trying to make the equivalent of the Corman movies of the sixties. I had all sorts of ideas—including comic books. I talked to Stan Lee about doing a Marvel-Hammer connection. But it all came to nothing...because we had no money to afford to pay anybody to develop it."

Wicking's idea was to bear *some* fruit, though. "Stan Lee had this correspondence thing in the comics—the reader was the most important person in the world to Stan Lee, and it seemed to me that the *viewer* was the most important person for Hammer. But nobody seemed to understand that." Michael understood. In a desperate bid to appeal to the fans where they lived, he took the unusual step of placing a full-page advertisement in the August 1975 issue of Forrest Ackerman's *Famous Monsters of Filmland* magazine, under the headline, "What Will Hammer Do Next?" Among Warren Publishing's other titles was another Ackerman creation—a hugely popular comic book about the adventures of a female vampire from outer space. Hammer's answer was quick in coming: *Vampirella*!

As *To the Devil—A Daughter* finally got underway at Elstree, Michael embarked on securing the rights to the character from publisher James Warren. By the first week in November, he would be attending a New York "Monstercon," and parading Barbara Leigh in the designer bat garb of the extraterrestrial blood drinker and adolescent male fantasy figure in question.

"It is *not* heresy...And I will *not* recant!"

—Father Michael Rayner
To the Devil—A Daughter

What had begun in 1974 as a £430,000 feature with 54 scheduled sets (30 of which had been used up in the first 14 pages of the screenplay) and location work in France commenced filming on September 1, 1975, as a £360,000 feature with a great many fewer sets and a couple of sequences shot at Lake Herrenchiemsee, near Munich. A suitable ending had still not been hammered out, but Skeggs had assured Nat Cohen that despite being "in the middle of extensive script rewrites," *To the Devil—A Daughter* was ready to go. It was anything but.

Warning sirens were sounded during the shooting: "Michael Carreras is well aware that the so-called Hammer 'product' is no longer viable today," the film's director vouchsafed to an inquisitive journalist. Notions such as "blood and guts horror" and "Hammer cult audience" (in Sykes's words) were apparently anathema to the new intelligentsia holding the reins of what was now to be the biggest-budgeted Hammer horror of them all. As the "virtue" of improvization was added to the idea of attracting a more "discerning" cinemagoer, a rat could be smelled. "We all feel that films should…be worked at and be reworked on the floor," Sykes added. To the cynically inclined, it sounded more like the blind leading the blind.

What would pass for horror in Sykes's decidedly anemic version of Wheatley's novel were the cavortings of a perambulating fetus created by Les Bowie. Given an effects budget that did not appear to have increased perceptibly since the days of *The Quatermass Experiment,* the result was to be an abortion, in more ways than one.

> *Occult expert John Verney is asked to protect Catherine Beddows from a Satanic cult led by excommunicate priest Father Michael. Verney enlists the help of Anna and her lover, David, to guard the girl. Father Michael has delivered one of his followers of a monstrous devil baby, which he intends to fuse with Anna to create the demon-god, Astaroth; the plan is part of a pact made between the priest and Catherine's father when she was born. In terror of his life, Beddows reveals Catherine's hiding place to Father Michael. Under the priest's influence, Catherine kills Anna and flees Verney's flat. But it is David who is burned to death in place of Beddows. The pact ended, Beddows tells Verney where the ceremony is to take place. Verney vanquishes the Satanist using ritual magic, but the process of incarnation may already be complete . . .*

With all and sundry contributing to the ever-changing plot, *To the Devil—A Daughter* was never going to be plain sailing. To give the subject some spurious resonance, its simple premise is rigged out in all manner of purposeful (and purposeless) confusions, but the central flaw is the incredible complexity by which the demon Astaroth is supposedly to be given human form. The notional possession (of Catherine Beddows) is *literalized,* with the devil baby first delivered of a willing acolyte, then crawling *into* the girl, in order to achieve the fusion. This repulsive nonsense had no precedent in Wheatley's original, leading him to label the film "thoroughly disgusting." "Dennis Wheatley said to me, 'I cannot understand how they could take my story and completely degrade it'," Lee confirmed. The curious result was a cross between *Rosemary's Baby* (1968) and *It's Alive* (1974), but lacking the conviction of either.

This sin is doubly injurious, in that Lee delivers his finest-ever performance for Hammer in the role of the excommunicate priest, nicely underplaying throughout to impart a chill sense of menace similar to that achieved by Vincent Price in *Witchfinder General*. There the similarity between the two ends, though. *To the Devil—A Daughter* is otherwise slack, slow-moving, and short on style.

The film remains notorious for its climax, or *lack* of it. What was originally intended to be shot in the crypt of St. Martin's-in-the-Field in Trafalgar Square was hastily relocated to the chapel over the Hellfire Caves, on the Dashwood estate at High Wycombe in Buckinghamshire. Here, the final battle between good and evil was to be enacted. But any repeat of the kind of ritualistic duel that had proved so effective in *The Devil Rides Out* was given nowhere to go in a film that had already eschewed the taint of such fantastical goings-on. Wheatley was always careful to ensure that readers of his novels were well aware of the rules by which the mystical game was to be played, but in Hammer's reconstructed version, the conflict is conducted in a mumbo-jumbo of obscure ceremonial to which only the combatants are privy, further depriving what climax there is of any possibility of suspense. To cap it off, the hapless priest is vanquished by a simple blow to the head from a stone hurled by Verney!

There *had* been more to it, however. The script had called for death "by metamorphosis," but according to Christopher Lee:

> "When we shot the film, I recovered, and staggered to my feet. I saw Widmark and Kinski out of the circle; I got up, and with the dagger in my hand, ran after them, forgetting the significance of crossing that circle of blood...The moment I touched it: divine retribution—there was a flash of lightning from on high, which struck me. I was thrown over backwards and I lay on the ground in a crucified position."

Well, it may have proved more exciting than what remained of it in the final cut.[16] But what had happened to it? Like Father Michael, Peter Sykes had been overruled by a higher authority. Lee again: "Somebody said, we'd better not have *that* as the end, because Christopher's done several films where he's been struck by lightning." He had done *one* (*Scars of Dracula*), and the producer of *To the Devil—A Daughter* might well have been referencing recent memory. But the idea of an archsatanist felled by a thud on the head was in keeping with the concept of devil worship as espoused in what was now to be Hammer's last horror film: terminally dull.

> "In Light all things thrive and bear fruit. In Darkness they decay and die. That is why we must follow the teachings of the Lords of Light"—Dennis Wheatley.

> —Screen caption
> *To the Devil—A Daughter*

At the "Monstercon," Michael was tired and dispirited. The painful passage of *To the Devil—A Daughter* from script to screen had taken its toll. But the price exacted was to be higher still when he finally came to view the fine cut on his return to England.

Appalled at the weak ending, Michael had Chris Wicking reprise his *original* concept in which the Devil was to have appeared in the guise of Hammer regular Shane Briant—"The idea was to have these two men battling naked in a field," explains Wicking. "To me, that went into Marvel country"—and promptly went to Cohen for additional funds to reshoot. Cohen screened the existing film to a bevy of EMI executives. It met with general approval, and he pronounced himself content with things as they stood. No further money would be forthcoming. Michael's instincts told him this was a mistake, as it turned out to be. First returns were good, but interest soon evaporated with poor word of mouth.[17]

The whole affair was a catalog of misfortune and mismanagement. Michael Carreras was not aware of all the ins and outs that had brought about such a half-hearted conclusion, but he ought to have been. Richard Widmark was still a star of some importance, yet Michael and he had not met once throughout the entire shoot. While Hammer's managing director had chosen to assume that all was well, Roy Skeggs had been dancing attendance on the disgruntled actor, to dissuade him from walking out on the production over what he felt was the "amateurishness" of it all. For a long time afterward, Michael was to believe that Peter Sykes had "betrayed" him—that while Chris Wicking and he "were making one film in head office, Sykes and Roy Skeggs were making another one at the studio." There was some truth in that. "Suddenly these rushes started turning up on the screen that bore no resemblance to anything I had anything to do with," said Wicking, who had been appointed by Michael to look after production on his behalf while he was in New York. And no wonder. "We are known as the Pink Page Production Company because we're changing the script so rapidly," director Sykes had confessed to *Screen International* in an interview that would expose his ambivalence about *To the Devil—A Daughter*.

It is the film's resolute desire to maintain a grounding in reality that is its downfall, finally. What Wheatley had achieved in the novel through the expeditious use of black magic is communicated here by the ludicrous device of what looks like a microwaved red jelly baby trying to negotiate its predestined way from one surrogate mother to another. The terrible anticlimax only compounds the injury. "Together, they ruined the film," said Lee, who needed only a timely word of encouragement from Richard Widmark to persuade him to pack his bags for good and all and leave Blighty for Los Angeles. But there was more to it than that. The spectacle of so many professional filmmakers so profoundly at odds with one another was confirmation that Hammer's race was run.

The BFI's *Monthly Film Bulletin* liked *To the Devil—A Daughter*. "It suggests that Hammer is at last finding successful ways of reworking the Gothic idiom," predicted Tony Rayns. If that was not enough to send a chill down the spine of anyone hopeful of a good commercial return, the *Evening Standard* was ready with the ice bucket. "*To the Devil—A Daughter* reduces Dennis Wheatley's novel to an obsession with gynaecological deliveries, bloodstained wombs, sacrificed babies and a scene where a slimy red gremlin appears to crawl into a naked woman," it advised.

Roy Skeggs's resignation as a director followed the close of production. He would return to supervising the sales ledger with Lawrence, but also from the safer haven of a self-owned company: Cinema Arts International. For the few who remained, all eyes may have been turning to *Vampirella*, but it was already a minute after midnight, and with the whimpering demise of Father Michael in *To the Devil—A Daughter* had echoed the last note in the barely audible swan song of Hammer Horror.

The Hammers That Never Were

"I have to tell you that we have irrefutable evidence that not only does the Loch Ness Monster exist, it is at present at large on the high seas."

Shooting script
Nessie

Hammer had experienced an unbroken series of commercial setbacks since 1971. Only a handful of its films had received decent distribution in America, and several had seen no release at all. Even in the U.K., a realistic circuit booking could no longer be assured. Yet Michael Carreras had felt no compunction about stepping in and saving *To the Devil—A Daughter.* While a coterie of hired hands crucified the film along with its villain, he was still playing the studio boss and pursuing the next big deal (*Vampirella*), and soon, a project that would prove to be even more elusive to the grasp: *Nessie.*

As the New Year issue of *Screen International* went to press, complete with a seasonal motto from Roy Skeggs that it was "going to be a good 1976," he, in turn, was now being replaced at Hammer by one-time film publicist Euan Lloyd, who was himself a creditor of PFS. By March 1976, with Lloyd in place and *Vampirella*, *Nessie*, and a large-scale western called *Death Rattle* all competing for attention on the drawing board, Britain was facing bankruptcy, and a humiliating meeting with the IMF had been arranged to bail it out of trouble.[18] The signs did not bode well, and the next three years were to witness the collapse of all these major projects, as well as sundry other minor ones along the way.

By June, Columbia had turned down the first of the big three— *Vampirella.* The project then went through numerous script rewrites (from an initial treatment by the trusty Jimmy Sangster), and ended, after more than a year, with the all-purpose Henry Younger combining the contributions of Chris Wicking, John Starr, and Lew Davidson. John Hough was set to direct and AIP was once again in the running as a potential coproducer, but wrangles with James Warren over the merchandising rights to the character eventually saw her slink back into the panels of the comic from whence she

had come, taking even more of Hammer's fast-depleting funds
with her.

Next on the list was *Death Rattle*, a $1.3 million coproduction
with MOS films, to be shot on location in South Africa. Again,
Michael sought the reassuring hand of Jimmy Sangster—but as
associate producer on a Bima Stagg script, this time. The film was
rejected by all the stars to whom it was pitched: Robert Mitchum,
James Coburn, Candice Bergen, and even Joni Mitchell.

In the meanwhile, Hammer had gained the services of ex-pro-
duction manager Tom Sachs, whose association with the company
went back to the days of *The Flanagan Boy*. Sachs had traveled the
same route through the industry as Aida Young, and having re-
joined Hammer as production manager on *The Vampire Lovers*, he
had worked on other horrors of the early seventies before following
an independent career as an associate producer. "I had scripts that
I was trying to push, and Michael and I would talk and I would
spend time with him," Sachs recalls. One was *The Sellout* (1975),
which he had hoped that Michael and Hammer might do—but
they "couldn't get it off the ground." Sachs finally went to Joe
Schaftel, "who managed it in the end."

Like Wicking, Sachs had come equipped with his own ideas
about the road that Hammer should take. But where Wicking saw
the future in comic book fantasy on a modest scale, Sachs saw it in
a return to high class horror, after the appearance of big budget
fright films like *The Omen* (1976). "I said to Michael, '*this* is where
Hammer ought to be.' He agreed in principle, but he always
dragged his feet; I suspect it was because he actually couldn't raise
that sort of money." Michael couldn't raise that sort of enthusiasm,
either. There was no shortage of ideas, only a shortage of resources
to action them.

In Tom Sachs, Hammer had been handed a replacement for Roy
Skeggs on the production side. "Michael had nobody else," observed the company's latest recruit. "He needed somebody to do
the nuts-and-bolts, because that wasn't really his bag. I was prepared to do it in order to get things moving." But there was no
guarantee of financial reward. "If there wasn't any money, you did
it in the hope that you could launch something," Sachs said. When
his hopes were dashed after abortive attempts to launch *Vlad the
Impaler* and *The Scavengers*, he would be offered recompense by
way of a directorship. By then, the value of that was to be much the

same. "Michael felt it would be beneficial if I became a director, but
I didn't want to do it. It was a very uncertain situation and I didn't
feel I wanted to get involved."

As reserves dwindled, ideas conversely became bigger and
bolder. "It was one desperate act after another," Michael would
judge in retrospect. With two down and one to go, far and away
the biggest of them was *Nessie,* a special-effects fantasy about the
legendary beast of Loch Ness, in which the monster grows to
gigantic proportions through ingesting a toxic chemical called
Mutane 4, escapes from the confines of the Loch, demolishes a
hovercraft and a North Sea oil rig, and is eventually brought to
book in the Sunda Straits of the South China Sea.

Michael and Euan Lloyd had provided the storyline, John Starr
the treatment, and Chris Wicking the screenplay. The film was
originally to have been a joint venture between Columbia, Hammer, Toho of Japan, Lloyd, and David Frost's Paradine Productions.
"Paradine had a lot of 'clout' and they managed to come up with
quite a bit of cash to get it moving," said Sachs. "The problem was
that the script wasn't good enough to raise the rest of the cash, and
all sorts of people had a go at rewriting it." With Paradine came
Bryan Forbes (through his involvement on *The Slipper and the Rose*;
1976), and by July 1976, Forbes had provided a shooting script on
condition that he could also direct the film if he so chose. With a
budget of $7 million, principal photography had been due to start
on May 1, 1977, but musical chairs in the Columbia boardroom put
the project into turnaround and, by the following March, with Toho
and everyone else subsequently pulling out of the picture, *Nessie*
would be dead in the water.[19]

The latter half of the seventies may have seen the dawning of a
cinema of spectacle and special effects, but British studios and
technicians were now being looked on merely as ancillary to Hollywood production, rather than an investment opportunity in their
own right. Times were hard, and it was becoming more difficult by
the week to finance a half-decent film in the shrinking economc
environment of the U.K. That none of these projects would see the
light of day had as much to do with bad luck as bad judgment, in
the final analysis—something that had dogged Michael throughout most of his career in films. Even Chris Wicking, a source of
strength and support for three years (on nothing more than a
retainer for much of that time) could no longer be afforded. Ham-

mer was reduced to a duo of Michael and Tom Sachs (though Euan Lloyd was to remain on the board to the end), with Jimmy Carreras, the second of Michael's three sons, providing the helping hand around the office.

With *Nessie* floundering and little return on their investment so far, the managers of Pension Funds Securities began to tighten their grip. Brian Lawrence and Roy Skeggs, through their individual companies, were doing what they could to keep the vulpine mortgagor from the door of Hammer House. But this was to leave Michael out in the cold. Aside from administration fees, the money coming in to Hammer was increasingly being debited to PFS in repayment of the loan. "Hammer was *owned* by the Pension Fund," Sachs explains. "And it was getting progressively more difficult to get them to contribute. Every bit of money that came in—like front monies on *Nessie* at that time—helped not only to launch the picture, but bolster the company's finances as well." Having now been cut adrift from the arterial supply, Michael and Sachs were to be forced to vacate Hammer's offices in Wardour Street and Elstree and move to the Coach House—a converted stable at Pinewood.

> "He has asked us to a final meeting with him—a *last supper* in a sense..."
>
> —Edward Hyde
> *The Two Faces of Dr. Jekyll*[20]

Michael Carreras battled gamely on into 1978 by digging into his own pocket to fund the day-to-day running of Hammer. But with his back right to the wall, he at last managed to find a "live" one. When things had begun to sour with EMI, Michael had nurtured a relationship with Rank—in particular, with distribution head Frank Poole, and this had led to the development of *The Lady Vanishes*, which Rank owned, several years before.[21] All else having failed, the George Axelrod script was dusted down and looked at afresh, but bad sense was again to get the better of good judgment. Tom Sachs was lined up to produce on this occasion, but the film that was to result would suffer from the by now predictable compromise between intent and actuality.

With PFS putting the squeeze on, what was originally to have been done for American TV was now blown out of all proportion into a major feature, with neither of the stars (Cybill Shepherd and

Elliott Gould) being first choice for the roles they were to play. "We set it up with Sam Arkoff," said Sachs. "But Sam wanted it 'Americanized,' and the Rank Organisation didn't see that at all; they saw it as an indigenous British product...So there was this difference of opinion, and Sam dropped out." Had it worked, *Mistress of the Seas* was to have followed it. But an old Hitchcock is an old Hitchcock, even when it goes way over an already inflated budget of £2,100,000!

In August 1978, the account of Hammer Film Productions was frozen on instruction from PFS, and hived off as a repository for all outstanding residuals, with Pension Funds Securities as sole beneficiary. This move effectively prevented Hammer from functioning, and to continue on, one of the "bird" companies that had remained inactive—Jackdaw—was dug out of the drawer to undergo a change of name to Hammer Films Limited, for the purpose of providing a new corporate umbrella. It was indeed a bird of ill-omen, and though *The Lady Vanishes* would go into production at Pinewood and Salzburg (Southern Austria) in September, the end was beginning. "*Lady Vanishes* was like M-G-M's *Ben Hur*," Sachs notes. "It was either going to get Hammer out of trouble or it was going to sink them. 'Shit or bust,' as Michael put it. And he did everything possible to make the best picture that he could." But the ailing concern was already overtrading. "I didn't steer what I had left in the right direction," Michael would reflect. "I tried to hang on; I tried to revitalize. I shouldn't. I should have chucked it all away and said, 'okay—it's a new world'."

It was a new world, alright. A new day.

By April 1979, the financial pressure being applied to the fractured operation that was all that now remained of Hammer Films had become intolerable. *The Lady Vanishes* was ready for a release in May, and while big things could no longer be expected of it, it was felt that the film would engender sufficient revenue to at least stave off foreclosure. The preceding two years had seen only £20,000 paid over to Pension Funds Securities Limited against the loan, but for the first time since 1976, Hammer had a film *in release*, and the possibility of light at the end of the tunnel was real at last. "It *will* be alright—won't it, Michael?" had become a regular entreaty from Brian Lawrence throughout the darkest days. For once, Michael felt he could reassure his associate of thirty years standing with some conviction.

This time, the monthly meeting with Hammer's paymasters was scheduled to take place at the offices of Thompson McKlintock in the City of London. Michael Carreras—his habitual trepidation tempered by hope for a change—was accompanied, as usual, by Skeggs and Lawrence. On arrival, the three separated, and Michael was ushered into another office for a private discussion with Tom Heyes and David Watts, acting for PFS. But the time for discussion was past. Michael was told that the company was to be placed in the hands of the Official Receiver. It was the end of the road. "What will you do when you leave here, Mister Carreras?" came the polite, though faintly embarrassed inquiry. Michael shrugged, but felt obliged to deliver an appropriate riposte. "Sell my house," he replied. Ironically, he had done that seven years before.

Skeggs and Lawrence were duly informed of what had taken place and were invited to continue with the collection of what residuals they could to reduce Hammer's indebtedness. The company was declared insolvent to the tune of £800,000. Stunned, but not entirely surprised by the turn of events, they agreed. It was an offer that neither man could reasonably refuse. (Both were subsequently reinstated as directors, in place of Michael Carreras and Euan Lloyd respectively.)

Within days of the meeting that was effectively to bring Hammer to an end, *The Lady Vanishes* opened at the Odeon Leicester Square—but the fact that it was "A Hammer Film" had already been relegated to the status of an afterthought on the credits.

After the Fall

Michael Carreras's resignation as a director of Hammer Films became effective on April 30, 1979. There had been no corporate wrangles to herald the final dissolution. There were disagreements and disappearances, but no boardroom battles had been fought and lost.

Skeggs and Lawrence continued with their roles as administrators on behalf of PFS and structured a proposal that would prevent liquidation and bring about a return to solvency. As the first step toward buying its way back out of debt, the company made two film series for the home screen in association with Lew Grade's ITC and Fox: "The Hammer House of Horror" in 1980, and "The Hammer House of Mystery and Suspense." Despite the odd episode that would produce an intermittent sparkle in glassing eyes, the bulk of them were little more than a death rattle. They did the trick, however. By the time PFS tired of the arrangement, the nominee directors found themselves in a position to bid for the company. Hammer was sold at last—lock, stock, and barrel—for £100,000.

The premier incarnation of "Hammer House" thrashed about in the treacherous waters of an ITV network slot that seemed to come and go with an unnerving suddenness. With its faddish affectation for punning titles, the series veered between a committee concept of classic Hammer Horror—"Guardian of the Abyss," "Children of the Full Moon"—and a hotchpotch of derivative "shockers" that were more akin to reject episodes from an Amicus portmanteau production—"Silent Scream," "A Visitor From the Grave" (from a script by John Elder), "Rude Awakening." Two of them were genuinely frightening; the rest were simply frightful. Style and content were overhauled during shooting when it was realized that a problem would arise with the American networks over the explicit nudity and the less-than-explicit gore, and the watering down that resulted diluted the second batch of shows to such an extent that they became indistinguishable from any other TV "Mystery Movie of the Week."

Brian Lawrence finally relinquished *his* hold on a part of Hammer in May 1985. Since that time, there has been the recurrent banshee wail portending of imminent revival, but after a decade, it seems that even this is merely an echo in the darkness. The company may have been laid to rest in an unquiet grave, but it appears singularly unable to break free from the constraints of the garlic flower. Much has been heard in the interim, but nothing whatever has been *seen*.

> Dracula's screams of agony echo and re-echo. . . . and suddenly cease.
>
> Prem: "Nothing will be left. The memory, nothing more."
>
> —From John Elder's unfilmed
> *Dracula—High Priest of Vampires*

As M. R. James wrote in "Casting The Runes" (*More Ghost Stories*, Edward Arnold, 1911), "one detail shall be added..."

On August 5, 1993, more than fourteen years after Michael's departure, a bulletin made the BBC's six o' clock news: "Hammer horror films—coming back from the dead?" The item went on to reveal a deal between Hammer and Warner Brothers, whereby Warners (after paying what the *Hollywood Reporter* referred to in its July 26 issue as a "high six-figure sum") planned a $100 million program of remakes of some of Hammer's greatest horrors, beginning with *The Quatermass Experiment* at $40 million (as opposed to some £40,000, forty years before).

The *Reporter* clarified the situation thus. Warners (and *The Omen*'s Richard Donner) had apparently taken up option rights on "the more than 200 mainly horror, terror, and suspense-genre films in the Hammer library," and explained that the fee had included "rights to original novels and short stories, screenplays, plays, and material that was optioned and developed by Hammer but never produced."

Could a stirring be detected in *Nessie*'s breast?

In the film business, nothing is ever as it seems. The deal may have been the culmination of many years of painstaking negotiation to provide a new future for Hammer—or it may have had more to do with the last sentence in the *Reporter*'s feature: "Hammer's British offices are located at Elstree Studios...which is due for demolition in September."[22] Whichever, the wheel comes full circle, and we end where we began in 1954—with *The Quatermass Experiment.*

As it used to say on the screen captions of old, before the final fade-out: *is it the end...or the beginning?* Only time will tell.

FACE OF CHANGE: *The Two Faces of Dr. Jekyll* (1959).

Michael Carreras and Paul Massie (with their wives) attend the premier of *The Two Faces of Dr. Jekyll.*

FACE OF FEAR: *The Brides of Dracula* — Yvonne Monlaur (1960).

Press reception for *The Terror of the Tongs:* L to R: Christopher Lee, Yvonne Monlaur, Ken Hyman, Michael Carreras, Jimmy Sangster.

Jimmy Sangster and Susan Strasberg on the set of *Taste of Fear*.

Advertising artwork for *The Curse of the Werewolf* (1960).

Glenn Corbett, Marla Landi, and producer Anthony Nelson Keys on the set of *The Pirates of Blood River*.

FACE OF DEATH: *The Phantom of the Opera*—Heather Sears, David Birks (1961).

Advertising artwork for *Maniac* (1962).

Michael and James Carreras welcome Anthony Hinds to his Tribute dinner at London's Café Royal.

DEATH LIVES: *The Plague of the Zombies* (1965).

Lieutenant-Colonel James Carreras, in his office at Hammer House in Wardour Street.

James Carreras, Arthur Banks, Peter Cushing, Christopher Lee, and Anthony Hinds (holding the Queen's Award to Industry), on the set of *Dracula Has Risen From the Grave*.

MAD MONSTER MAKER: *Frankenstein Must Be Destroyed*—Freddie
Jones, Peter Cushing (1969).

DEATH LURKS: *Crescendo*—James Olsen (1969).

James Carreras and the Duke of Edinburgh attend a Variety Club International fundraising function in Toronto, Canada.

Publicity pose for *Taste the Blood of Dracula*—Christipher Lee (1969).

SEX AND HORROR: *The Vampire Lovers*—Kate O'Mara, Pippa Steele, Madeline Smith, Ingrid Pitt, Kirsten Lindholm (1970)

Jimmy Sangster and Dave Prowse on the set of *The Horror of Frankenstein.*

DEATH LOVES: *Countess Dracula*—Ingrid Pitt (1970).

SOFTCORE SEX: *Lust For a Vampire*—Mike Raven, Michael Johnson, Yutte Stensgaard.

HARDCORE HORROR: *Blood From the Mummy's Tomb*—Mark Edwards, Hugh Burden (1971).

SEX(-CHANGE) AND HORROR: *Dr. Jekyll and Sister Hyde*—Ralph Bates, Martine Beswick (1971).

Dave Prowse and Terence Fisher on the set of *Frankenstein and the Monster From Hell.*

KUNG-FU, SEX, AND HORROR: *The Legend of the 7 Golden Vampires*— Chan Shen, John Forbes-Robertson (1973).

SHADOWS AND LIGHT: *To the Devil—A Daughter*—Christopher Lee (1975).

The Spirit of Hammer

by Michael Carreras

Like the "Sin Eater" of old, I have just had to digest 32 years of my life, as laid out by Denis Meikle. And now he asks me to recall my personal "highs" and "lows"—what a task! If one puts aside the films which have already spoken for themselves in every possible way to four different generations of audiences and the fact that from nowhere, Hammer became an international household name, then I am left with the people and the events. Family, friends, artists, technicians—all of whom either worked on, or lived with, the films in the making.

Friendships are forged deep in short time spans, then put aside perhaps for years, and renewed again as if only a weekend had gone between. Most are finally lost along the way. Some are still with me. My wife of 45 years—Jo—has seen it all. My younger children, Jimmy and Anthony, tried it for short periods but moved on, while Christopher took to it like a duck to water, and is still swimming strongly outside of Hammer.

How can I ever forget being stranded on the "Nab" Tower (*The Dark Light*) with Jack and Steve, electricians who taught me how to play poker the hard way? Or being chased by baboons in Namibia, watching Raquel Welch acting to thin air in Lanzarote, or working with Robert Aldrich in the wartorn sections of Berlin. Or meeting the "giants"—Harry Cohn, Spyros Skouras, Jack Warner. Or *The Hound of the Baskervilles* licking my hand between takes. Or the Blackpool Tower, Monica Hustler, dear Tom Conway, Peter Bryan, Ursula Andress, Dennis Wheatley—working in Hong Kong, driving a steam train in Austria, and my many trips to New York and Los Angeles. Alex Paal, Bob Lippert, Eliot and Kenny Hyman. Or doing a government-sponsored location survey of Kenya and Western Australia for the British Film Finance Corporation. Magical experiences, all.

Then there was knowing Bette Davis, Jack Palance, the "Slave Girls of the White Rhino," the "Seven Golden Vampires," and "Sister Hyde." "Mrs. T," who looked after my inner man for so many years at Bray Studios. The young Tony Hinds and Jimmy Sangster, who will always be part of me. Brian Lawrence, who came from a cloistered world to join us and stayed the longest. Roy Skeggs, who joined last, and now controls the company. And at the very start, the three Grayson brothers (director Godfrey, writer Ambrose, and composer Rupert), Francis Searle, and Vernon Sewell, who guided us through the first 19 films between them. They made us professionals and set us on our way to join other filmmakers. Terence Fisher, Val Guest, Jack Asher, Roy Ward Baker, and Don Chaffey (*One Million Years BC*)—all were good friends.

Molly and Rosemary in wardrobe, Hugh and Pauline Harlow, Len Harris, Phil Martell—the man with a metronome in his head, Esther Harris, who made our "trailers" (and better films than we did!), costumer Monty Berman, Aida Young, Tom Sachs, Chris Wicking, and, of course, Anthony Nelson Keys, who contributed greatly in so many ways. And the hundreds of others who at one time or another became "family" members. How can I fit them all in in such a short space? ("Don't go rabbiting on," Denis said.)

As for the highs and the lows—just going to the studio each morning was the highest of highs! Anything else was just a little, or a lot, lower than that—and I'm not saying which was which. But I cannot end without admitting that the early days (1949-1954) "BF"—Before Frankenstein) were my own favorites. Working on 43 productions in 6 years in the house studios with the family units. The learning and growing period.

After that, 1959 was my *own* vintage year.

I produced *The Mummy, The Two Faces of Dr. Jekyll, Hell Is a City,* and *Yesterday's Enemy*—two of which are still my favorite films— and before the year was out, three were playing simultaneously at major cinemas in the West End of London. I was then 32.

And now—the almost 160 films, the Founding Fathers, the officers and staff of the company, the business deals and everything else about the inner workings of Hammer are all documented and intellectualized in *A History of Horrors* for those who want to know.

Thank you, Denis, for your devotion to this work—but I honestly believe that of equal importance to all of this in the fortunes of Hammer was the family of friends who generated the underlying "Spirit of Hammer" that made it all work. They know who they are—and I say Thank You to all of them for letting me in on it.

Michael Carreras
Isla De La Palma, Canaries, 1993

Notes

Chapter 1: The Rebirth of Frankenstein

1. The British "X" (for Adults Only) certificate restricted viewing to persons of 16 and over; the "A" restricted viewing to those of 14 years of age, but children could see "A" certificate films if they were accompanied by a parent or guardian; the "U" was the certificate of general exhibition.

2. As with Will *Hammer, George Mozart* was actually the adopted stage name of music hall comedian Dave Gillings, brother of George.

3. "Logging and barring" was the means of keeping tabs on films currently in release, in order to help underpin the monopoly status of the circuit chains. By *logging* playdates on a national basis, the smaller independent theaters could be *barred* from playing a film while it was running on one of the major circuit houses in the same area.

4. "Quota quickies" were short program fillers, often made in three weeks or under, produced to comply with the 1927 Cinematograph Film Act, whereby theaters were obliged to screen a given percentage of entirely home-grown films (the quota) to maintain continuity of production in the indigenous industry.

5. National Film Finance Company, later to be Corporation.

6. One of several Medals of Honor awarded for outstanding service to the nation. M.B.E. stands for Member of the British Empire; O.B.E. is Officer of the British Empire.

7. This situation was particularly to apply to the arrangement with Universal. When 7-Arts came on the scene, Hammer invariably took a percentage of the domestic and commonwealth gross but sold its interest in the rest of the world to 7-Arts/Warners. The rights to the 7-Arts films (including the later Draculas) reside with Warners to this day.

8. Several other radio-inspired subjects were cancelled in prospect of the move into the American market: *Inspector Hornleigh, Miss Dangerfield, Taxi, The Robinson Family, Armchair Detective,* and a second *Dr. Morelle: The Case Of The Crooked Steeple.*

9. In October 1950, Sol Lesser was negotiating for the rights to *Murders in the Rue Morgue.* Had the deal with Lesser and RKO been more fruitful, Hammer might have found itself in the horror market a good deal sooner.

10. Association of Ciné-Technicians—which was to become the Association of Cinematograph, Television and allied Technicians in March 1956, and BECTU (Broadcasting, Entertainment, Cinematograph and Theatre Union) in 1991.

11. Union restrictions made it necessary to employ a British director to "sit in" on the set if an American (or foreign national) director was used—as was sometimes the case with the contractual packaging on Lippert coproductions; consequently, it

made better economic sense to have the films directed by a Briton in the first place, whenever possible.

12. AB Pathé was the distribution arm of ABPC--Associated British Pictures Corporation.

13. A word of explanation for American readers in particular. *Picture Post* was a photo-based news journal, successor to the *Illustrated London News; Reveille* (and *Tit-Bits*) were weekly tabloid newspapers along the lines of *The National Enquirer*—news, gossip, articles of the "strange but true" variety, outlandish features "exposing" the truth about everything from space aliens to yetis, and peppered throughout with pinups of scantily-clad girls (such as Marie Devereux). The *Eagle* was a popular boys' comic whose star character was "Dan Dare—Pilot of the Future," with his *Heinkel*-inspired spaceship and skull-headed archenemy, the "Mekon." "Archie Andrews" was a ventriloquist's dummy (the ventriloquist being Peter Brough). "The Goons" were collectively Peter Sellers, Spike Milligan, Harry Secombe, and Michael Bentine. "Have A Go" was a radio quiz show hosted by Pickles (who would go on to act in films like *The Family Way* in 1966, with John and Hayley Mills), with "Mabel"—Violet Carson—on an accompanying piano. "Fabian of the Yard" was a TV series (and several spin-off second features) purportedly based on the exploits of Chief Inspector Robert Fabian. Edgar Lustgarten was a writer and criminologist who narrated a long-running series of "true crime" second features, which were also culled from the files of Scotland Yard, and who served as the basis for Charles Gray's send-up as "The Narrator" in *The Rocky Horror Picture Show* (1976).

14. The serial's Quatermass—Reginald Tate—was not even considered for the film version, due to the need for an American lead to guarantee U.S. distribution. Just as well; Tate died suddenly, only weeks before he was due to reprise the role in the television sequel, and he was replaced in that by John Robinson.

15. A supporting role in the 1950 police drama *The Blue Lamp*, that of P. C. George Dixon, was to produce such an affectionate archetype of the British bobby that Warner was eventually to recreate the part some five hundred times more in a long-running BBC TV series, "Dixon Of Dock Green," the first six episodes of which were to have gone on air by the time *The Quatermass Experiment* was released.

16. The episode by the canal with the little girl (shot at the East India Docks with a young Jane Asher) exactly parallels the famous sequence in the original Universal *Frankenstein* (1931) and consequently prefigures Hammer's revival of the story. In a similar vein, Wordsworth's makeup for the monster was also to reflect the Shelley concept—more so than that devised for Lee: "His yellow skin scarcely covered the work of muscles and arteries beneath; his hair was of a lustrous black…but these luxuriances only formed a more horrid contrast with his watery eyes…his shrivelled complexion and straight black lips."—*Frankenstein,* Mary W. Shelley; 1818.

17. Until now, Hammer's films had played as second features on the major circuits, but as *first* features in independent houses—some 2,000 bookings in total for each film—and they had been further guaranteed anything up to 1,800 bookings each in America.

18. This was FIDO—the Film Industry Defence Organization—whose purpose was to "regulate" the release of films to television, and thus protect the interests of the industry. The sanction-busting sale of 55 features direct to the BBC by Romulus Films and producer Daniel Angel at the end of 1959 was effectively to herald the end of this self-imposed restrictive practice.

19. The first two episodes of "The Quatermass Experiment" *were* Kinescoped during transmission (*filmed* off a high-resolution monitor screen using a conven-

tional camera) and now reside in the National Film Archive. Sadly for posterity, a technician's strike intervened to prevent the recording of the remaining four.

20. This idea came from *Rocketship X-M,* which had started life as *Rocketship Expedition Moon.*

21. This was corrected in *Quatermass II,* where Quatermass *is* government-funded—in fact, it is the cutback of those very funds which sets the entire plot in motion.

22. Independent producers Edward J. and Harry Lee Danziger, who specialized in low-budget thrillers. The Danzigers had made 1954's *Devil Girl From Mars* and would return to the form in 1955 with the science-fiction shennanigans of *Satellite In the Sky.* In 1960, they would also produce a version of Poe's *The Tell-Tale Heart* from a script cowritten by Brian Clemens.

23. For completists, these were variously *Captain Morgan, Buccaneer* (to star Forrest Tucker) *Friar Tuck, Breakout, Stand and Deliver, Charter to Danger, The Cavalier* (aka *King Charles and the Roundheads*), the featurette *Dance Band Story,* James Fennimore Cooper's *The Deerslayer, Chorus of Echoes, Black Chiffon, A Holiday For Simon,* further outings for both the Lyons and The Saint, and *Brat Farrar*—which would eventually resurface in 1962 as *Paranoiac.*

24. London: Arrow-Hutchinson, 1979.

25. Kneale's forebodings, as predicated in *Quatermass II,* were to prove alarmingly accurate. In 1955, an explosion at the Soviet nuclear facility in Chelyabinsk was ultimately to affect nearly half a million Russians—and in October 1957, a release of radiation caused by a fire in one of the Windscale reactors would result in some 200 cases of thyroid cancer being diagnosed among workers and inhabitants of the local community; it would be many years before the full extent of this disaster became public knowledge.

26. It was left to Eliot Hyman to break the news that Hammer was to write its own script for *Frankenstein.* According to Rosenberg, he and Subotsky received $5,000 and 20 percent of the proceeds in respect of their extant contribution and to obviate any "nuisance" suit—but this would come from Hyman, not Hammer.

27. British Film Producers Association.

28. By the time *The Curse of Frankenstein* finished shooting, "The 6-5 Special" was already on air, and Bill Haley and the Comets would be jetting in to the U. K. for their first nationwide tour.

29. The exception is *Frankenstein Must Be Destroyed* (1969), where screenwriter Bert Batt took his cue from *The Curse of Frankenstein,* rather than its successors in the series, to make the baron's ruthless streak his dominant attribute.

30. It would ultimately fall to Roger Corman to tease out of Court the wanton allure and moral decadence that her portrayals for Hammer had done their best to stifle, when he came to cast her in several of his later Poe adaptions—*The Premature Burial* (1961), *The Raven* (1962), *The Masque of the Red Death* (1964).

Chapter 2: New Blood For Old

1. The producer of *Night of the Demon,* Columbia executive Hal E. Chester, was the recipient of an invitation from Carreras to an introductory expense-account lunch at one of the exclusive West End eateries now being regularly pressed into service for this very purpose. Unimpressed by the Colonel's waving-away of the à

la carte menu in favor of the speciality of the house, the former *East Side Kid* would call for a steak sandwich and a beer, instead!

2. The term *Gothic* as applied to these films has its origins in the Gothic horror novels of the 18th and 19th centuries, whose authors were to borrow piecemeal from German (and other European) folklore in a determinedly populist attempt to break down the barriers of literary convention and produce a new and more vibrant form of story-telling. This meant the wholesale employment of all the mechanics of melodrama, and the German influence ensured that the results were dark in tone and invariably obsessed with the grim appurtenances of death, and what lay beyond it. The prime movers in this new school of "raw-head and bloody bones" were Horace Walpole, Mrs. Anne Radcliffe, Matthew Gregory Lewis, and Charles Maturin, with novels such as *The Castle of Otranto* (1765), *The Mysteries of Udolpho* (1794), *The Monk* (1796), and *Melmoth The Wanderer* (1820), respectively. The Gothic tradition found many forms, from the high art of Wilkie Collins to the low common denominator of the Victorian "penny dreadful" (such as James Malcolm Rymer's *Varney The Vampire*; 1847), before expiring at its height during the Gothic Revival of the late 1800s, when it was overtaken by the exotics of H. Rider Haggard—*King Solomon's Mines* (1885), *She* (1887)—and the detective fiction of, among others, Sir Arthur Conan Doyle. This latter departure had effectively been begun by Edgar Allan Poe in his "The Murders in the Rue Morgue" (1841), whose fictional sleuth, Auguste Dupin, had served as a model in part for Doyle's Sherlock Holmes. Scholars generally agree that the true Gothic horror novel began with *The Castle of Otranto* in 1765, but they are less in concert about its effective demise in "pure" form. Concensus tends to lie somewhere between 1825 and 1865, when the upsurge of the penny dreadful sullied the genre by exploitative repetition. *Frankenstein* is a pure example of Gothic art, whereas *Dracula* (which was written in 1897, during the Gothic Revival that also produced Robert Louis Stevenson's *Dr. Jekyll and Mr Hyde* [1886] and Oscar Wilde's *The Picture of Dorian Gray* [1891]) is Gothic artifice.

3. When modernist Wolf Mankowitz came to elaborate on this very theme for Fisher's *The Two Faces of Dr. Jekyll*, he was to turn Jekyll's spouse into just as much of a sexual predator as the rakish Hyde. Fisher thought *that* script an imbroglio, referring to the same trait that he had considered so attractive in Dracula as producing a wife "who was no good anyway" when manifested in a woman.

4. Lee had played minor roles in some three dozen films before appearing in *The Curse of Frankenstein*—but then Boris Karloff before him had appeared in over eighty before his *Frankenstein* in 1931.

5. The Comics Code Authority—a self-regulating U.S. body set up in 1954 to stem the floodtide of horror comics in response to the backlash that had been created after the publication of Dr. Frederic Wertham's condemnatory *Seduction of the Innocent*, a tract that had primarily been aimed at the graphic excess typified by the output of publisher William S. Gaines, notably *Tales From the Crypt* and *The Vault of Horror*.

6. *Fangoria:* "Monster Moguls—Hammer's Michael Carreras: Horror As a Family Business"/Steve Swires/February, 1987.

7. Tony Hinds would continue to commission story ideas for *Tales of Frankenstein* until May 1958. After the series was abandoned, two of these outlines (by Peter Bryan and Cyril Kersh) would find their way into the plots of *The Evil of Frankenstein* and *Frankenstein Created Woman*.

8. James Carreras would blow the lid off this "subterfuge" for good in the January 6, 1960, issue of *Variety*, in an article carrying his own byline. "We decided there was only one way to really scare the crowds—by giving them plausible horror and

human monsters with a taste for *sex*," Carreras revealed. "Like handsome Christopher Lee who played Dracula as a sex-fiend as well as a blood-lapper!"

9. Among the other subsidiaries were Travel, Atalanta and Saturn Films, Key *Distributors*, Concanen *Recordings*, and Kingfisher, Hawfinch, Hammer Television and even "Cloister" Productions—the last, no doubt a joke at Brian Lawrence's expense!

10. Peter Cushing was often less than happy with the quality of Hammer's scripts, and he would invariably fine-tune his dialogue, politely but persuasively ensuring that the roles he played were up to his exacting requirements. To *The Hound of the Baskervilles*, he added this line and other bits of business from Conan Doyle to give the production some Holmesian rectitude.

11. Woodfall was the teaming of Tony Richardson and John Osborne, and Bryanston was one of several independents operating under the umbrella of Sir Michael Balcon and British Lion.

12. Peter Bryan had been Hammer's camera operator before the advent of Len Harris in 1952. Bryan had left to make documentaries for Cinevision Productions, which he had formed with recordist Edgar Vetter, and some of these would eventually find their way into the Hammer catalog. Tony Hinds would reemploy Bryan from time to time on scriptwriting chores, to help him with his medical bills; Bryan was to die of throat cancer.

13. Cushing would reprise the role of Holmes on BBC Television between September and December of 1968, in a series of fifteen story adaptions which would also include *The Hound of the Baskervilles* in two parts. Douglas Wilmer had been the BBC's Holmes in 1965, but Cushing was to be drafted on the strength of his Hammer persona, for a series that would concern itself more with the "lurking horror and callous savagery" of the Victorian half-world, according to BBC publicity.

14. "The Final Problem," *Strand Magazine*, Vol. V, December, 1893.

15. After *Ten Seconds to Hell*, two more projects requiring exotic locations were shelved: *Build Us a Dam* and *The Mercenaries*, from novels by Jon Manchip White, who had coscripted *The Camp on Blood Island*. But both were kept on the stocks for a time, and White produced a draft of *The Mercenaries* as late as September 1962.

16. This mysterious nobleman had been reported alive and well at dates as disparate as 1660 and 1820. He was known to *Otranto*'s Horace Walpole, was an inventor of chemical techniques (his immense wealth purportedly being due to his discovery of the Philosopher's Stone), and he taught magic to Mesmer and Cagliostro.

17. Coauthored with H. P. Lovecraft and first published in *Weird Tales* in 1935.

18. Hammer's film, with its powerful but above all *agile* example of the breed, is the only one to capture the dynamic of this particular weird tale, whose mummy bounds "like a tiger...with blazing eyes and one stringy arm out-thrown."

19. Jimmy Sangster's confessed antipathy toward doing research was never a virtue: Karnak was a *locale*—site of the Temple of Amun—and not a God, as in the film.

20. *The Mummy*'s title cards make no such allusions as to its source, and in a letter to *Time* magazine of April 27, 1959, Nina Wilcox Putnam wrote: "Thank you for your April 6 exposé of the horror motion pictures that are currently being made in England at the Hammer studios. Without this review I might not have known that my story, *The Mummy*, was being remade in a debased form. This story, as originally written by me, was a perfectly clean and decent archaeological "chiller" which I wrote expressly for Boris Karloff. This disgusting English remake was done without

my knowledge or consent, and it has been a terrible shock, at the age of 75, to find such a work attributed to me, however wrongly and by indirection."

21. In some territories, this entire sequence was eliminated to improve the pace; paradoxically, it would bring the film back in line with Sangster's original concept.

22. The design of many of the sequences featuring the mummy itself (in particular, the asylum attack on Stephen Banning) is uncannily reminiscent of situations in *The Ghoul*, which Boris Karloff had made for Gaumont-British in 1933. Fisher had no connection with that film, but he was working in the industry at the time of its release, and its highly charged *mise-en-scène* seems to have infected his subconscious somewhere along the line.

23. Raymond Huntley had the distinction of beating Christopher Lee to an English interpretation of Dracula when, in 1927, as a young actor of 22, he had essayed the role of the count on the West End stage in the British production of Hamilton Deane's adaption of the novel. Felix Aylmer's film career stretched back to the early thirties, but his quiet and beneficent manner had removed him from subjects of *gravitas*—*Henry V* (1944); *Hamlet* (1948)—and led him to play a succession of Jewish patriarchs in a series of historical epics for M-G-M, inaugurated by *Quo Vadis* (1951). He was to be knighted in 1965, but he was already in possession of an O.B.E. by the time his presence graced *The Mummy* (and soon *Never Take Sweets From a Stranger*).

24. Industry pundits were now predicting the imminent demise of the resurgent cycle, and it was a view not lost on Hammer. During lunch with the BBFC's newly appointed Secretary, John Trevelyan, James Carreras had asked the censor if he thought the horror boom would last another twelve months. "No," Trevelyan had replied. It was to prove a self-fulfilling prophecy.

25. British Film Academy, now Academy of Film *and Television* Arts (BAFTA).

26. Joseph Losey was contracted to direct *Brat Farrar* with Dirk Bogarde starring, but Columbia hated the very idea of it: "It was too *mummy darling*," Hinds said— "Jim Carreras was very devious. He would never actually come out and say, 'I don't think we should do this'; he'd say, 'I had a word with the circuits and *they* don't fancy it'. So I couldn't argue with that." With the loss of such high-caliber talent, Hinds would ask Jimmy Sangster to rewrite the script, and the resulting film was to be relegated to B-feature status as *Paranoiac* (1962).

27. *Never Take Sweets (Candy) From a Stranger* was to be denied a Production Code "Seal of Approval" in the United States. Columbia appealed the decision and lost, and the film was subsequently dropped. As a result, it received only limited distribution through the Omat Corporation.

Chapter 3: Diminishing Returns

1. Originally, "Tin Pan Alley" was 28th Street in New York City, where most of the popular songs were published as sheet music, but the term is generally taken to mean any commercial center of popular music, like London's Denmark Street.

2. Monty Norman and David Heneker, who had written the music for *Expresso Bongo*, would join Mankowitz on *The Two Faces of Dr. Jekyll* and provide an excellent and evocative score, as well as a lively overture composed of Victorian music-hall melodies.

3. *Films and Filming*: "Horror Is My Business"/Raymond Durgnat, John Cutts/July, 1964.

4. In a speech which has as much to say about censorship now as then, Gerald Gardiner Q.C., closing for the defense, said of the charges against the book: "Nobody suggests that the Director of Public Prosecutions becomes depraved or corrupted. Counsel read the book; they do not become depraved or corrupted. Witnesses read the book; they do not become depraved or corrupted. Nobody suggests the judge or the jury becomes depraved or corrupted. It is always *somebody else*; it is never ourselves..." (Fenton Bressler, *Sex and the Law*. London: Muller-Century Hutchinson, 1988).

5. Even *The Nutty Professor* was to lose a major portion of its transformation scene in order to gain a "U" certificate in the U.K.

6. A one-time Tory MP for Ashford in Kent, Edward Percy had been a playwright since 1922; his most notable works were *Ladies in Retirement* (1939) and *The Shop at Sly Corner* (1941), which was made into a film in 1946 by George King and on which Bernard Robinson had acted as art director.

7. Greta's line, "He's got to come back here...before cock-crow," was to signal to the audience the means by which Marianne would subsequently escape the vampire's fangs; its retention in the final cut was made incidental by the changes.

8. In his formative years, Michael Carreras supped on a diet of Harry James and Jesse James, and his debut as a feature-director—*The Steel Bayonet* (1956)—owed much of its storyline to the Republic western, *The Last Command* (1955): the Alamo, in the case of the Carreras film, being transported to the plains of Tunisia, circa 1943.

9. The American release of *Peeping Tom* was to be held up for two years, and then the film would be shorn of 23 minutes running time.

10. Even William Castle, the producer-director of essentially harmless exploitation quickies such as *The Tingler* (1959) and *13 Ghosts* (1960) would fall victim to the backlash. His *Mr. Sardonicus* (1961), an otherwise minor excursion into the Gothic cycle that had plucked Ronald Lewis and Guy Rolfe from recent Hammer fare, was to be so comprehensively emasculated as to be made unintelligible, both in storyline *and* central conceit.

11. Despite its cancellation, the idea behind this film was to persist, and Michael would later incorporate much of the imagery of *The Inquisitor* into his own script for *The Lost Continent*.

12. To bolster yet another period of flagging British production, the ACTT had agreed to sponsor some of its own; BHP (formed in February 1960 by screenwriter George Baxt, theatrical agent Richard Finlay Hatton, and director Jon Penington) had been one of several companies set up to take advantage of the situation, and as an act of goodwill toward the union, Hammer extended facilities and personnel to the film on a nominal fee-paying basis.

13. The novel's antihero was named Bertrand Chaillet; for the film, this was changed to Bernardo to suit the Spanish setting, before finally becoming Leon.

14. Tey's novel *A Shilling in Time* had been the basis of Alfred Hitchcock's *Young and Innocent*(1937), and *The Franchise Affair* had also reached the screen in 1950 with Michael Denison, Dulcie Gray, and Hy Hazell starring.

15. John Trevelyan placed much store by the advice of the various psychiatrists that the board consulted, and blood *on breasts* was considered to be a psychopathic "trigger."

16. Corman's Poe films aped the Hammer product in more ways than one: they were also the product of a bevy of brilliantly original talents—Daniel Haller (art

direction), Les Baxter (music), Richard Matheson (scriptwriting), and Floyd Crosby (camerawork), among others. The sixth Poe variant, *The Haunted Palace* (1963)—in reality, H. P. Lovecraft's *The Case of Charles Dexter Ward*—even prefigured Hammer's Gothics of the seventies by having a motley of disaffected villagers storm the ancestral castle!

17. *Conversations With Losey.* London: Methuen, 1985.

18. London: Michael Joseph, 1973.

19. In addition to providing *The Kiss of the Vampire* with its prologue and climax, *The Disciple of Dracula* also graced the film's Professor Zimmer with Sangster's original characterization of Latour: brandy-swigging, shabbily-dressed, laconic—and bent on revenge for the loss of a daughter. Here is a sample exchange.

Latour (to Pauline): "You're a very sensible young lady...you remind me of my daughter."

Pauline: "I wouldn't have thought you..."

Latour: I haven't always been a wanderer. She's dead now."

Chapter 4: The House of Horror

1. In addition to Hinds and his partner James Carreras, there were sixty guests—including the "Hammer" contingent (Michael, Jimmy Sangster, Tony and Basil Keys, editor Jim Needs, directors Fisher and Francis, construction manager Arthur Banks, publicist Dennison Thornton, and the two "Peters"—Cushing and Bryan). They represented the *crème de la crème* of the British industry. Among their number were Columbia's Bill Graf and Mike Frankovich, Rank's George Pinches and Fred Thomas, director Vernon Sewell, Jack Goodlatte, Nat Cohen, Stuart Levy, and film censor John Trevelyan.

2. *The Brigand of Kandahar* would fall back on stock footage from *Zarak* (1956) to supplement a leaner production at Elstree. The expedient was to persuade its star to leave Hammer for good. "I had heard that things were falling to pieces, and I saw what was happening to Peter and Christopher...in terms of being cast in those sort of roles all the time. So I called it a day," said Oliver Reed.

3. An attempt to disguise the fact that two actresses played the role of *The Gorgon* was carried over into the cast roller, where Prudence Hyman was referred to as "Chatelaine"—literally, "mistress of the chateau."

4. The sequel to *The Camp on Blood Island* would be delivered to Universal with no mention of the fact that its predecessor had suffered in distribution due to a series of territorial embargoes imposed at the instigation of the Japanese government. When *The Secret of Blood Island* met with similar resistance, Universal were less than pleased—it was the end of a beautiful friendship.

5. The precredits sequence was a last-minute inclusion, to bring the new film up to the required running time.

6. Peter Bryan's screenplays were tuned specifically to Hammer. He could turn in the occasional cutting line or exchange ("Well?" the squire inquires of the purpose behind a visit by Forbes in *The Plague of the Zombies*; "Thank you, yes," reproves the imperturbable physician), but even a cursory glance at *The Blood-Beast Terror* (aka *The Deathshead-Vampire/The Vampire-Beast Craves Blood*; 1967), directed by Vernon Sewell and a Hammer by another name—Tigon—reveals the flat and functional nature of their construction, when deprived of the part played by Hammer's

production ensemble. Hinds could afford only *one* Bryan script for the Cornish duo; the *Deathshead-Vampire* idea, remarkably similar to *The Reptile* in every way, was subsequently sold to Tony Tenser.

7. Coincidentally, Harry Spalding was the name of the screenwriter on two Lippert quickies made in England while Bray had been closed for renovation: *Witchcraft* (1964) and *Curse of the Fly* (1965).

8. When Bray was eventually sold in 1971, it was to Redspring Ltd for £250,000, in a three-way split among Hammer, Columbia, and EMI. (The asking price had been £75,000 in 1967.) Bray International Film Centre, as it would become, was then sold on to Samuelsons in 1984 for a cool £700,000.

9. Damned if you do, and damned if you don't department: *Curse of the Crimson Altar* (aka *The Crimson Cult*), Tigon's black magic opus, made the following year and modelled on H. P. Lovecraft's "The Dreams in the Witch-House," was less restrained in its approach—but all the film's satanic sex-and-sadism sequences were deleted on its British release.

10. Gwen Ffrangcon-Davies, who had also appeared in *The Witchess*, had her scenes as the Countess (and therefore her relationship with Tanith) cut for pace in *The Devil Rides Out*. As an incidental, this venerable actress was to live to the ripe old age of 101!

11. London: Secker and Warburg, 1967.

12. Foremost among the victims of the Manson cult's murder spree was actress Sharon Tate, wife of film director Roman Polanski. Tate had starred in the witchcraft thriller *Eye of the Devil* (1967) and Polanski's own *Dance of the Vampires* (aka *The Fearless Vampire Killers*; 1968), and in a macabre twist, Polanski's film of Ira Levin's *Rosemary's Baby*—about a cult of Satanists operating from the Bramford apartment building in New York—had opened in London on March 2, 1969, six months before the murders.

Chapter 5: Last Rites

1. Bernard Robinson had maintained a prodigious output, despite recurrent health problems. On March 2, 1970, he died, disillusioned and dispirited. Hammer had come to admire his economy, though not his artistry: he had given the films their soul. "Bernie was the *real* star of Hammer films," Christopher Lee freely concedes.

2. *Films and Filming*: "Hammering the Box Office"/Colin Heard/June, 1959.

3. Hammer was regularly dunking its feet in the murky waters of sexploitation by now: a skin-dip for Victoria Vetri in *When Dinosaurs Ruled the Earth* (cut in American *and* British prints), the titillating brothel sequence in *Taste the Blood of Dracula* (also cut in the U.S.), and topless scenes for both Jane Lapotaire *and* Stefanie Powers in *Crescendo*.

4. In later years, Roy Ward Baker would attribute this dictate to "cold feet" on the part of AIP, rather than the BBFC—but Brian Lawrence had sought commentary on Gates's script from all quarters, *including* AIP; Deke Heyward was less concerned by the lesbianism in *Vampire Lovers* that he was by the fact that with the departure of Hinds, Hammer was behaving like a headless chicken.

5. ABC-EMI distribution was subsequently to be split in two: M-G-M-EMI (domestic) and Anglo-EMI (overseas), the latter being headed up by Nat Cohen.

6. After appearing in *The Vampire Lovers* and *The Horror of Frankenstein*, Jon Finch would play the lead in Roman Polanski's *Macbeth* (1971), Alfred Hitchcock's British-made *Frenzy* (1972), and Robert Fuest's *The Final Programme* (aka *The Last Days of Man on Earth* [1973])—as Michael Moorcock's oddball antihero, Jerry Cornelius—but his career was to stall with the collapse of the domestic industry in the mid-seventies.

7. Mike Raven would feature in only two more horrors: *Crucible of Terror* (1971) and *Disciple of Death* (1972), both of which he would coproduce himself, before effectively retiring from public life to a hill farm in North Cornwall.

8. During a party at Court-in-Holmes, the East Sussex home of Sir James Carreras at the time, *Countess Dracula* producer Alex Paal tried to interest Carreras in the idea of a film about the *real* "Dracula," Vlad Tepes, using original locations in Romania and with *Mike Raven* playing the lead. Carreras expressed a reluctance to upset his most bankable star at this delicate stage in their dealings (Lee's own desire was to do exactly the same—and he would, for television, in "In Search Of Dracula"). Carreras declined, but the idea was to remain on the stocks. It would later surface (though never be filmed) as *Lord Dracula* (from a radio play by Brian Hayles) and *Vlad the Impaler*.

9. The statuesque Valerie Leon—who was actually second choice to Amy Grant for Margaret/Tera in *Blood From the Mummy's Tomb*—would find wider-reaching fame in a series of television commercials for *Hai Karate* aftershave. She (or according to the actress, a body double) had contributed a brief rear nude to the film, but American audiences were to be denied that moment of light relief.

10. Alleyn's was the sister school of Dulwich College, both in Southeast London; it was ex-College master Michael Croft who had founded the National Youth Theatre.

11. The Laurie Marsh Group's plans in the film business were dealt a terminal blow by its failure to acquire Hammer. Tony Tenser was to resign his seat on the LMG board at the end of 1972 (and form Team Productions) and the Tigon name would be reduced to a utility for distribution purposes only. By the end of 1973, Laurie Peter Marsh would have sold off both his LMG film distributors *and* his Classic cinema chain.

12. Sir James Carreras subsequently took up a consultancy post with EMI (in conjunction to one with Studio Film Labs which became effective on April 3, 1973) and set his sights on the vacancy for head of production which had come about with the sudden end of Bryan Forbes's tenure at Elstree. The job would go to Nat Cohen, and, Variety Club notwithstanding, all the years of friendship between Carreras and Cohen ended then and there.

13. When Robert Quarry and Vincent Price were reunited for *Madhouse* (aka *The Revenge of Doctor Death*) after *Dr. Phibes Rises Again*, their combative egos had to be compressed into the tiny stages of Twickenham.

14. Terence Fisher, alone, attended the sparsely supported press screening for *Frankenstein and the Monster From Hell*. The few critics present ignored him, preferring to chat among themselves about the new Woody Allen film that they had seen earlier in the day. The 70-year-old director sat impassively on the sidelines, only too aware that the concluding installment in the saga had now been enacted.

15. *Kali, Devil-Bride of Dracula* (formerly *Dracula, High Priest of Vampires*) had been intended as a companion piece to *The Legend of the 7 Golden Vampires*. The film got as far as the casting, but it was wholly dependent on frozen rupees—which were

suddenly unfrozen by the Indian government and hurriedly withdrawn to Warners' bank account, instead.

16. The "missing" scenes fell between two consecutive reaction close shots of Verney as he turned back to face the altar after having rescued Catherine; there is a clear mismatch in these shots as they appear in the extant print.

17. Nat Cohen subsequently asked Roy Skeggs to reinstate any censored material for a foreign version, but time had moved on, and under new Secretary Stephen Murray, the BBFC had found nothing to warrant cutting in the first place. Skeggs could only suggest lengthening "the orgy sequence" with outtakes, but this was felt to be more trouble than it was worth, and export prints ultimately remained the same.

18. The International Monetary Fund.

19. As late as May 1979, Michael was still attempting to float *Nessie.* By that time, the budget would have been increased to $10 million. Lindsay Anderson was said to have agreed to direct, Richard Harris and Katherine Ross had been approached to star, and filming was planned on the stages of Pinewood to meet a release date of summer 1980. Unlike the beast in the story, the film would never surface.

20. The phrase, "a last supper in a sense," was deleted from the script at the request of the BBFC.

21. When *The Lady Vanishes* was being planned for American television (with director John L. Moxey), Michael Carreras had set his sights on James Garner, but according to Wicking, a more *camp* cast version had come nearer to fruition. "The whole thing came down to casting and nobody could ever agree who they should be. And one day a cable came from ABC in America saying, '*Can get* Lyndsay Wagner and Henry Winkler' (of "Happy Days"). You'd have had 'The Fonz' and 'The Bionic Woman' in *The Lady Vanishes,* and the least it would have done was make money. Michael had to try and tell Frank Poole that Henry *Winkler* (who, at that time, nobody here had ever heard of) was a good idea! That was the problem Michael was up against working out of England: people not knowing things of that nature."

22. At the time of writing (April 1995), demolition has been delayed—temporarily at least.

Appendix 1

The Hammer Horrors: Cast and Credits

The 60 films listed in this appendix are those considered most eligible to be designated as Hammer Horror. Where they are not obvious from the subject matter (or the fact that they contain elements of *grand guignol*), consideration has been given to how they were sold, and the British censor's "X" certificate has also been taken as a rule of thumb. Several psychothrillers are included, where they enjoy an air of the fantastic, but others are not (such as *The Nanny*, which is little more than a psychological case-study). But a great many films are borderline, nevertheless: *Four Sided Triangle* is included because of its position as the first Hammer film to use the trappings of science-horror, as is *The Damned* because of its "importance," but *The Camp on Blood Island* (which was sold as an atrocity piece) is not, nor is *The Old Dark House,* which was based on a Universal horror film but designed and marketed as a comedy—or *The Horror of Frankenstein,* which was also intended to be a comedy. *Nightmare* and *Straight on Till Morning* are two more exceptions, but a line has to be drawn somewhere. Essential details of all Hammer's films can be found in Appendix 2.

Produced dates are those of the *actual* commencement of production, i.e., when principal photography commenced, and have been given as the Monday of the first week, though shooting, in a few instances, may have begun a day or two later. (This applies equally to Appendix 2.)

Released dates are those of the films' British general release (except where * denotes a premier engagement); ** denotes the date of review in the BFI's *Monthly Film Bulletin,* and although this has been given as a date of release in some cases, it is not necessarily correct in that context; *** denotes trade show. (This also applies to Appendix 2.)

ROOM TO LET

Hammer 68 minutes Black-and-white Cert A
Produced October 3, 1949/Released May 15, 1950**
Distributor Exclusive

CAST

Curly Minter	Jimmy Hanley
J. J.	J. A. La Penna
Harding	Aubrey Dexter
Sergeant	Reginald Dyson
P. C. Smith	Charles Mander
Mansfield	Cyril Conway
Doctor Fell	Valentine Dyall
Alice	Merle Tottenham
Molly	Constance Smith
Mrs. Musgrave	Christine Silver
Editor	Lawrence Naismith
Michael	Charles Hawtrey
Atkinson	John Clifford
Porter	Stewart Saunders
Tom	Charles Houston
Matron	Harriet Petworth
Butler	F. A. Williams

CREDITS

Directed by	Godfrey Grayson
Produced by	Anthony Hinds
Screenplay by	John Gilling/Godfrey Grayson
Based on the BBC feature by	Margery Allingham
Music Composed/Conducted by	Frank Spencer
Director of Photography	Cedric Williams
Camera Operator	Peter Bryan
Art Director	Denis Wreford
Editor	James Needs
Cutter	Alfred Cox
Production Manager	Arthur Barnes
Assistant Director	Jimmy Sangster
Continuity	Renee Glynn
Recordist	Edgar Vetter
Makeup	Phil Leakey
Hairstylist	Monica Hustler
Dress Designer	Myra Cullimore
Casting	Prudence Sykes

FOUR SIDED TRIANGLE

Hammer 81 (USA 74) minutes Black-and-white Cert A
Produced July 28, 1952/Released May 25, 1953
Distributor Exclusive/Astor (USA)

CAST

Lena/Helen	Barbara Payton
Dr. Harvey	James Hayter
Bill	Stephen Murray
Robin	John Van Eyssen
Sir Walter	Percy Marmont
Lena as a Child	Jennifer Dearman
Bill as a Child	Glyn Dearman
Robin as a Child	Sean Barrett
Lord Grant	Kynaston Reeves
Solicitor	John Stuart
Lady Grant	Edith Saville

CREDITS

Directed by	Terence Fisher
Produced by	Michael Carreras/Alexander Paal
Screenplay by	Paul Tabori/Terence Fisher
Adaption by	Paul Tabori
Based on the novel by	William F. Temple
Music Composed by	Malcolm Arnold
Music Conducted by	Muir Mathieson
Director of Photography	Reginald Wyer
Camera Operator	Len Harris
Art Director	J. Elder Wills
Editor	Maurice Rootes
Sound Recordist	Bill Salter
Production Manager	Victor Wark
Assistant Director	Bill Shore
Second Asst Director	Aida Young
Makeup	D. Bonnor-Moris
Hair Stylist	Nina Broe
Dialogue Director	Nora Roberts
Continuity	Renee Glynn
Stills Cameraman	John Jay

THE QUATERMASS EXPERIMENT
(American Titles: Shock/The Creeping Unknown)

Hammer 82 (USA:78) minutes Black-and-white Cert X
Produced November 1954/Released November 20, 1955
Distributor Exclusive/United Artists (USA)
Original Second Feature (UK/USA):*Rififi/The Black Sleep*

CAST

Professor Bernard Quatermass	Brian Donlevy
Inspector Lomax	Jack Warner
Judith Carroon	Margia Dean
Victor Carroon	Richard Wordsworth
Rosie	Thora Hird
Gordon Briscoe	David King-Wood
Christie	Harold Lang
Blake	Lionel Jeffries
Marsh	Maurice Kauffman
TV Producer	Gordon Jackson
Green	Gron Davies
Reichenheim	Stanley Von Beers
BBC Announcer	Frank Phillips
Sergeant Bromley	Arthur Lovegrove
Major	John Sterling
Young Man	Eric Corrie
Maggie	Margaret Anderson
Maggie's Father	Henry Longhurst
Fireman	Michael Godfrey
Inspector	Fred Johnson
Local Policeman	George Roderick
Fire Chief	Ernest Hare
Laboratory Assistant	John Kerr
Best	John Wynn
Chemist	Toke Townley
Zoo Keeper	Bartlett Mullins
Mother (at Zoo)	Molly Glessing
Zoo Official	Mayne Lynton
Night Porter	Harry Brunsing
Tucker	Barry Lowe
Mrs. Lomax	Jane Aird
Station Sergeant	Sam Kydd
Floor Boy	Arthur Gross
Sound Engineer	James Drake
Station Policeman	Edward Dane
Sir Lionel	Basil Dignam
First Nurse	Betty Impey
Second Nurse	Marianne Stone
Young Girl	Jane Asher

CREDITS

Directed by	Val Guest
Produced by	Anthony Hinds
Screenplay by	Richard Landau/Val Guest
Based on the BBC TV serial by	Nigel Kneale
Music Composed by	James Bernard
Music Conducted by	John Hollingsworth
Director of Photography	Walter Harvey BSC
Camera Operator	Len Harris
Art Director	J. Elder Wills
Editor	James Needs
Asst Editor	Henry Richardson
Sound Recordist	H. C. Pearson
Production Manager	T. S. Lyndon-Haynes
Assistant Director	Bill Shore
2nd Asst Director	Aida Young
Makeup	Phil Leakey
Hairdresser	Monica Hustler
Wardrobe	Molly Arbuthnot
Continuity	Renee Glynne
Special Effects	Les Bowie

X THE UNKNOWN

Hammer 78 minutes Black-and-white Cert X
Produced January 9, 1956/Released November 5, 1956
Distributor Exclusive/Warner Bros (USA)
Original Cofeature (UK/USA): *Les Diaboliques/The Curse of Frankenstein*

CAST

Dr. Adam Royston	Dean Jagger
Elliott	Edward Chapman
McGill	Leo McKern
Pte. "Spider" Webb	Anthony Newley
Jack Harding	Jameson Clark
Peter Elliott	William Lucas
Lt. Bannerman	Peter Hammond
Zena	Marianne Brauns
"Haggis"	Ian MacNaughton
Sgt. Grimsdyke	Michael Ripper
Major Cartwright	John Harvey
Old Soldier	Edwin Richfield
Vi Harding	Jane Aird
Old Tom	Norman Macowan
Unwin (Radiographer)	Neil Hallet
Pte. Lancing	Kenneth Cope
Willie Harding	Michael Brook

Ian Osbourne	Fraser Hines
Russel	Neil Wilson
Gerry	John Stone
Police Sgt Yeardye	Archie Duncan
Police Car Driver	John Stirling
Police Radio Operator	Shaw Taylor
P. C. Williams	Frank Taylor
Vicar	Brown Derby
Hospital Director	Max Brimmell
Dr. Kelly	Robert Bruce
Nurse	Stella Kemball
Gateman	Anthony Sager
Security Man	Phillip Levene
Soldier in Trench	Barry Steel
Second Guard	Lawrence James
First Soldier	Brian Peck
Second Soldier	Edward Judd
First Reporter	Stephenson Lang

CREDITS

Directed by	Leslie Norman (who replaced Joseph Losey [Joseph Walton])
Produced by	Anthony Hinds
Story and Screenplay by	Jimmy Sangster
Music Composed by	James Bernard
Musical Director	John Hollingsworth
Director of Photography	Gerald Gibbs
Camera Operator	Len Harris
Editor	James Needs
Sound Mixer	Jock May
Dubbing Editor	Alfred Cox
Production Manager	Jimmy Sangster
Assistant Director	Christopher Sutton
Makeup/Special Makeup Effects	Phil Leakey
Wardrobe	Molly Arbuthnot
Continuity	June Randall
Special Effects	Jack Curtis/Bowie Margutti Ltd
Executive Producer	Michael Carreras

QUATERMASS II

(American Title: Enemy From Space)

Hammer 85 minutes Black-and-white Cert X
Produced May 21, 1956/Released June 17, 1957
Distributor United Artists

CAST

Professor Quatermass	Brian Donlevy
Lomax	John Longden
Jimmy Hall	Sidney James
Marsh	Bryan Forbes
Brand	William Franklyn
Sheila	Vera Day
Dawson	Charles Lloyd Pack
Vincent Broadhead MP	Tom Chatto
The PRO	John Van Eyssen
Gorman	Percy Herbert
Ernie	Michael Ripper
E. J. McLeod	John Rae
Mrs. McLeod	Jane Aird
Secretary	Marianne Stone
Kelly	Betty Impey
Inspector	Lloyd Lamble
Commissioner	John Stuart
Banker	Gilbert Davies
Woman MP	Joyce Adams
Peterson	Edwin Richfield
Michaels	Howard Williams
Lab Assistants	Philip Baird, Robert Raikes
Intern	John Fabian
Superintendent	George Merritt
Constable	Arthur Blake
Harry	Michael Balfour
Young Man in Car	Ronald Wilson
Young Woman in Car	Jan Holden

CREDITS

Directed by	Val Guest
Produced by	Anthony Hinds
Screenplay by	Nigel Kneale/Val Guest
Based on the BBC TV serial by	Nigel Kneale
Music Composed by	James Bernard
Music Conducted by	John Hollingsworth
Director of Photography	Gerald Gibbs
Camera Operator	Len Harris
Art Director	Bernard Robinson
Editor	James Needs
Sound Recordist	Cliff Sandell
Sound Editor	Alfred Cox
Production Manager	John Workman
Assistant Director	Don Weeks
Makeup	Phil Leakey
Wardrobe	Rene Coke
Continuity	June Randall

Special Effects	Bill Warrington/Les Bowie/ Henry Harris/Frank George
Production Supervisor	Anthony Nelson Keys
Executive Producer	Michael Carreras

THE CURSE OF FRANKENSTEIN

Hammer/Clarion 82 minutes Eastmancolor Cert X
Produced November 19, 1956/Released May 20, 1957
Distributor Warner Bros.
Original Second Feature (UK/USA): *Woman of Rome/X The Unknown*

CAST

Victor Frankenstein	Peter Cushing
Elizabeth	Hazel Court
Paul Krempe	Robert Urquhart
Creature	Christopher Lee
Young Victor	Melvyn Hayes
Justine	Valerie Gaunt
Professor Bernstein	Paul Hardtmuth
Aunt Sophia	Noel Hood
Grandpa	Fred Johnson
Little Boy	Claude Kingston
Priest	Alec Gallier
Warder	Michael Mulcaster
Burgomeister	Andrew Leigh
Burgomeister's Wife	Anne Blake
Young Elizabeth	Sally Walsh
Lecturer	Middleton Woods
Uncle	Raymond Ray
Mother	Marjorie Hume
Fritz	Joseph Behrman
Undertaker	Ernest Jay

The following roles were originally cast, then recast as above or eliminated:

Schoolmaster	Henry Caine
Kurt	Patrick Troughton
Burgomeister	Hugh Dempster
Father Felix	Raymond Rollett
Uncle	J. Trevor Davis
A Tramp	Bartlett Mullins
Second Priest	Eugene Leahy

CREDITS

Directed by	Terence Fisher
Produced by	Anthony Hinds

Screenplay by   Jimmy Sangster
Based on the classic story by Mary W. Shelley
Associate Producer   Anthony Nelson-Keys
Music Composed by   James Bernard
Musical Director   John Hollingsworth
Director of Photography   Jack Asher BSC
Camera Operator   Len Harris
Focus Puller   Harry Oakes
Production Designer   Bernard Robinson
Art Director   Ted Marshall
Supervising Editor   James Needs
Assistant Editor   Roy Norman
Sound Recordist   W. H. May
Sound Camera Operator   Michael Sale
Boom Operator   Jimmy Parry
Production Manager   Don Weeks
Assistant Director   Derek Whitehurst
Second Asst Director   Jimmy Komisarjevsky
Third Asst Director   Hugh Harlow
Makeup   Phil Leakey
Hair stylist   Henry Montsash
Continuity   Doreen Soan
Casting Director   Dorothy Holloway
Stills Cameraman   John Jay/Tom Edwards
Production Secretary   Faith Frisby
Executive Producer   Michael Carreras

THE ABOMINABLE SNOWMAN

(American Title: The Abominable Snowman of the Himalayas)

Hammer 90 (USA:85) minutes Black-and-white/Regalscope Cert A
Produced January 28, 1957/Released August 26, 1957
Distributor Warner Bros.
Original Second Feature (UK): *Untamed Youth*

CAST

Tom Friend   Forrest Tucker
Dr. John Rollason   Peter Cushing
Helen Rollason   Maureen Connell
Peter Fox   Richard Wattis
Ed Shelley   Robert Brown
McNee   Michael Brill
Kusang   Wolfe Morris
Lhama   Arnold Marle
Major Domo   Anthony Chin
Yeti   Jock Easton, Joe Powell

CREDITS

Directed by	Val Guest
Produced by	Aubrey Baring
Screenplay by	Nigel Kneale
Based on his BBC TV play "The Creature"	
Associate Producer	Anthony Nelson Keys
Music Composed by	Humphrey Searle
Musical Director	John Hollingsworth
Director of Photography	Arthur Grant
Camera Operator	Len Harris
Production Designer	Bernard Robinson
Art Director	Ted Marshall
Editor	Bill Lenny
Sound Recordist	Jock May
Production Manager	Don Weeks
Assistant Director	Robert Lynn
Makeup	Phil Leakey
Hairdressing	Henry Montsash
Dress Designer	Beatrice Dawson
Wardrobe	Molly Arbuthnot
Continuity	Doreen Soan
Executive Producer	Michael Carreras

DRACULA

(American Title: Horror of Dracula)

Hammer 82 minutes Technicolor Cert X
Produced November 11, 1957/Released June 16, 1958
Distributor Rank/Universal-International (USA)
Original Second Feature (UK/USA): *There's Always a Price Tag/The Thing That Couldn't Die*

CAST

Dr. Van Helsing	Peter Cushing
Count Dracula	Christopher Lee
Arthur Holmwood	Michael Gough
Mina Holmwood	Melissa Stribling
Lucy Holmwood	Carol Marsh
Gerda	Olga Dickie
Jonathan Harker	John Van Eyssen
Vampire Woman	Valerie Gaunt
Tania	Janine Faye
Inga	Barbara Archer
Dr. Seward	Charles Lloyd Pack
Policeman	George Merritt

Landlord	George Woodbridge
Frontier Official	George Benson
Marx, the Undertaker	Miles Malleson
Porter	Geoffrey Bayldon
Lad	Paul Cole
Coach Driver	Guy Mills
Driver's Companion	Dick Morgan
Hearse Driver	John Mossman

The following roles were originally cast and filmed but eliminated during post-production:

Woman in Coach	Judith Nelmes
Man in Coach	Stedwell Fulcher
Fat Merchant	Humphrey Kent
Priest	William Sherwood

CREDITS

Directed by	Terence Fisher
Produced by	Anthony Hinds
Screenplay by	Jimmy Sangster
Based on the novel by Bram Stoker	
Associate Producer	Anthony Nelson Keys
Music Composed by	James Bernard
Music Conducted by	John Hollingsworth
Director of Photography	Jack Asher BSC
Camera Operator	Len Harris
Production Designer	Bernard Robinson
Supervising Editor	James Needs
Editor	Bill Lenny
Sound Recordist	Jock May
Production Manager	Don Weeks
Assistant Director	Robert Lynn
Makeup	Phil Leakey/Roy Ashton
Hairstylist	Henry Montsash
Wardrobe	Molly Arbuthnot
Continuity	Doreen Dearnaley
Special Effects	Sydney Pearson/Les Bowie
Stills Cameraman	Tom Edwards
Executive Producer	Michael Carreras

THE REVENGE OF FRANKENSTEIN

Hammer/Cadogan 89 minutes Technicolor Cert X
Produced January 6, 1958/Released August 28, 1958*
Distributor BLC/Columbia (USA)
Original Second Feature (USA): *Curse of the Demon*

CAST

Dr. Victor Stein	Peter Cushing
Dr. Hans Kleve	Francis Matthews
Margaret	Eunice Gayson
The Creature (Karl)	Michael Gwynn
Bergman	John Welsh
Fritz	Lionel Jeffries
The Dwarf/Karl	Oscar Quitak
Up Patient	Richard Wordsworth
President	Charles Lloyd Pack
Inspector	John Stuart
Molke	Arnold Diamond
Countess Barscynska	Margery Cresley
Vera Barscynska	Anna Walmsley
Janitor	George Woodbridge
Kurt	Michael Ripper
Boy	Ian Whittaker
Girl	Avril Leslie
Tattooed Patient	Michael Mulcaster
Priest	Alec Gallier

CREDITS

Directed by	Terence Fisher
Produced by	Anthony Hinds
Screenplay by	Jimmy Sangster
Additional Dialogue	H. Hurford Janes
Associate Producer	Anthony Nelson Keys
Music Composed by	Leonard Salzedo
Musical Director	Muir Mathieson
Director of Photography	Jack Asher BSC
Camera Operator	Len Harris
Production Designer	Bernard Robinson
Supervising Editor	James Needs
Editor	Alfred Cox
Sound Recordist	Jock May
Production Manager	Don Weeks
Assistant Director	Robert Lynn
Makeup	Phil Leakey/Hal Lesley
Hairstylist	Henry Montsash
Wardrobe	Rosemary Burrows
Continuity	Doreen Dearnaley
Executive Producer	Michael Carreras

Tales of Frankenstein:
"The Face in the Tombstone Mirror"

Hammer 26 minutes Black-and-white

Produced January/February 1958
Distributor Columbia/Screen Gems

CAST

Baron Von Frankenstein	Anton Diffring
Christine Halpert	Helen Westcott
The Monster	Don Megowan
Wilhelm	Ludwig Stossel
Max Halpert	Richard Bull
Doctor	Raymond Greenleaf
Gottfried	Peter Brocco

CREDITS

Directed by	Curt Siodmak
Produced by	Michael Carreras
Story by	Curt Siodmak
Teleplay by	Catherine & Henry Kuttner
Associate Producer	Curt Siodmak
Director of Photography	Gert Andersen ASC
Art Director	Carl Anderson
Set Decorator	James M.Crowe
Supervising Editor	Richard Fanti ACF
Film Editor	Tony DeMarco
Production Assistant	Seymour Friedman
Assistant Director	Floyd Joyer
Makeup by	Clay Campbell SMA
Hair Styles by	Helen Hunt

THE HOUND OF THE BASKERVILLES

Hammer 87 minutes Technicolor Cert A
Produced September 15, 1958/Released May 3, 1959
Distributor United Artists

CAST

Sherlock Holmes	Peter Cushing
Dr. Watson	André Morell
Sir Henry Baskerville	Christopher Lee
Cecile Stapleton	Marla Landi
Sir Hugo Baskerville	David Oxley
Dr. Richard Mortimer	Francis De Wolff
Bishop Frankland	Miles Malleson
Stapleton	Ewen Solon
Barrymore	John Le Mesurier
Mrs. Barrymore	Helen Goss
Perkins	Sam Kydd

Lord Caphill	Michael Hawkins
Servant Girl	Judi Moyens
Selden, the Convict	Michael Mulcaster
Servant	David Birks
Lord Kingsblood	Ian Hewitson
Mrs. Goodlippe	Elizabeth Dott

CREDITS

Directed by	Terence Fisher
Produced by	Anthony Hinds/Kenneth Hyman
Screenplay by	Peter Bryan
Associate Producer	Anthony Nelson Keys
Music Composed by	James Bernard
Music Conducted by	John Hollingsworth
Director of Photography	Jack Asher BSC
Camera Operator	Len Harris
Production Designer	Bernard Robinson
Supervising Editor	James Needs
Editor	Alfred Cox
Sound Recordist	Jock May
Production Manager	Don Weeks
Assistant Director	John Peverall
Second Asst Director	Tom Walls
Makeup	Roy Ashton
Hairstyles	Henry Montsash
Wardrobe	Molly Arbuthnot
Continuity	Shirley Barnes
Special Effects	Sydney Pearson
Executive Producer	Michael Carreras

THE MAN WHO COULD CHEAT DEATH

Hammer/Cadogan 83 minutes Technicolor Cert X
Produced November 17, 1958/Released November 28, 1959*
Distributor Paramount
Original Second Feature (UK): *The Evil That is Eve*

CAST

Dr. Georges Bonner	Anton Diffring
Janine Dubois	Hazel Court
Pierre Gerrard	Christopher Lee
Professor Ludwig Weiss	Arnold Marle
Margo	Delphi Lawrence
Inspector Legris	Francis de Wolff
Street Girl	Gerda Larsen
Little Man	Middleton Woods
Tavern Customer	Denis Shaw

Footman	Frederick Rawlings
Woman	Marie Burke
Man	Charles Lloyd Pack
Servant	John Harrison
Second Doctor	Ronald Adam
Third Doctor	Barry Shawzin

The following roles were originally cast and filmed but eliminated during post-production:

Morgue Attendant	Michael Ripper
Roget	Ian Hewitson
First Doctor	Lockwood West

CREDITS

Directed by	Terence Fisher
Produced by	Michael Carreras
Screenplay by	Jimmy Sangster
Based on a play by	Barré Lyndon
Associate Producer	Anthony Nelson Keys
Music Composed by	Richard Rodney Bennett
Musical Supervisor	John Hollingsworth
Director of Photography	Jack Asher BSC
Camera Operator	Len Harris
Production Designer	Bernard Robinson
Supervising Editor	James Needs
Sound Recordist	Jock May
Editor	John Dunsford
Production Manager	Don Weeks
Assistant Director	John Peverall
Makeup	Roy Ashton
Hairstylist	Henry Montsash
Wardrobe	Molly Arbuthnot
Continuity	Shirley Barnes
Special Effects	Les Bowie
Executive Producer	Michael Carreras

THE MUMMY

Hammer 88 minutes Technicolor Cert X
Produced February 25, 1959/Released November 2, 1959
Distributor Rank/Universal-International (USA)
Original Second Feature (UK/USA): *Bed Without Breakfast/Curse of the Undead*

CAST

| John Banning | Peter Cushing |
| The Mummy/Kharis | Christopher Lee |

Isobel/Ananka	Yvonne Furneaux
Stephen Banning	Felix Aylmer
Joseph Whemple	Raymond Huntley
Inspector Mulrooney	Eddie Byrne
Mehemet Akir	George Pastell
Poacher	Michael Ripper
Police Constable	George Woodbridge
Pat	Harold Goodwin
Mike	Denis Shaw
Irish Customer	Gerald Lawson
Dr. Reilly	Willoughby Gray
Coroner	John Stuart
Police Sergeant	David Browning
Bill	Frank Sieman
Attendant	Stanley Meadows
Head Porter	Frank Singuineau
First Libation Priest	John Harrison
Second Libation Priest	James Clarke

CREDITS

Directed by	Terence Fisher
Produced by	Michael Carreras
Screenplay by	Jimmy Sangster
Associate Producer	Anthony Nelson Keys
Music Composed by	Franz Reizenstein
Musical Supervisor	John Hollingsworth
Director of Photography	Jack Asher BSC
Camera Operator	Len Harris
Production Designer	Bernard Robinson
Art Director	Don Mingaye
Supervising Editor	James Needs
Editor	Alfred Cox
Sound Recordist	Jock May
Sound Editor	Roy Hyde
Production Manager	Don Weeks
Assistant Director	John Peverall
Second Asst Director	Tom Walls
Makeup	Roy Ashton
Hairstylist	Henry Montsash
Wardrobe Mistress	Molly Arbuthnot
Continuity	Marjorie Lavelly
Special Effects	Bill Warrington/Les Bowie
Technical Advisor	Andrew Low
Egyptian masks made by	Margaret Carter

THE STRANGLERS OF BOMBAY

Hammer 80 minutes Black-and-white/Megascope Cert A

Produced July 6, 1959/Released December 4, 1959*
Distributor BLC/Columbia (USA)
Original Second Feature (UK): *Kill Her Gently*

CAST

Captain Lewis	Guy Rolfe
Connaught-Smith	Allan Cuthbertson
Colonel Henderson	Andrew Cruickshank
High Priest	George Pastell
Patel Shari	Marne Maitland
Mary	Jan Holden
Silver	Paul Stassino
Ram Das	Tutte Lemkow
Gopali	David Spenser
Burns	John Harvey
Bundar	Roger Delgado
Karim	Marie Devereux
Flood	Michael Nightingale
Dorothy Flood	Margaret Gordon
Walters	Steven Scott
Corporal Roberts	Jack McNaughton
Camel Vendor	Ewen Solon
Merchant	Warren Mitchell

CREDITS

Directed by	Terence Fisher
Produced by	Anthony Hinds
Screenplay by	David Z. Goodman
Associate Producer	Anthony Nelson Keys
Music Composed by	James Bernard
Musical Director	John Hollingsworth
Director of Photography	Arthur Grant BSC
Camera Operator	Len Harris
Production Designer	Bernard Robinson
Art Director	Don Mingaye
Supervising Editor	James Needs
Editor	Alfred Cox
Sound Recordist	Jock May
Sound Editor	Arthur Cox
Production Manager	Don Weeks
Assistant Director	John Peverall
Second Asst Director	Tom Walls
Makeup	Roy Ashton
Hair Stylist	Henry Montsash
Wardrobe Mistress	Molly Arbuthnot
Continuity	Tilly Day
Historical Adviser	Michael Edwardes
Executive Producer	Michael Carreras

In association with   Kenneth Hyman

THE TWO FACES OF DR. JEKYLL
(American Titles: Jekyll's Inferno/House of Fright)

Hammer 88 (USA:80) minutes Technicolor/Megascope Cert X
Produced November 23, 1959/Released October 7, 1960*
Distributor BLC/Columbia/American-International (USA)
Original Second Feature (UK/USA): *Hot Hours/Terror in the Haunted House*

CAST

Dr. Henry Jekyll/Edward Hyde	Paul Massie
Kitty Jekyll	Dawn Addams
Paul Allen	Christopher Lee
Ernst Litauer	David Kossoff
Inspector	Francis de Wolff
Maria	Norma Marla
First Brass	Joy Webster
Second Brass	Roberta Kirkwood
Sphinx Girl	Magda Miller
Second Sphinx Girl	Doreen Ismail
Clubman	William Kendall
Nanny	Helen Goss
Jane	Janine Faye
Coroner	Percy Cartwright
Major Domo	Joan Tyrill
Corinthian	"Tiger" Joe Robinson
Boxer	Douglas Robinson
Plainclothes Man	Donald Tandy
Groom	Frank Atkinson
Tough	Oliver Reed
First Gambler	Felix Felton
Second Gambler	Walter Gotell
Third Gambler	Anthony Jacobs
Tavern Customer	Denis Shaw
Tavern Girl	Pauline Shepherd
Tavern Women	Prudence Hyman, Lucy Griffiths
Singers	Ralph Broadbent, Laurence Richardson, Alex Miller, Archie Baker
Gypsy Girl	Maria Andippa
Cabby	Arthur Lovegrove
Nurse	Joyce Wren
Sphinx Girls	Patricia Sayers, Carole Haynes, Gene Long, Marilyn Ridge, Hazel Graeme, Moyna Sharwin, Pauline Dukes, Josephine Jay, Bandana Das Gupta, Gundel Sargent, Shirli Scott-James

CREDITS

Directed by	Terence Fisher
Produced by	Michael Carreras
Screenplay by	Wolf Mankowitz
Based on the novel by Robert Louis Stevenson	
Associate Producer	Anthony Nelson Keys
Music/Songs Composed by	Monty Norman/David Heneker
Musical Supervisor	John Hollingsworth
Dance Director	Julie Mendez
Director of Photography	Jack Asher BSC
Camera Operator	Len Harris
Production Designer	Bernard Robinson
Art Director	Don Mingaye
Supervising Editor	James Needs
Editor	Eric Boyd-Perkins
Sound Recordist	Jock May
Sound Editor	Archie Ludski
Production Manager	Clifford Parkes
Assistant Director	John Peverall
Second Asst Director	Hugh Harlow
Makeup	Roy Ashton
Hairdresser	Ivy Emmerton
Costume Designer	Mayo
Wardrobe Mistress	Molly Arbuthnot
Continuity	Tilly Day
Casting	Dorothy Holloway

THE BRIDES OF DRACULA

Hammer/Hotspur 85 minutes Technicolor Cert X
Produced January 26, 1960/Released July 4, 1960*
Distributor Rank/Universal-International (USA)
Original Second Feature (UK/USA): *Teenage Lovers/The Leech Woman*

CAST

Dr. Van Helsing	Peter Cushing
Baroness Meinster	Martita Hunt
Marianne Danielle	Yvonne Monlaur
Greta	Freda Jackson
Baron Meinster	David Peel
Dr. Tobler	Miles Malleson
Herr Lang	Henry Oscar
Frau Lang	Mona Washbourne
Gina	Andree Melly
Hans	Victor Brooks
The Curé	Fred Johnson

Coachman	Michael Ripper
Landlord	Norman Pierce
Landlord's Wife	Vera Cook
Village Girl/Vampire	Marie Devereux
Severin	Harold Scott
Latour	Michael Mulcaster

CREDITS

Directed by	Terence Fisher
Produced by	Anthony Hinds
Screenplay by	Jimmy Sangster/Peter Bryan/ Edward Percy
Associate Producer	Anthony Nelson-Keys
Music Composed by	Malcolm Williamson
Musical Supervisor	John Hollingsworth
Director of Photography	Jack Asher BSC
Camera Operator	Len Harris
Production Designer	Bernard Robinson
Art Director	Thomas Goswell
Supervising Editor	James Needs
Editor	Alfred Cox
Sound Recordist	Jock May
Sound Editor	James Groom
Production Manager	Don Weeks
Assistant Director	John Peverall
Second Asst Director	Hugh Harlow
Makeup Artist	Roy Ashton
Hairstylist	Freda Steiger
Wardrobe Mistress	Molly Arbuthnot
Continuity	Tilly Day
Special Effects	Sydney Pearson
Executive Producer	Michael Carreras

THE TERROR OF THE TONGS

Hammer/Merlin 77 minutes Technicolor Cert X
Produced April 18, 1960/Released October 1, 1961
Distributor BLC/Columbia (USA)
Original Cofeature (UK/USA): *Homicidal*

CAST

Chung King	Christopher Lee
Captain Jackson Sale	Geoffrey Toone
Lee	Yvonne Monlaur
Harcourt	Brian Worth
Inspector Dean	Richard Leech
Beggar	Marne Maitland

Helena	Barbara Brown
Maya	Marie Burke
Anna	Bandana Das Gupta
Ming	Burt Kwouk
Wang How	Roger Delgado
Guardian	Milton Reid
Doctor Chow	Charles Lloyd Pack
Confucius	Eric Young
Priest	Michael Hawkins
Executioner	Johnny Arlan
Tang How	Ewen Solon
Sergeant	Santos Wong
Lee Chung	Andy Ho
Spokesman	Arnold Lee
Sailor	Harold Goodwin

CREDITS

Directed by	Anthony Bushell
Produced by	Kenneth Hyman
Screenplay by	Jimmy Sangster
Associate Producer	Anthony Nelson Keys
Music Composed by	James Bernard
Musical Supervisor	John Hollingsworth
Director of Photography	Arthur Grant BSC
Camera Operator	Len Harris
Production Designer	Bernard Robinson
Art Director	Thomas Goswell
Supervising Editor	James Needs
Editor	Eric Boyd-Perkins
Sound Recordist	Jock May
Sound Editor	Alban Streeter
Production Manager	Clifford Parkes
Assistant Director	John Peverall
Second Asst Director	Joe Levy
Makeup	Roy Ashton/Colin Garde
Hairdresser	Freida Steiger
Wardrobe Mistress	Molly Arbuthnot
Continuity	Tilly Day
Executive Producer	Michael Carreras

THE CURSE OF THE WEREWOLF

Hammer/Hotspur 88 (USA:91) minutes Technicolor Cert X
Produced September 12, 1960/Released April 30, 1961
Distributor Rank/Universal-International (USA)
Original Second Feature (UK/USA): *The Shadow of the Cat*

CAST

Don Alfredo Carido	Clifford Evans
Leon Carido	Oliver Reed
Servant girl	Yvonne Romain
Cristina Fernando	Catherine Feller
The Marques Siniestro	Anthony Dawson
The Marquesa	Josephine Llewellyn
The Beggar	Richard Wordsworth
Teresa	Hira Talfrey
Young Leon	Justin Walters
The Priest	John Gabriel
Pepe Valiente	Warren Mitchell
Dominique	George Woodbridge
Old Soaker	Michael Ripper
Don Fernando	Ewen Solon
Don Enrique	Peter Sallis
José	Martin Matthews
Rico Gomez	David Conville
Rosa	Anne Blake
Yvonne	Renny Lister
Isabel	Joy Webster
Jailer	Denis Shaw
Senora Zumara	Serafina di Leo
Vera	Sheila Brennan
First Footman	Desmond Llewelyn
Second Footman	Gordon Whiting
Landlord	Hamlyn Benson
Sergeant	Alastair Williamson
Policeman	John Bennett
Chef	Charles Lamb
Midwife	Kitty Attwood
Farmers	Howard Lang, Stephen W. Scott, Max Butterfield, Michael Peake
Tavern Customers	Rodney Burke, Alan Page, Richard Golding
Official	Ray Browne
Gardener	Frank Sieman
Page	Michael Lewis
Child (Servant girl)	Loraine Caruana

CREDITS

Directed by	Terence Fisher
Produced by	Anthony Hinds
Screenplay by	John Elder (Anthony Hinds)
Associate Producer	Anthony Nelson Keys
Music Composed/Conducted by	Benjamin Frankel
Director of Photography	Arthur Grant BSC
Camera Operator	Len Harris

Production Designer	Bernard Robinson
Art Director	Don Mingaye
Supervising Editor	James Needs
Editor	Alfred Cox
Sound Recordist	Jock May
Sound Editor	Alban Streeter
Production Manager	Clifford Parkes
Assistant Director	John Peverall
Second Asst Director	Dominic Fulford
Makeup	Roy Ashton/Colin Garde
Hairstylist	Frieda Steiger
Wardrobe Mistress	Molly Arbuthnot
Continuity	Tilly Day
Casting	Stuart Lyons
Special Effects	Les Bowie
Executive Producer	Michael Carreras

TASTE OF FEAR

(American Title: Scream of Fear)

Hammer 82 minutes Black-and-white Cert X
Produced November 7, 1960/Released November 1961
Distributor BLC/Columbia (USA)

CAST

Penny Appleby	Susan Strasberg
Bob	Ronald Lewis
Jane Appleby	Ann Todd
Dr. Gerrard	Christopher Lee
Spratt	Leonard Sachs
Marie	Anne Blake
Inspector Legrand	John Serret
Father	Fred Johnson

CREDITS

Directed by	Seth Holt
Produced by	Jimmy Sangster
Screenplay by	Jimmy Sangster
Music Composed by	Clifton Parker
Musical Supervisor	John Hollingsworth
Director of Photography	Douglas Slocombe
Camera Operator	Desmond Davis
Production Designer	Bernard Robinson
Art Director	Thomas Goswell
Asst Art Director	Bill Constable
Supervising Editor	James Needs

Editor	Eric Boyd-Perkins
Sound Recordist	Leslie Hammond
Production Manager	Bill Hill
Assistant Director	David Tomblin
Second Asst Director	Terry Lens
Makeup	Basil Newall
Hairdresser	Eileen Bates
Wardrobe Mistress	Dora Lloyd
Continuity	Pamela Mann
Casting Director	Stuart Lyons
Stills Cameraman	George Higgins
Asst to Exec Producer	Ian Lewis
Executive Producer	Michael Carreras

THE DAMNED

(American Title: These Are the Damned)

Hammer 96/87 (USA:77) minutes Black-and-white/Hammerscope Cert X
Produced May 8, 1961/Released May 19, 1963
Distributor BLC/Columbia (USA)
Original Cofeature (UK): *Maniac*

CAST

Simon Wells	MacDonald Carey
Joan	Shirley Anne Field
Freya	Viveca Lindfors
Bernard	Alexander Knox
King	Oliver Reed
Major Holland	Walter Gotell
Captain Gregory	James Villiers
Ted	Thomas Kempinski
Sid	Kenneth Cope
Mr. Dingle	Brian Oulton
Miss Lamont	Barbara Everest
Mr. Stuart	Alan McClelland
Mr. Talbot	James Maxwell
Victoria	Rachel Clay
Elizabeth	Caroline Sheldon
Anne	Rebecca Dignam
Mary	Siobhan Taylor
Richard	Nicholas Clay
Henry	Kit Williams
William	Christopher Witty
George	David Palmer
Charles	John Thompson

CREDITS

Directed by	Joseph Losey
Produced by	Anthony Hinds
Screenplay by	Evan Jones
From the novel *The Children of Light* by H. L. Lawrence	
Associate Producer	Anthony Nelson Keys
Music Composed by	James Bernard
Song "Black Leather Rock," by	James Bernard/Evan Jones
Musical Director	John Hollingsworth
Director of Photography	Arthur Grant BSC
Camera Operator	Len Harris
Production Designer	Bernard Robinson
Art Director	Don Mingaye
Production Layout	Richard MacDonald
Supervising Editor	James Needs
Editor	Reginald Mills
Sound Recordist	Jock May
Sound Editor	James Groom
Production Manager	Don Weeks
Assistant Director	John Peverall
Second Asst Director	Dominic Fulford
Makeup	Roy Ashton
Hair Stylist	Frieda Steiger
Costumes	Molly Arbuthnot
Continuity	Pamela Davies
Casting	Stuart Lyons
Sculptures	Elisabeth Frink
Executive Producer	Michael Carreras

CAPTAIN CLEGG

(American Title: Night Creatures)

Hammer-Major 82 minutes Technicolor Cert A
Produced September 25, 1961/Released August 26, 1962*
Distributor Rank/Universal-International (USA)
Original Cofeature (UK/USA): *The Phantom of the Opera*

CAST

Dr. Blyss/Nathaniel Clegg	Peter Cushing
Imogene	Yvonne Romain
Captain Collier	Patrick Allen
Harry	Oliver Reed
Mipps	Michael Ripper
Rash	Martin Benson
Bosun	David Lodge
Squire	Derek Francis

Mrs. Rash	Daphne Anderson
Mulatto	Milton Reid
Frightened Man	Jack Macgowran
First Sailor	Peter Halliday
Second Sailor	Terry Scully
Tom Ketch	Sydney Bromley
Gerry	Rupert Osborn
Wurzel	Gordon Rollings
Peg-leg	Bob Head
Pirate Bosun	Colin Douglas

CREDITS

Directed by	Peter Graham Scott
Produced by	John Temple-Smith
Screenplay by	John Elder
Additional Dialogue	Barbara S. Harper
Music Composed by	Don Banks
Musical Director	Philip Martell
Director of Photography	Arthur Grant BSC
Camera Operator	Len Harris
Production Designer	Bernard Robinson
Art Director	Don Mingaye
Supervising Editor	James Needs
Editor	Eric Boyd-Perkins
Sound Recordist	Jock May
Sound Editor	Terry Paulton
Production Manager	Don Weeks
Assistant Director	John Peverall
Second Asst Director	Peter Medak
Makeup	Roy Ashton
Hairstylist	Frieda Steiger
Wardrobe Supervisor	Molly Arbuthnot
Wardrobe Mistress	Rosemary Burrows
Special Effects	Les Bowie
Fight sequences supervised by	Bob Simmons

THE PHANTOM OF THE OPERA

Hammer/Laverstock 84 minutes Technicolor Cert A
Produced November 20, 1961/Released August 26, 1962*
Distributor Rank/Universal-International (USA)
Original Second Feature (UK/USA): *Captain Clegg (Night Creatures)*

CAST

The Phantom/Professor Petrie	Herbert Lom
Christine Charles	Heather Sears
Harry Hunter	Edward de Souza

Lattimer	Thorley Walters
Lord Ambrose D'Arcy	Michael Gough
Bill	Harold Goodwin
Rossi	Martin Miller
Maria	Liane Aukin
Teresa	Leila Forde
Yvonne	Sonia Cordeau
Xavier	Marne Maitland
Charwoman	Miriam Karlin
Rat-catcher	Patrick Troughton
Mrs. Tucker	Renee Houston
Weaver	Keith Pyott
Sergeant Vickers	John Harvey
First Cabby	Michael Ripper
Second Cabby	Miles Malleson
Frenchman in Tavern	Geoff L'Cise
The Dwarf	Ian Wilson

CREDITS

Directed by	Terence Fisher
Produced by	Anthony Hinds
Screenplay by	John Elder
Based on a composition by Gaston Leroux	
Associate Producer	Basil Keys
Music Composed/Conducted by	Edwin Astley
Director of Photography	Arthur Grant BSC
Camera Operator	Len Harris
Production Designer	Bernard Robinson
Art Director	Don Mingaye
Supervising Editor	James Needs
Editor	Alfred Cox
Sound Recordist	Jock May
Sound Editor	James Groom
Production Manager	Clifford Parkes
Assistant Director	John Peverall
Second Asst Director	Peter Medak
Makeup	Roy Ashton
Hair Stylist	Frieda Steiger
Wardrobe Supervisor	Molly Arbuthnot
Wardrobe Mistress	Rosemary Burrows
Continuity	Tilly Day/Pauline Wise
Opera Scenes staged by	Dennis Maunder
	By permission of the General Administrator, Royal Opera House, Covent Garden Ltd.

MANIAC

Hammer 86 minutes Black-and-white Cert X
Produced May 27, 1962/Released May 19, 1963
Distributor BLC/Columbia (USA)
Original Cofeature (UK/USA): *The Damned/The Old Dark House*

CAST

Geoff Farrell	Kerwin Mathews
Eve Beynat	Nadia Gray
Georges Beynat	Donald Houston
Annette Beynat	Liliane Brousse
Salon (Gendarme)	Norman Bird
Inspector Etienne	George Pastell
Giles	Jerold Wells
Janiello	Arnold Diamond
Blanchard	Leon Peers
Grace	Justine Lord

CREDITS

Directed by	Michael Carreras
Produced by	Jimmy Sangster
Screenplay by	Jimmy Sangster
Music Composed/Conducted by	Stanley Black
Director of Photography	Wilkie Cooper
Camera Operator	Harry Gillam
Art Director	Edward Carrick
Supervising Editor	James Needs
Editor	Tom Simpson
Sound Recordist	Cyril Swern
Sound Editor	Roy Baker
Production Manager	Bill Hill
Assistant Director	Ross MacKenzie
Second Asst Director	Terry Lewis
Makeup	Basil Newall
Hairdresser	Pat McDermott
Wardrobe Supervisor	Molly Arbuthnot
Wardrobe Mistress	Jean Fairlie
Continuity	Kay Rawlings
Stills Cameraman	James Swarbrick
Asst to Producer	Ian Lewis

PARANOIAC

Hammer 80 minutes Black-and-white Cert X
Produced July 23, 1962/Released January 26, 1964

Distributor Rank/Universal-International (USA)
Original Cofeature (UK/USA): *The Kiss of the Vampire*

CAST

Eleanor Ashby	Janette Scott
Simon Ashby	Oliver Reed
Francoise	Liliane Brousse
Tony	Alexander Davion
Harriet	Sheila Burrell
John Kossett	Maurice Denham
Keith Kossett	John Bonney
Williams	John Stuart
Vicar	Colin Tapley
RAF Type	Harold Lang
First Woman	Laurie Leigh
Second Woman	Marianne Stone
Tramp	Sydney Bromley
Sailor	Jack Taylor

CREDITS

Directed by	Freddie Francis
Produced by	Anthony Hinds
Screenplay by	Jimmy Sangster
Associate Producer	Basil Keys
Music Composed by	Elisabeth Lutyens
Musical Supervisor	John Hollingsworth
Production Designer	Bernard Robinson
Art Director	Don Mingaye
Director of Photography	Arthur Grant
Camera Operator	Moray Grant
Supervising Editor	James Needs
Sound Recordist	Ken Rawkins
Sound Editor	James Groom
Production Manager	John Draper
Assistant Director	Ross MacKenzie
Second Asst Director	Hugh Harlow
Makeup	Roy Ashton
Hairdresser	Freida Steiger
Wardrobe Supervisor	Molly Arbuthnot
Wardrobe Mistress	Rosemary Burrows
Continuity	Pauline Wise
Special Effects	Les Bowie
Stills Cameraman	Curtis Reeks

THE KISS OF THE VAMPIRE
(American TV Title: Kiss of Evil)

Hammer 88 minutes Eastmancolor Cert X
Produced September 17, 1962/Released January 26, 1964
Distributor Rank/Universal-International (USA)
Original Second Feature (UK/USA): *Paranoiac*

CAST

Professor Zimmer	Clifford Evans
Dr. Ravna	Noel Willman
Gerald Harcourt	Edward de Souza
Marianne Harcourt	Jennifer Daniel
Carl Ravna	Barry Warren
Sabena Ravna	Jacquie Wallis
Tania	Isobel Black
Bruno	Peter Madden
Anna	Vera Cook
Father Xavier	Noel Howlett
Hans	Stan Simmons
First Disciple	Brian Oulton
Police Sergeant	John Harvey
Woman at Graveyard	Olga Dickie
First Girl Disciple	Margaret Read
Second Girl Disciple	Elizabeth Valentine

CREDITS

Directed by	Don Sharp
Produced by	Anthony Hinds
Screenplay by	John Elder
Music composed by	James Bernard
Musical Supervisor	John Hollingsworth
Director of Photography	Alan Hume
Camera Operator	Moray Grant
Production Designer	Bernard Robinson
Art Director	Don Mingaye
Supervising Editor	James Needs
Sound Recordist	Ken Rawkins
Sound Editor	James Groom
Production Manager	Don Weeks
Assistant Director	Douglas Hermes
Second Asst Director	Hugh Harlow
Makeup	Roy Ashton
Hair Stylist	Frieda Steiger
Wardrobe Supervisor	Molly Arbuthnot
Wardrobe Mistress	Rosemary Burrows

Continuity   Pauline Wise
Special Effects   Les Bowie

THE EVIL OF FRANKENSTEIN

Hammer 84 minutes Eastmancolor Cert X
Produced October 14, 1963/Released May 31, 1964
Distributor Rank/Universal-International (USA)
Original Second Feature (UK/USA): *Nightmare*

CAST

Frankenstein   Peter Cushing
Zoltan   Peter Woodthorpe
Chief of Police   Duncan Lamont
Hans   Sandor Elès
Beggar Girl   Katy Wild
Burgomaster   David Hutcheson
Priest   James Maxwell
Drunk   Howard Goorney
Policemen   Anthony Blackshaw, David Conville
Burgomaster's Wife   Caron Gardner
Body Snatcher   Tony Arpino
Landlord   Alistair Williamson
Manservant   Frank Forsyth
Curé   Kenneth Cove
Little Girl   Michele Scott
Hypnotised Man   Timothy Bateson
Roustabouts   Derek Martin, Robert Flynn,
                                      Anthony Poole, James Garfield
The Creature   Kiwi Kingston

CREDITS

Directed by   Freddie Francis
Produced by   Anthony Hinds
Screenplay by   John Elder
Music Composed by   Don Banks
Musical Supervisor   Philip Martell
Director of Photography   John Wilcox BSC
Camera Operator   Ronnie Maasz
Focus Puller   G. Glover
Art Director   Don Mingaye
Supervising Editor   James Needs
Editor   Chris Barnes
Sound Recordist   Ken Rawkins
Sound Camera Operator   A. Thorne
Sound Editor   Roy Hyde
Dubbing Mixer   Michael Sale

Boom Operator	T.Buchanan
Production Manager	Don Weeks
Assistant Director	Bill Cartlidge
Second Asst Director	Hugh Harlow
Third Asst Director	Stephen Victor
Makeup	Roy Ashton/Richard Mills
Hair Stylist	Frieda Steiger
Wardrobe Mistress	Rosemary Burrows
Continuity	Pauline Harlow
Special Effects	Les Bowie
Construction Manager	Arthur Banks
Production Secretary	Maureen White
Stills Cameraman	Tom Edwards

THE GORGON

Hammer 83 minutes Eastmancolor Cert X
Produced December 9, 1963/Released October 18, 1964
Distributor BLC/Columbia (USA)
Original Cofeature (UK/USA): *The Curse of the Mummy's Tomb*

CAST

Namaroff	Peter Cushing
Professor Meister	Christopher Lee
Paul	Richard Pascoe
Carla Hoffman	Barbara Shelley
Professor Heitz	Michael Goodliffe
Kanof	Patrick Troughton
Coroner	Joseph O'Conor
Megaera/The Gorgon	Prudence Hyman
Ratoff	Jack Watson
Hans	Redmond Phillips
Bruno Heitz	Jeremy Longhurst
Sascha	Toni Gilpin
Martha	Joyce Hemson
Policeman	Michael Peake
Cass	Alistair Williamson
Nurse	Sally Nesbitt

CREDITS

Directed by	Terence Fisher
Produced by	Anthony Nelson Keys
Screenplay by	John Gilling
Original Story by	J. Llewellyn Devine
Music Composed by	James Bernard
Musical Supervisor	Marcus Dodds
Director of Photography	Michael Reed

Camera Operator	Cece Cooney
Production Designer	Bernard Robinson
Art Director	Don Mingaye
Supervising Editor	James Needs
Editor	Eric Boyd-Perkins
Sound Recordist	Ken Rawkins
Sound Editor	Roy Hyde
Production Manager	Don Weeks
Assistant Director	Bert Batt
Second Asst Director	Hugh Harlow
Makeup Artist	Roy Ashton
Hairstylist	Frieda Steiger
Wardrobe Mistress	Rosemary Burrows
Continuity	Pauline Harlow
Special Effects	Syd Pearson
Fight Arranger	Peter Diamond

THE CURSE OF THE MUMMY'S TOMB

Hammer/Swallow 80 minutes Technicolor/Techniscope Cert X
Produced February 24, 1964/Released October 18, 1964
Distributor BLC/Columbia (USA)
Original Cofeature (UK/USA): *The Gorgon*

CAST

Adam Beauchamp/Be	Terence Morgan
John Bray	Ronald Howard
Alexander King	Fred Clark
Annette Dubois	Jeanne Roland
Hashmi Bey	George Pastell
Sir Giles Dalrymple	Jack Gwillim
Inspector Mackenzie	John Paul
Professor Dubois	Bernard Rebel
Ra-Antef	Michael McStay
The Mummy	Dickie Owen
Jenny	Jill Mai Meredith
Jessop	Vernon Smythe
Nightwatchman	Michael Ripper
First Workman	Jimmy Gardner
Second Workman	Harold Goodwin
Landlady	Marianne Stone

CREDITS

Directed/Produced by	Michael Carreras
Screenplay by	Henry Younger (Michael Carreras/ Alvin Rakoff)
Associate Producer	Bill Hill

Music Composed by	Carlo Martelli
Musical Supervisor	Philip Martell
Director of Photography	Otto Heller BSC
Camera Operator	Bob Thompson
Production Designer	Bernard Robinson
Supervising Editor	James Needs
Editor	Eric Boyd-Perkins
Sound Recordist	Claude Hitchcock
Sound Editor	James Groom
Assistant Director	Bert Batt
Second Asst Director	Hugh Harlow
Makeup	Roy Ashton
Hair Stylist	Iris Tilley
Wardrobe	Betty Adamson/John Briggs
Continuity	Eileen Head
Casting	David Booth
Technical Adviser	Andrew Low

FANATIC

(American Title: Die! Die! My Darling!)

Hammer 96 (USA:105) minutes Technicolor Cert X
Produced September 7, 1964/Released March 21, 1965
Distributor BLC/Columbia (USA)
Original Second Feature (UK): *The Killers*

CAST

Mrs. Trefoile	Tallulah Bankhead
Patricia Carroll	Stephanie Powers
Harry	Peter Vaughan
Alan Glentower	Maurice Kauffman
Anna	Yootha Joyce
Joseph	Donald Sutherland
Gloria	Gwendolyn Watts
Ormsby	Robert Dorning
Oscar	Philip Gilbert
Shopkeeper	Winifred Dennis
Woman in Shop	Diana King
Vicar	Henry McGee

CREDITS

Directed by	Sivio Narrizano
Produced by	Anthony Hinds
Screenplay by	Richard Matheson
From the novel *Nightmare* by Anne Blaisdell	
Music Composed by	Wilfred Josephs

Musical Supervisor	Philip Martell
Director of Photography	Arthur Ibbetson
Camera Operator	Paul Wilson
Production Designer	Peter Proud
Art Director	Don Mingaye
Supervising Editor	James Needs
Editor	John Dunsford
Sound Recordist	Ken Rawkins
Sound Editor	Roy Hyde
Production Manager	George Fowler
Assistant Director	Claude Watson
Second Asst Director	Hugh Harlow
Makeup Artist	Roy Ashton/Richard Mills
Hairstylist	Olga Angelinetta
Wardrobe Mistress	Mary Gibson
Continuity	Renee Glynn
Special Effects	Syd Pearson
Fight Arranger	Peter Diamond

DRACULA—PRINCE OF DARKNESS

Hammer/7-Arts 90 minutes Technicolor/Techniscope Cert X
Produced April 26, 1965/Released January 9, 1966
Distributor Warner-Pathé/Fox (USA)
Original Second Feature (UK/USA): *The Plague of the Zombies*

CAST

Dracula	Christopher Lee
Helen Kent	Barbara Shelley
Father Sandor	Andrew Keir
Charles Kent	Francis Matthews
Diana Kent	Suzan Farmer
Alan Kent	Charles Tingwell
Ludwig	Thorley Walters
Klove	Philip Latham
Brother Mark	Walter Brown
Landlord	George Woodbridge
Brother Peter	Jack Lambert
Priest	Philip Ray
Mother	Joyce Hemson
Coach Driver	John Maxim

CREDITS

Directed by	Terence Fisher
Produced by	Anthony Nelson Keys
Screenplay by	John Sansom (Jimmy Sangster)
From an idea by John Elder,	

Based on characters created by Bram Stoker

Music Composed by	James Bernard
Musical Supervisor	Philip Martell
Director of Photography	Michael Reed
Camera Operator	Cece Cooney
Production Designer	Bernard Robinson
Art Director	Don Mingaye
Supervising Editor	James Needs
Editor	Chris Barnes
Sound Recordist	Ken Rawkins
Sound Editor	Roy Baker
Production Manager	Ross Mackenzie
Assistant Director	Bert Batt
Second Asst Director	Hugh Harlow
Makeup	Roy Ashton
Hair Stylist	Frieda Steiger
Wardrobe	Rosemary Burrows
Continuity	Lorna Selwyn
Special Effects	Bowie Films Ltd

RASPUTIN—THE MAD MONK

Hammer/7-Arts 91 minutes Technicolor/Cinemascope Cert X
Produced June 7, 1965/Released March 6, 1966
Distributor Warner-Pathé/Fox (USA)
Original Second Feature (UK/USA): *The Reptile*

CAST

Grigori Yefimovich Rasputin	Christopher Lee
Sonia	Barbara Shelley
Dr. Zargo	Richard Pasco
Ivan	Francis Matthews
Vanessa	Suzan Farmer
Peter	Dinsdale Landen
Tsarina	Renee Asherson
Innkeeper	Derek Francis
The Bishop	Joss Ackland
Tsarevitch	Robert Duncan
Patron	Alan Tilvern
The Abbott	John Welsh
Court Physician	John Bailey
Burly Brute	Brian Wilde
Son	Michael Cadman
Daughter	Fiona Hartford
Tough	Bryan Marshall
Waggoner	Bartlett Mullins
Doctor	Michael Godfrey
First Tart	Helen Christie

Second Tart	Maggie Wright
Fat Lady	Celia Ryder
Girl	Veronica Nicholson
Foxy Face	Cyril Shaps
Wide Eyes	Lucy Fleming

CREDITS

Directed by	Don Sharp
Produced by	Anthony Nelson Keys
Screenplay by	John Elder
Music Composed by	Don Banks
Musical Supervisor	Philip Martell
Director of Photography	Michael Reed
Camera Operator	Cece Cooney
Production Designer	Bernard Robinson
Art Director	Don Mingaye
Supervising Editor	James Needs
Editor	Roy Hyde
Sound Recordist	Ken Rawkins
Sound Editor	Roy Baker
Production Manager	Ross Mackenzie
Assistant Director	Bert Batt
Second Asst Director	Hugh Harlow
Makeup	Roy Ashton
Hair Stylist	Frieda Steiger
Wardrobe	Rosemary Burrows
Continuity	Lorna Selwyn

THE PLAGUE OF THE ZOMBIES

Hammer/7-Arts 91 minutes Technicolor Cert X
Produced July 26, 1965/Released January 9, 1966
Distributor Warner-Pathé/Fox (USA)
Original Cofeature (UK/USA): *Dracula—Prince of Darkness*

CAST

Sir James Forbes	André Morell
Sylvia	Diane Clare
Dr. Peter Tompson	Brook Williams
Alice	Jacqueline Pearce
Clive Hamilton	John Carson
Denver	Alex Davion
Sergeant Jack Swift	Michael Ripper
Martinus	Marcus Hammond
Constable Christian	Dennis Chinnery
Colored Servant	Louis Mahoney
Vicar	Roy Royston

John Martinus — Ben Aris
The Young Bloods — Tim Condron, Bernard Egan,
Norman Mann, Francis Willey

CREDITS

Directed by	John Gilling
Produced by	Anthony Nelson Keys
Screenplay by	Peter Bryan
Music Composed by	James Bernard
Musical Supervisor	Philip Martell
Director of Photography	Arthur Grant BSC
Camera Operator	Moray Grant
Production Designer	Bernard Robinson
Art Director	Don Mingaye
Supervising Editor	James Needs
Editor	Chris Barnes
Sound Recordist	Ken Rawkins
Sound Editor	Roy Baker
Production Manager	George Fowler
Assistant Director	Bert Batt
Makeup	Roy Ashton
Hair Stylist	Frieda Steiger
Wardrobe	Rosemary Burrows
Continuity	Lorna Selwyn
Special Effects	Bowie Films Ltd

THE REPTILE

Hammer/7-Arts 91 minutes Technicolor Cert X
Produced September 13, 1965/Released March 6, 1966
Distributor Warner-Pathé/Fox (USA)
Original Cofeature (UK/USA): *Rasputin—The Mad Monk*

CAST

Dr. Franklyn	Noel Willman
Valerie Spalding	Jennifer Daniel
Harry Spalding	Ray Barrett
Anna Franklyn	Jacqueline Pearce
Tom Bailey	Michael Ripper
Mad Peter	John Laurie
Malay	Marne Maitland
Charles Spalding	David Baron
The Vicar	Charles Lloyd Pack
Solicitor	Harold Goldblatt
Old Garnsey	George Woodbridge

CREDITS

Directed by	John Gilling
Produced by	Anthony Nelson Keys
Screenplay by	John Elder
Music Composed by	Don Banks
Musical Supervisor	Philip Martell
Director of Photography	Arthur Grant BSC
Camera Operator	Moray Grant
Production Designer	Bernard Robinson
Art Director	Don Mingaye
Supervising Editor	James Needs
Editor	Roy Hyde
Sound Recordist	William Bulkley
Sound Editor	Roy Baker
Production Manager	George Fowler
Assistant Director	Bill Cartlidge
Makeup	Roy Ashton
Hair Stylist	Frieda Steiger
Wardrobe	Rosemary Burrows
Continuity	Lorna Selwyn
Special Effects	Bowie Films Ltd

THE WITCHES

(American Title: The Devil's Own)

Hammer/7-Arts 91 minutes Technicolor Cert X
Produced April 18, 1966/Released December 11, 1966
Distributor Warner-Pathé/Fox (USA)
Original Second Feature (UK/USA): *Death Is a Woman/The Kremlin Letter*

CAST

Gwen Mayfield	Joan Fontaine
Stephanie Bax	Kay Walsh
Alan Bax	Alec McCowen
Linda	Ingrid Brett
Dowsett	John Collin
Mrs. Dowsett	Carmel McSharry
Ronnie Dowsett	Martin Stephens
Granny Rigg	Gwen Ffrangcon-Davies
Bob Curd	Duncan Lamont
Mrs. Curd	Viola Keats
Dr. Wallis	Leonard Rossiter
Sally	Ann Bell
Valerie	Michelle Dotrice
Mrs. Creek	Shelagh Fraser
Tom	Bryan Marshall

CREDITS

Directed by	Cyril Frankel
Produced by	Anthony Nelson Keys
Screenplay by	Nigel Kneale
From the novel *The Devil's Own* by Peter Curtis	
Music Composed by	Richard Rodney Bennett
Musical Supervisor	Philip Martell
Choreographer	Denys Palmer
Director of Photography	Arthur Grant
Camera Operator	Cece Cooney
Production Designer	Bernard Robinson
Art Director	Don Mingaye
Supervising Editor	James Needs
Editor	Chris Barnes
Sound Recordist	Ken Rawkins
Sound Editor	Roy Hyde
Production Manager	Charles Permane
Assistant Director	David Tringham
Makeup	George Partleton
Hair Stylist	Frieda Steiger
Wardrobe Supervisor	Molly Arbuthnot
Wardrobe Master	Harry Haynes
Continuity	Anne Deeley
Casting	Irene Lamb

FRANKENSTEIN CREATED WOMAN

Hammer/7-Arts 86 minutes Technicolor Cert X
Produced July 4, 1966/Released June 18, 1967
Distributor Warner-Pathé/Fox (USA)
Original Second Feature (UK/USA): *The Mummy's Shroud*

CAST

Baron Frankenstein	Peter Cushing
Christina	Susan Denberg
Dr. Hertz	Thorley Walters
Hans Baumer	Robert Morris
Anton	Peter Blythe
Karl	Barry Warren
Johann	Derek Fowlds
Kleve	Alan MacNaughton
Chief of Police	Peter Madden
Mayor	Philip Ray
Landlord	Ivan Beavis
Priest	Colin Jeavons
Bystander	Bartlett Mullins
Spokesman	Alec Mango

Hans as a Boy	Stuart Middleton
Prisoner/Hans's Father	Duncan Lamont
Sergeant	John Maxim
Gaoler	Kevin Flood

CREDITS

Directed by	Terence Fisher
Produced by	Anthony Nelson Keys
Screenplay by	John Elder
Music Composed by	James Bernard
Musical Supervisor	Philip Martell
Director of Photography	Arthur Grant BSC
Camera Operator	Moray Grant
Production Designer	Bernard Robinson
Art Director	Don Mingaye
Supervising Editor	James Needs
Editor	Spencer Reeve
Asst Editor	Elizabeth Redstone
Sound Recordist	Ken Rawkins
Sound Editor	Roy Hyde
Production Manager	Ian Lewis
Assistant Director	Douglas Hermes
2nd Asst Director	Joe Marks
3rd Asst Director	Christopher Neame
Makeup	George Partleton
Hair Stylist	Frieda Steiger
Wardrobe Mistress	Rosemary Burrows
Wardrobe Master	Larry Stuart
Continuity	Eileen Head
Scenic Artist	Felix Sergejak
Casting	Irene Lamb
Special Effects	Les Bowie

THE MUMMY'S SHROUD

Hammer/7-Arts 90 minutes Technicolor Cert X
Produced September 12, 1966/Released June 18, 1967
Distributor Warner-Pathé/Fox (USA)
Original Cofeature (UK/USA): *Frankenstein Created Woman*

CAST

Sir Basil Walden	André Morell
Stanley Preston	John Phillips
Paul Preston	David Buck
Barbara Preston	Elizabeth Sellars
Claire	Maggie Kimberley
Longbarrow	Michael Ripper

Harry Newton	Tim Barrett
Inspector Barrani	Richard Warner
Hasmid Ali	Roger Delgado
Haiti	Catherine Lacey
Prem, the Mummy	Eddie Powell
Prem (in Flashback)	Dickie Owen
Pharaoh	Bruno Barnabe
Pharaoh's Wife	Toni Gilpin
Kah-To-Bey	Toolsie Persaud
The Curator	Andreas Malandrinos

CREDITS

Directed by	John Gilling
Produced by	Anthony Nelson Keys
Screenplay by	John Gilling
From an original story by	John Elder
Music Composed by	Don Banks
Musical Supervisor	Philip Martell
Director of Photography	Arthur Grant BSC
Camera Operator	Moray Grant
Production Designer	Bernard Robinson
Art Director	Don Mingaye
Supervising Editor	James Needs
Editor	Chris Barnes
Sound Recordist	Ken Rawkins
Sound Editor	Roy Hyde
Production Manager	Ed Harper
Assistant Director	Bluey Hill
Makeup	George Partleton
Hairstylist	Frieda Steiger
Wardrobe Mistress	Molly Arbuthnot
Wardrobe Master	Larry Steward
Continuity	Eileen Head
Casting	Irene Lamb
Special Effects	Bowie Films Ltd.

QUATERMASS AND THE PIT

(American Title: Five Million Years to Earth)

Hammer/7-Arts 98 minutes Technicolor Cert X
Produced February 27, 1967/Released November 19, 1967
Distributor Warner-Pathé/Fox (USA)
Original Second Feature (UK/USA): *Circus of Fear/The Viking Queen*

CAST

Dr. Roney	James Donald

Quatermass	Andrew Keir
Barbara Judd	Barbara Shelley
Colonel Breen	Julian Glover
Sladden	Duncan Lamont
Captain Potter	Bryan Marshall
Howell	Peter Copley
Minister	Edwin Richfield
Police Sergeant Ellis	Grant Taylor
Sergeant Cleghorn	Morris Good
Watson	Robert Morris
Journalist	Sheila Steafel
Sapper West	Hugh Futcher
Elderly Journalist	Hugh Morton
Vicar	Thomas Heathcote
Abbey Librarian	Noel Howlett
Pub Customer	Hugh Manning
Blonde	June Ellis
Johnson	Keith Marsh
Corporal Gibson	James Culliford
Miss Dobson	Bee Duffell
Electrician	Roger Avon
Technical Officer	Brian Peck
Inspector	John Graham
Newsvendor	Charles Lamb

CREDITS

Directed by	Roy Ward Baker
Produced by	Anthony Nelson Keys
Screenplay by	Nigel Kneale
Based on the BBC TV serial by	Nigel Kneale
Music Composed by	Tristram Cary
Musical Supervisor	Philip Martell
Director of Photography	Arthur Grant BSC
Camera Operator	Moray Grant
Supervising Art Director	Bernard Robinson
Art Director	Ken Ryan
Supervising Editor	James Needs
Editor	Spencer Reeve
Sound Recordist	Sash Fisher
Sound Editor	Roy Hyde
Production Manager	Ian Lewis
Assistant Director	Bert Batt
Makeup	Michael Morris
Hair Stylist	Pearl Tipaldi
Wardrobe Mistress	Rosemary Burrows
Continuity	Doreen Dearnaley
Casting	Irene Lamb
Special Effects	Bowie Films Ltd

THE DEVIL RIDES OUT
(American Title: The Devil's Bride)

Hammer/7-Arts 95 minutes Technicolor Cert X
Produced August 7, 1967/Released July 7, 1968
Distributor Warner-Pathé/Fox (USA)
Original Second Feature (UK/USA): *Slave Girls (Prehistoric Women)*

CAST

Duc de Richleau	Christopher Lee
Mocata	Charles Gray
Tanith	Nike Arrighi
Rex van Ryn	Leon Greene
Simon Aron	Patrick Mower
Countess	Gwen Ffrangcon-Davies
Marie	Sarah Lawson
Richard	Paul Eddington
Peggy	Rosalyn Landor
Malin	Russell Waters
The Devil	Eddie Powell

CREDITS

Directed by	Terence Fisher
Produced by	Anthony Nelson Keys
Screenplay by	Richard Matheson
From the classic novel by Dennis Wheatley	
Associate Producers	Michael Stainer-Hutchins/P. Daw
Music Composed by	James Bernard
Musical Supervisor	Philip Martell
Choreographer	David Toguri
Director of Photography	Arthur Grant BSC
Camera Operator	Moray Grant
Supervising Art Director	Bernard Robinson
Supervising Editor	James Needs
Editor	Spencer Reeve
Recording Supervisor	A.W.Lumkin
Sound Recordist	Ken Rawkins
Sound Editor	Arthur Cox
Production Manager	Ian Lewis
Assistant Director	Bert Batt
Makeup	Eddie Knight
Hairstylist	Pat McDermott
Wardrobe Supervisor	Rosemary Burrows
Wardrobe Mistress	Janet Lucas
Continuity	June Randall

Casting   Irene Lamb
Special Effects   Michael Stainer-Hutchins

THE LOST CONTINENT

Hammer/7-Arts 98 minutes Technicolor Cert X
Produced September 11, 1967/Released July 14, 1968
Distributor Warner-Pathé/Fox (USA)
Original Second Feature (UK/USA): *Young and Eager/The Vengeance of She*

CAST

Lansen	Eric Porter
Eva	Hildegarde Knef
Unity	Suzanna Leigh
Tyler	Tony Beckley
Webster	Nigel Stock
Hemmings	Neil McCallum
Ricaldi	Benito Carruthers
Pat	Jimmy Hanley
Chief	James Cossins
Sarah	Dana Gillespie
Mate	Victor Maddern
Helmsman	Reg Lye
Jonathan	Norman Eshley
Sea Lawyer	Michael Ripper
Sparks	Donald Sumpter
Jason	Alf Joint
Braemar	Charles Houston
Hurri Curri	Shivendra Sinha
El Diablo	Darryl Read
Inquisitor	Eddie Powell
Sergeant	Frank Hayden
Customs Men	Mark Heath, Horace James

CREDITS

Directed/Produced by	Michael Carreras
Screenplay by	Michael Nash (Michael Carreras)
Based on the novel *Uncharted Seas* by Dennis Wheatley	
Associate Producer	Peter Manley
Music Composed by	Gerard Schurmann
Musical Supervisor	Philip Martell
Songs by Roy Philips; sung by	The Pedlars
Director of Photography	Paul Beeson BSC
Camera Operator	Russell Thomson
Art Director	Arthur Lawson
Assistant Art Director	Don Picton
Supervising Editor	James Needs

Editor	Chris Barnes
Recording Supervisor	A. W. Lumkin
Sound Editor	Roy Hyde
Sound Mixer	Dennis Whitlock
Assistant Director	Dominic Fulford
Makeup	George Partleton
Hairdresser	Elsie Alder
Costume Designer	Carl Toms
Wardrobe	Mary Gibson
Continuity	Doreen Soan
Casting	Irene Lamb
Special Effects	Robert A. Mattey/Cliff Richardson
Consultant	Arthur Hayward
Modeller	Arthur Fehr

DRACULA HAS RISEN FROM THE GRAVE

Hammer/7-Arts 92 minutes Technicolor Cert X
Produced April 22, 1968/Released November 7, 1968*
Distributor Warner-Pathé/Warner-7-Arts (USA)
Original Second Feature (UK): *A Covenant with Death*

CAST

Dracula	Christopher Lee
Monsignor Ernst Muller	Rupert Davies
Maria	Veronica Carlson
Zena	Barbara Ewing
Paul	Barry Andrews
Priest	Ewan Hooper
Anna	Marion Mathie
Max	Michael Ripper
Student	John D. Collins
Landlord	George A. Cooper
Farmer	Chris Cunningham
Boy	Norman Bacon
Girl in Bell	Carrie Baker

CREDITS

Directed by	Freddie Francis
Produced by	Aida Young
Screenplay by	John Elder
Based on the character created by Bram Stoker	
Music Composed by	James Bernard
Musical Supervisor	Philip Martell
Director of Photography	Arthur Grant BSC
Camera Operator	Moray Grant

Supervising Art Director	Bernard Robinson
Supervising Editor	James Needs
Editor	Spencer Reeve
Sound Recordist	Ken Rawkins
Sound Editor	Wilfred Thompson
Production Manager	Christopher Sutton
Assistant Director	Dennis Robertson
Makeup	Heather Nurse/Rosemarie McDonald-Peattie
Hair Stylist	Wanda Kelley
Wardrobe Mistress	Jill Thompson
Continuity	Doris Martin
Special Effects	Frank George
Matte Artist	Peter Melrose
Construction Manager	Arthur Banks

FRANKENSTEIN MUST BE DESTROYED

Hammer 97 minutes Technicolor Cert X
Produced January 13, 1969/Released June 8, 1969
Distributor Warner-Pathé/Warner-7-Arts (USA)
Original Second Feature (UK): *Sons of Satan*

CAST

Baron Frankenstein	Peter Cushing
Anna Spengler	Veronica Carlson
Professor Richter	Freddie Jones
Karl Holst	Simon Ward
Inspector Frisch	Thorley Walters
Ella Brandt	Maxine Audley
Doctor Brandt	George Pravda
Police Doctor	Geoffrey Bayldon
Mad Woman	Colette O'Neil
Guests	Frank Middlemass, George Belbin, Norman Shelley, Michael Gover
Principal	Peter Copley
Dr. Heidecke	Jim Collier
Police Sergeants	Allan Surtees, Windsor Davies
Burglar	Harold Goodwin

CREDITS

Directed by	Terence Fisher
Produced by	Anthony Nelson Keys
Screenplay by	Bert Batt
From an original story by	Anthony Nelson Keys
Director of Photography	Arthur Grant
Camera Operator	Neil Binney

Music Composed by	James Bernard
Musical Supervisor	Philip Martell
Art Director	Bernard Robinson
Supervising Editor	James Needs
Editor	Gordon Hales
Recording Supervisor	Tony Lumkin
Sound Recordist	Ken Rawkins
Sound Editor	Don Ranasinghe
Production Manager	Christopher Neame
Assistant Director	Bert Batt
Makeup	Eddie Knight
Hairstylist	Pat McDermott
Wardrobe Supervisor	Rosemary Burrows
Wardrobe Mistress	Lotte Slattery
Continuity	Doreen Dearnaley
Construction Manager	Arthur Banks
Special Effects	Studios Locations Ltd

CRESCENDO

Hammer 95 minutes Technicolor Cert X
Produced July 14, 1969/Released May 7, 1970*
Distributor Warner-Pathé/Warner Bros. (USA)
Original Cofeature (UK/USA): *Taste the Blood of Dracula*

CAST

Susan Roberts	Stephanie Powers
Georges/Jacques	James Olson
Danielle Ryman	Margaretta Scott
Lillianne	Jane Lapotaire
Carter	Joss Ackland
Catherine	Kirsten Betts

CREDITS

Directed by	Alan Gibson
Produced by	Michael Carreras
Screenplay	Alfred Shaughnessy/Jimmy Sangster
Music Composed by	Malcolm Williamson
Musical Supervisor	Philip Martell
Solo Piano	Clive Lythgoe
Solo Saxophone	Tubby Hayes
Director of Photography	Paul Beeson
Camera Operator	John Winbolt
Art Director	Scott MacGregor
Assistant Art Director	Don Picton
Set Dresser	Freda Pearson
Property Buyer	Ron Baker

Editor   Chris Barnes
Recording Supervisor   A. W. Lumkin
Sound Editor   Roy Hyde
Sound Mixer   Claude Hitchcock
Dubbing Mixer   Len Abbott
Production Manager   Hugh Harlow
Assistant Director   Jack Martin
Makeup   Stella Morris
Hairdresser   Ivy Emmerton
Wardrobe   Jackie Breed
Continuity   Lillian Lee
Construction Manager   Arthur Banks

TASTE THE BLOOD OF DRACULA

Hammer 95 minutes Technicolor Cert X
Produced October 27, 1969/Released May 7, 1970*
Distributor Warner-Pathé/Warner Bros. (USA)
Original Second Feature (UK/USA): *Crescendo/Trog*

CAST

Dracula   Christopher Lee
William Hargood   Geoffrey Keene
Martha Hargood   Gwen Watford
Alice Hargood   Linda Hayden
Samuel Paxton   Peter Sallis
Paul Paxton   Anthony Corlan
Lucy Paxton   Isla Blair
Jonathon Secker   John Carson
Jeremy Secker   Martin Jarvis
Lord Courtley   Ralph Bates
Weller   Roy Kinnear
Sergeant Cobb   Michael Ripper
Felix   Russell Hunter
Hargood's Maid   Shirley Jaffe
Father   Keith Marsh
Son   Peter May
Vicar   Reginald Barratt
Dolly   Maddy Smith
Chinese Girl   Lai Ling
Snake Girl   Malaika Martin

CREDITS

Directed by   Peter Sasdy
Produced by   Aida Young
Screenplay by   John Elder

Based on the character created by Bram Stoker

Music Composed by	James Bernard
Musical Supervisor	Philip Martell
Director of Photography	Arthur Grant BSC
Art Director	Scott Macgregor
Editor	Chris Barnes
Recording Supervisor	Tony Lumkin
Dubbing Mixer	Dennis Whitlock
Sound Recordist	Ron Barron
Sound Editor	Roy Hyde
Production Manager	Christopher Sutton
Assistant Director	Derek Whitehurst
Makeup Supervisor	Gerry Fletcher
Hairdressing Supervisor	Mary Bredin
Wardrobe Master	Brian Owen-Smith
Continuity	Geraldine Lawton
Special Effects	Brian Johncock
Construction Manager	Arthur Banks

THE VAMPIRE LOVERS

Hammer/American-International 91 minutes Technicolor Cert X
Produced January 19, 1970/Released September 3, 1970*
Distributor MGM-EMI/American-International (USA)
Original Second Feature (UK/USA): *Angels from Hell/Cult of the Damned*

CAST

Mircalla Karnstein	Ingrid Pitt
Marcilla Karnstein	
Carmilla Karnstein	
General Spielsdorf	Peter Cushing
Laura	Pippa Steele
Emma	Madeline Smith
Roger Morton	George Cole
The Countess	Dawn Addams
Governess	Kate O'Mara
Baron Hartog	Douglas Wilmer
Carl	Jon Finch
Renton	Harvey Hall
Doctor	Ferdy Mayne
First Vampire	Kirsten Betts
Man in Black	John Forbes Robertson
Gretchen	Janet Key
Landlord	Charles Farrell

CREDITS

Directed by	Roy Ward Baker

| Produced by | Harry Fine/Michael Style |
| Screenplay by | Tudor Gates |

Adapted from J. Sheridan Le Fanu's story "Carmilla" by Harry Fine, Tudor Gates, and Michael Style

Music Composed by	Harry Robinson
Musical Supervisor	Philip Martell
Director of Photography	Moray Grant
Camera Operator	Neil Binney
Art Director	Scott MacGregor
Editor	James Needs
Recording Director	Tony Lumkin
Sound Recordist	Claude Hitchcock
Sound Editor	Roy Hyde
Dubbing Mixer	Dennis Whitlock
Production Manager	Tom Sachs
Assistant Director	Derek Whitehurst
Makeup Supervisor	Tom Smith
Hairdressing Supervisor	Pearl Tipaldi
Costume Designer	Brian Box
Wardrobe Mistress	Laura Nightingale
Continuity	Betty Harley
Construction Manager	Bill Greene

SCARS OF DRACULA

Hammer 96 minutes Technicolor Cert X
Produced May 11, 1970/Released October 8, 1970*
Distributor MGM-EMI/Continental (USA)
Original Cofeature (UK/USA) :*The Horror of Frankenstein*

CAST

Dracula	Christopher Lee
Simon	Dennis Waterman
Sarah	Jenny Hanley
Paul	Christopher Matthews
Klove	Patrick Troughton
Priest	Michael Gwynn
Landlord	Michael Ripper
Julie	Wendy Hamilton
Tania	Anouska Hempel
Alice	Delia Lindsay
Burgomaster	Bob Todd
Elderly Waggoner	Toke Townley
First Officer	David Leland
Second Officer	Richard Durden
Farmer	Morris Bush

Landlord's Wife	Margo Boht
Fat Young Man	Clive Barrie

CREDITS

Directed by	Roy Ward Baker
Produced by	Aida Young
Screenplay by	John Elder
Based on the character created by	Bram Stoker
Music Composed by	James Bernard
Musical Supervisor	Philip Martell
Director of Photography	Moray Grant
Art Director	Scott MacGregor
Supervising Editor	James Needs
Recording Supervisor	Tony Lumkin
Sound Recordist	Ron Barron
Sound Editor	Roy Hyde
Dubbing Mixer	Dennis Whitlock
Production Manager	Tom Sachs
Assistant Director	Derek Whitehurst
Makeup Supervisor	Wally Schneidermann
Makeup Assistant	Heather Nurse
Hairdressing Supervisor	Pearl Tipaldi
Wardrobe Mistress	Laura Nightingale
Continuity	Betty Harley
Special Effects	Roger Dicken/Brian Johncock
Construction Manager	Arthur Banks

LUST FOR A VAMPIRE

Hammer 95 minutes Technicolor Cert X
Produced July 6, 1970/Released January 17, 1971
Distributor MGM-EMI/Continental (USA)
Original Second Feature (UK): *The Losers*

CAST

Countess Herritzen	Barbara Jefford
Giles Barton	Ralph Bates
Janet Playfair	Suzanna Leigh
Mircalla	Yutte Stensgaard
Richard Lestrange	Michael Johnson
Miss Simpson	Helen Christie
Count Karnstein	Mike Raven
Coachman	Christopher Cunningham
Inspector Heinrich	Harvey Hall
Landlord	Michael Brennan
Susan Pelley	Pippa Steele
Amanda	Judy Matheson

Isabel	Caryl Little
Raymond Pelley	David Healy
Biggs	Jonathan Cecil
Professor Hertz	Eric Chitty
Bishop	Jack Melford
Hans	Christopher Neame
Peasant Girl	Kirsten Lindholm
Trudi	Luan Peters
First Villager	Nick Brimble
Second Villager	David Richardson
Schoolgirls	Melinda Churcher, Melita Clarke, Vivienne Chandler, Erica Beale, Jackie Leapman, Sue Longhurst, Christine Smith, Patricia Warner

CREDITS

Directed by	Jimmy Sangster
Produced by	Harry Fine/Michael Style
Screenplay by	Tudor Gates
Based on characters created by J. Sheridan Le Fanu	
Music Composed by	Harry Robinson
"Strange Love" sung by Tracy; lyrics by Frank Godwin	
Musical Supervisor	Philip Martell
Choreographer	Babbie McManus
Director of Photography	David Muir
Camera Operator	R. Anstiss
Art Director	Don Mingaye
Editor	Spencer Reeve
Recording Director	Tony Lumkin
Sound Recordist	Ron Barron
Sound Editor	Terry Poulton
Dubbing Mixer	Len Abbott
Boom Operator	John Hall
Production Manager	Tom Sachs
Assistant Director	David Bracknell
Makeup Supervisor	George Blackler
Hairdressing Supervisor	Pearl Tipaldi
Wardrobe Mistress	Laura Nightingale
Continuity	Betty Harley
Construction Manager	Bill Greene

COUNTESS DRACULA

Hammer 93 minutes Eastmancolor Cert X
Produced July 27, 1970/Released February 14, 1971
Distributor Rank/Fox (USA)
Original Second Feature (UK/USA): *Hell's Belles/Vampire Circus*

CAST

Countess Elisabeth	Ingrid Pitt
Captain Dobi	Nigel Green
Imre Toth	Sandor Elès
Master Fabio	Maurice Denham
Julie	Patience Collier
Captain Balogh	Peter Jeffrey
Ilona	Lesley-Anne Downe
Sergeant of Bailiffs	Leon Lissek
Rosa	Jessie Evans
Ziza	Andrea Lawrence
Teri	Susan Brodrick
Clown	Ian Trigger
Gypsy Girl	Nike Arrighi
Janco	Peter May
Priest	John Moore
Second Cook	Joan Haythorne
Kitchen Maid	Marianne Stone
The Seller	Charles Farrell
Bertha	Sally Adcock
Pregnant Woman	Anne Stallybrass
Man	Paddy Ryan
Young Man	Michael Cadman
Belly Dancer	Hulya Babus
Gypsy Dancers	Lesley Anderson, Biddy Hearne, Diana Sawday
First Boy	Andrew Burleigh
Second Boy	Gary Rich
Circus Midgets	Albert Wilkinson, Ismed Hassan

CREDITS

Directed by	Peter Sasdy
Produced by	Alexander Paal
Screenplay by	Jeremy Paul
Story by	Alexander Paal/Peter Sasdy
Based on an idea by	Gabriel Ronay
Music Composed by	Harry Robinson
Musical Supervisor	Philip Martell
Choreographer	Mia Nardi
Director of Photography	Ken Talbot BSC
Camera Operator	Ken Withers
Art Director	Philip Harrison
Editor	Henry Richardson
Sound Recordist	Kevin Sutton
Sound Editor	Al Streeter
Dubbing Mixer	Ken Barker
Production manager	Christopher Sutton
Assistant Director	Ariel Levy

Makeup Supervisor	Tom Smith
Hairdressing Supervisor	Pat McDermot
Costume Designer	Raymond Hughes
Wardrobe Master	Brian Owen-Smith
Continuity	Gladys Goldsmith
Special Effects	Bert Luxford
Construction Manager	Arthur Banks

BLOOD FROM THE MUMMY'S TOMB

Hammer 93 minutes Technicolor Cert X
Produced January 11, 1971/Released November 7, 1971
Distributor MGM-EMI/American-International (USA)
Original Cofeature (UK/USA): *Dr. Jekyll and Sister Hyde/Night of the Blood Monster*

CAST

Fuchs	Andrew Keir
Margaret/Tera	Valerie Leon
Corbeck	James Villiers
Dandridge	Hugh Burden
Berigan	George Coulouris
Tod Browning	Mark Edwards
Helen Dickerson	Rosalie Crutchley
Doctor Putnum	Aubrey Morris
Doctor Burgess	David Markham
Mrs. Caporal	Joan Young
Older Male Nurse	James Cossins
Young Male Nurse	David Jackson
Saturnine Young Man	Jonathan Burn
Youth in Museum	Graham James
Veronica	Tamara Ustinov
Nurse	Penelope Holt
Nurse	Angela Ginders
Patient	Tex Fuller
Priests	Madina Luis, Omar Amoodi, Abdul Kader, Oscar Charles, Ahmed Osman, Soltan Lalani, Saad Ghazi
Tod's cat	Sunbronze Danny Boy

CREDITS

Directed by	Seth Holt
(shooting completed by Michael Carreras)	
Produced by	Howard Brandy
Screenplay by	Christopher Wicking
Based on *The Jewel of the Seven Stars* by Bram Stoker	
Music Composed by	Tristram Cary
Director of Photography	Arthur Grant

Camera Operator	Neil Binney
Production Designer	Scott MacGregor
Assistant Art Director	Don Picton
Editor	Peter Weatherley GBFE
Sound Recordist	Tony Dawe
Sound Editor	Roy Hyde GBFE
Production Manager	Christopher Neame
Assistant Director	Derek Whitehurst
Makeup Supervisor	Eddie Knight
Hairdressing Supervisor	Ivy Emmerton
Wardrobe Supervisor	Rosemary Burrows
Wardrobe Mistress	Diane Jones
Continuity	Betty Harley
Special Effects	Michael Collins
Construction Manager	Bill Greene
Production Supervisor	Roy Skeggs

DR. JEKYLL AND SISTER HYDE

Hammer 97 minutes Technicolor Cert X
Produced February 15, 1971/Released November 7, 1971
Distributor MGM-EMI/American-International (USA)
Original Second Feature (UK): *Blood From the Mummy's Tomb*

CAST

Dr. Jekyll	Ralph Bates
Sister Hyde	Martine Beswick
Professor Robertson	Gerald Sim
Howard	Lewis Fiander
Mrs. Spencer	Dorothy Alison
Older Policeman	Neil Wilson
Burke	Ivor Dean
Sergeant Danvers	Paul Whitsun-Jones
Byker	Philip Madoc
Hare	Tony Calvin
Susan	Susan Brodrick
Town Crier	Dan Meaden
Betsy	Virginia Wetherell
First Policeman	Jeffrey Kenion
Yvonne	Irene Bradshaw
Julie	Anna Brett
Jackie	Margie Poole
Marie	Rosemary Lord
Petra	Petula Portell
Helen	Pat Brackenbury
Emma	Liz Romanoff
Mein Host	Will Stampe

Knife grinder	Roy Evans
First Sailor	Derek Steen
Second Sailor	John Lyons
Jill	Janette Wilde
Young Apprentice	Bobby Parr
Street Singer	Julia Wright

CREDITS

Directed by	Roy Ward Baker
Produced by	Albert Fennell/Brian Clemens
Screenplay by	Brian Clemens
Based upon the story by Robert Louis Stevenson	
Music Composed by	David Whitaker
Musical Supervisor	Philip Martell
Song "He'll Be There," words and music by Brian Clemens	
Director of Photography	Norman Warwick BSC
Camera Operator	Godfrey Godar
Production Designer	Robert Jones
Assistant Art Director	Len Townsend
Editor	James Needs GBFE
Recording Director	A. W. Lumkin
Sound	Bill Rowe
Sound Editor	Charles Crafford GBFE
Production Manager	Don Weeks
Assistant Director	Bert Batt
Makeup	Trevor Crole-Rees
Hairdressing	Bernie Ibbetson
Wardrobe Supervisor	Rosemary Burrows
Wardrobe Mistress	Kathleen Moore
Continuity	Sally Ball
Casting Director	Jimmy Liggat
Construction Manager	Bill Greene
Production Supervisor	Roy Skeggs

HANDS OF THE RIPPER

Hammer 85 minutes Technicolor Cert X
Produced January 25, 1971/Released October 17, 1971
Distributor Rank/Universal (USA)
Original Cofeature (UK/USA): *Twins of Evil*

CAST

Dr. John Pritchard	Eric Porter
Anna	Angharad Rees
Laura	Jane Merrow
Michael Pritchard	Keith Bell

Dysart	Derek Godfrey
Mrs. Golding	Dora Bryan
Mrs. Bryant	Marjorie Rhodes
Long Liz	Lynda Baron
Dolly	Marjie Lawrence
Police Inspector	Norman Bird
Madame Bullard	Margaret Rawlings
Mrs. Wilson	Elizabeth Maclennan
Mr. Wilson	Barry Lowe
Rev. Anderson	A. J. Brown
Catherine	April Wilding
First Cell Whore	Anne Clune
Second Cell Whore	Vicki Woolf
First Pub Whore	Katya Wyeth
Second Pub Whore	Beulah Hughes
Third Pub Whore	Tallulah Miller
Pleasants	Peter Munt
Seamstress	Ann Way
Police Constable	Philip Ryan
Maid	Molly Weir
Guard	Charles Lamb

CREDITS

Directed by	Peter Sasdy
Produced by	Aida Young
Screenplay by	L. W. Davidson
From an original story by	Edward Spencer Shew
Music Composed by	Christopher Gunning
Musical Supervisor	Philip Martell
Director of Photography	Kenneth Talbot BSC
Camera Operator	Robert Kindred
Art Director	Roy Stannard
Editor	Chris Barnes
Sound Recordist	Kevin Sutton
Dubbing Mixer	Ken Barker
Production Manager	Christopher Sutton
Assistant Director	Ariel Levy
Make Up Supervisor	Bunty Phillips
Hairdressing Supervisor	Pat McDermott
Wardrobe Supervisor	Rosemary Burrows
Wardrobe Mistress	Eileen Sullivan
Continuity	Gladys Goldsmith
Special Effects	Cliff Culley
Construction Manager	Arthur Banks

TWINS OF EVIL

Hammer 87 minutes Eastmancolor Cert X

Produced March 22, 1971/Released October 17, 1971
Distributor Rank/Universal (USA)
Original Cofeature (UK/USA): *Hands of the Ripper*

CAST

Gustav Weil	Peter Cushing
Frieda Gellhorn	Madeleine Collinson
Maria Gellhorn	Mary Collinson
Anton Hoffer	David Warbeck
Count Karnstein	Damien Thomas
Countess Mircalla	Katya Wyeth
Ingrid Hoffer	Isobel Black
Katy Weil	Kathleen Byron
Franz	Harvey Hall
Hermann	Alex Scott
Joachim	Roy Stewart
Gerta	Luan Peters
Dietrich	Dennis Price
Alexa	Maggie Wright
Lady in Coach	Sheelah Wilcox
Woodman	Inigo Jackson
Woodman's Daughter	Judy Matheson
Girl at Stake	Kirsten Lindholm
Jailer	Peter Thompson

CREDITS

Directed by	John Hough
Produced by	Harry Fine/Michael Style
Screenplay by	Tudor Gates
Based on characters created by	J. Sheridan Le Fanu
Music Composed by	Harry Robinson
Musical Supervisor	Philip Martell
Director of Photography	Dick Bush BSC
Camera Operator	Dudley Lovell
Second Unit/Special Effects Photography	Jack Mills BSC
Art Director	Roy Stannard
Editor	Spencer Reeve
Sound Recordist	Ron Barron
Sound Camera Operator	Stan Samworth
Sound Editor	Bill Trent
Dubbing Mixer	Ken Barker
Production Manager	Tom Sachs
Assistant Director	Patrick Clayton
Chief Makeup	George Blackler
Makeup Assistant	John Webber
Hairdressing	Pearl Tipaldi
Wardrobe	Rosemary Burrows

Continuity	Gladys Goldsmith
Dialogue Coach	Ruth Lodge
Casting Director	Jimmy Liggat
Special Effects	Bert Luxford
Construction Manager	Arthur Banks

VAMPIRE CIRCUS

Hammer 87 minutes Eastmancolor Cert X
Produced August 9, 1971/Released June 1972**
Distributor Rank/Fox (USA)
Original Cofeature (UK/USA): *Explosion/ Countess Dracula*

CAST

Gypsy Woman	Adrienne Corri
Burgermeister	Thorley Walters
Emil	Anthony Corlan
Anton	John Moulder-Brown
Mueller	Laurence Payne
Kersh	Richard Owens
Dora	Lynne Frederick
Gerta	Elizabeth Seal
Hauser	Robin Hunter
Anna	Domini Blythe
Count Mitterhouse	Robert Tayman
Schilt	John Brown
Elvira	Mary Wimbush
Rosa	Christina Paul
Heinrich	Robin Sachs
Helga	Lala Ward
Michael	Skip Martin
Strongman	Dave Prowse
Jon	Roderick Shaw
Gustav	Barnaby Shaw
The Webbers	Milovan and Serena
Jenny Schilt	Jane Derby
Mrs. Schilt	Sybilla Kay
Grandma Schilt	Dorothy Frere
First Soldier	Sean Hewitt
Sexton	Giles Fibbs
Foreman	Jason James
Old Villager	Arnold Locke
Bradforts-Amaros by courtesy of	Billy Smarts Circus

CREDITS

Directed by	Robert Young
Produced by	Wilbur Stark

Screenplay by	Judson Kinberg
Music Composed by	David Whitaker
Musical Supervisor	Philip Martell
Director of Photography	Moray Grant BSC
Camera Operator	Walter Byatt
Art Director	Scott MacGregor
Assistant Art Director	Don Picton
Editor	Peter Musgrave
Sound Recordist	Claude Hitchcock
Sound Camera Operator	Laurie Reed
Sound Editor	Roy Hyde
Dubbing Mixer	Ken Barker
Production Manager	Tom Sachs
Assistant Director	Derek Whitehurst
Makeup	Jill Carpenter
Hairdressing	Ann McFadyen
Wardrobe Supervisor	Brian Owen-Smith
Continuity	June Randall
Casting Director	James Liggat
Special Effects	Les Bowie
Construction Manager	Arthur Banks
Animal Adviser	Mary Chipperfield
Production Supervisor	Roy Skeggs

DEMONS OF THE MIND

Hammer/Frank Godwin 89 minutes Technicolor Cert X
Produced August 16, 1971/Released November 1972
Distributor M-G-M-EMI/International Co-Productions (USA)
Original Cofeature (UK/USA): *Tower of Evil/Fear in the Night*

CAST

Count Zorn	Robert Hardy
Emil	Shane Briant
Elizabeth	Gillian Hills
Hilda	Yvonne Mitchell
Carl Richter	Paul Jones
Dr. Falkenburg	Patrick Magee
Klaus	Kenneth J.Warren
Priest	Michael Hordern
Inge	Virginia Wetherell
Fischinger	Robert Brown
Ernst	Barry Stanton
Magda	Deirdre Costello
Zorn's Wife	Sidonie Bond
Coachman	Thomas Heathcote
First Villager	John Atkinson
Second Villager	George Cormack

Matronly Woman	Mary Hignett
Old Crone	Sheila Raynor
First Girl	Jan Adair
Second Girl	Jane Cardew

CREDITS

Directed by	Peter Sykes
Produced by	Frank Godwin
Screenplay by	Christopher Wicking
Original Story by	Frank Godwin/Christopher Wicking
Music Composed by	Harry Robinson
Musical Supervisor	Philip Martell
Director of Photography	Arthur Grant
Camera Operator	Neil Binney
Production Designer	Michael Stringer
Assistant Art Director	Bill Brodis
Editor	Chris Barnes
Recording Director	A. W. Lumkin
Sound Recordist	John Purghess
Sound Editor	Terry Poulton
Dubbing Mixer	Len Abbott
Production Manager	Christopher Neame
Assistant Director	Ted Morley
Makeup	Trevor Crole-Rees
Hairdressing	Maud Onslow
Wardrobe Supervisor	Rosemary Burrows
Wardrobe Mistress	Eileen Sullivan
Continuity	Gladys Goldsmith
Casting	James Liggat
Construction Manager	Bill Greene
Production Supervisor	Roy Skeggs

DRACULA AD 1972

Hammer 97 minutes Eastmancolor Cert X
Produced September 27, 1971/Released October 1, 1972
Distributor Columbia-Warner/Warner Bros. (USA)
Original Second Feature (UK/USA): *Trog/Crescendo*

CAST

Count Dracula	Christopher Lee
Professor Van Helsing	Peter Cushing
Jessica Van Helsing	Stephanie Beacham
Johnny Alucard	Christopher Neame
Inspector Murray	Michael Coles
Gaynor	Marsha Hunt
Laura	Caroline Munro

Anna	Janet Key
Joe Mitchum	William Ellis
Bob	Philip Miller
Greg	Michael Kitchen
Detective Sergeant	David Andrews
Matron	Lally Bowyers
Mrs. Donnelly	Constance Luttrell
Charles	Michael Daly
Police Sergeant	Arturo Morris
Crying Matron	Jo Richardson
Hippie Girl	Penny Brahms
Hippie Boy	Brian John Smith
Rock Group	Stoneground

CREDITS

Directed by	Alan Gibson
Produced by	Josephine Douglas
Screenplay by	Don Houghton
Music Composed by	Michael Vickers
Musical Supervisor	Philip Martell
Songs: "Alligator Man" by Sal Valentino	
"You Better Come Through" by Tim Barnes	
Director of Photography	Dick Bush BSC
Camera Operator	Bernie Ford
Production Designer	Don Mingaye
Assistant Art Director	Ron Benton
Editor	James Needs
Recording Director	A. W. Lumkin
Sound Recordist	Claude Hitchcock
Sound Editor	Roy Baker
Dubbing Mixer	Bill Rowe
Production Manager	Ron Jackson
Assistant Director	Robert Lynn
Makeup	Jill Carpenter
Hairdressing	Barbara Ritchie
Wardrobe Supervisor	Rosemary Burrows
Continuity	Doreen Dearnaley
Casting Director	James Liggat
Special Effects	Les Bowie
Construction Manager	Bill Greene
Production Supervisor	Roy Skeggs

FEAR IN THE NIGHT

Hammer 86 minutes Technicolor Cert X
Produced November 15, 1971/Released October 1972
Distributor M-G-M-EMI/International Co-Productions (USA)
Original Second Feature (UK/USA): *Straight on Till Morning/Demons of the Mind*

CAST

Peggy Heller	Judy Geeson
Molly Carmichael	Joan Collins
Robert Heller	Ralph Bates
Michael Carmichael	Peter Cushing
Mrs. Beamish	Gillian Lind
Doctor	James Cossins
First Policeman	John Brown
Second Policeman	Brian Grellis

CREDITS

Produced by	Jimmy Sangster
Directed by	Jimmy Sangster
Screenplay by	Jimmy Sangster/Michael Syson
Music Composed by	John McCabe
Director of Photography	Arthur Grant
Camera Operator	Neil Binney
Art Director	Don Picton
Set Dresser	Penny Struthers
Editor	Peter Weatherley
Recording Director	Tony Lumpkin
Sound Editor	Roy Hyde
Production Manager	Christopher Neame
Assistant Director	Ted Morley
Makeup	Bill Partleton
Hairdresser	Helen Lennox
Wardrobe	Rosemary Burrows
Continuity	Gladys Goldsmith
Casting	James Liggat
Production Supervisor	Roy Skeggs
Executive Producer	Michael Carreras

CAPTAIN KRONOS—VAMPIRE HUNTER

Hammer 91 minutes Eastmancolor Cert AA
Produced April 10, 1972/Released April 1974**
Distributor Bruton-EMI/Paramount (USA)
Original Cofeature (UK/USA): *The Girl With the Thunderbolt Kick/Frankenstein and the Monster From Hell*

CAST

Kronos	Horst Janson
Dr. Marcus	John Carson
Paul Durward	Shane Briant
Carla	Caroline Munro
Grost	John Cater

Sarah Durward	Lois Daine
Kerro	Ian Hendry
Lady Durward	Wanda Ventham
Hagen	William Hobbs
George Sorell	Brian Tully
Pointer	Robert James
Barlow	Perry Soblosky
Giles	Paul Greenwood
Vanda Sorell	Lisa Gollings
Barman	John Hollis
Isabella Sorell	Susanna East
Barton Sorell	Stafford Gordon
Ann Sorell	Elisabeth Dear
Mira	Joanna Ross
Priest	Neil Seiler
Lilian	Olga Anthony
Blind Girl	Gigi Gurpinar
Big Man	Peter Davidson
Tom	Terence Sewards
Deke	Trevor Lawrence
Barmaid	Jacqui Cook
Whore	Penny Price

CREDITS

Directed/Written by	Brian Clemens
Produced by	Albert Fennell/Brian Clemens
Music Composed by	Laurie Johnson
Musical Supervisor	Philip Martell
Director of Photography	Ian Wilson
Camera Operator	Godfrey Godar
Production Designer	Robert Jones
Assistant Art Director	Kenneth McCallum Tait
Editor	James Needs
Recording Director	A. W. Lumkin
Sound Recordist	Jim Willis
Sound Editor	Peter Lennard
Dubbing Mixer	Bill Rowe
Production Manager	Richard Dalton
Assistant Director	David Tringham
Makeup	Jim Evans
Hairdressing	Barbara Ritchie
Wardrobe Supervisor	Dulcie Midwinter
Continuity	June Randall
Casting Director	James Liggat
Fight Arranger	William Hobbs
Production Supervisor	Roy Skeggs

FRANKENSTEIN AND THE MONSTER FROM HELL

Hammer 99 minutes Technicolor Cert X
Produced September 18, 1972/Released May 12, 1974
Distributor Avco Embassy/Paramount (USA)
Original Second Feature (UK/USA): *Fists of Vengeance/Captain Kronos—Vampire Hunter*

CAST

Baron Frankenstein	Peter Cushing
Simon	Shane Briant
Sarah	Madeline Smith
Monster	Dave Prowse
Asylum Director	John Stratton
Transvest	Michael Ward
Wild One	Elsie Wagstaff
Police Sergeant	Norman Mitchell
Judge	Clifford Mollison
Body Snatcher	Patrick Troughton
Ernst	Philip Voss
Hans	Chris Cunningham
Professor Durendel	Charles Lloyd Pack
Old Hag	Lucy Griffiths
Tarmut	Bernard Lee
Muller	Sydney Bromley
Brassy Girl	Andrea Lawrence
Landlord	Jerold Wells
Gerda	Sheila D'Union
Twitch	Mischa de la Motte
Smiler	Norman Atkyns
Letch	Victor Woolf
Mouse	Winifred Sabine
Chatter	Janet Hargreaves
Coach Driver	Peter Madden
Inmate	Tony Harris

CREDITS

Directed by	Terence Fisher
Produced by	Roy Skeggs
Screenplay by	John Elder
Music Composed by	James Bernard
Musical Supervisor	Philip Martell
Director of Photography	Brian Probyn BSC
Camera Operator	Chic Anstiss
Art Director	Scott MacGregor
Assistant Art Director	Don Picton
Editor	James Needs

A History of Horrors

Sound Recordist	Les Hammond
Sound Editor	Roy Hyde
Dubbing Mixer	Morris Askew
Production Manager	Christopher Neame
Assistant Director	Derek Whitehurst
Makeup	Doug Knight
Hairdresser	Maude Onslow
Wardrobe Supervisor	Dulcie Midwinter
Continuity	Kay Rawlings
Casting Director	James Liggat
Construction Manager	Arthur Banks

THE SATANIC RITES OF DRACULA

(American Title: Count Dracula and His Vampire Bride)

Hammer 87 minutes Technicolor Cert X
Produced November 13, 1972/Released January 1974
Distributor Columbia-Warner/Dynamite! Entertainment (USA)
Original Second Feature (UK): *Blacula*

CAST

Count Dracula	Christopher Lee
Van Helsing	Peter Cushing
Inspector Murray	Michael Coles
Torrence	William Franklyn
Professor Keeley	Freddie Jones
Jessica	Joanna Lumley
Mathews	Richard Vernon
Chin Yang	Barbara Yu Ling
Lord Carradine	Patrick Barr
Porter	Richard Mathews
Freeborne	Lockwood West
Jane	Valerie Van Ost
Hanson	Maurice O'Connell
Doctor	Peter Adair
Vampire Girls	Maggie Fitzgerald, Pauline Peart, Finnuala O'Shannon, Mia Martin
Commissionaire	John Harvey
Guards	Marc Zuber, Paul Weston, Ian Dewar, Graham Rees

CREDITS

Directed by	Alan Gibson
Produced by	Roy Skeggs
Screenplay by	Don Houghton
Associate Producer	Don Houghton

378

Music Composed by	John Cacavas
Musical Supervisor	Philip Martell
Director of Photography	Brian Probyn
Camera Operator	Chic Anstiss
Art Director	Lionel Couch
Assistant Art Director	Don Picton
Editor	Chris Barnes
Sound Recordist	Claude Hitchcock
Sound Editor	Terry Poulton
Dubbing Mixer	Dennis Whitlock
Production Manager	Ron Jackson
Assistant Director	Derek Whitehurst
Makeup	George Blackler
Hairdresser	Maude Onslow
Wardrobe Supervisor	Rebecca Breed
Continuity	Elizabeth Wilcox
Casting Director	James Liggat
Special Effects	Les Bowie
Construction Manager	Ken Softley
Stills Cameraman	Ronnie Pilgrim
Production Secretary	Sally Pardo

THE LEGEND OF THE 7 GOLDEN VAMPIRES

(American Title: The Seven Brothers Meet Dracula)

Hammer/Shaw 89 minutes Technicolor/Panavision Cert X
Produced October 22, 1973/Released October 6, 1974
Distributor Columbia-Warner/Dynamite! Entertainment (USA)

CAST

Professor Van Helsing	Peter Cushing
Hsi Ching	David Chiang
Vanessa Buren	Julie Ege
Leyland Van Helsing	Robin Stewart
Mai Kwei	Shih Szu
Dracula	John Forbes-Robertson
British Consul	Robert Hanna
Kah	Chan Shen
Hsi Ta	James Ma
Hsi Kwei	Liu Chia Yung
Hsi Sung	Feng Ko An
Hsi San	Chen Tieng Loong
Leung Hon	Wong Han Chan

CREDITS

Directed by	Roy Ward Baker

Produced by	Don Houghton/Vee King Shaw
Screenplay by	Don Houghton
Music Composed by	James Bernard
Musical Supervisor	Philip Martell
Director of Photography	John Wilcox BSC/Roy Ford
Camera Operator	Roy Ford
Focus Puller	Keith Jones
Art Director	Johnson Tsau
Editor	Chris Barnes
Assistant Editor	Larry Richardson
Sound Recordist	Les Hammond
Sound Editor	Frank Golding
Boom Operator	Tommy Staples
Sound Maintenance	Dan Grimmel
Production Manager	Chua Lam
Assistant Director	Erh Feng
Makeup	Wu Hsu Ching
Hairdresser	Peng Yen Lien
Costumes	Liu Chi-Yu
Continuity	Renee Glynne
Props Master	Li Wu
Special Effects	Les Bowie
Martial arts sequences staged by	Tang Chia/Liu Chia-Liang
Assistant to Producer	Christopher Carreras
Production Secretary	Jean Walter
Unit Manager	Shen Chung
Floor Manager	Peng Cheng

TO THE DEVIL—A DAUGHTER

Hammer-Terra 92 minutes Technicolor Cert X
Produced September 1, 1975/Released March 4, 1976
Distributor EMI/Cine Artists (USA)

CAST

John Verney	Richard Widmark
Father Michael Rayner	Christopher Lee
Anna	Honor Blackman
Henry Beddows	Denholm Elliott
George de Grass	Michael Goodliffe
Catherine Beddows	Nastassja Kinski
Eveline de Grass	Eva Maria Meineke
David	Anthony Valentine
Bishop	Derek Francis
Margaret	Isabella Telezynska
Kollde	Konstantin de Goguel
Isabel	Anna Bentinck

German Matron	Irene Prador
Black Room Attendant	Brian Wilde
Sister Helle	Petra Peters
Airport Porter	William Ridout
Critic	Howard Goorney
Salvation Army Major	Frances de la Tour
First Girl	Zoe Hendry
Second Girl	Lindy Benson
Third Girl	Jo Peters
Fourth Girl	Bobby Sparrow

CREDITS

Directed by	Peter Sykes
Produced by	Roy Skeggs
Screenplay by	Christopher Wicking
Adaption by	John Peacock
From the novel by Dennis Wheatley	
Music Composed by	Paul Glass
Musical Supervisor	Philip Martell
Director of Photography	David Watkin
Camera Operator	Ron Robson
Art Director	Don Picton
Editor	John Trumper
Recording Director	Tony Lumkin
Sound Recordist	Dennis Whitlock
Sound Editor	Mike le Mare GBFE
Dubbing Mixer	Bill Rowe
Production Manager	Ron Jackson
Assistant Director	Barry Langley
Second Asst Director	Mike Higgins
Third Asst Director	Roy Stevens
Production Assistant	Jean Clarkson
Makeup	Eric Allwright/George Blackler
Hairdressing Supervisor	Jeanette Freeman
Wardrobe Supervisor	Laura Nightingale
Wardrobe Master	Eddie Boyce
Continuity	Sally Jones
Casting Director	Irene Lamb
Special Effects	Les Bowie
Construction Manager	Wag Hammerton
Gaffer	Ted Hallows
Stills Cameraman	Ray Hearne
Publicist	Mike Russell
Production Accountant	Ken Gordon

Appendix 2

HAMMER FILMOGRAPHY

1946-1979

P:Producer/**D**:Director/**S**:Screenplay/**RT**:Running Time
The Hammer Horrors are in **bold**.
(American Titles in parentheses.)

1946

CRIME REPORTER
P:Hal Wilson/D:Ben R. Hart/S:Jimmy Corbett/*Stars:John Blythe/Jackie Brent*/RT: 36 mins
Released March 6, 1947***

1947

RIVER PATROL
P:Hal Wilson/D:Ben R. Hart/S:Jimmy Corbett/*Stars:John Blythe/Wally Patch*/RT:46 mins
Released January 28, 1948***

WHO KILLED VAN LOON?
P:Anthony Hinds/D: Gordon Kyle/Lionel Tomlinson/*Stars:Raymond Lovell/Kay Bannerman* /RT:48 mins
Released June 30, 1948

DEATH IN HIGH HEELS
P:Henry Halsted/D:Lionel Tomlinson/S: Christianna Brand/*Stars:Don Stannard/Patricia Laffan*/RT:70 mins
Released June

THE DARK ROAD
P:Henry Halsted/D:Alfred Goulding/*Stars:Charles Stuart/Michael Ripper*/RT:70 mins

Released October 1, 1948

DICK BARTON, SPECIAL AGENT (Dick Barton, Detective)
P:Henry Halsted/D:Alfred Goulding/S:Alan Stranks/Alfred
Goulding/*Stars:Don Stannard/George Ford*/RT:70 mins
Released May 9, 1948

1948

DICK BARTON AT BAY
P:Henry Halsted/D:Godfrey Grayson/S:J. C. Budd/E. Trechmann/Ambrose
Grayson/*Stars:Don Stannard/Meinhart Maur*/RT:68 mins
Released October 2, 1950

THE JACK OF DIAMONDS
P-D:Vernon Sewell/S:Nigel Patrick/Cyril Raymond/*Stars: Nigel Patrick/Joan Carol*/RT:74 mins
Released May 23, 1949

DICK BARTON STRIKES BACK (1)
P:Anthony Hinds/D:Godfrey Grayson/S:Ambrose Grayson/*Stars:Don Stannard/Sebastian Cabot*/RT:73 mins
Released July 18, 1949

DR MORELLE—"The Case of the Missing Heiress"
P:Anthony Hinds/D:Godfrey Grayson/S:Roy Plomley/Ambrose
Grayson/*Stars:Valentine Dyall/Julia Lang*/RT:73 mins
Produced November/Released June 27, 1949

Shooting (or preproduction) title(s) as follows:
(1) DICK BARTON AND THE SILENT PLAGUE

1949

THE ADVENTURES OF P.C. 49
P:Anthony Hinds/D:Godfrey Grayson/S:Alan Stranks/Vernon
Harris/*Stars:Hugh Latimer/Patricia Cutts*/RT:67 mins
Produced February/Released January 2, 1950

CELIA (2)
P:Anthony Hinds/D:Francis Searle/S:A. R. Rawlinson/Edward J. Mason/
Francis Searle/*Stars:Hy Hazell/Bruce Lester*/RT:67 mins
Produced April 4/Released August 29

MEET SIMON CHERRY (3)
P:Anthony Hinds/D:Godfrey Grayson/S:A. R. Rawlinson /Godfrey
Grayson/*Stars: Hugh Moxey/Zena Marshall*/RT:67 mins
Produced June/Released April 10, 1950

THE MAN IN BLACK
P:Anthony Hinds/D:Francis Searle/S:John Gilling/*Stars: Betty Ann Davies/Sidney James*/RT:75 mins
Produced August 8/Released March 6, 1950

ROOM TO LET

SOMEONE AT THE DOOR
P:Anthony Hinds/D:Francis Searle/S:A. R. Rawlinson/*Stars:Yvonne Owen/ Michael Medwin*/RT:65 mins
Produced November 21/Released August 21, 1950

Shooting (or preproduction) title(s) as follows:
(2) THE SINISTER AFFAIR OF POOR AUNT NORA
(3) MEET THE REV.

1950

WHAT THE BUTLER SAW
P:Anthony Hinds/D:Godfrey Grayson/S:A. R. Rawlinson/Edward J. Mason/*Stars:Edward Rigby/Henry Mollison*/RT:61 mins
Produced January/Released September 11

THE BLACK WIDOW (4)
P:Anthony Hinds/D:Vernon Sewell/S:Allan MacKinnon/*Stars: Christine Norden/Robert Ayres*/RT:62 mins
Produced January 16/Released October 22

THE LADY CRAVED EXCITEMENT
P:Anthony Hinds/D:Godfrey Grayson/S:John Gilling/Edward J.Mason/Francis Searle/*Stars:Hy Hazell/Michael Medwin*/RT:69 mins
Produced March 13/Released October 16

THE ROSSITER CASE
P:Anthony Hinds/D:Francis Searle/S:Kenneth Hyde/John Hunter/ Francis Searle/*Stars:Helen Shingler/Sheila Burrell*/RT:75 mins
Produced May/Released January 29, 1951

TO HAVE AND TO HOLD
P:Anthony Hinds/D:Godfrey Grayson/S:Reginald Long/*Stars:Patrick Barr/ Avis Scott*/RT:63 mins
Produced June 26/Released April 2, 1951

THE DARK LIGHT
P:Michael Carreras/D-S:Vernon Sewell/*Stars:Albert Lieven/ David Greene*/RT:66 mins
Produced July 10/Released April 23, 1951

A CASE FOR P.C. 49
P:Anthony Hinds/D:Francis Searle/S:Alan Stranks/Vernon Harris/*Stars:Brian Reece/Joy Shelton*/RT:66/80 mins
Released July 23, 1951

Shooting (or preproduction) title(s) as follows:
(4) RETURN FROM DARKNESS

1951

CLOUDBURST
P:Anthony Hinds/D:Francis Searle/S:Francis Searle/Leo Marks/*Stars:Robert Preston/Elizabeth Sellars*/RT:92 (USA:83) mins
Produced January 8/Released December 10

DEATH OF AN ANGEL
P:Anthony Hinds/D:Charles Saunders/S:Reginald Long/*Stars:Patrick Barr/Jane Baxter*/RT:64 mins
Produced March/Released March 24, 1952

WHISPERING SMITH HITS LONDON
(Whispering Smith VS Scotland Yard) (5)
P:Anthony Hinds/D:Francis Searle/S:John Gilling/*Stars: Richard Carlson/Greta Gynt*/RT:82 (USA:77) mins
Produced May/Released February 3, 1952

THE LAST PAGE (Man Bait) (6)
P:Anthony Hinds/D:Terence Fisher/S:Frederick Knott/*Stars:George Brent/Marguerite Chapman* /RT:84 (USA:78) mins
Produced July 9/Released May 19, 1952

WINGS OF DANGER (7)
P:Anthony Hinds/D:Terence Fisher/S:John Gilling/*Stars: Zachary Scott/Robert Beatty*/RT:73 mins
Produced September 3/Released May 26, 1952

NEVER LOOK BACK
P:Michael Carreras/D:Francis Searle/S:John Hunter/Guy Morgan/Francis Searle/*Stars:Rosamund John/Hugh Sinclair*/RT:73 mins
Produced September 17/Released May 26, 1952

STOLEN FACE
P:Anthony Hinds/D:Terence Fisher/S:Richard H. Landau /
Martin Berkeley/*Stars:Paul Henreid/Lizabeth Scott*/RT:72 mins
Produced October 22/Released June 23, 1952

Shooting (or preproduction) title(s) as follows:
(5) WHISPERING SMITH INVESTIGATES

(6) MURDER IN SAFETY
(7) DEAD ON COURSE

1952

LADY IN THE FOG (Scotland Yard Inspector)
P:Anthony Hinds/D:Sam Newfield/S:Orville H. Hampton/*Stars:Cesar Romero/Lois Maxwell*/RT:82 (USA:73) mins
Released October 13

THE GAMBLER AND THE LADY
P:Anthony Hinds/D:Sam Newfield/Patrick Jenkins/*Stars: Dane Clark/ Kathleen Byron*/RT:74 (USA:71) mins
Released January 26, 1953

MANTRAP (Man in Hiding)
P:Michael Carreras/D:Terence Fisher/S:Paul Tabori/Terence Fisher/*Stars:Paul Henreid/Lois Maxwell*/RT:79 mins
Released March 16, 1953

FOUR SIDED TRIANGLE

THE FLANAGAN BOY (Bad Blonde)
P:Anthony Hinds/D:Reginald Le Borg/S:Guy Elmes/Richard H. Landau/*Stars:Barbara Payton/Tony Wright* /RT:81 mins
Produced September 9/Released October 12, 1953

SPACEWAYS
P:Michael Carreras/D:Terence Fisher/S:Paul Tabori/Richard H. Landau/*Stars:Howard Duff/Eva Bartok*/RT:76 mins
Released December 21, 1953

1953

THE SAINT'S RETURN (The Saint's Girl Friday) (8)
P:Anthony Hinds/D:Seymour Friedman/S:Allan MacKinnon/*Stars:Louis Hayward/Sidney Tafler*/RT:73 (USA:68) mins
Released October 12

BLOOD ORANGE (Three Stops to Murder)
P:Michael Carreras/D:Terence Fisher/S:Jan Read/*Stars: Tom Conway/ Mila Parely*/RT:76 mins
Released November 3

36 HOURS (Terror Street)
P:Anthony Hinds/D:Montgomery Tully/S:Steve Fisher/*Stars:Dan Duryea/ Elsy Albiin*/RT:80 (USA:84) mins
Produced May/Released October 25

FACE THE MUSIC (The Black Glove)(9)
P:Michael Carreras/D:Terence Fisher/S:Ernest Borneman/*Stars:Alex
Nicol/Eleanor Summerfield*/RT:84 mins
Produced June 29/Released February 22, 1954

THE HOUSE ACROSS THE LAKE (Heat Wave)
P:Anthony Hinds/D-S:Ken Hughes/*Stars:Alex Nicol/Hillary Brooke*/RT:68 mins
Released June 21, 1954

LIFE WITH THE LYONS
P-S:Robert Dunbar/D-S:Val Guest/*Stars:Ben Lyon/Bebe Daniels*/RT:81 mins
Released May 25, 1954

MURDER BY PROXY (Blackout)
P:Michael Carreras/D:Terence Fisher/S:Richard H. Landau/*Stars:Dane Clark/
Belinda Lee*/RT:87 mins
Released March 28, 1955

FIVE DAYS (Paid to Kill)
P:Anthony Hinds/D:Montgomery Tully/S:Paul Tabori/*Stars: Dane Clark/
Paul Carpenter*/RT:72 mins
Released May 12, 1954

Shooting (or preproduction) title(s) as follows:
(8) THE SAINT RETURNS
(9) THE TRUMPET STORY

1954

THE STRANGER CAME HOME (The Unholy Four)
P-S: Michael Carreras/D:Terence Fisher/*Stars:Paulette Goddard/William
Sylvester*/RT:80 mins
Released August 9

THIRD PARTY RISK (Deadly Game)
P-S:Robert Dunbar/D-S:Daniel Birt/*Stars:Lloyd Bridges/Finlay Currie*/RT:70
(USA:63) mins
Released April 4, 1955

MASK OF DUST (A Race for Life)
P:Mickey Delamar/D:Terence Fisher/S:Richard H. Landau/*Stars:Richard
Conte/Mari Aldon*/RT:79 (USA:69) mins
Released December 27

THE MEN OF SHERWOOD FOREST
P:Michael Carreras/D:Val Guest/S:Allan MacKinnon/*Stars: Don Taylor/
Reginald Beckwith*/RT:77 mins
Released December 6

THE LYONS IN PARIS
P:Robert Dunbar/D-S:Val Guest/*Stars:Ben Lyon/Bebe Daniels*/RT:81 mins
Released January 5, 1955

THE GLASS CAGE (The Glass Tomb)
P:Anthony Hinds/D:Montgomery Tully/S:Richard H. Landau /*Stars:John Ireland/Honor Blackman*/RT:59 mins
Released August 29, 1955

BREAK IN THE CIRCLE
P:Michael Carreras/D-S:Val Guest/*Stars:Forrest Tucker/Eva Bartok*/RT:91 (USA:69) mins
Released February 28, 1955

THE QUATERMASS EXPERIMENT

1955

WOMEN WITHOUT MEN (Blonde Bait)
P:Anthony Hinds/D:Elmo Williams/S:Val Guest/Richard H. Landau/*Stars: Beverley Michaels/Joan Rice* /RT:73 mins
Released June 14, 1956***

CYRIL STAPLETON AND THE SHOW BAND
P-D:Michael Carreras/RT:29 mins
Released June**

JUST FOR YOU
P-D:Michael Carreras/RT:30 mins
Released January 16, 1956

THE ERIC WINSTONE BAND SHOW
P-D:Michael Carreras/RT:29 mins
Released August 26

PARADE OF THE BANDS
P-D:Michael Carreras/RT:30 mins
Released April 17, 1956***

ERIC WINSTONE'S STAGECOACH
P-D:Michael Carreras/RT:30 mins
Released February 25, 1956

THE EDMUNDO ROS HALF HOUR
P-D:Michael Carreras/RT:30 mins
Released May 18, 1956

DICK TURPIN—HIGHWAYMAN
P:Michael Carreras/D:David Paltenghi/S:Joel Murcott/*Stars:Philip Friend/
Diane Hart*/RT:26 mins
Released December 12, 1956***

A MAN ON THE BEACH
P:Anthony Hinds/D:Joseph Losey/S:Jimmy Sangster/*Stars: Donald Wolfit/
Michael Medwin*/RT:29 mins
Released March 26, 1956

COPENHAGEN
P-D:Michael Carreras/RT:16 mins
Released February 4, 1956

THE RIGHT PERSON
P:Michael Carreras/D:Peter Cotes/S:Philip Mackie/*Stars: Margo
Lorenz/Douglas Wilme*r/RT:30 mins
Released December 26

1956

X THE UNKNOWN

DAY OF GRACE
P-D:Francis Searle/S:Jon Manchip White/Francis Searle/*Stars:Vincent
Winter/John Laurie*/RT:27 mins
Released July 20

THE STEEL BAYONET
P-D:Michael Carreras/S:Howard Clewes/*Stars:Leo Genn/Kieron Moore*/RT:85 mins
Released June 3, 1957

QUATERMASS II

THE CURSE OF FRANKENSTEIN

1957

THE ABOMINABLE SNOWMAN

A CLEAN SWEEP
P:Anthony Hinds/D:Maclean Rogers/*Stars:Eric Barker/Thora Hird*/RT:29 mins
Produced March 11

DANGER LIST
P:Anthony Hinds/D:Leslie Arliss/S:J. D. Scott/*Stars: Philip Friend/Honor
Blackman*/RT:22 mins
Produced March 15/Released December 26

MAN WITH A DOG
P:Anthony Hinds/D:Leslie Arliss/*Stars:Maurice Denham/Sarah Lawson/*
RT:20 mins
Produced March 25/Released November 3

THE CAMP ON BLOOD ISLAND
P:Anthony Hinds/D:Val Guest/S:Jon Manchip White/Val Guest/*Stars:André Morell/Carl Mohner*/RT:82 mins
Produced July 29/Released April 18, 1958*

THE SNORKEL
P:Michael Carreras/D:Guy Green/S:Peter Myers/Jimmy Sangster/*Stars:Peter Van Eyck/Betta St John*/RT:90 (USA:74) mins
Produced September 9/Released July 7, 1958

DRACULA

1958

THE REVENGE OF FRANKENSTEIN

FURTHER UP THE CREEK
P:Henry Halsted/D:Val Guest/S:John Warren/Len Heath/Val Guest/*Stars:David Tomlinson/Frankie Howerd*/RT:91 mins
Produced May 19/Released October 20

I ONLY ARSKED
P:Anthony Hinds/D:Montgomery Tully/S:Sid Colin/Jack Davies/*Stars:Bernard Bresslaw/Michael Medwin*/RT:82 mins
Produced July 21/Released November 7*

SEVEN WONDERS OF IRELAND
P-D:Peter Bryan

ITALIAN HOLIDAY
P-D:Peter Bryan

OPERATION UNIVERSE
P-D-S:Peter Bryan/RT:28 mins

THE HOUND OF THE BASKERVILLES

TEN SECONDS TO HELL (10)
P:Michael Carreras/D:Robert Aldrich/S:Robert Aldrich/Teddi
Sherman/*Stars:Jeff Chandler/Jack Palance* /RT:94 mins
Produced October/Released September 1959

THE MAN WHO COULD CHEAT DEATH

Shooting (or preproduction) title(s) as follows:
(10) THE PHOENIX

_____

1959

YESTERDAY'S ENEMY
P:Michael Carreras/D:Val Guest/S:Peter R. Newman/*Stars: Stanley Baker/*
Guy Rolfe/RT:95 mins
Produced January 12/Released October 12

TICKET TO HAPPINESS
P-D:Peter Bryan/RT:30 mins
Produced January 12/Released November

THE MUMMY

THE UGLY DUCKLING
P:Michael Carreras/D:Lance Comfort/S:Sid Colin/Jack Davies/*Stars:Bernard*
Bresslaw/Reginald Beckwith /RT:84 mins
Produced March 4/Released August 10

DON'T PANIC CHAPS!
P:Teddy Baird/D:George Pollock/S:Jack Davies/*Stars: Dennis Price/*
George Cole/RT:85 mins
Released January 1960**

THE STRANGLERS OF BOMBAY

HELL IS A CITY
P:Michael Carreras/D-S:Val Guest/Stars:*Stanley Baker/Donald Pleasance*/RT:98
mins
Produced September 21/Released May 9, 1960

NEVER TAKE SWEETS FROM A STRANGER
(Never Take Candy From a Stranger)
P:Anthony Hinds/D:Cyril Frankel/S:John Hunter/*Stars: Gwen Watford/*
Patrick Allen/RT:81 mins
Produced September 14/Released October 2, 1960

THE TWO FACES OF DR JEKYLL

_____

1960

THE BRIDES OF DRACULA

THE FULL TREATMENT (Stop Me Before I Kill)
P-D:Val Guest/S:Val Guest/Ronald Scott Thorn/*Stars: Ronald Lewis/*
Diane Cilento/RT:109 mins
Produced March 21/Released March 1961**

THE TERROR OF THE TONGS

SWORD OF SHERWOOD FOREST
P:Richard Greene/Sidney Cole/D:Terence Fisher/S:Alan Hackney/*Stars:Richard Greene/Peter Cushing*/RT:80 mins
Produced May 23/Released February 1961**

VISA TO CANTON (Passport To China)
P-D:Michael Carreras/S:Gordon Wellesley/*Stars:Richard Basehart/Lisa Gastoni*/RT:75 mins
Produced June 9/Released February 1961**

THE CURSE OF THE WEREWOLF

A WEEKEND WITH LULU
P-S:Ted Lloyd/D:John Paddy Carstairs/*Stars:Bob Monkhouse/Leslie Phillips*/RT:89 mins
Produced October 3/Released May 1961**

TASTE OF FEAR

1961

WATCH IT, SAILOR
P:Maurice Cowan/D:Wolf Rilla/S:Falkland Cary/Philip King/*Stars:Dennis Price/Liz Fraser*/RT:81 mins
Produced January 30/Released August**

CASH ON DEMAND (The Gold Inside)
P:Michael Carreras/D:Quentin Lawrence/S:David T. Chantler/Lewis Greifer/*Stars:Peter Cushing/André Morell*/RT:66 mins
Produced April 4/Released November 15, 1963

HIGHWAY HOLIDAY
P-D:Ian Lewis/RT:25 mins

THE DAMNED

THE PIRATES OF BLOOD RIVER
P:Anthony Nelson Keys/D:John Gilling/S:John Hunter/John Gilling/*Stars:Christopher Lee/Kerwin Mathews*/RT:84 mins
Produced July 3/Released August 19, 1962*

CAPTAIN CLEGG

THE PHANTOM OF THE OPERA

1962

THE OLD DARK HOUSE
P:Anthony Hinds/William Castle/D:William Castle/S:Robert Dillon/*Stars:Tom Poston/Robert Morley*/RT:86 (USA:77) mins
Produced May 14, 1962/Released September 16, 1966

MANIAC

PARANOIAC

THE KISS OF THE VAMPIRE

NIGHTMARE
P-S:Jimmy Sangster/D:Freddie Francis/*Stars:David Knight/ Moira Redmond*/RT:82 mins
Produced December 17/Released May 31, 1964

1963

THE SCARLET BLADE (The Crimson Blade)
P:Anthony Nelson Keys/D-S:John Gilling/*Stars:Lionel Jeffries/Oliver Reed*/RT:82 mins
Produced March 1/Released August 11

THE DEVIL SHIP PIRATES
P:Anthony Nelson Keys/D:Don Sharp/S:Jimmy Sangster/*Stars:Christopher Lee/John Cairney*/RT:86 mins
Produced August 19/Released August 9, 1964

THE EVIL OF FRANKENSTEIN

THE GORGON

1964

HYSTERIA
P-S:Jimmy Sangster/D:Freddie Francis/*Stars:Robert Webber/Lelia Goldoni*/RT:85 mins
Produced February 10/Released July 27, 1965

THE CURSE OF THE MUMMY'S TOMB

THE SECRET OF BLOOD ISLAND
P:Anthony Nelson Keys/D:Quentin Lawrence/S:John Gilling/*Stars:Barbara Shelley/Jack Hedley*/RT:84 mins
Produced July 23/Released July 14, 1965

SHE
P:Michael Carreras/D:Robert Day/S:David T. Chantler/*Stars:Ursula Andress/Peter Cushing*/RT:105 mins
Produced August 24/Released April 18, 1965

THE BRIGAND OF KANDAHAR
P:Anthony Nelson Keys/D-S:John Gilling/*Stars:Oliver Reed/Ronald Lewis*/RT:81 mins
Produced October 6/Released August 8, 1965

FANATIC

1965

THE NANNY
P-S:Jimmy Sangster/D:Seth Holt/*Stars:Bette Davis/Jill Bennett*/RT:93 mins
Produced April 5/Released November 14

DRACULA—PRINCE OF DARKNESS

RASPUTIN—THE MAD MONK

THE PLAGUE OF THE ZOMBIES

THE REPTILE

ONE MILLION YEARS BC
P-S:Michael Carreras/D:Don Chaffey/*Stars:Raquel Welch/John Richardson*/RT:100 (USA:91) mins
Produced October 18/Released December 30, 1966

1966

SLAVE GIRLS (Prehistoric Women)
P-D-S:Michael Carreras/*Stars:Martine Beswick/Edina Ronay*/RT:74 (USA:95) mins
Produced January 22/Released July 7, 1968

THE WITCHES

THE VIKING QUEEN
P:John Temple-Smith/D:Don Chaffey/S:Clarke Reynolds /*Stars:Don Murray/Carita*/RT:91 mins
Produced June 15/Released March 26, 1967

FRANKENSTEIN CREATED WOMAN

THE MUMMY'S SHROUD

1967

QUATERMASS AND THE PIT

THE ANNIVERSARY
P-S:Jimmy Sangster/D:Roy Ward Baker/*Stars:Bette Davis/Sheila Hancock*/RT:95 mins
Produced May 1/Released February 18, 1968

THE VENGEANCE OF SHE
P:Aida Young/D:Cliff Owen/S:Peter O'Donnell/*Stars:John Richardson/Olinka Berova*/RT:101 mins
Produced June 26/Released May 1968**

THE LOST CONTINENT

THE DEVIL RIDES OUT

1968

DRACULA HAS RISEN FROM THE GRAVE

A CHALLENGE FOR ROBIN HOOD (11)
Producer:C. M. Pennington-Richards/D:Clifford Parkes /S:Peter Bryan/*Stars: Barrie Ingham/James Hayter*/RT:96 mins
Produced May 1/Released December 22

WHEN DINOSAURS RULED THE EARTH
P:Aida Young/D-S:Val Guest/*Stars:Victoria Vetri/Robin Hawdon*/RT:100 (USA:96) mins
Produced October 14/Released October 25, 1970

Shooting (or preproduction) title(s) as follows:
(11) ROBIN HOOD'S CHALLENGE

1969

FRANKENSTEIN MUST BE DESTROYED

MOON ZERO TWO
P-S:Michael Carreras/D:Roy Ward Baker/*Stars:James Olson/Catherina von Schell*/RT:100 mins
Produced March 31/Released October 26

CRESCENDO

TASTE THE BLOOD OF DRACULA

1970

THE VAMPIRE LOVERS

THE HORROR OF FRANKENSTEIN
P-D:Jimmy Sangster/S:Jeremy Burnham/Jimmy Sangster/*Stars:Ralph Bates/
Veronica Carlson*/RT:95 mins
Produced March 16/Released October 8*

SCARS OF DRACULA

CREATURES THE WORLD FORGOT
P-S:Michael Carreras/D:Don Chaffey/*Stars:Julie Ege/Brian
O'Shaughnessy*/RT:95 mins
Produced June 1/Released April 25, 1971

LUST FOR A VAMPIRE

COUNTESS DRACULA

1971

BLOOD FROM THE MUMMY'S TOMB

HANDS OF THE RIPPER

DR JEKYLL AND SISTER HYDE

ON THE BUSES
P-S:Ronald Wolfe/Ronald Chesney/D:Harry Booth/*Stars:Reg Varney/Doris
Hare*/RT:88 mins
Produced March 8/Released August

TWINS OF EVIL

VAMPIRE CIRCUS

DEMONS OF THE MIND

DRACULA AD 1972

STRAIGHT ON TILL MORNING
P:Michael Carreras/D:Peter Collinson/S:Michael Peacock/*Stars:Rita
Tushingham/Shane Bryant*/RT:96 mins
Produced November 1/Released October 1972

FEAR IN THE NIGHT

1972

MUTINY ON THE BUSES
P-S:Ronald Wolfe/Ronald Chesney/D:Harry Booth/*Stars:Reg Varney/Doris Hare*/RT:89 mins
Produced February 21/Released September**

CAPTAIN KRONOS—VAMPIRE HUNTER

THAT'S YOUR FUNERAL
P:Michael Carreras/D:John Robins/S:Peter Lewis/*Stars: Bill Fraser/Raymond Huntley*/RT:82 mins
Produced June 5/Released July 1973**

NEAREST AND DEAREST
P:Michael Carreras/D:John Robins/S:Tom Brennand/Roy Bottomley/*Stars:Hylda Baker/Jimmy Jewel*
Produced July 10/Released April 1973**

FRANKENSTEIN AND THE MONSTER FROM HELL

THE SATANIC RITES OF DRACULA

1973

LOVE THY NEIGHBOUR
P:Roy Skeggs/D:John Robins/S:Vince Powell/Harry Driver/*Stars:Jack Smethurst/Rudolph Walker*/RT:85 mins
Produced January 20/Released July**

MAN AT THE TOP
P:Peter Charlesworth/Jock Jacobsen/D:Mike Vardy/S:Hugh Whitemore/*Stars:Kenneth Haigh/Nanette Newman*/RT:87 mins
Produced March 13/Released October**

HOLIDAY ON THE BUSES (12)
P:Ronald Wolfe/Ronald Chesney/D:Brian Izzard/*Stars:Reg Varney/Doris Hare*/
Produced May 19/Released December**

THE LEGEND OF THE 7 GOLDEN VAMPIRES

Shooting (or preproduction) title(s) as follows:
(12) STILL AT IT ON THE BUSES

1974

SHATTER (Call Him Mr Shatter)
P:Michael Carreras/Vee King Shaw/D:Michael Carreras /S:Don Houghton/*Stars:Stuart Whitman/Peter Cushing*/RT:90 mins

Produced January 17

MAN ABOUT THE HOUSE
P:Roy Skeggs/D:John Robins/S:Johnnie Mortimer/Brian Cooke/*Stars:Richard O'Sullivan/Paula Wilcox*/RT:90 mins
Produced March 16/Released December

1975

TO THE DEVIL—A DAUGHTER

1978

THE LADY VANISHES
P:Tom Sachs/D:Anthony Page/S:George Axelrod/*Stars: Cybill Shepherd/Elliott Gould*/RT:97 mins
Produced September 16/Released May 8, 1979*

Other Short Films

1946

OLD FATHER THAMES
CANDY'S CALENDER
CORNISH HOLIDAY

1947

SKIFFY GOES TO SEA
WE DO BELIEVE IN GHOSTS
BRED TO STAY

1950

MONKEY MANNERS
YOGA AND YOU

1951

KEEP FIT WITH YOGA
YOGA AND THE AVERAGE MAN
VILLAGE OF BRAY

1952

QUEER FISH

1953

RIVER SHIPS
SKY TRADERS

1955

NATIONAL SPORTING CLUB

1958

SUNSHINE HOLIDAY
ENCHANTED ISLAND
LAND OF THE LEPRECHAUNS
MODERN IRELAND
SPORTSMAN'S PARADE
O'HARA'S HOLIDAY

Bibliography

Over the last 35 years, every book or magazine that has dealt with the subject of horror films has had occasion to mention Hammer. To list them all would serve no purpose, as these same titles appear time and again in the bibliographies of each new work about the genre. I have decided instead to confine myself to those titles which were of particular material help in the writing of this book. My thanks go to their authors.

AURUM FILM ENCYCLOPEDIA, THE: Horror
Editor: Phil Hardy/*Aurum Press*/London/1985

AURUM FILM ENCYCLOPEDIA, THE: Science Fiction
Editor Phil Hardy/*Aurum Press*/London/1984

CHARM OF EVIL, THE: Terence Fisher
Wheeler W. Dixon/*Scarecrow Press*/Metuchen, NJ/1991

CINEFANTASTIQUE/Vol 4:3/"TERENCE FISHER—The Human Side
/Underlining"/*Harry Ringel*/1975

DEAD THAT WALK, THE
Leslie Halliwell/*Collins*/*Grafton Books*/London/1986

DREADFUL PLEASURES
James B.Twitchell/*Oxford University Press*/New York/1985

FANDOM'S FILM GALLERY/3: The Curse Of The Werewolf
Jan Van Genechten/Belgium/1978

HALLIWELL'S FILM GUIDE/8th Edition
Editor: John Walker/*Collins/Grafton Books*/London/1991

HAMMER: A Cinema Case Study
David Pirie/*BFI Education Books*/London/1980

HAMMER HORROR/Issues 1-7
Editor: Marcus Hearn/*Marvel Comics UK Limited*/London/1994-1995

HERITAGE OF HORROR, A
David Pirie/*Gordon Fraser*/London/1973

HORROR FILM HANDBOOK, THE
Alan Frank/*B. T. Batsford Limited*/London/1982

HORROR MOVIES: An Illustrated Survey
Carlos Clarens/*Secker & Warburg Limited*/London/1968

HOUSE OF HAMMER, THE (HALLS OF HORROR, THE)/Issues1-30
Editors: Dez Skinn/Dave Reeder/*General Book Distribution/Quality Communications Limited*/London/1976-1984

HOUSE OF HORROR, THE
Allen Eyles, Robert Adkinson, Nicholas Fry/*Lorrimer Publishing Limited*/London/1973

ILLUSTRATED WHO'S WHO OF THE CINEMA, THE
Editors: Ann Lloyd, Graham Fuller/*Orbis Publishing*/London/1983

KEEP WATCHING THE SKIES/Vols1 and 2
Bill Warren/*McFarland*/Jefferson, NC/1982

LITTLE SHOPPE OF HORRORS/Issues1-12
Richard Klemensen/*U.S.Press and Allen Printing Company*/Des Moines, IA/1978-present

MONSTER MANIA/Issues 1-3
Editor: Russ Jones/*Renaissance Productions*/New York /1966

PHOTON/27/"HORROR OF DRACULA—An Analysis of the Hammer Film Classic"/Ronald V. Borst/1977

REFERENCE GUIDE TO FANTASTIC FILMS/3 Vols
Walter W. Lee/*Chelsea-Lee Books*/Los Angeles/1974

SCIENCE FICTION FILM HANDBOOK, THE
Alan Frank/*B. T. Batsford Limited*/London/1982

SUPERNATURAL HORROR FILMING/Issues 1 and 2
Editor: Tim Stout/*Dorset Publishing Company*/Bournemouth, Dorset, England /1969

Index

Knight, Eddie, 263
Korda, Alexander, 13
Kubrick, Stanley, 231
Kuttner, Henry, 69

Ladd, Alan, 18, 41
Lady Chatterley's Lover, 75, 107, 120
Lady Craved Excitement, The, 9, 385
Lady in the Fog, 387
Lady Vanishes, The, 168, 288, 289, 290, 399
Lair of the White Worm, The (novel), 196
Landau, Richard H., 20, 25
Landi, Marla (Marcella Scorafia), 80
Landis, Carole, 200
Lapotaire, Jane, 308
Last Frontier, The, 181
Last Page, The, 14, 136, 386
Latta, C. J., 17
Laurie Marsh Group, 266, 268
Lawrence, Anthony E., 4, 5, 7, 10, 77; and end of Exclusive Films, 103, 166, 206, 214, 219, 229, 245, 259; and sale of Hammer Films, 266-269, 279, 284; and collapse of Hammer Films, 288-292
Lawrence, H. L., 151
Lawrie, James, 11
Lazarus, Paul, 94, 95, 263
Le Fanu, Joseph S., 231-234
Leakey, Philip, 45, 46, 63, 85, 87
Lean, David, 129
Leaver, Philip, 8
Lee, Belinda, 136
Lee, Birgit, 159
Lee, Bruce, 275
Lee, Christopher, 11, 21, 45, 47; and *Dracula*, 58-60, 62-64, 83, 84; and Bray Studios, 86-88, 92, 93, 95, 115, 128; and *The Terror of the Tongs*, 132-133, 136, 141, 145, 154, 159, 166, 172, 174, 178, 179; and *Dracula—Prince of Darkness*, 186-196, 214; and *Dracula Has Risen From the Grave*, 216-219, 225, 226; and *Taste the Blood of Dracula*, 228-229, 233, 234, 236; and *Scars*

of Dracula, 238-239, 242, 243, 257, 260, 263, 271, 272, 274, 276; and *To the Devil—A Daughter*, 278-279, 281-282, 284
Lee, Stan, 279, 280
Leech Woman, The, 131
Legend of Sleepy Hollow, The, 157
Legend of the 7 Golden Vampires, The, 243, 275-276, 379
Legion of Decency, 46, 109, 121
Leigh, Barbara, 280
Lejeune, Caroline A., 74
Leon, Valerie, 243
Leroux, Gaston, 160
Lesser, Julian, 17
Lesser, Sol, 13, 32
Lester, Richard, 182
Levine, Joseph E., 154, 199
Levy, Eliphas, 212
Levy, Stuart, 113
Lewis, Jerry, 122
Lewis, Ronald, 145
Lewton, Val, 167
Life With the Lyons, 20, 388
Lippert, Robert L., 13, 14, 16, 32, 56, 136, 172
Lloyd, Euan, 285, 287, 288, 290
Lloyd, Fred, 81
Lock Up Your Daughters, 219
Lodger, The (novel), 12
Lofts, Nora, 201
Lollobrigida, Gina, 75
Lom, Herbert, 163
London, Julie, 90
Look Back In Anger, 41
Lorne, Peter, 266
Losers, The, 253
Losey, Joseph, 28, 30, 39; and *The Damned*, 151-153, 185
Loss, Joe, 11
Lost Continent, The, 203, 207, 210, 211, 213, 214, 220, 248, 356
"Lot No. 249" (short story), 96
Lous, Hugo, 180
Love in Smokey Regions, 181
Love Me Tender, 41
Love Thy Neighbour, 274, 398
Low, Andrew, 98